CHICAGO PUBLIC LIBRARY
BUSINESS / SCIENCE / TECHNOLOGY
400 S. STATE ST.   60605

D0205564

HC
427.8
.P67
1994

Porter, Robin.

Industrial reformers
 in Republican
China.

$55.00

DATE			

BAKER & TAYLOR BOOKS

INDUSTRIAL REFORMERS IN REPUBLICAN CHINA

Studies on Modern China

INDUSTRIAL REFORMERS IN REPUBLICAN CHINA
Robin Porter

THE KWANGSI WAY IN KUOMINTANG CHINA, 1931–1939
Eugene William Levich

"SECRET SOCIETIES" RECONSIDERED
*Perspectives on the Social History of
Early Modern South China and Southeast Asia*
Edited by David Ownby and Mary Somers Heidhues

THE SAGA OF ANTHROPOLOGY IN CHINA
From Malinowski to Moscow to Mao
Gregory Eliyu Guldin

MODERN CHINESE WRITERS
Self-Portrayals
Edited by Helmut Martin and Jeffrey C. Kinkley

MODERNIZATION AND REVOLUTION IN CHINA
June Grasso, Jay Corrin, and Michael Kort

PERSPECTIVES ON MODERN CHINA
Four Anniversaries
*Edited by Kenneth Lieberthal, Joyce Kallgren,
Roderick MacFarquhar, and Frederic Wakeman, Jr.*

READING THE MODERN CHINESE SHORT STORY
Edited by Theodore Huters

UNITED STATES ATTITUDES TOWARD CHINA
The Impact of American Missionaries
Edited by Patricia Neils

Studies on Modern China

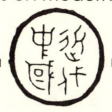

INDUSTRIAL REFORMERS IN REPUBLICAN CHINA

ROBIN PORTER

An East Gate Book

M.E. Sharpe
Armonk, New York
London, England

An East Gate Book

Copyright © 1994 by M. E. Sharpe, Inc.

All rights reserved. No part of this book may be reproduced in any form
without written permission from the publisher, M. E. Sharpe, Inc.,
80 Business Park Drive, Armonk, New York 10504.

Published simultaneously as Vol. 27, Nos. 3–4 of *Chinese Studies in History.*

Library of Congress Cataloging-in-Publication Data

Porter, Robin
Industrial reformers in Republican China / Robin Porter.
p.   cm.—(Studies on modern China)
"An East Gate book."
Includes bibliographical references and index.
ISBN 1-56324-393-8
1. China—Economic conditions—1912–1949.
2. China—Industries—1912–1949.
3. China—Social conditions—1912-1949.
I. Title.
II. Series.
HC427.8.P67   1994
338.951—dc20
94-16349
CIP

Printed in the United States of America

The paper used in this publication meets the minimum requirements of
American National Standard for Information Sciences—
Permanence of Paper for Printed Library Materials,
ANSI Z 39.48-1984.

EB (c)   10   9   8   7   6   5   4   3   2   1

CHICAGO PUBLIC LIBRARY
BUSINESS / SCIENCE / TECHNOLOGY
400 S. STATE ST.   60605

R00966 90982

REF

For Jan and Katie

Contents

Preface   ix

Introduction: The Nature of Liberal Reform   xi

Part I : The Task Defined

1. Modern Industry and Its Human Implications   3

Part II : The Movement for Industrial Reform

2. The YMCA   29

3. The YWCA   47

4. The National Christian Council of China   73

5. The Shanghai Municipal Council   98

6. Wartime Work   122

7. China and the International Labor Organization   145

8. Between Capital and Labor   160

Conclusion   172

Appendixes

Appendix 1A. The Usual Range of Adult Wages in Certain Chinese Industries, 1931–1932   179

Appendix 1B. Average Monthly Earnings of Workers in Shanghai, 1930–1940   180

Appendix 1C. Indices of Actual Earnings, Cost of Living, and Real Wages, 1930–1940   182

Appendix 1D. Regional Differences in Factory Wages, 1933   183

Appendix 2A. Peking Provisional Factory Regulations, 1923   184

Appendix 2B. Factory Act of the Nanking Government, 1931   189

Appendix 3. Shanghai Child Labor Commission Enquiry Form,
    with Sample Responses, 1923   203

Notes   205

Glossary of Chinese Names   255

Select Bibliography   257

Index   265

Preface

In the past decade much has been written about the process of modernization that has followed China's reopening to the outside world. The debate, both inside and outside China, has embraced many aspects of the central dilemma of modernization anywhere: how to achieve a transformation and upgrading of the productive life of the country while passing on as equitably as possible the benefits of change. An important part of this concern must be the conditions of work and life of the progressively larger numbers of people caught up in the modern sector of the economy. For China, as for the newly industrialized Taiwan, South Korea, Hong Kong, and Singapore, the ability to attend successfully to these matters may ultimately be the key to political stability.

But China's modernization did not begin in 1979, nor even in 1949. In reality the process began with the earliest significant Western contact in the 1840s. By the collapse of the Ch'ing dynasty and the founding of the republic in 1912, it was well under way. Undercurrents of change in economic activity in both the countryside and the cities had already thrown up social problems crying out for attention, and these were exacerbated by the fluctuations caused by the Great War in Europe. It is no coincidence that after China was denied justice at the Versailles peace conference in 1919, during the May Fourth protests and the New Culture Movement that followed, the plight of workers in the transitional economy formed the subject of much debate.

There is a good case to be made that the failure of liberalism in early-twentieth-century China came about, not through any inadequacy in the level of debate during the New Culture Movement, but rather in the course of attempts by liberals to come to grips with the enormous practical difficulties in improving the lot of ordinary people as China slowly entered the modern age. Charles Hayford's recent work on James Yen highlights the problems encountered by one determined individual in his attempts to introduce mass education and rural reconstruction into China. In his efforts, Yen increasingly focused on the countryside, and ultimately it was there that his campaign was fought and lost.

The present work looks at the other main arena of endeavor, modern industry.

Although the number of people working in modern industry in China in the Republican period was very small in absolute terms, the significance of the urban industrial working class far outweighed their numbers. For these people were the first to experience as a group the full impact of the modern age in every aspect of their lives. They were of the class whose condition had moved Marx and Engels, in another place and at another time, to predict and to urge revolution. Could Western experience generate solutions to the problems it had created for these people that were anything short of revolutionary?

Curiously, although the Chinese industrial proletariat played its part in the Communist victory in 1949, it was not to have the leading role. Turned back from its course of mass activism by the Kuomintang terror and purges of 1927, for another twenty years it would remain a minor player in the political events unfolding in China, apparently unchanged in its demeanor and its ability to influence its fate. Yet it would be during the three decades prior to Liberation that the "heroes and harridans" of the industrial reform movement would attempt to make their mark on China's intractable industrial problems, fail, and in their failure sow the seeds among working people of much more radical and self-directed change. This above all was the legacy of industrial reformers in Republican China.

Many friends and colleagues have contributed to this book in a variety of ways. In particular I would like to thank the archivists of the World YWCA, the World YMCA, the International Labour Organization, and the World Council of Churches, all in Geneva, and librarians at Friends House, London, and at the YWCA and YMCA in New York. In Geneva Mrs. Katherine Strong and her husband Robbins Strong offered their support and personal recollections, while in London Mrs. Hilda Brown kindly gave me access to the papers of her father, J. B. Tayler. Thanks go too to friends in China who have assisted with material. In the more distant past, meetings in China with Rewi Alley and Ma Haide (George Hatem) remain etched in my memory. I am indebted to Jack Gray and his wife Maisie for their particular help and encouragement, and to others who over the years have formed my view of China—especially Paul Lin, Jerome Ch'en, and Charles Curwen. Former colleagues at Concordia University in Montreal and current colleagues at Keele University in England have contributed ideas. I am grateful to the Department of Political Science at the University of Melbourne for kindly affording me hospitality and facilities during a period of intensive revision.Thanks to those of you out there who in the 1980s have through your work put modern Chinese social and labor history on the map. Finally, to Jan and Katie, thank you for waiting. To one and all I am most grateful.

Introduction
The Nature of Liberal Reform

The story of attempts to reform early industrial conditions in China takes place against a background of incomplete Chinese sovereignty and the competing influence and interests of the foreign powers. China's treaty port cities, legendary meeting places of East and West, have always been regarded with ambivalence by Chinese people themselves. Foreigners in the treaty ports lived in them as if they were their own, and the physical appearance of Shanghai in particular came to symbolize both modernity and the anticipated permanence of the foreign presence. In the 1920s the Bund and the waterfront, Nanking Road with its great department stores, and the vast stone houses of the French Concession all combined to rank Shanghai as one of the world's leading cities and the most cosmopolitan place in Asia—a Western city run by Westerners with Chinese labor, for Westerners and very wealthy Chinese.

In microcosm, the British and American communities in Shanghai reflected the full range of opinions that might be found in the expatriates' home countries. Thus it was that, among the foreigners, not only advocates of the most conservative view on labor matters wrote to the papers, but also many of a more liberal persuasion, and some even whose views would have been regarded as radical at home. The same held true of the Chinese community in Shanghai. Not only was there, in 1920, an untouched territory in terms of labor conditions, but also an atmosphere and a relative freedom from political constraint not present elsewhere in China, which encouraged the reformers to act boldly and to believe in the possibility of achieving results.

However, even among the individuals and organizations involved in the effort to improve the lot of industrial working people there were important nuances of difference. Thus the YMCA's approach to industrial matters and its brand of liberalism were quite different from those of its supposed sister organization, the YWCA. The Nationalist government and the Shanghai Municipal Council had their own distinct reasons for taking an interest. The incentive for involvement in China by the International Labour Organization (ILO) was different again. The liberal objective of a better life for working people was not always supported for liberal reasons, or even because it was thought that it would come true.

The principal organizations involved from the start in the industrial welfare movement were Christian. The YMCA's general objectives in China have been well documented,[1] and it has been aptly observed that President McKinley's famous remarks on his intentions toward the Philippines in 1898, "to uplift and civilize and Christianize," could equally be applied to the YMCA's program in China.[2] Prior to the First World War, the YMCA had confined its attention to the sons of the elite within society, the children of the upper class and the emerging middle class, whose power and influence in the new China would make them rewarding candidates for Christian evangelism. Service to Chinese laborers in France during the war extended education, recreation, and health care to working people, with a clear view to ensuring the docility of the work force.

After the war, the YMCA embarked on similar work with returned laborers in China, and, as with James Yen's Mass Education Movement, it was this activity that gave rise to the YMCA's industrial program. Similar work was begun in the United States. It is noteworthy, however, that in contrast to developments within the YWCA, the World's Committee of the YMCA did not appoint a Commission on Labor Problems until 1927.[3] The work developed haphazardly from one country to another, and for most YMCA officials it seems to have been motivated largely by a belief that a worker who could read and write and was well rested was likely to be more responsible and more amenable to the teachings of Christ than one who was not. The YMCA's belief in democracy did not, it would seem, extend to Chinese industrial workers, despite experiments undertaken on the rural side at Tinghsien.

The YWCA for its part traced its interest in service to working people to a recognition by its World's Committee, meeting in Berlin in 1910, that "present social and industrial conditions militate against the highest development of Christian womanhood."[4]

At Champery in France in 1920 the World's Committee made a firm commitment to get in touch with industrial women in far larger numbers through the establishment of a network of centers close to their places of work.

The YWCA further unequivocally recognized the right of working women to organize "to improve their status and voice their needs"[5] and endorsed a series of draft conventions and recommendations adopted at the first International Labor Conference in Washington in 1919.[6] The World's YWCA set up a permanent Industrial Advisory Committee and placed the "industrial question" firmly on the agenda of its national associations.

The approach of the YWCA in its industrial work was later summed up in the following terms :

> 1. The World's YWCA and a number of national associations have accepted the need of industrial standards and have pledged themselves to work for their adoption.

2. The Association recognizes the principle of opportunities for all workers and education for a group that often has had no other real chance at education.

3. In promoting industrial work the World's YWCA recognizes the need of developing leadership among industrial girls, so that they may themselves take an active part in working to bring about better conditions in industry. Hence the program for industrial girls should be built with this aim in view.[7]

These areas of concern came each in turn to be the principal peacetime emphasis of YWCA industrial work in China. By the early 1930s, YWCA industrial secretaries had concluded that "the development of class consciousness is fundamental to the improvement of workers' conditions."[8]

The liberalism of the YWCA therefore amounted to far more than "uplift" and evangelism, or the "Transpacific liberalism" of James Yen.[9] While the YMCA in China was influenced and largely funded by the International Committee of the YMCA in New York, and therefore tended to be more American in its inspiration, the YWCA in its work in China relied heavily on the World's YWCA organization, based at that time in London. It attracted to the work in China women from Britain and Australia, as well as from the United States. These women's knowledge of the techniques of industrial welfare derived from professional training, and they drew more in inspiration from the British Christian Socialist and Labour party traditions than from the business and free enterprise traditions that moved the YMCA. Indeed, some did not even consider themselves Christian at all.[10]

The National Christian Council (NCC) of China, a protestant umbrella organization, for a time helped to promote standards in industry, and some of those involved in this work went on to contribute to industrial reform in other ways. Here the distinction between the activists and their constituency, notable to a degree with all the organizations involved, was particularly significant. The NCC's constituency was the church and its membership.

The rationale for involvement of the church in efforts to improve the lives of working people was given clear expression at the meeting of the International Missionary Council in Jerusalem in 1928: "[A]ny form of economic organization which involves the treatment of men primarily as instruments of production or which sacrifices the opportunity of full personal development which should be the right of every child, is evidently anti-Christian." Christ's teaching as to the need for brotherhood "would seem to preclude such struggle for gain or self-advancement as snatches opportunities for personal success at the expense of the community or of its weaker members, and the organization of economic life primarily with a view to the enrichment of individuals."[11]

Yet even in the 1920s, the church in China tended to be conservative. Few missionaries, and perhaps fewer Chinese clergy, would have understood or sympathized much with the plight of industrial workers. The industrial reform work of the NCC was peripheral to the interests of the church, the more so as a renewed commitment to evangelism became the main focus of church activity in the 1930s.

Neither the Shanghai Municipal Council nor the Nationalist government was a liberal organization. That the Municipal Council should come to be engaged in the regulation of industrial conditions in the 1930s was attributable to the dedication of two individuals—an Australian and a New Zealander—and to the council's pragmatic desire to defuse potential sources of social unrest. It was simply not possible by this time for any government of Shanghai to ignore completely the labor conflict, unemployment, and poverty that characterized industrial life, let alone potential industrial hazards to health and safety in the confines of a vastly overcrowded city. To these concerns were added the many new problems created by the influx of refugees into the International Settlement, especially after 1937. The Municipal Council became involved because it really had no choice.

The Nanking government saw its Factory Act of 1929–31 and complementary Trade Union Law as a means of extending its influence over industrial production. Coming as it did on the heels of the purge of independent labor union activity in 1927–28, the legislation can hardly be seen as likely to bolster workers' rights, despite the intentions of its independent-minded author. It did, however, serve as a further stick with which to beat the foreign powers over the continued existence of the treaty port system.

Many people regarded the International Labour Organization as the repository of liberal values on labor matters. Yet the ILO's concern for Chinese workers was at best half-hearted and hypothetical. In the period under review the ILO was often accused of being Eurocentric, and there is evidence to suggest that as a body it was more anxious about the impact of goods made with cheap labor on European production than about the actual condition of Chinese workers.

In sum, therefore, while promoters of industrial reform were pursuing a liberal objective in that they sought "reasonable and orderly change" in conditions of life and labor for industrial workers, they differed in the lengths to which they were prepared to go to achieve it, and even in the degree of sincerity with which they sought it. In this, the movement for industrial reform mirrored the larger debate over the future form of Chinese society.

The National Question

In the years after 1919, the whole framework of extraterritoriality undergirding the existence of concession areas, settlements, and other foreign privileges in China came increasingly under attack, from workers who bore the brunt of foreign exploitation reinforced by troops and police, from Chinese merchants threatened by foreign competition, and from intellectuals who had come to feel that a more complete national independence would have to be realized before any government would be in a position to make and implement policy on other matters of pressing concern.

The patriotic movement, triggered by the unfair treatment of China at the Versailles peace conference of 1919, was perhaps a predictable response to decades of unequal interaction between China and the powers. It was also fed by specific issues, like the extension of the authority of the foreign-controlled Mixed Court in Shanghai, the lack of any representation of Chinese ratepayers on the Shanghai Municipal Council, and the attempt of the foreign council to expand its control over

Chinese territory adjacent to a series of roads, built with dubious legality even under the terms of the unequal treaties, outside the area of the International Settlement.

Inevitably the national question, in its various manifestations, had a major impact on industrial welfare work. Just as modern industry itself was a foreign invention, so largely was the campaign to reform conditions in industry. Since the first Factory Act had been passed in Britain in 1847, movements for the reform of factory life had grown up in the world's leading industrialized countries, and there was a body of opinion and expertise in the area. For this reason, and because modern industry in China was so new, the attempt to reform conditions in industry in China in the 1920s was led, with one exception in the YMCA, by foreigners. Here there was a marked difference with the Mass Education Movement and with rural reconstruction, where the leadership had from the beginning been Chinese.[12]

In the 1930s, when sinicization was the order of the day, the National Christian Council and the YMCA effectively dropped out of industrial welfare work. Only in the YWCA did the work of training industrial leaders flourish, under Cora Deng. This is not to say that there were no Chinese "foot soldiers" in the industrial reform movement, but rather that as a cause among educated Chinese, a healthy industrial work environment, requiring an increasing degree of technical competence to monitor, was a foreign concept that never really seemed to take.

Perhaps the explanation for this lies in the degree of frustration felt by Chinese people over China's inability effectively to implement legislation to regulate industrial conditions, or indeed anything else where foreign interests were involved. The industrial reform movement ran straight up against the rise of Chinese nationalism. Many Chinese people came to feel that as most of the larger factories were foreign-owned and protected from regulation by the unequal treaties, their anger should be directed against the treaties rather than against industrial conditions per se. The trade unions, while genuinely concerned about conditions, had their own agenda.

The reactions of foreign industrial reformers to the growing desire of Chinese people for the realization of their full national integrity were varied. Perhaps most sympathetic were officials of the YWCA, though even these women, while protesting the indignity that extraterritorial jurisdiction imposed upon Chinese, nonetheless enjoyed the special protection accorded to all foreigners in times of crisis.[13] Within the constituency of the National Christian Council, foreigners were divided in their feelings about extraterritoriality, their desire to support their Chinese colleagues in arguing for its abolition competing with anxiety about what the future might hold for foreign missionaries in China after its discontinuation. As the church in China was sinicized, however, its ambivalence disappeared. Chinese Christians, lay and clergy, generally supported the government's demand that the system be brought to an end.[14]

It is with the YMCA that the national question becomes most troublesome. While the prime mover of YMCA industrial work in the 1920s was a Chinese, it is apparent that from the beginning the work was closely supervised by older, American staff, both on the spot in China and on the International Committee back in New York.[15] With much of the money for YMCA work in China also coming from the

United States, there was a strong sense, supported by the correspondence, that the YMCA's industrial program was regarded as a charitable work undertaken by Americans on behalf of the Chinese.

Perhaps the clearest indication of where the foreign staff's national sentiments lay came with the invasion of Shanghai by Nationalist forces in the early spring of 1927. At this time, anxiety within the association about the possible collapse of the social order in China and an end to extraterritoriality reached its highest point, moving one official to write home, "We are having martial times in Shanghai, as you have heard. To-day I was thrilled to see twelve hundred American marines march through the city. Their splendid bearing and energetic step and fine form filled me with pride and emotion. They marched like soldiers."[16] The YMCA apparently counted on support from the U.S. government in the event of any violation of its property by Chinese troops.[17]

In all, therefore, the unresolved national question to a marked degree determined what could be achieved in the way of industrial reform.

The Legal Context

It was, of course, in Shanghai and in other treaty port cities that the greater part of China's modern industry came to be located. If the system of extraterritoriality and unequal treaties worked to confound the application of Chinese labor law where it was most needed, the legal position of foreigners and their factories operating in the treaty ports was of particular significance.[18]

The treaty port system dated back to the signing in 1842 of the first of the unequal treaties between China and the foreign powers, in the first instance Britain, following China's defeat in the First Opium War. Among the provisions of the Treaty of Nanking was the right of foreigners to "reside, lease land, and build houses"[19] in certain concession areas in designated treaty ports. This right was extended to other foreign nationalities, just as the number of treaty ports was also increased following further conflict between China and the powers in the Second Opium War of 1856 to 1860.

Although in the beginning there had been a prohibition on Chinese living in the concession areas, this proved impossible to enforce, and foreigners rapidly became involved in the regulation of matters affecting the lives of Chinese living in and frequenting the concessions. As the Ch'ing dynasty went into further decline, finally collapsing in 1911, the foreign powers increased their grip on the concession areas, and the most important of them took on many of the attributes of full colonies, with complex laws, courts, and paramilitary forces.

Shanghai was divided jurisdictionally into three during the period under review, the constituent parts being the essentially Anglo-American International Settlement, the French Concession, and the Chinese-administered areas known as Chapei, Nantao, and Woosung. These latter were brought together as the Municipality of Greater Shanghai under the direct supervision of Nanking in 1927.[20]

The International Settlement was governed by a Municipal Council whose legitimacy was held to be derived from the Land Regulations of 1845. The council ruled through promulgation and enforcement of bylaws enacted from time to time as the need arose. Amendment of the Land Regulations could only be achieved through diplomatic negotiation between China and the powers involved, though by the 1920s any extension of the council's influence by this means was out of the question. Enactment or amendment of bylaws required a two-thirds majority of those present and voting at a special meeting of the ratepayers of the settlement, and the approval of the consular and diplomatic bodies of the powers concerned.

Foreigners enjoying extraterritorial privileges in China, whether they lived inside or outside the settlement, were exempt from the jurisdiction of the Chinese courts and were subject instead to special consular courts that applied to them the law of their country of origin. Despite the contention of Chinese authorities that extraterritoriality was "of the person" and should not afford protection from Chinese law to enterprises owned by foreigners, in practice it did afford such protection. It was also the case, however, that the labor legislation obtaining in an employer's country of origin was not generally applied to the factory that person operated in China, so that foreign manufacturing enterprises benefited from the law while suffering none of its constraints. Two actions brought against American companies for failing to comply with the terms of the Workmen's Compensation Act of the District of Columbia, heard in the United States Court for China in 1936, led to inconclusive results.[21]

Chinese citizens residing in the International Settlement were subject to the jurisdiction of the Mixed Court between 1911 and 1927, and subsequently that of the Provisional Court, and after 1930 the First Special District Court. While the earlier arrangements provided for foreign "assessors" to sit with Chinese judges, after 1930 the jurisdiction was exclusively Chinese. The court tried cases brought before it by the Shanghai Municipal Police arising out of infringements of all duly enacted laws of the Chinese government and infractions of Shanghai Municipal Council bylaws, committed both by Chinese and by those categories of foreigners not enjoying extraterritorial status.

The court was not, however, in a position to apply regulations promulgated by the various ministries of the Chinese government. Into this class fell the provisions of the Factory Act and related legislation of 1929–31. Furthermore, the "competent authorities" charged with the task of enforcing this legislation throughout China were the various municipal and hsien governments. However, the Shanghai city government, its police, and other organs of enforcement had no power to bring offenders within the settlement before the First Special District Court, while the court, for its part, refused to try cases under the labor laws brought to it by the Shanghai Municipal Police or any other organ of the Municipal Council. Thus a stalemate existed.[22]

The jurisdiction dispute proved an obstacle to the implementation of legislated reform of labor conditions in Shanghai throughout the period under review. In 1925 many Chinese, even some among the reform lobby, turned against the Municipal Council's proposed legislation to limit the use of child labor in settlement factories because it represented an attempt by the foreign council to extend its jurisdiction.

Nor would the council yield any authority on the matter of labor legislation to the Chinese, asserting upon promulgation of Nanking's Factory Act in 1929 its right to jurisdiction in the International Settlement, subject only to the limitations imposed by the Land Regulations and to the ultimate sanction of the consular body in Shanghai and of the ministers of the powers.

That foreigners were unreceptive to suggestions by the Chinese that they should give up their privileged position is amply illustrated in testimony before the Feetham Commission on the status of the International Settlement in Shanghai in 1931.[23] Indeed, Feetham's conclusion that the status of the settlement was legitimate because it had been freely negotiated in a diplomatic treaty was narrowly legalistic and bound not to impress Chinese opinion. It showed how wide a gap remained on extraterritoriality well into the 1930s.

Attempts by the ILO and others to find a compromise solution that would enable enforcement of uniform labor legislation throughout China met with no success. In due course it became clear that legislation would not be the way to improve the lot of working people in China's "special circumstances."

Part I
The Task Defined

1

Modern Industry and Its Human Implications

The year 1895 was in several ways a watershed for China. The defeat by Japan in that year precipitated both a movement for reform in all phases of Chinese life, culminating in the abortive "hundred days of reform" in 1898, and the scramble for further concessions and spheres of influence on the part of the foreign powers, which helped to provoke the Boxer Uprising in 1899. Not least among the consequences of China's defeat was the provision of the Treaty of Shimonoseki that permitted for the first time the construction and operation of modern factories by the Japanese in the principal treaty ports. According to the most-favored-nation principle, this privilege came to apply automatically to the other powers having treaty relations with China. While illegal foreign investment in industry in China predated the 1895 treaty,[1] there can be no doubt that it paved the way for a significant influx of foreign capital. This in turn led to increased Chinese investment in industry, especially when the flow of foreign goods into China was disrupted during the First World War. Thus have the years 1914 to 1922 been described as the "golden age" of Chinese industry.[2]

The precise pattern of industrial development in China before Liberation was largely determined by the prospects for a rapid return on investment as they appeared to Chinese and foreign entrepreneurs. Capital was therefore invested in those industries where there was the greatest likelihood of a quick profit, with little attention being given to attaining industrial self-sufficiency. Labor was widely regarded as limitless and expendable. A typical appeal to shareholders by the agents of one cotton mill in the mid-1920s claimed that "the company is in an exceptionally favorable position. With the raw product at their doors, an abundant and absurdly cheap labor supply to draw on, and no vexatious factory laws to observe, it is not surprising that their annual profits should have exceeded their total capital on at least three occasions."[3] It was in this climate that the industrial welfare movement in China came into being.

The Scope of Modern Industry

The flow of investment into an industry naturally tended to be reflected in the size of the actual factories in which the workers and machinery were housed, and indeed

3

in the extent to which modern machinery was used at all. Thus industries that were "modern," as this term would be understood in the West—those "in which large factories may be found where large numbers of workers are gathered in large buildings and power machinery is used"[4]—were cotton spinning, silk reeling, cigarette and tobacco manufacture, the manufacture of matches, flour milling, oil pressing, sugar refining, the making of egg products, printing, the manufacture of machine parts, and the manufacture of items from rubber.[5]

Certain of these industries were also carried on in smaller workshops with fewer employees and a lesser degree of modernization; in particular silk reeling, the manufacture of rubber and matches, and printing were also carried on on this smaller scale. Other manufacturing processes were undertaken principally at this level, notably the production of knitted garments and woolen textiles, electrical items, glassware, and paper.[6] Indeed, the great majority of factories in China before Liberation were of this smaller type, and as a consequence of this fragmentation of industry, observation of conditions, reform, and the application of legislation were all made more difficult than they might otherwise have been.[7]

A third level of manufacturing enterprise was true handicraft industry, production of domestic wares and other relatively simple items using age-old techniques. Handicraft work was carried on both in the cities and, particularly during the slack season afforded by the agricultural cycle, in the countryside by peasants. Here production was usually related more directly to local needs, and the influence of the money economy and considerations of profit were felt much less, with the result that the handicraft worker, though poor, was more his or her own master, and the pace of work was less arduous. Exceptions to this rule might be those hand industries that produced for a wider market or for export, such as the lacquerware industry, notably in Canton and Foochow, and the porcelain industry at Kingtechen in Kiangsi. Handicraft industry, although involving many more people than the modern sector, commanded little attention among those seeking to reform conditions of industry in China in the period under review and therefore will not be considered here.

The three levels of production were by no means mutually exclusive, and processes might be carried on at different levels within one industry.[8] It is even possible that the growth in the market for certain goods, consequent on the introduction of modern industry, may have forestalled a decline in handicraft production.[9]

Deployment of Resources

It is difficult to estimate accurately how many workers were employed in the various industries, how many and how large were the factories in which they worked, or even the extent of capitalization for any but the most prominent enterprises. Although statistics were kept by the Peking government between 1914 and 1920, and again by the Nationalist Ministry of Industries in Nanking and by the Bureau of Social Affairs of the Municipality of Greater Shanghai after 1928, they were in the early years incomplete, inadequately qualified, and inconsistent.[10] Efforts by the Nankai University Statistical Service, the contemporary economist

D. K. Lieu, and others to make sense of government figures tended to founder because of the haphazardness with which the data had been collected.[11] Partial but probably more accurate information was sometimes provided for researchers by employers' associations or by individual firms and was also kept, though rarely made public, by the consular officers of the various powers enjoying treaty privileges in China.[12] In the late 1930s the Shanghai Municipal Council's Industrial Section began to keep comprehensive data on industry in the International Settlement, but this activity was soon cut short by the Japanese occupation of Shanghai at the end of 1941.[13]

While statistics for the period in question must therefore be treated as only a very imprecise indication of the true state of affairs, some attempt to define the scope of Chinese industry at this time would seem in order. Among contemporary sources, the last survey prepared by the Peking government, in 1920, estimated that there were some 420,000 workers in Chinese industry in that year, of whom by far the largest element were workers in cotton spinning and related occupations—some 144,000. "Textile weaving" employed some 80,000 workers, silk reeling 54,000, tobacco processing nearly 7,000, the manufacture of matches and gunpowder nearly 10,000, and printing over 4,000, to name but a few. It was estimated that of the total of 6,524 factories in China at this time, 80 percent employed between 7 and 29 workers, while only 1,312, or 20 percent, contained 30 workers or more. In only 499 factories, or 7.6 percent, were there said to be 100 workers or more.[14] Augusta Wagner, writing in 1938, estimated that there were by that time "probably not more than 2,000" factories with 30 or more employees, and that of these there were "probably not more than 500 large factories." Wagner cites a census taken in Shanghai in 1934 that showed that only 375 factories there averaged 100 employees or more. In her estimation there were between 900,000 and 1 million workers employed in "industrial establishments which can be considered factories," by which she would appear to mean those employing 30 or more.[15] Wagner puts the development of industry into perspective when she points out that even by the time of the outbreak of war with Japan, less than one-fifth of 1 percent of China's people were engaged in industrial production in any modern sense.

More recent estimates tend to confirm the overall impression given by contemporary observers. Thomas Rawski, drawing on the work of Liu and Yeh, accepts a figure of 921,000 workers in China's most important industries in 1933, working in factories that were "manufacturing establishments of all sizes using mechanical power." Rawski's observation that in 1933 modern industry accounted for only 3 percent of China's estimated GDP places industrial activity in perspective.[16]

China's most important modern industry was cotton. This included both spinning and weaving: Bush notes that the vertical integration of these two functions within a single mill tended to be greatest in the larger mills.[17] A burst of activity in this industry, marked by an increase in the number of cotton mills in operation from 49 to 120 between 1918 and 1923,[18] was slowing down by the early 1920s, as evidenced by a decline in the value added in cotton textiles in 1921–22.[19] The industry also suffered along with other industries during the depression in China, from 1933 to 1936, as noted below.

For most of the rest of the period under review, however, the industry prospered. A 1928 report by the Chinese Cotton Mill Owners' Association claimed that in that year the industry as a whole, still with 120 mills, employed 241,559 people and was capitalized at 297.4 million taels (460.97 million yuan).[20] A subsequent report, in 1937, found that there were then 143 mills employing 232,846 workers.[21]

These figures may not be inconsistent with Liu and Yeh's data, which show 317,000 workers employed in the cotton textile industry as a whole in 1933, immediately before the impact of the depression.[22] For that year in Shanghai, however, where more than half the mills were located, Emily Honig posits a working population in the city's cotton mills of 113,766. Honig believes 1930 to be the year of highest employment in the cotton industry, when 131,038 were employed.[23] Many of these were women and young girls.[24]

In the silk industry one source estimates that there were 495 steam-worked silk filatures throughout China in 1929, of which 299 were in Kwangtung, while in Shanghai there were 104 and in Wusih 37. Others were located elsewhere in Kiangsu and in Chekiang, Szechuan, Hupeh, and Shantung. No proper contemporary estimate seems to exist of the total number employed in the silk industry at the time of this survey, though Shanghai filatures are reported as giving employment to 63,900.[25] A different source places the number employed in the filatures in Wusih at 23,604.[26] If these figures are projected, it is possible to speculate that there may have been as many as 237,000 workers employed in silk filatures throughout China, most of them women and girls.[27] Liu and Yeh's more recent study puts the number employed in 1933 in silk textiles at 108,000, and in silk piece goods at a further 87,000.[28]

The investment of capital in the silk industry needed to be on a much smaller scale than was the case with cotton. If Ho and Fong are reasonably accurate in asserting that the "mode size filature" in Shanghai was capitalized at this time at about 30,000 taels,[29] then the capital invested in the silk industry throughout China might be estimated at 14.85 million taels (23.02 million yuan).

Consumption of cigarettes in China is said to have reached 100 billion a year by the early 1930s. Most cigarettes were supplied by the domestic tobacco industry.[30] The industry could claim some 58 factories by 1937, of which those of the British-American Tobacco (BAT) Company and the Nanyang Brothers were by far the largest and the best known. The BAT Company and most of the Chinese factories were situated in Shanghai, where the 45 Chinese factories alone employed some 17,000 workers.[31] A full complement at the BAT works would bring this figure up to a likely 25,000, while in China as a whole there were perhaps 30,000 working in the industry in 1937. Liu and Yeh put forward a higher total for the industry, 44,000, for the year 1933.[32] In tobacco factories, it was common for both men and women to be employed.

Capitalization of Chinese cigarette factories stood, according to one source, at 20,452,667 yuan in 1937.[33] If the BAT interests are taken into account, it is possible to conceive of capitalization for the industry standing at about 30 million yuan.

In the match industry, there were said to be some 73 factories in existence in 1937, substantially fewer than another study had uncovered nine years earlier.[34]

Neither of these contemporary sources attempts to estimate the number of people working in match factories, which were scattered throughout almost all the provinces of China, though Liu and Yeh believe the figure to be 37,000 in 1933.[35] Total capitalization for the industry was put at 16,852,570 yuan in 1937.[36] Most factories were said to be quite small, and many apparently used little or no power machinery. Their importance to any consideration of industrial welfare lies in the particular notoriety they gained in the 1920s for their extensive use of poisonous white phosphorous and their widespread employment of children.

These industries held much of the attention of industrial reformers, but also significant in terms of the pattern of industry at the time were machine tool works (49,000 employed), printing works (42,000 employed), transport equipment factories (27,000 employed), brick and shingle plants (23,000 employed), iron and steel works (22,000 employed), rubber factories (16,000 employed), and food-processing plants of different kinds (60,000 employed).[37] Carpet manufacture was an important smaller-scale industry local to Peking, Tientsin, and Shanghai.[38]

Growth and Retrenchment

The inadequacy of statistical information about Chinese industry at this time, and in particular its lack of continuity, also makes it difficult to assess with any precision the pattern of growth or retrenchment in Chinese industry during the period under review. For example, Eastman sees the age of greatest expansion and prosperity, consequent on temporary freedom from foreign competition, as lasting from 1914 right up until late 1922, when an "industrial crisis" brought on by poor cotton harvests, high world prices of cotton, and a fall in world prices of silver put an end to it.[39] Thereafter growth resumed, but at a slower rate. Rawski, however, maintains that the years 1920–22 produced the only instance of a contraction in industrial output for the whole period 1912–36.[40] Apart from this brief reversal, Rawski holds that growth in manufacturing, while not constant, was steady. Yet at a time when most analysts agree manufacturing industry was buoyant, in 1924, the chairman of the Foreign Cotton Mill Owners Association could declare of business prospects that they were "very bad at present, and would probably become worse."[41]

It is true that there were changes in the context for business that were experienced by all the various categories of manufacturing industry. The early 1920s were characterized by political strife, growing labor militancy, and renewed competition for Chinese products from goods manufactured in Europe.[42] It is no coincidence that this period also happened to see the first wave of concern among foreigners over questions of industrial welfare in China.

Most Chinese manufacturers welcomed the coming of the Kuomintang to Shanghai in 1927 and the purges of the labor unions that followed. The new government was established in Nanking, and between 1929 and 1931, with the victory of the Nationalist forces and suppression of the unions guaranteeing industrialists a respite from labor troubles, Chinese industry experienced a resurgence. As Coble and Bush have both shown, however, relations between Chinese industrialists and the Nationalist government were far from close, and their interests proved in many areas not to coincide.[43] Taxation and "squeeze" to fund endless wars against the Communists and the Kuomintang's tolerance of Green Gang interference with labor practices were just two major sources of conflict. Even the Factory Act of 1931, which the Kuomintang saw as a means of defusing industrial causes of potentially threatening social unrest, was opposed by Chinese cotton mill owners as a constraint on their right to manage.[44]

In September 1931 Japan invaded Manchuria, and in the spring of 1932 it bombarded and invaded Shanghai, causing widespread if temporary disruption of industrial production. Floods also brought distress to the Yangtze valley in 1931. These events combined with developments overseas to bring the full impact of the world depression to China in 1933.

In 1931 Britain, Germany, Japan, and Canada, already hard hit by the effects of the depression, abandoned the gold standard. In March 1933 the United States did the same. The world price of silver rapidly increased, taking China's currency up with it. Between 1931 and 1935 the foreign exchange value of the yuan almost doubled, which, along with the loss of Manchuria, contributed to a decline in the value of China's exports from 1,417 million yuan in 1931 to only 535 million yuan in 1935.[45] Cotton and silk products, with substantial export markets, were particularly affected. Simultaneously foreign investment in China was drastically cut, while in 1934 the adoption by the United States of a silver purchase policy caused silver to pour out of China through Shanghai, and especially through the foreign-owned banks.[46]

The rural depression, exacerbated by the floods, had begun in 1932 and led to a slackening in domestic demand for manufactured products, causing wholesale prices to fall by 26.4 percent between 1931 and 1935. Prior to the depression, many industrialists had expanded production, borrowing heavily from the banks to do so. Loans were secured by product, raw materials, factory building, and site. The declining value of all these, in the face of rising interest rates, placed many manufacturers in an impossible position from the spring of 1933. The predicament was made worse in the case of the Shanghai textile industry by increased competition from plants in the interior; Chinese-owned plants additionally suffered both from intense competition from Japanese-owned plants in China and from the Nanking government's own tax policies.[47]

The effect of the depression on most industries, certainly in the short term, was very serious. Between 1932 and 1935 many factories reduced the number of workers they employed and cut the working hours and pay of those who remained. Others closed down altogether, some never to reopen. In 1934 only 5 out of more than 100 silk filatures in Shanghai were functioning normally, and 70,000 silk workers in Chekiang and Kiangsu were out of work. In 1935 nine cotton mills in various parts of China with a capital value of nearly 14 million yuan were driven to bankruptcy.[48] Government commissions were established to assist in reviving the fortunes of both the cotton and silk industries, but neither had any great impact.

In the longer term, the effect of the depression on the Chinese economy may have been less severe than in the case of other countries. Government measures to stabilize the currency and nationalize the major Chinese banks taken in the autumn of 1935 brought a return of confidence in the new year, and industrial production had begun to approach predepression levels by mid-1937. Moreover, it has been shown that except for 1933, Chinese industrial output continued to expand right through the depression years despite all temporary setbacks.[49]

The outbreak of war with Japan changed the position yet again. One after another of the cities in eastern China fell to the armies of occupation and industrial production came, for the time being, to a halt. In Shanghai, Japanese bombing of factories in areas under Chinese jurisdiction and the enormous influx of refugees into the International Settlement rendered normal economic life impossible well into 1938.[50] In due course, however, factories in territory under Japanese control were mobilized more or less effectively in support of the Japanese war effort, while in the International Settlement Chinese and foreign entrepreneurs took advantage of the enclave's extraordinary neutrality to revive production and profit, probably from both sides, in the war. Over the next two years the economy of the settlement experienced an unprecedented recovery, although decline had again set in by 1941. Away to the west, attempts by the Nationalists to reestablish production around Chungking with machinery and refugees brought from the cities of the east met with only limited success.

These developments formed the context for growth or retrenchment in Chinese industry and might be supposed to have favored one or the other. Yet, with the possible exception of the impact of the depression, as Rawski has observed, it is still difficult to generalize in any valid way about the progress of industry as a whole. Rather Rawski attempts to identify growth in individual industries over the period from 1912, the beginning of the republic, to 1936, close to the beginning of all-out war with Japan. Thus, building on the work of John Chang, he is able to determine an overall rate of growth in the most important sectors of Chinese manufacturing industry (see Table 1.1).

Growth in most of these industries for the period as a whole is quite significant. Rawski also notes certain particular causes of fluctuation in individual industries, observing that as some waned, others flourished. In cotton textiles, the years 1923–27 were a time of dramatic growth in output, to meet demand from an expanded domestic market. Performance over the following decade was mixed. By comparison, cotton yarn made more modest gains, with growth after 1927 dependent on exports. In the silk industry, output rose between 1912 and 1926, only to fall right back by 1936, for a net gain of zero. A substantial drop in exports during the depression years helped to account for this poor performance. Nearly all cigarette production was for the domestic market; except for the years 1920–22, Rawski infers an overall steady growth in this industry, where output was increasingly dominated by the British-American Tobacco Company. In the match industry, through flexible use of technology to suit the assets of different firms, the industry as a whole expanded rapidly until the early 1930s. Thereafter, growth was checked by the depression. The rubber industry presents almost an opposite case, developing

Table 1.1

**Estimated Growth Rate of
Manufacturing Output, 1912–1936**

Sector Average Annual Growth Rate	Percent
Pig iron	20
Steel	23
Cotton yarn	9.1
Cotton cloth	17.5
Cement	11.6
Cigarettes	20
Rubber	30
Matches	8
Machinery/transport equipment	10
Bricks and shingles	10
Silk and silk pieces	0
Edible oil	3
Rice milling	1
Flour	6.7

Source: Adapted from Rawski, *Economic Growth in Prewar China*, table A.1.

more slowly until around 1930, and then leaping ahead throughout the years up to 1936.

Rawski concludes that the long-term growth rate of the Chinese manufacturing industry between 1912 and 1936, based on all the industries noted in table 1.1, was 8.1 percent. The industries used in this study accounted for 73 percent of value added, and 88 percent of employment in industry in 1933.[51]

Ownership

To what extent was China's industry foreign-owned during the period under review? Perhaps the best contemporary study of foreign investment at this time remains that by C. F. Remer, first published in 1933. Remer found that of all foreign money invested in China in the early 1930s, a total he estimated at U.S. $3,242,500,000, only slightly over 10 percent, some $376,300,000, was invested in the manufacturing industry, with the remainder, nearly 90 percent, representing interests in transport, mining, real estate, banking, and the export and import trade. Of this $376,300,000, all but $4,000,000 was taken up by the interests of four major powers, Britain, Japan, the United States, and Russia, with Britain's share being U.S. $173,400,000; Japan's, $165,600,000; the United States', $20,500,000; and Russia's, $12,800,000. British investment in manufacturing was by far the most diversified: in addition to cotton and silk products, British-owned factories in China made cigarettes, candles, flour, bean oil, chemicals, soap, cement, lumber, and rope, as well as processing skins, furs, bristles, and wool. There were also British-owned printing works. British manufacturing interests were represented in some measure in almost every major treaty port. By contrast, much of Japan's investment was concentrated in cotton and silk mills, particularly in Shanghai, though Japanese capital was also present in cigarette and match factories, paper factories, sawmills and woodworking plants, flour mills, and vegetable oil pressing mills. American investment was principally in the manufacture of carpets, while White Russians had owned flour mills, distilleries, sawmills, and vegetable oil pressing mills, chiefly in Manchuria where they were lost to the Japanese in 1931.[52] Thus the range of foreign investment covered nearly all of China's most important industries.

More recent work gives a further perspective on foreign ownership. Eastman notes that in 1933, foreign firms represented 63 percent of all industrial capital in China and Manchuria.[53] Rawski finds for the same year that in terms of value of industrial output, which he puts at a total of 2,645.5 billion yuan for China and Manchuria, just over 27 percent was produced by factories owned or partially owned by foreigners.[54]

Where advanced technology or a new product was the hallmark of an industry, Chinese investment often followed foreign investment. Thus, as Cochran has observed, in the cigarette industry the market was really created through the initiative of the British-American Tobacco Company between 1902 and 1915, but thereafter an effective challenge was mounted by the Nanyang Brothers well into the 1920s. Cochran's study highlights the complexity of the relationship between Chinese and foreign entrepreneurship. Thus it was BAT's Chinese staff who in fact had brought about the company's success by going into the interior, persuading peasants to grow the new "bright" tobacco, and using the techniques of what now would be called saturation advertising to encourage consumption of cigarettes.[55] Nanyang was then able to exploit the new taste for cigarettes and, using the latest technology and patriotic advertising, make substantial gains at BAT's expense. Beyond the mid-1920s, Nanyang succumbed to internal feuds and capital problems that made it less effective.

The experience varied from industry to industry, but the example of the cigarette industry is sufficient to show that not in all cases did the thesis of imperialist exploitation hold good in any straightforward way.[56] While foreign firms had access to technology, and capital from foreign banks, Chinese firms had local knowledge, often cheaper labor costs combined with more labor intensive production, and, for much of the period, the nationalist movement on their side.[57] The latter showed itself in strikes and boycotts against foreign-owned enterprises and appeals to support Chinese-made goods.[58] For Rawski, responsiveness to "changing market requirements" was the factor that outweighed all others in determining individual firms' success.[59]

One advantage that foreign industrialists did enjoy, however, was extraterritorial protection from Chinese law. Many of their factories were in any case situated in the foreign settlements of major treaty ports, but even where they operated in territory nominally under Chinese jurisdiction, there was no clear agreement that their operation should be governed by Chinese law. Thus all foreign concerns in reality enjoyed a residual protection from the vagaries of Chinese politics. One important result of extraterritoriality was the lack of progress on the implementation of laws for factory inspection because the Chinese government claimed that it could not enforce its will on factories outside the concession areas if it was prevented from enforcing it inside the settlement boundaries. In fact, on this particular point there was no significant benefit to either side.

Some observers of the industrial scene in China at this time suggested that there was a link between industrial conditions and management practice, on one hand, and whether the factory was Chinese- or foreign-owned, on the other.[60] In reality, whether a factory was Chinese- or foreign-owned seemed to have no necessary impact on conditions unless the size and degree of modernization of the factory were also taken into account. There were wide variations in the management practices of foreign concerns, just as there were among Chinese firms, and no hard and fast conclusions can be drawn. Much depended on the conviction of individual factory owners and on their inclination to provide better wages and conditions or other palliatives. Such an inclination might be based on a philanthropic motive or, more likely, the hard calculation that this was what management needed to do to get the staff.

Human Factors

Where did the people come from to fill the factories, and what were their conditions of work? Much of the labor employed in treaty port factories was attracted from rural areas in the hinterland of the cities, or from farther afield in neighboring provinces. In general, the flow from villages was greatest when the weather, or political unrest, made it harder than usual to scratch a living from the soil. At first most workers, often male heads of household, would be likely to spend only part of the year in the factory, returning to the country to practice their former livelihood for the remainder of the time. This was true not only for industrial workers but also for other groups, like rickshaw pullers.[61] Some mills took this into account and closed down for a month or so at harvest time. "Rural-urban mobility" might also occur on the occasion of religious holidays, marriages and birthdays, funeral ceremonies, the illness of a parent, a desire to consult a local medicine man or fortune-teller, and so forth, for voluntary and social as well as for economic reasons.

In due course, the tendency was for the entire family to migrate to the city and remain there on a year-round basis. Traffic back and forth to the countryside became less frequent. Thus in centers such as Shanghai, Tientsin, Hankow, and Canton, sizable urbanized laboring classes came into existence. Shanghai, for example, drew many of its workers from the depressed area of Kiangsu north of the Yangtze River known as Supei, or the "Kompo."[62] Nonetheless, both Hershatter and Honig find the continuance of rural ties and identification with native place of great significance in the lives of workers, and especially of women. Place of origin could even determine life's possibilities in Shanghai, providing the informal network through which one might get a job, find protection, or even organize for better conditions of work.[63]

The trend overall was in the direction of the cities, though the flow was by no means unbroken—in the case of Shanghai the influx of permanent immigrants during the period of civil strife in the mid-1920s was followed by a forced, if temporary, exodus by tens of thousands of unemployed during the lean years of the early 1930s—the countryside acting as "unemployment insurance" for city workers.[64] This trend continued up to Liberation and resumed, though without official sanction, in the 1980s. In this, China is not unlike other countries where the city is the symbol of modern life and the streets are assumed to be paved with gold.

Recruitment

The particular methods of recruiting workers into industry in China in the early twentieth century played no small part in hastening the flow from the countryside and in making sure that workers remained in city mills and factories as long as they were needed. Jean Chesneaux has described the three principal methods of recruitment as apprenticeship, the labor contract, and the "freely negotiated agreement," a broad division also used by Eastman.[65] While this categorization may not describe all the possible variations, as will be noted below, it is a useful starting point for this discussion.

Apprenticeship was a concept that had been inherited from the traditional Chinese guild. It was used by employers essentially to hold down labor costs and to limit the mobility of workers.[66] While it was not widely used as a method of recruitment in Shanghai, it was much in evidence elsewhere, Chesneaux citing its use in the cotton mills of Tientsin and Hankow, the silk filatures of Wusih, the match factories of Peking and Tientsin, the glassworks of Peking and Hong Kong, and the workshops on the Ching-Han railway line.[67] Hershatter found apprenticeship widely used in Tientsin in carpet factories, among handloom weavers, button makers, and hosiery knitters, and in electroplating, soapmaking, tanning, iron-working, and machine-making—the processes carried on in smaller plants with less complex equipment.[68]

Under this system, a company agent would be sent to the villages in a city's hinterland to urge male children to return with him to the city and become apprenticed to a trade or industry.[69] Parents would be encouraged to sign their offspring over to the agent by promises that factory work was not hard, and that schooling would be given to all workers. The decisive factor must often have been the bleakness of the prospects in the countryside. Once the contract was signed, the young apprentice would be obliged to go to work for his company for board and lodging, and frequently no salary at all. An apprentice was often virtually a prisoner in the factory where he worked, eating and sleeping there, and requiring special permission to go out. If an apprentice abandoned his company before his time was served, his family would in all likelihood be subject to a fine. In most cases, the promised schooling failed to materialize, and because of the continual induction of new recruits into the system the possibilities for employment at the end of the term were severely limited.[70]

Most true apprentices were boys aged between fourteen and eighteen, but observers agree that there was substantial overlap between formal apprenticeship and the practice of hiring child workers to perform unskilled tasks, and that one tended to blur into the other.[71] Management of some of the larger mills apparently disliked the apprenticeship system, which they claimed was forced upon them by parents, and the system was less in evidence by the early 1930s. It experienced a resurgence later in the decade, however, and was sufficiently common once more by the late 1930s for the Bureau of Social Affairs of the Tientsin city government to draw up a model contract for apprentices in that city, to try to reduce abuse of the system.[72]

The *pao-kung*, or contract labor system, the second of the three methods of recruitment, was the one that prevailed in Shanghai until Liberation. It was used extensively in the cotton mills and silk filatures, and by foreign employers such as the Public Works Department of the International Settlement, the French Tramway Company, and the British-American Tobacco Company. While it is frequently suggested that foreign entrepreneurs, upon coming to China, may have adopted this method of recruitment because it was an easy way of handling Chinese labor, Chesneaux points out that there was precedent for the hiring of workers through intermediary agencies not only in certain precapitalist industries such as flour-milling, construction, and tin-mining, but also in agriculture in certain parts of the country.[73]

According to this system, a *pao-kung-t'ou* or *lao-pan*, essentially a middle man who had made a contract with the manager of an enterprise to supply a certain quantity of labor, would in turn make contracts with workers, both adults and children, who would then become his employees. They might then work in a factory designated by the contractor for three or four years or more for nothing more than board, lodging, and clothing provided by the contractor, and perhaps a bonus of from ten to forty yuan at the end of the contract. Young women workers were often locked in their dormitories during their leisure hours and escorted to and from work by "guards" employed by the contractor specially for the purpose.[74]

The profits made by some labor contractors were quite handsome. Where a worker had been so unfortunate as to get into debt with his contractor, exorbitant rates of interest ensured that he would have to go on working for nothing well after the expiry of his original contract. When days were lost through illness or for some other reason, they had to be made up at the expiry of the contract. Augusta Wagner, an authoritative contemporary observer, suggests that compensation of one month's work for one day lost was not uncommon.[75]

Where the labor contract system was used to recruit children from the countryside there was, as the Shanghai Child Labor Commission was to observe, ample scope for abuse. Children were often housed in the most miserable quarters and fed scarcely enough to keep them alive; while the contractor might pay the parents of a child two yuan per month for the right to exploit its labor, he would probably collect six yuan per month from the company for the work that the child had done.[76] The findings of the Child Labor Commission with respect to the conditions that children endured in the factories stand as testimony to the desperate circumstances that prompted their parents to send them there in the first place. (The issue of child labor will be dealt with more fully in chapter 5.)

Emily Honig, in her exhaustive study of women cotton workers in Shanghai, draws a distinction between the contract labor system and what she calls the contract work system. According to Honig, under the contract work system, "the owner and manager of an enterprise relinquished all decisions concerning production to a foreman, who was paid a flat fee for producing a certain amount of the finished product," and who handled recruitment using subordinate foremen. This system was common in the early 1920s in Shanghai but gave way from around 1928 to a true contract labor system, in which contractors who had no firm connection with the factory acted as middlemen, mounting expeditions into the countryside to look for prospective young women workers, a process referred to colloquially as "plucking mulberry leaves." This development she sees as a direct consequence of the increasing involvement of the Green Gang in labor recruiting, following their participation in the purges by the Kuomintang of the Communist movement in 1927.[77]

Honig is undoubtedly correct in identifying a trend to the "institutionalization" of the role of the middleman in recruitment in the late 1920s and in linking this to the Green Gang, but it is not clear that labor contractors, as distinct from factory foremen, were not active before that point. Both the report of the Shanghai Child Labor Commission, published in 1925, and unpublished testimony to the commission dating from 1923, for example, make reference to labor contractors as facilitators of the problem of child labor. What these sources do not indicate is whether these individuals were working for the factory or for themselves, though the strong implication is that some of them at least may have been working for themselves.

The "freely negotiated agreement" was the third form of recruitment, according to which the worker was, in theory, taken on and paid directly by the factory and was free to quit at any time. The actual hiring was usually done by the factory foreman or forewoman in control of the factory floor, however, and it was common for this individual to exact a commission of two weeks' or a month's wages for taking on a new recruit. Once employed, the "free laborer" in many cases had to continue to ply the foreman with gifts if he wished to keep his job. The tyranny of the overseer was common among enterprises of all kinds, and a hierarchy of authority and patronage existed even in those factories where recruits were hired on a supposedly free basis.

In all forms of recruitment in Shanghai the role of the Green Gang should not be underestimated. As Honig and others have shown, after 1927 especially the Green Gang effectively controlled much of the economic life of Shanghai, a situation employers and employees alike were obliged to endure.[78] Thus factory workers frequently got a job through the connections of a Green Gang member, worked for a foreman or a labor contractor who was a gang member, paid protection money to gang members, and, if all else failed, might be buried through the good offices of a gang member. The rule of the gangs was only marginally less severe in other cities.

The Green Gang maintained a stranglehold on industrial life, as on all other areas of activity; not to show deference was to court disaster.

Hours and Rates of Pay

As in other spheres, information about hours and rates of pay in Chinese industry in the 1920s is fragmented and incomplete. Some data were collected, largely as a result of the initiative of Christian reformers, who had as a rule no training in statistics. In the early 1930s, however, the interest in gathering statistical information increased, and several studies were published that attempted to describe the range of wages in various industries.[79] Some, more importantly, tried to relate the wages paid to the cost of living for working-class families.[80]

First, with respect to hours, a study published in 1935 showed that in Shanghai, even by that late date, workers in the cotton spinning mills worked on average an eleven and one-half-hour day, as did those in the silk reeling mills. Workers in these two industries probably accounted for almost half of all the workers in the city. In the flour mills the length of the average working day was eleven and one-half hours, in cotton weaving mills eleven and one-quarter, in wool weaving ten, in silk weaving ten and one-half, in machine shops nine and one-quarter, and in tobacco and match factories under eight hours, according to this report.[81] A separate study by the Nanking Ministry of Industries in 1937 purported to show that the overall average for hours of work in Shanghai industries was nine and one-quarter, which compared favorably with an average of ten hours for Hankow and Peking, eleven hours for Soochow and Chefoo, and twelve hours for Tientsin and Tsingdao. In one city, Tsungchow, the average working day was said to be thirteen hours long.[82] During his trip to China in 1924 the ILO official Pierre Henry found small factories in Peking where a sixteen-hour day was normal practice,[83] and there is little reason to suppose that where a single shift was worked it would not be well over twelve hours in length even into the late 1930s. In the larger plants, where children were employed at certain stages in the process of production, it was necessary for them to work the same hours as adults in order to keep up the pace of manufacture.

In cotton mills this often meant rotating shifts every week, working a twelve-hour day shift one week and a twelve-hour night shift the next.[84] Despite having to meet quotas, workers resorted to a variety of subterfuges to take a rest while nominally at work, a practice known as "soaking mushrooms."[85] Skilled craftsmen, such as machinists or printers, tended to work shorter hours, a fact that reflected the expendable character of unskilled labor.[86]

One of the earliest attempts to make a comprehensive estimate of wages in a wide range of industries throughout China was the study undertaken by Dorothy Orchard over the years 1931–32.[87] Orchard conducted a survey that yielded information for 168 establishments employing some 73,000 workers in 34 cities from Harbin to Canton. Her findings with respect to the "usual" basic wage for workers in various industries are reproduced in appendix 1A and show a range for particular industries, and a relationship between industries not dissimilar to what is suggested by the more partial surveys undertaken in the 1920s.[88] Nonetheless, her findings suffer the disadvantages of any attempt at generalization—precisely that they are not specific enough with respect to variations in wage according to place and the sex, age, and function of the worker to be of much use. Nor does she relate earnings to the cost of living, an equation that would be difficult to make with any validity over so vast a geographical area. A study published in December 1934 showing that for Shanghai alone, where wage rates were generally agreed to be better than elsewhere in China, the average annual expenditure of a laborer was 454 yuan, while the average annual income was 416 yuan, clearly pointed up the need for the relation to be made.[89]

Perhaps the most sophisticated of the contemporary attempts to portray the standard of living of Chinese workers resulted from studies undertaken in Shanghai by organs of the Municipal Council of the International Settlement, studies that suggest the influence of Eleanor Hinder and Rewi Alley of the Council's Industrial Section. The council's Housing Committee reported in 1937 that in a sample of the expenditure of working-class families, those families where the head of the household was unskilled regularly spent an average of 11.63 percent more than the income of the head of the household just for the basic necessities of food, rent, and clothing. For the whole sample of 670 families, if expenditures other than food, rent, and clothing were taken into account, none of the families was able to live within the income of the head of the household. The difference was made up in a few cases by profit from money-lending, or from rent for land in the country, but in most cases by the income of other members of the family, and by borrowing. Some 185 families, covering the full spectrum of unskilled, semi-skilled, and skilled heads of household, had to borrow to meet their deficit, from which it is possible to conclude that more than a quarter of working-class families in Shanghai may have been permanently in debt.[90]

The Industrial Section of the Municipal Council began itself to publish figures on hours, wages, and the cost of living for workers under its jurisdiction in 1938. The process of gathering data was supervised by T. Y. Tsha, formerly chief of the Statistical Division of the Bureau of Social Affairs of the Municipality of Greater Shanghai, who took up his duties with the council when the Japanese occupation made it impossible to carry on his work outside the settlement.[91] His data for the years 1938–40 therefore represent an extension of that compiled over the previous decade for factories in Greater Shanghai, but now apparently covered only factories in the settlement. It is further evident that only Chinese-owned factories were surveyed, and it was not until 1940 that the possibility of gathering data for foreign-owned enterprises began seriously to be broached. In a report in that year it was suggested that the proportionally higher use of men in foreign-owned factories, rather than women workers, would if it were taken into account be reflected in an improved overall picture of wages.[92] It had long been established practice in China, as elsewhere, that in general men were paid more than women, and women were paid more than children.

The average monthly earnings for workers in a variety of industries for the years 1930 to 1940 inclusive in Shanghai are presented in tabular form in appendix 1B.

They are perhaps more useful than simple hourly wage rates, in that they reflect the level of activity in an industry, and the hours and days actually worked, rather than a normative rate of pay. There will nonetheless be some correspondence between earnings and rates of pay. Tsha's data show that those industries where the average monthly earnings were consistently lowest were silk reeling, match making, and cotton spinning, with the tobacco industry offering only a little more. At the other end of the scale, workers in the printing and shipbuilding industries earned the most, sometimes in excess of four times as much on average as their lowest-paid colleagues in the silk industry. In between were workers in industries such as wool weaving, flour milling, hosiery knitting, and oil pressing.

While there was some fluctuation in the relative earning capacity of workers in various industries over the years, broadly speaking the pattern was little changed by 1940. What had changed was the purchasing power of workers as represented by their real wages, the reflection of the relationship between their actual earnings and the cost of living. A study in 1940 showed that real wages, from an index of 96.19 in 1930, had increased to 11.57 by 1933, declined to 96.8 by 1935 because of the depression, rose slightly to the base of 100 in 1936, and then plummeted to 55.3 in 1940 because of the war.[93] Thus, it must be clear that for workers in the lowest-paid occupations, where the hold on life was already marginal with all members of the family working, the impact on their livelihood of recession or civil strife was most significant. When the pace of industry slowed down, those who were not thrown out of work altogether often had their hours reduced with a corresponding drop in their earnings, while some even had to endure a reduction in their rate of pay.[94]

More recent accounts have confirmed the impression given by contemporary sources and have added detail. Rawski calculates a range of annual wages for seven industries in 1933, showing that Shanghai workers were paid consistently better than those in other places, highlighting regional variations.[95] Cochran notes that except for the most highly skilled, who were paid more at BAT, cigarette workers at the Chinese Nanyang Brothers factories and those at BAT were paid broadly the same.[96] Strand puts the average wage of rickshaw pullers in Beijing in the 1920s at ten to twelve yuan a month, placing them on a par with the lower band of industrial workers at the time.[97]

Hershatter found that in Tientsin in 1930 millhands spent 63.8 percent of their wages on food, 6.7 percent on clothing, 7.1 percent on rent, 9.7 percent on fuel, leaving 12.7 percent for "miscellaneous" expenditures.[98] Honig found that at Shanghai's Shen Xin Number Nine cotton mill during the depression years 1932 to 1936, as workers were laid off, the percentage of women workers increased; however, as the wages of women workers were drastically cut, those of their male counterparts actually rose slightly.[99] Eastman concludes that women and child workers were prepared to work for low wages because their incomes were "merely supplemental" to the family budget, a position with which I could not possibly agree.[100]

The broad picture, therefore, is of an industrial work force that put in long hours to earn a living that was neither adequate nor secure. In this, China was no different from other countries in the early stages of industrialization.

Unemployment

There were, of course, those who had no work at all. Because of the constant flow of people back and forth from the city to the countryside, exaggerated in times of stress, and because government agencies were in any case little inclined to monitor the movements of the industrial population, it is almost impossible to estimate in retrospect the extent of unemployment in industry in China at any given time or place during the period under consideration. Some fragmentary evidence is available: for example, 75,219 out of a total of 394,154 workers registering with the Bureau of Social Affairs of Greater Shanghai in 1928 were said to be unemployed, while in the same year 96,050 laborers were said to be unemployed in Hankow.[101] Undoubtedly these totals include not only unemployed workers in manufacturing industry, but also many "coolie" laborers and handicraft workers. Another estimate, by the All China Labor Federation (ACLF) in 1930, put the total of unemployed in both modern and handicraft industry at about 10 million, or 60 percent of what the ACLF considered to be the work force in all branches of industry throughout China.[102]

It will be apparent that figures such as these are inadequate as a guide to unemployment in modern industry. Nonetheless, they are an indication that unemployment of a substantial order probably existed, even at a time of relatively normal commercial activity.

It is generally conceded that the level of unemployment dramatically increased during the slump of 1934–35 throughout the country, and again in late 1937, particularly in Shanghai as a result of the outbreak of hostilities between China and Japan. The emergency facing the authorities of the International Settlement in 1937 because of the simultaneous destruction of some industry in the area under their jurisdiction, with the consequent loss of jobs, and the influx of workers from outside the settlement boundaries, where destruction had been more systematic, led to a survey of the extent of unemployment. Partial estimates suggested that in the eastern and northern districts of the settlement alone, the destruction during the last half of 1937 had put some 95,000 workers out of work.[103]

Revised figures presented the following year showed that the number of industrial workers employed in the settlement had dropped from some 200,000 before the outbreak of hostilities to only 27,000 in December 1937, but that because of rapid rebuilding and clever exploitation of markets formerly supplied by industries elsewhere, the number employed by December 1938 had increased to 237,000.[104] Despite this extraordinary recovery in the settlement, it is very probable that a large measure of unemployment continued to exist among industrial workers in Shanghai, particularly among those previously employed by enterprises in areas now under Japanese occupation. Here reconstruction was slower, if undertaken at all, and it is likely that many tens of thousands of workers were permanently displaced from their jobs, some probably returning to the countryside and others drifting into the settlement, where they might find refuge but few extra jobs.[105] The refugee question is dealt with more fully in chapter 6.

With respect to unemployment, loss of income, and personal disruption to people's lives, therefore, it is hard to accept Rawski's assertion that "historians often exaggerate the negative economic consequences of political turmoil."[106] In Peking the machinations of warlords threatened the jobs and livelihood of workers throughout the 1920s.[107] In Tientsin in 1922 and from 1926 to 1929, conflicts between rival armies caused the cotton mills to be squeezed for cash until many had to shut down, throwing their employees out of work.[108] In Shanghai the ubiquitous Green Gang, itself a product of political turmoil, placed workers' jobs permanently at risk and dependent on gifts and favors that laborers could ill afford.[109] Japan's projects of expansion constituted a threat to life and labor through much of the 1930s. On this level at least, political turmoil was a significant cause for concern to urban workers, who were, if anything, even more exposed than their rural counterparts.

Health and Safety

The level of health and industrial safety among working people and the quality of housing available to them were other considerations with an important bearing on their overall well-being.

In many industries occupational hazards were to be found that adversely affected the health or threatened the safety of workers. In cotton mills, workers frequently suffered from a high level of dust and fluff in the air, while in one typical mill 14 percent of women and 22 percent of children had tuberculosis.[110] In silk filatures, the humid atmosphere necessary to preserve the quality of the silk also made for a high incidence of tuberculosis among employees.[111] In match factories, the extensive use of white phosphorous in the process of manufacture in the 1920s often gave rise to phosphorous poisoning among workers, the disease known as "phossy-jaw," which caused the progressive disintegration of the bone structure of the face and in many cases death.[112] An outcry against the continued use of white phosphorous in the late 1920s saw its gradual replacement by a less poisonous phosphorous. In rug factories and embroidery workshops, young workers frequently went blind after a few years because they were required to work in cramped quarters with insufficient light.[113] In rubber factories and chemical plants, inadequate ventilation to clear away the fumes meant that employees often had to live with recurring bouts of nausea,[114] while of one glass factory visited by the ILO official Pierre Henry in 1924 it was observed that if a visitor spent a morning there he would emerge unable to speak because of the number of particles of glass he had absorbed.[115]

Almost all workers had to endure the effects of some degree of malnutrition and fatigue from long hours of work. Sanitary facilities in the factories were usually of the most primitive kind, and dysentery was widespread. Beri-beri, skin diseases, and sore feet that would not heal were common.[116] As Hershatter has noted, each time of life had its own illnesses—diarrhea and enteritis up to the age of one, typhoid, typhus, dysentery, smallpox, diptheria, measles, sores, fevers, rashes, convulsions, and digestive illnesses from one to five, and tuberculosis and respiratory illnesses after the age of sixteen.[117] To all these had to be added the effects of beatings frequently received by workers, especially women, from contractors, factory fore-men, and gang members for transgressions real or imagined.[118]

Very few inquiries were undertaken into the health of industrial workers; those that stand out are the investigation into phosphorous poisoning in the match indus-try conducted by Dr. G. T. Maitland for the National Christian Council in 1924 (see chapter 4) and the studies undertaken for the Industrial Section of the Shang-hai Municipal Council between 1934 and 1937 by Dr. H. S. Gear into lead poison-ing in the printing industry, by Dr. S. C. Hatem (Ma Hai-teh) into acid poisoning in the chrome and metal plating industry, by Dr. Bernard Read into the diet of workers, and by Dr. B. S. Platt into the deleterious effects of handling lead and antimony in type-founding for the printing industry, in soldering, and in the manu-facture of storage batteries and enamel. An experiment in 1937 designed to en-courage the provision by employers of more nutritious food for their workers was cut short by the war.[119]

It was not only the health of workers that was frequently in jeopardy in their places of work, but also their safety. Unguarded power machinery moving at high speed was a hazard in many factories, but especially in the cotton mills where the swing of the plait of a woman's hair or a hand carelessly extended could result in a scalping or maiming, or the loss of fingers or an arm.[120] The risk of fire was always present, especially in chemical plants, textile mills, and match factories, and in one conflagration in a rubber plant in Shanghai in 1933 eighty-one workers lost their lives.[121] Frequently no precautions were taken against fire, and exits were blocked, preventing escape. Explosions caused by faultily constructed boilers and pressure vessels were another cause of injury and death, while in the construction industry workers were prone to suffer mis-adventure by falling as a result of haste or negligence, or loose scaffolding.[122] In many manufacturing processes, the mishandling of dangerous substances was a common cause of mishap.

The Industrial Section of the Shanghai Municipal Council kept a record of all industrial accidents reported in the settlement between 1934 and 1940. During these years there was an annual average of 1,886 accidents reported, of which on average 92.3, or 4.9 percent, were fatal.[123] It must be emphasized, however, that employers often did not report misadventures in their factories to the section, and therefore the accident figures offered in the annual reports represent only a partial picture, being based on the submissions of hospitals, the police, ambu-lance services, and those employers who would cooperate. It is not possible to say from these annual reports that misadventure was most common in any one industry, as the industry most subject to mishap varied from year to year.[124]

Housing

If industrial accidents contributed to the burden of working-class life only occa-sionally, the lack of a decent place to live was a constant and inescapable trial. A survey of workers' housing by M. T. Tchou of the YMCA in 1926 revealed such conditions of squalor and overcrowding in workers' accommodation in Shanghai that for a time a token interest was aroused in "model villages" as a panacea for the physical and spiritual degeneration of workers' lives.[125] The interest was to be short-lived, however, and conditions had changed little by the outbreak of hostilities with Japan in 1937.

The average two-story "Chinese house" in Shanghai was partitioned into a rabbit warren of compartments and subcompartments by means of vertical and horizontal boards. It might contain two dozen or more people who all had to eat, cook, and sleep within its limited confines. Of a sample of 113,286 families living in 41,160 houses in a congested part of Shanghai in 1935, the greatest number of families, the modal group, lived four families to a house. By 1938, as a result of the influx of refugees into the settlement, an estimate based on a much smaller sample suggested that the modal point might be 7.22 families to a house.[126] In Tientsin, where houses were more usually one story, families might be able to afford one room, around ten feet by eight feet.[127] In most city housing of this kind, the principal tenant often sought to extract the maximum possible rent from subtenants.

Many workers could not afford even this kind of accommodation and were driven to occupy shacks and shanties on the outskirts of the city. In the case of Shanghai, these were often farther along the banks of the Soochow Creek or the Whangpoo River, away from the city center, and were made of matting, straw, and broken boards. In Tientsin many workers also lived in shacks, made of wood and coated with mud and grass. Some industrial workers in Shanghai lived on boats moored in the river.[128] Recommendations by the Municipal Council's Housing Committee in 1937, which might have eased the situation in Shanghai, were never put into effect because of the outbreak of war, though the council took certain initiatives in 1941 to ease the accommodation dilemma somewhat (see chapter 6).

For single workers, dormitory accommodation, an idea imported from Japan, provided an alternative. Some prosperous labor contractors had their own dormitories, but usually the dormitories were built and operated by the company. The dormitories might house both workers hired directly by the factory and those engaged by labor contractors, who would rent space for them.

Sometimes dormitories seemed to work well. Subsidized dormitory accommodation was provided by both the British-American Tobacco Company and Nanyang Brothers for their workers in the cigarette industry in the 1920s and was widely seen as a benefit of working in that industry.[129] In other cases the employee became almost a prisoner of the company or of the labor contractor. Employees would have their movements severely restricted, and the tendency was for the quality of the lodging, and board if provided, to decline. In the late 1930s in Shanghai this trend was reinforced by the flow of refugees into the settlement in search of accommodation and employment, so that the call for "one worker, one bed" became common among dormitory residents resisting the practice of assigning two workers to every bunk in the daytime, and two other workers at night.[130]

Palliatives

Employers' Welfare Schemes

One employer to recognize the need for supplementary assistance for its workers was the Commercial Press, a large publishing house with branches in several major cities. As early as 1924, the Commercial Press provided a comprehensive program of benefits for its employees, which, in addition to the usual annual and monthly attendance bonuses, offered participation in a savings scheme with 9 percent interest on fixed accounts, assistance from the company benevolent fund in case of retirement, death, or extreme need, hospital care at no charge and facilities for vaccination, two months maternity leave on reduced pay, recreation and bathing facilities, English- and Chinese-language evening classes available to adult workers for a nominal charge, and subsidized kindergarten and primary school education for the children of workers.[131] The Commercial Press was run by the Chinese Christian industrialist Fong Sec, who was closely associated with the YMCA.[132]

Less likely to have been motivated by altruistic considerations were British-American Tobacco and the Nanyang Brothers, rivals in the cigarette industry. By the late 1920s, BAT provided its workers with dormitories, clinics, schools, a savings fund, and a rice allowance. Hours were shorter, work lighter, and night shifts less frequent than in the cotton and silk industries. Nanyang offered similar facilities and conditions.[133] The Japanese firm Naigai Wata Kaisha provided its workers with a hospital, a dispensary, and educational facilities.[134] In Tientsin, some cotton mills were "planned communities," one even having "dormitories, dining hall, clinic, schools for workers and their children, consumers' co-operative, bathhouse, athletic field, and martial arts society . . . paid maternity leave, disability benefits, funeral subsidy, and the bonus paid to workers so they could purchase melons in the summer."[135]

Hershatter observes that there were precedents for the provision of this kind of infrastructure by factories in eighteenth-century Britain and nineteenth-century Russia. She also notes that the creation of a closed company environment helped to extend factory discipline. Strand finds that more generally the concept of the "moral economy," a shared concern for the people's livelihood, or *minsheng*, has strong roots in Chinese tradition, in Confucian civic activism. He points to the traditional charitable activities of the guilds, transposed to 1920s Peking and extended to the provision of charitable factories for the poor, such as that opened for unemployed rickshaw pullers in 1929.[136]

Whatever the motivation, it is important to realize that the provision of benefits of this kind was very unusual. Most concerns, whether Chinese or foreign, offered their workers nothing more than the conventional bonus at Chinese New Year. The Nanking government's Factory Act of 1929 urged upon employers an enlightened attitude toward the provision of welfare benefits for their employees, but it seems to have had little effect. Likewise, some labor unions at various times sought to offer welfare and educational facilities to their members, but after 1927 the unfavorable disposition of the authorities toward the unions and the need for them to exist at least in part clandestinely discouraged this kind of initiative. By and large, in hard times the Chinese worker was without recourse.

Factory Legislation

Although legislation played little part in the regulation of working conditions in industry, it is appropriate to review briefly at least such initiatives as were taken in this direction. China's first Factory Act was promulgated by the Peking government in 1923 as a result of a campaign for legislation mounted by organized labor and insistence in Geneva that China should take a first step toward implementation of standards agreed upon at the first International Labor Conference in Washington in 1919. Essentially, the act provided that in factories employing one hundred workers or more, and in factories where dangerous work was carried on, the employment of boys under ten and girls under twelve should be prohibited, while boys under seventeen and girls under eighteen should be permitted only light work. Juvenile workers were to work no more than eight hours per day, with three days of rest per month and no night work allowed, while adults were to work no more than ten hours per day, with at least two rest days per month. Other provisions related to the manner of payment of wages: although no minimum wage was specified, the payment of compensation upon the death of a worker, the provision of facilities for education at the factories, and various precautions against industrial accidents and disease and to ensure the health of workers, including arrangements for maternity leave, were included in the act.[137]

Quite apart from the fact that application of the act only to those factories with one hundred workers or more omitted consideration of the vast majority of enterprises where fewer than this number were employed, the actual terms of the act were so far in advance of what could be expected to be immediately enforceable within the context of a capitalist economy as to invite wholesale evasion on the part of employers. Indeed, as the act neither contained nor was followed by any provision for the establishment of an inspectorate to compel compliance, it is possible to question the commitment of the Peking government to the principle of industrial regulation. A survey of labor conditions conducted by officers of the British Consular Service in various cities in 1924 revealed that most employers claimed not even to be aware of the legislation.[138]

In South China, at its First National Congress in 1924 the Kuomintang agreed in principle to a program of legislation providing for freedom of association, the right to strike, an eight-hour day and a six-day week, regulation of the employment of women and children, unemployment insurance, an old-age pension, maternity leave, and compensation for sickness, accident, and death. Little seems to have been done by the Canton government to implement these proposals, however. At its Second Congress in 1926, the Kuomintang reaffirmed its commitment to this program and added to it a call for arbitration courts to settle labor disputes, legal holidays with pay, regulation of apprenticeship, the abolition of contract labor, improved housing and sanitation, and provision of education for workers and their children.[139] Implementation of these measures, though, was now apparently explicitly deferred until the Nationalist revolution had been achieved.[140] Elsewhere, legislation was enacted between 1926 and 1929 by local or provincial governments in Hupeh, Shansi and Kansu, Kwangtung, and Wuhan. Described by Wagner as "an odd chop suey," the provisions of these pieces of legislation included such items as the prohibition of child labor, limitation on the working day, maternity leave, and procedures for dismissal with compensation.[141] Again, there is no evidence that any attempt was made to enforce them.[142]

Ironically, the most comprehensive effort to enact legislation on labor questions came only after the Kuomintang had veered sharply to the right under the direction of Chiang Kai-shek and the labor movement, except for the "yellow" unions under the government's tutelage, had been all but crushed. At the end of 1929 the government in Nanking promulgated its Factory Act, Factory Inspection Act, and Trade Union Law, and with amendments these were formally passed in 1931. Over the next five years further amendments and enabling legislation were introduced, along with supplementary regulations on workers' education, health and safety hazards, and a minimum wage.[143] The Factory Act was made to apply to all factories employing thirty workers or more. It contained provisions dealing with women and child workers, apprenticeship, working hours, rest days and holidays, dismissal procedures, welfare facilities, safety precautions, compensation for injury, sickness, and death, and the creation of "factory councils" of workers' and employers' representatives whose function would be to improve relations between labor and management and to facilitate production (see appendix 2B). Although the Factory Act was acclaimed by many as a significant step forward, more than a few of its elements could be seen as a two-edged sword, cutting as much against the laborer as in his or her favor.[144]

A Central Factory Inspection Bureau was established under the Ministry of Industries in 1933 in order that the conditions of the act could be enforced. Little had been achieved, however, when the government decided in April 1934 that it could not hope to apply the act all at once and resolved to apply it in five distinct stages, beginning with the most urgent requirements, such as the keeping of factory records, reporting of accidents, supervision of apprentices, and banning of women and juveniles from dangerous work. By May 1936, when the government reported that this first stage had been successfully completed, Wagner found that all that had been accomplished was the sporadic reporting of industrial accidents and the allocation by only a few of the municipal and provincial governments that Nanking had charged with the task of inspection of money for that purpose.[145] With the outbreak of war scarcely more than a year later, the Factory Act became a dead letter.

Part II

The Movement for Industrial Reform

2

The YMCA

In 1841 the religious fervor and ambition of a young London apprentice, George Williams, led him to found an organization dedicated to providing young men with an opportunity for Christian fellowship, recreation, and self-improvement. Within ten years, the Young Men's Christian Association movement had caught the public imagination, and branches of the YMCA existed in cities throughout Britain and had begun to be established in the United States and Canada. In due course, the idea formed among YMCA members in the United States that they had a mission to accomplish in China, and after limited success had been achieved elsewhere in the Far East the first organizer, D. W. Lyon, was sent to China in 1895. By 1920 the association had "city" and "student" branches throughout eastern China and was firmly established in its religious and educational work, with a principal ministry among the more affluent youth of the treaty ports.[1]

The work of James Yen, the American-educated Chinese recruited during the First World War for work among Chinese laborers in France, widened this concern. Back in China Yen embarked on literacy work among returned laborers, and in due course this expanded to become the Mass Education Movement, spreading to the villages through the large-scale experiment in Tinghsien County. Yen's work was only incidentally concerned with industry, however, and it would remain for others to take up this challenge.[2]

After the First World War the extension of service to industrial workers became an accepted feature of the YMCA program in the United States. In contrast to developments within the YWCA, this work was not promoted by any international committee of the association and tended to develop haphazardly from one country to another. In China the beginnings of YMCA industrial work were to be found in the continuation of service to laborers, now returned to China, whom the association had helped in France during the war. This "returned laborer work" picked up toward the end of 1919 as thousands of workers passed through the major treaty ports on their way home. Most possessed little money and were uncertain of their future plans. The YMCA undertook to offer advice to those who sought it, to write letters for the illiterate, and to arrange introductions for those looking for work. Others they assisted to secure back pay from the government or medical attention from local hospitals.[3] Meetings were held at which lectures were given on matters of health and hygiene, thrift, and "moral and practical topics." Some attempt was made to transmit a religious message to the laborers, although "those who have come to Shanghai seem to be of a roving disposition and uninterested in our efforts to get them into groups for educational work and Bible study."[4]

Extension Work

By 1922 work for the returned laborers was rapidly nearing its completion, but out of this work there had evolved in the meantime an interest in the plight of urban factory workers as a whole. Discussions were held with employers in Shanghai and elsewhere, and some were found to be sympathetic to the YMCA's desire to bring a new morality to the relationship between employers and employed. In November 1920 "extension work" had been started in seven factories on the Shanghai side of the Whangpoo River, while the erection of a large mat shed on the other side of the river had brought the YMCA program to the factory workers of Pootung.[5] In the factories, weekly meetings were held, beginning about 7 P.M., or whenever the factory closed. "Those who attend are taught the singing of patriotic songs and hymns and are given short talks on some inspirational theme."[6] After half an hour of this communal activity, those assembled would break up into small groups for "club work" or study, a central feature of the educational effort being literacy classes conducted mainly by volunteer teachers.

After the erection of the Pootung hut, meetings of a "semi-educational and semi-entertainment nature" were held there every night, and an average of almost a thousand workers a night were said to attend.[7] There was also a free day school for workers' children, with an initial registration of about sixty, a reading room, a letter-writing service for the illiterate, and religious meetings on Sundays. Lectures and films were an important part of the program. Themes for lectures included "The Purpose of the YMCA," "Hygiene," "The Relation Between the Laborer and the YMCA," and "The Citizen's Morality." Films were shown on such subjects as "The European War," "The Far East Olympics," "Industry," "The Life of Jesus," and "A Visit to an American City."[8] The object was to strike a balance between what was likely to appeal and the message that the association wanted to transmit.

Some months after the Pootung project had begun, the highly inflammable hut burned down, and the YMCA was obliged to seek quarters in rented accommodation in the main street of Pootung, which effectively reduced the size of meetings that could be held to an attendance of 250.[9] Nonetheless, the program continued and was augmented by the provision of evening classes for workers and day classes for their children. A regular clinic was also established at the Pootung center, under the direction of the Chinese Dr. Mary Stone. One immediate concern of the clinic was to vaccinate as many workers as possible against smallpox, scarlet fever, and diphtheria, which were all of epidemic proportions in the community. The clinic was said to be vaccinating an average of nearly one hundred persons a day.[10]

Elsewhere in Shanghai, the educational program was pursued where funds and facilities permitted, and evening classes given by the YMCA in a hut in Hongkew, at Kashing Road School, and at Hwei Han School in Hong Kong Road were said to have an enrollment of 57, 28, and 164, respectively, in 1921.[11]

One other aspect of the YMCA's industrial work in Shanghai in this early stage was the holding of an "industrial seminar," a course of study on industrial questions, for an hour and a half each week, presided over by persons locally available and with a degree of expertise on the subject. Among those called in to help were C. F. Remer of St. John's University, later to become well known for his work on foreign investment in China; D. H. Kulp of Shanghai College; and Agatha Harrison of the Industrial Department of the YWCA. The seminar was arranged for the benefit of the eight regular industrial secretaries and other staff. The YMCA as yet had no personnel of its own with the experience to undertake the training of its industrial staff. The seminar ran from the autumn of 1921 to the summer of 1922.[12]

In Wuhan, work similar to that being undertaken in Shanghai was launched in 1920 under the direction of YMCA Secretary C. C. Shedd, and it would appear that some industrial work may also have been commenced in Tientsin, Tsinan, and other cities, though no record has survived of this.[13]

As the industrial program brought YMCA officials closer to the lives of working people, those involved began to reflect more carefully on the role they should be playing. Although the Chinese YMCA never formulated any definite set of principles to guide its industrial work, it is possible to discern certain underlying assumptions on the basis of which it went forward. The first was that the work should be "a co-operative effort in which both employers and employees join."[14] It was expected that once initial suspicions had been laid to rest, employers would come forward to provide facilities to enable the YMCA to carry on its program, and that workers would not hesitate to take advantage of the program and would advise others to do so too. There was secondly the conviction that the YMCA could maintain the attitude of "a neutral agency with the confidence of both sides, labourer and capitalist."[15] It was felt that as a Christian agency the association had no particular axe to grind and sought only to bring the theory and practice of Christ to the lives of ordinary men. A logical consequence of this was that "the Association should not take part in the discussion of questions that are issues between the employers and the employees but should in its program in the mill or factory confine itself to questions that fall within the recognized province of the Association."[16] It was frequently reiterated that in all the association's work with industrial laborers, "the definite religious objective should be emphasized from the first." As one official put it, "Had we been able to go into Russia thirty years ago with our city and student program, had we been able to follow this ten years ago with an industrial and rural program, the history of the world would be different. How can we fail to do for China at this moment when it is as sure as fate that a failure to do so and to do quickly may, and I feel will surely, lead to the repetition in China of what has happened in Russia."[17] Paradoxically, in spite of the fact that most association personnel considered evangelism to be their primary task, and industrial work only a means to that end, many of those involved most directly with the work felt that they ought somehow to be helping to introduce modern American industrial techniques to China. One such secretary called for surveys and experiments, literature and conferences, to explain to employers and government officials how modern industry could be efficient and still "conserve human welfare."[18] It was widely felt that an expert ought to be brought in to direct the association's industrial work, if necessary from outside the movement. The man required would be "well balanced, not a faddist, warm-hearted and with real religion, adaptable to new situations, able to work with others, without race prejudice, a student."[19] By 1922 the National Committee of the YMCA in China had found such a man in the person of Thomas Tchou, a graduate in engineering of the University of Glasgow. The conflict of moral imperatives in the thinking of YMCA staff was never resolved, however, and contributed materially to Tchou's early resignation only four years later.

Surveys and Seminars

For the time being, at least, the YMCA's Industrial Department had firm leadership, and the program was given a boost by two other developments occurring in the course of 1922. At the National Christian Conference in Hangchow in May, three recommendations were approved relating to standards in industrial life. The passage of these resolutions effectively committed the new National Christian Council of China to an ongoing consideration of industrial problems. In the late autumn the American "industrial evangelist" Sherwood Eddy came to China for a short visit at the invitation of the YMCA.

In preparation for Eddy's visit, a questionnaire was circulated in June to groups and individuals in the principal urban centers throughout China, including those where the YMCA had established local industrial departments. Among the cities from which information was drawn were Hankow, Shanghai, Tientsin, Chefoo, Changsha, Nanking, Tsinan, Tongshan, Peking, Wuhu, Chengchow, and Wusih.[20] The questionnaire, which Eddy himself had drawn up, asked for details of wages, hours, and conditions of labor in various industries, unemployment, health problems, accidents, housing, the existing state of welfare work, the activity of trade unions, the extent of democratic control in industry, and the incidence of police repression in labor disputes. Information was also sought on the position of women and child workers, the nature of any labor regulations in force, and broader social questions such as poverty, child marriage, prostitution, and slavery, the influence of traditional Chinese religions, and signs of awakening social consciousness among students, women, and other groups.[21] It was by far the most comprehensive questionnaire circulated in China on labor and related problems up to that time.

The answers obtained varied considerably in quality according to the level of understanding of the different respondents, usually local YMCA secretaries, and with the methods used to gather information. In Wuhan, for example, the secretary brought together "a few of the most thoughtful people" to discuss the questions raised. Apart from the U.S. consul-general, those present at the three-hour meeting were two railway men (a locomotive superintendent, and a construction engineer), the head of a flour mill and also a cotton mill, the head of the Independent News Agency and also representative for the Weekly Review of the Far East and also the China Press, the head of the social service work of the Hankow YMCA and a man who has been closely connected with the settlement of a recent rickshaw strike and the accompanying complications, and three of us connected with the industrial work of this centre. Then too we had with us the one clergyman who is really getting next to the industrial people.[22]

In Wuhan at least, no attempt was made to consult the rank-and-file worker directly, and it is likely that this omission was repeated elsewhere. In Chefoo a twelve-page report was submitted that contained almost no account of wages paid in local industries, although a comparison of wages and cost of living was central to the purpose of the survey.[23]

The information received in response to the questionnaire was edited by Thomas Tchou and made available at the end of 1922 as a typed manuscript, "Report on Industrial and Social Survey," copies of which went into limited circulation.[24] It is not surprising that the survey revealed a consistent pattern of very low wages, long hours, and appalling conditions of labor among urban working people, varying only slightly in degree according to the nature of the work performed and the geographic location. Tchou estimated that 40 percent of workers in Shanghai lived below the poverty line, while in North China and the interior cities the figure was put at 50 percent. Ministering to the needs of this vast army of underprivileged workers were various social service organizations such as the YM and YWCA, the Yangtzepoo Social Center and the Nantao Christian Institute in Shanghai, and the Chefoo Christian Women Workers' Society. Little had been done by individual firms toward the provision of social welfare schemes for their workers, though the Commercial Press and Yangtze Engineering Works in Shanghai were exceptions to this rule, and the Chung Hwa Book Company claimed to be considering a welfare scheme. In Chefoo Christian influence in the hair net and embroidery industries was said to have brought about a paid day off on Sundays in many factories. Throughout China, it was found that larger factories were more likely to offer some educational or medical facilities to their employees than were smaller concerns.

While Tchou concluded that more employers could be expected in the future to recognize their social responsibility toward their workers, he doubted whether the workers themselves would accept any further arbitrary intervention: "Labour leaders are beginning to resent these paternalistic and charitable schemes and there is already an increasing feeling that employees should have a voice in determining the kind of welfare work that is to be performed amongst them and that they consider as their due."[25]

Shortly after his arrival in China, Sherwood Eddy addressed a meeting of industrial staff and senior officers of the YMCA and urged upon them implementation of "a progressive program of education and welfare work," in the spirit of the principles adopted at the National Christian Conference and ratified by the YMCA.[26] He subsequently spent three months visiting some twenty Chinese cities, holding evangelical meetings "chiefly among government students and non-Christian young men," preaching industrial reform, and seeking to study conditions in factories and workshops across the country. Eddy too found "a growing spirit of unrest among the masses," an attitude "changing from passive subjection to resentment."[27]

Theory and Practice

In the spring and summer of 1923, Thomas Tchou embarked upon an extended tour of North America and Europe to study industrial conditions, paying particular attention to the workings of the cooperative movement and to experimental housing projects for factory workers. Apart from having the opportunity to observe industry in a different setting, Tchou was able to have discussions with a number of prominent people concerned with social reform, among them John D. Rockefeller in the United States and George Bernard Shaw, Seebohm Rowntree, and Arthur Greenwood in England. It may be supposed that these conversations helped to mold his perspective on what was desirable, or possible, in China. Tchou returned to China with heightened conviction as to the necessity of creating public opinion in favor of industrial legislation and of evolving a new economic order based on "the Christian principles of justice, brotherly love, and service." "The result should be an industrial and economic structure of which cooperation and goodwill shall form the cornerstone and in which distinctions based on wealth, class or race should not hamper the full realization of cooperative democracy embracing the economic and political as well as social life of the country."[28] At the YMCA's annual convention in Canton in October, resolutions were passed broadly supporting the application of these principles in the association's industrial work.

Toward the end of the year Tchou spent a month visiting cities in North and Central China reporting on his trip abroad and trying to stimulate the industrial welfare efforts of local YMCA secretaries. In each city meetings were held with Christian laymen and officials, students and employers, and occasionally workers to discuss the needs of the district. In many cases there was felt to be a dearth of information, and study committees were therefore set up to gather information and make specific recommendations as to what might be done locally. In Peking, J. B. Tayler undertook to prepare several pamphlets for the Commission on Church and Industry of the National Christian Council, and to try to interest the various Christian colleges and universities in the industrial question.

Staff in all the centers visited expressed the need for published material ranging from general texts on the industrial revolution and on Chinese economic history to more specific treatises on the methodology of social research, the organization of cooperatives, and the proposed role of the church and the Christian agencies in promoting a new economic order in China. It was decided that an appropriate method of transmitting information for the guidance of local committees would be the publication and distribution of short pamphlets on the subjects of most pressing concern, each with a list of works for further reference. To supplement this service, it was decided to implement an "Industrial Bulletin" that would give news of progress from time to time; this was put out under the auspices of the National Christian Council. Tchou's consultations with secretaries in the field also led to a plan for the convening of local industrial welfare conferences in 1924, regional or district conferences in 1925, and a national conference in 1926.[29]

During the next two years, 1923 to 1925, when the focus nationally was on the campaign to reform child labor conducted jointly by several Christian agencies, the YMCA's own record of achievement was in fact somewhat mixed. While the National Industrial Committee of the YMCA proceeded with the dissemination of information and an industrial seminar was held as part of the association's summer school at Kuling in 1924, other aspects of the program were not going so well. Efforts to persuade the provincial governments of Chekiang and Kiangsu to pass legislation restricting child labor resulted only in Kiangsu promulgating a law that was never enforced. Plans to invite the American experts Sherwood Eddy, Harry Ward, and Kirby Page and the Englishman Seebohm Rowntree to China for several months to lecture and study appear not to have reached fruition.[30] By mid-1925 the YMCA had begun industrial work in sixteen Chinese cities, in fourteen of which activity was continuing. There were thirteen YMCA secretaries with full-time responsibility for industrial programs, and ten with part-time responsibility.[31] Yet despite this apparent flurry of activity, by 1925 the YMCA had still not come to grips with the problem of how to tackle the appalling human consequences of the rapid development of modern industry. A typical industrial program in one Chinese city apparently consisted of "1,000-character classes for illiterates, citizenship classes for literates, boys' groups, Bible classes, educational lectures, and educational motion pictures showing industries in other lands." While other staff was recruited to help carry the local program, the function of the industrial secretary in each city was "to keep up to date on actual conditions, help plan new experiments, where necessary help enlist lay leadership, and cultivate the owners of the shops, as well as influential workmen."[32]

In a review of YMCA industrial work to date, undertaken in July 1925, Thomas Tchou recognized that it had many weak points. The association had not really developed a program specifically adapted to the needs of working people. Its relations with employers' associations and labor unions needed to be clarified. Its existing channels of approach to workers were not satisfactory. More attention would have to be paid in future to the relief of economic pressure on the working class.[33] Tchou also observed that the work was too thinly spread, and that lack of staff inhibited further development. As a means of rectifying some of these deficiencies, he urged the YMCA to press ahead with the promotion of cooperatives for consumption, production, banking and marketing, savings, insurance, and loan societies, and with vocational training facilities to increase workers' skill levels and earning power. More effort would be needed to bring about legislation to reform working conditions.

Tchou again raised the question of how to create a Christian social order in China. No ready answers were offered, but it is apparent that by this time the issue of the people's livelihood in its broadest sense had begun to occupy the minds of some of the YMCA's industrial staff. Tchou suggested that the association would do well to experiment toward the development of three separate industrial programs—one for workers in modern industry, one for handicraft workers, and one for rural workers—and to think how these might be correlated.[34]

The Model Village

As luck would have it, 1925 and 1926 were difficult years for all Christian industrial welfare work in China, and soon after Tchou's review was completed, the prospects for maintaining even the existing level of work seemed to have diminished. The campaign to put an end to child labor in Shanghai factories had twice ended in failure, while the May Thirtieth incident alienated many Chinese who might otherwise have supported the cause of reform. Against the background of these events, Tchou chose to embark on a project that would be practical, could be quickly realized, and would be highly visible. This was the YMCA's "Model Village" for industrial workers.

The decision to build the Model Village followed closely on completion by Tchou of a survey of existing workers' housing in Shanghai. "Outlines of Report on Housing and Social Conditions Among Industrial Workers in Shanghai" was based on a study conducted over a period of eight months by YMCA workers in Hongkew, Chapei, Ferry Road District, Yangtzepoo, and Pootung. Affirming that no accurate statistics on the average income of Shanghai workers were available, Tchou suggested that the average income of a working family would not exceed Mex. $20, and that of this one-sixth, or not more than $3.33, would be available for housing. Many families would spend much less. Prevailing rates of interest payable on property meant that the most expensive house the average family could afford to buy, or to make payments on, would cost $266, while the cheapest houses available were over $700, the key factor being the price of land, often valued at more than $4,000 per mou. This predicament compelled families to share accommodation and to tolerate deplorable living conditions.

Tchou found that workers' accommodation fell into five broad categories. The best available was in the form of rows of two-story terraced tenements, built mainly of brick with tile roofs, and separated by narrow passages. Each house had a small rear kitchen, but no toilet facilities. Rent was from $6 to $3 per month, making it necessary for from two to four families to live in every house, and usually affording each family 100 to 200 square feet of private floor area.

A second category of accommodation was the single-story house, renting for a sum between $2 and $4 per month, which would be subdivided by means of the improvisation of horizontal shelves up to eight feet wide on which would live one entire family, while perhaps two or three more families would live on the ground floor. These houses might frequently be built of wood, with mud floors, and were "as a rule situated in the neighbourhood of cesspools, graveyards, foul creeks or manure wharfs."

A third type of accommodation was the hostel or dormitory, usually for single men, run privately. Workers paid from 30 to 80 cents a month for a shelf on which to sleep and leave their things. Dormitories often also housed ricksha, wharf, and wheelbarrow coolies, as many as twenty men occupying a single house. Tchou found that the dormitories were "invariably infested by vermin" and, where no women or children were present, that gambling, opium smoking, and drinking were common.

Houses and dormitories built and owned by factory firms and rented to their employees formed a fourth category of accommodation. One firm that had done much toward the provision of living quarters for its workers was the Japanese Naigai Wata Kaisha cotton mill, which made available 1,400 two-story houses at $4 per month and 500 one-story houses at $2 per month. To save money, however, workers had divided and subdivided the accommodation with beams and shelves until it resembled the "overcrowded steerage quarters on a Chinese river boat." This was evidently no satisfactory solution.

The worst form of accommodation of all was the "mud hut," colonies of which around Shanghai housed the several hundred thousand northerners or "Kong-Peh" people among the city's population. These people had come to Shanghai from the depressed rural hinterland of northern Kiangsu to seek work. Initially without friends or relatives to help them, and regarded as a source of the cheapest labor for the worst jobs, they could not afford even to share the accommodation of the ordinary worker. Instead, they built huts of bamboo covered with mud and straw, with thatch for the roof. The building materials for one hut were estimated to cost between $12 and $30, which would have to be borrowed from friends or, more probably, from a loan shop at an annual rate of interest from 50 to 95 percent. In addition, the occupier of a mud hut would have to share with immediate neighbors the rental of the land on which their huts were built. Tchou cites the case of twenty-one families who were obliged to pay a rent of $200 per year for the land on which their huts stood. The contract ran for five years; if during that time the tenants wished to terminate the contract, they were obliged to pay five years' rent to the landlord, while if the landlord wished to end the agreement he supposedly needed to pay the tenants only one year's rent. As the value of land rose, mud hut dwellers were pushed farther and farther out by a process of development fueled by their very presence.

Mud huts were particularly prone to flooding in bad weather and to fire, seven hundred huts having been burned down in one month in 1925 in Chapei alone. Furthermore, the huts were considered dangerous by the authorities of the International Settlement, and some four hundred of them were burned by the municipal police in October 1925 on the grounds that they did not conform to the building regulations of the settlement.

Common to all forms of housing for workers, according to the report, were overcrowding and the lack of a clean water supply, adequate sanitation, facilities for recreation or education, or any opportunity for a dignified life. Working-class communities "usually receive no attention from the outside or from the authorities, until some crime has been committed which however would only be an occasion to inflict punishment." Observing that China was in an age of change, Tchou recalled the northern worker who had pointed to a $202,000 silk warehouse and remarked, "How well that go-down is built for the housing of goods, and what awful quarters we have for housing men."[35]

A Community of Brothers

Some months after the appearance of the housing report, Tchou published a second pamphlet, "Outlines of Plan for Model Villages for Working People." The pamphlet urged the construction of an experimental village that would meet many of the criticisms of the existing workers' accommodation and serve as an example to municipal authorities: "through this means to usher in a movement to promote a new social order based on the principles of brotherhood, mutual service, goodwill, cleanliness, economy, temperance, and purity."

The plan called for thirty-two houses to be built, together with a social center and a children's playground on three mou of land no more than half a mile from an area of major industrial employment. There were to be several types of houses to suit families of different sizes and different incomes, but all with separate kitchenette and separate toilet room. Construction was to be of wood and bamboo covered with plaster, with tiled roofs as a precaution against fire. Adequate clean water supply would be provided, and there would be strict regulations governing the disposal of waste. The community center, with an auditorium large enough to accommodate the entire inhabitants of the village, would afford facilities for recreation, literacy and other classes, and a regular clinic. It was understood that it would be through the community center that the YMCA would carry on its work in the village. Also envisaged were a consumers' cooperative society to keep the villagers supplied with daily necessities, and a cooperative savings society or bank.

To prevent profiteering, it was felt desirable that the inhabitants should buy over their properties within a definite period of time, so that ultimately the village would be self-owned and cooperatively governed. Tchou drew up an arrangement for the gradual transfer of administrative power from those who put up the money for the project to the inhabitants themselves. From the YMCA's point of view, "this plan would have the advantage of avoiding the odium of capitalistic control or selfish landlordism and of giving a fair opportunity of rendering altruistic social service through the social center without the motive of its program being misunderstood."[36]

By the autumn of 1926 sufficient funds had been raised to enable construction of the model village to begin on a one-acre site in the center of the factory district of Pootung across the Whangpoo River from Shanghai proper. While YMCA secretaries were now speaking in terms of fifty-four or sixty houses, initially only twelve houses were built, paid for by organizations and individuals—among them the American Friends Service Committee, the Shanghai Rotary Club, and the Commercial Press—while the British-American Tobacco Company provided the land.[37] Within two months the village was ready for occupation, and a Chinese YMCA secretary, "a Christian college graduate," installed with his family in one of the houses ready to direct the program of the social center. One senior YMCA official expressed the hope that the experiment would lead to the building of thousands of other such villages throughout China.[38]

To qualify for consideration for a house in the model village, a prospective tenant had to have an income of less than $30 per month, a legitimate occupation, and a reliable guarantor. He would then be accepted or rejected by the village board, made up of leaders from the Shanghai business community. If accepted, the tenant would be required to deposit Mex. $3 with the YMCA and would be responsible for the monthly rent of $3 and for the payment of taxes. Subletting was not permitted, and the tenant had to seek the YMCA secretary's approval before changing the "inside structure" of his house. Among regulations governing life in the village were those prohibiting opium smoking, gambling, and "other immoral practices," keeping contraband, and requiring tenants to keep their houses clean and to be within the village gates by ten o'clock at night.[39] The scale of repayments, allowing organizations that had put up the money annual interest of 5 percent on their investment, provided for ownership of the houses by the tenants after a period of fifteen years.[40]

While the Model Village did show what could be done to provide better housing for workers, the YMCA also saw it as an excellent opportunity to reach a working-class audience with its fourfold program of religious, educational, physical, and social activities. Personal evangelism, Bible storytelling, small discussion group meetings, and monthly lectures are described as being the outstanding features of the religious program.[41] One obstacle in the way of successful evangelization, however, was the high rate of illiteracy among workers, which prevented them from reading even the simplest Christian tracts. Some years later, when the village had doubled in size and some shift in population in and out must have taken place, only three families were reported to have taken the decision to become Christian.[42]

As might be expected, the popular education program proved to be much more successful. For workers' children there was a primary school, known as the industrial or trade school, which combined elementary education with practical work. For two hours of class time each day, boys would be taught to make paper flowers, for example, while girls would be trained to sew and to make handicrafts. Raw materials were supplied by the YMCA, which would endeavor to sell the work produced, dividing the profits among the children.[43] The academic program of the primary school was reported in 1933 to include Chinese writing, Mandarin, and simple arithmetic in the first three grades, with some English and conversation lessons in the fourth, fifth, and sixth.[44] School fees were $1 per term, rising in the 1930s to $2. Enrollment fluctuated according to political and economic circumstances and was reported as 101 in 1928, over 200 in 1933, but only 53 in 1935. From these figures, it would appear likely that the primary school in the Model Village was open to children living outside the village as well. To cope with the numbers involved, association secretaries encouraged older students to teach their younger classmates and to clean and decorate their own classrooms, and a genuine spirit of self-help was said to prevail.[45]

In addition to the children's primary school, the YMCA operated at the village men's popular education classes and English-language classes in the evening, and in conjunction with the YWCA popular education classes for women. By the mid-1930s there were also daily literacy classes for local ricksha coolies, actually held at the ricksha stations. The basis for literacy instruction was the text *One Thousand Common Characters*, published by the YMCA. Texts for English-language instruction are reported to have included *Anglo Chinese Commercial Conversation* and *Workmen's Practical Conversation*. Both the men's and women's popular education classes were free to workers, while for the English-language classes a nominal tuition fee was payable. As with the primary school, attendance fluctuated, and it was particularly noted that attendance would drop dramatically during strikes or labor disputes. On the whole, enrollment remained substantial, however, with figures for the men's classes at 31 in 1928 and 68 in 1935, and for the women's classes 45 in 1928 and 135 in 1935. Registration in English classes in 1928 stood at 20.[46]

Other aspects of the education program were the provision of a reading room, open daily until late in the evening, where average attendance was said in 1928 to be about sixty persons per day, and the holding of regular "citizenship" lectures. These lectures, given once a week, were on such subjects as "The Three Principles" (of Sun Yat-sen), "Thrift in Wedding and Funeral Ceremonies," "The Responsibility of Parents and Children," and "Life Problems." After the village had become well established, special Saturday classes were held in an attempt to reach out to the many thousands of "street children" in Pootung who could not be encompassed within the village primary school. "This Saturday gathering teaches them singing and games, helps them to recognize words, tells them stories to arouse their ambition to be good and useful."[47]

Rounding out the YMCA's religious and educational work in the village were the physical and social activities offered both to villagers and to the surrounding community. Among the sports organized were boxing, football, volleyball, handball, and Ping-Pong, usually carried on under supervision in the playground adjacent to the village social center. A dispensary supplied free medicine to villagers, while injections and vaccinations against cholera and other infectious diseases were undertaken at regular intervals. Lectures on health topics were reportedly given every two weeks, accompanied by slides, and special campaigns were mounted from time to time using dramatic performances, placards, and cartoons to dramatize particular problems of hygiene. Among social activities were performances offered by the village dramatic society and Chinese music club, movies, and other social gatherings of various kinds. There was also said to be a study group that met twice a week to discuss issues of common interest.[48]

Second Thoughts

In 1929 twelve new houses were added to the Model Village, bringing the total number to twenty-four, and the population in all likelihood to a little under one hundred.[49] In 1930 a social center resembling that in the Model Village but without the surrounding houses was built in Robison Road in the industrial western district of Shanghai, on land loaned by the Shanghai Power Company. Activities were promoted substantially similar to those at the Pootung center.[50]

The Model Village attracted attention from company and municipal officials in many parts of China, and similar schemes were reportedly promoted in Nanking and Foochow.[51] The most significant project to be based on the experience of the Model Village was the construction of four model villages by the government of the Municipality of Greater Shanghai in 1935 and 1936, in which the Shanghai government was said to have collaborated closely with the YMCA. This project was begun following the involvement of Y. L. Lee, formerly of the Canton YMCA, in a program of slum clearance for the Shanghai government and no doubt benefited also from M. T. Tchou's influence on industrial matters in the government in Nanking.[52] These villages, at Chung Shan Road, Chi Mei Road, Pao Shan Road, and Tai Mo Bridge, were on a much greater scale than the YMCA village. They incorporated "not only modern and sanitary homes but facilities for child welfare, general recreation, bathing, the operation of co-operative stores and other conveniences." They accommodated a total of 1,500 people. As with the YMCA village, the focal point of community life was to be the social center. As these villages quickly filled up, the Greater Shanghai government made plans to erect social centers in other areas, with a view to inviting workers to erect their own houses around them, under municipal direction and using specified materials made available to them cheaply by the government.[53] This plan had no time to come to fruition, however, before the outbreak of hostilities with Japan in mid-1937.

Although it may have been an inspiration to some, the YMCA Model Village was by no means an unqualified success. One critical visitor in 1929 expressed his view of the experiment in these terms:

> The only thing in the village that seemed good was the artesian well which brought up salt water. The whole thing is cheap, in the bad sense of that word. Walks are narrow and if a wheelbarrow came into the village with a heavy load, it would sink to the axle. The houses are already leaky and will not last [sic] at most ten years when they will be wrecks. The lack of drainage makes it anything but model for sanitation. . . . Families selected. . . . Government entirely by YMCA. . . . In 20 years the Y will have six acres of valuable property.[54]

The YMCA responded by reiterating the need to find solutions appropriate to the economic and political reality of China. "The promoters of the enterprise . . . were anxious to conduct an experiment on a business basis; that is, they wished to build houses at a price which they could rent [sic] for an amount within the means of the laborers and at the same time earn a modest profit on their investment. This I understand they have succeeded in doing."[55]

As it was, the fixing of the monthly rent at $3 at a time when many families could not afford to pay much more than half that amount for accommodation meant that no solution had yet been found to the problem of housing poorer workers. Furthermore, the scope of the Model Village was quite modest, given that the building of its twenty-four houses and the operation of the social centers in Pootung and at Robison Road was the principal piece of industrial work undertaken by the YMCA in the period under consideration. The evidence suggests that during the eleven years of its existence no progress was made toward bringing the Model Village's administration into the hands of its inhabitants, as had been envisaged by Thomas Tchou, and it would appear that the YMCA remained in strict control throughout. Nor was it possible to see what effect full ownership of their property might have had on the day-to-day life of the villagers, as in 1937, four years before the mortgages would have been fully paid up, the Model Village was bombed flat by the Japanese.[56]

Decline

Model Village apart, the YMCA's industrial work was by the mid-1920s approaching a crisis. Ironically, this would be precipitated by the engagement of the very foreign industrial expert whom Tchou and others had for some years regarded as essential to the success of their work.

In 1924 John D. Rockefeller had granted the Christian forces in China the sum of $25,000 gold per year over three years to advance their industrial welfare work. Of this, $10,000 per year was specifically allocated to the YMCA, partly to hire a foreign expert. After a search that lasted for some months, Sherwood Eddy, acting in the United States on behalf of the Chinese YMCA, engaged G. T. Schwenning to go to China. Schwenning was described as "a sound progressive man, a valuable adviser and leader in industrial work, a man with high admiration for the Chinese people and a good man to work with in all relations."[57]

Schwenning had most recently been professor of economics and industry in the YMCA College at Springfield, Massachusetts. He had worked in mines and factories for six years before going on to study theology, sociology, and economics at university, later becoming an association secretary with special responsibility for industrial workers in the New York Bowery. Schwenning arrived in China in November 1925. By the end of December he remarked that the situation was not what he had been led to expect, that conditions were "unspeakably bad," and that the prospects for serious investigation and for welfare work were severely limited.[58] He censured the Chinese YMCA for its "timidity," the only person he exempted from this judgment being his colleague Thomas Tchou, who he considered did not enjoy the confidence of the secretaries in the field.

At the end of March Schwenning resigned his position as foreign industrial secretary of the Chinese YMCA and returned with his wife to New York. In four months in China he had been outside Shanghai only twice, once on a short visit to Shantung and another time on a hunting trip to Hangchow. He had been plagued by illness and tormented by the thought that he had given up the offer of a job at Harvard to come to China. His disenchantment with Chinese nationalism had been rapid, and with Thomas Tchou only a little less so. Overriding all was Schwenning's misapprehension about the task he had been called upon to undertake: "He seems to have thought that the association had already in operation a strong, clearly conceived, enthusiastically supported industrial program and that he was being called upon to give it 'expert' advice and help to a going enterprise. He has found this not to be the case."[59]

The YMCA invited Carrington Goodrich, formerly of the Rockefeller Foundation office in Peking, to take Schwenning's place, but Goodrich declined the post. The loss of the foreign expert so soon after his acquisition dealt a serious blow to the YMCA's industrial program. A further consequence of this episode was the eclipse and resignation of Thomas Tchou, at a time when the association's industrial work might have benefited most from firm leadership.[60]

A trained engineer, Tchou was said to have been converted to Christianity after coming under the influence of Feng Yu-hsiang and had taught for a time at Wesley College in Ningpo before joining the staff of the YMCA in the early 1920s.[61] He was fluent in English, French, and German and was spoken of by one colleague as "a remarkable genius with some of the limitations geniuses are likely to have," the chief of which, according to this observer, pertained to his executive and administrative ability. Tchou had "shown power as the Prophet of a cause but not as its administrative and executive head."[62]

Pierre Henry of the ILO saw Tchou differently. He was a man ahead of his time, with "too much enthusiasm"[63] for the liking of some of those with whom he had to deal. Henry felt that many of Tchou's problems derived from the fact that he had too many masters to please, both in the association and in the business community.[64] The Schwenning affair apparently brought these tensions to the surface.

By December 1926, within a few months of Schwenning's departure, Tchou had taken on a new job as administrator of a large industrial school operated under the auspices of a Canton guild. While technically on a year's leave of absence from the YMCA, Tchou was in fact regarded as having withdrawn from the association, and the National Committee is reported to have begun looking for another industrial secretary.[65] Tchou continued his association with the Industrial Commission of the National Christian Council, though his involvement with it diminished with the passage of time. In 1928 he was still a member of the advisory committee of the Model Village, though no longer apparently a member of the YMCA's industrial staff.[66] By 1929 he had moved into the employment of the Nationalist government.[67]

With the departure of Thomas Tchou, the industrial program of the YMCA was left in 1927 without effective leadership. In 1928 two new national industrial secretaries were appointed, the American J. W. Nipps in place of the "foreign expert," and C. H. Lowe, a graduate of the University of Chicago, who took on Tchou's role as Chinese coordinator of the program. Both of these men had had some experience as local industrial secretaries, but neither at this stage possessed the degree of expertise or understanding that, it had become apparent, would be necessary to the successful prosecution of a more ambitious industrial effort. Nonetheless, payments were resumed from the Rockefeller Fund to underwrite their salaries and expenses.

In their first year Nipps and Lowe spent much of their time traveling from place to place, studying industrial and labor conditions in some twenty-one Chinese cities with a view to preparing yet another plan of action in the light of the changed political circumstances. On these tours of inspection the two men held talks, with national and municipal government officials, employers, and local YMCA personnel. It is evident that they attached considerable importance to discussions they had with senior Kuomintang officials and tended to accept at face value the protestations of good intention on the part of these officials with respect to economic reconstruction and social reform. Typically, the two secretaries found Nanking to be "an active and constructive capital in spite of considerable talking about its weaknesses," where the local authorities were "seriously carrying out important social reforms, [such] as the consolidation of all charitable institutions . . . under the direct control of the Municipal Government." Only in Canton did they encounter any trade unionists, and these, as they affirmed, were "anti-Communists."[68] In due course, these tours of inspection came in for criticism from the association hierarchy.[69] After more than a year, there were few places of any note left to visit, and the tours came to an end by mid-1929.

In the autumn of 1929 the sole innovation in industrial work was the holding of a "labor forum" in Shanghai, a series of discussions on labor topics chaired by well-known personalities, among them Ch'en Ta. A proposal for a YMCA Industrial Training Center, originating with Nipps, failed to come to fruition because no one could be found with the skill necessary to organize such a project.[70] The conclusion could no longer be avoided that no matter how many reports were drawn up or plans were made, the program could not be carried on without competent direction and qualified personnel. Whereas in 1925 the YMCA had been active in industrial work in fourteen Chinese cities, by 1929 this work was carried on in only five cities.[71] The events of 1925–27 and the failure in leadership had taken their toll.

Toward the end of 1929, C. H. Lowe was transferred to local industrial work in the Shanghai YMCA, where he later was put in charge of the new social center in Robison Road, opened late in 1930.[72] In due course, Lowe came to feel that his primary interest was in research and writing,[73] and it was to this that he turned his attention, becoming an acknowledged authority on labor matters. Nipps, now left alone, was faced early in 1930 with an urgent request from the YMCA's International Committee in New York for a comprehensive statement of progress to date in industrial work, along with an account of how the Rockefeller money had been spent. He submitted his report in April.

The report proved to be Nipps's undoing. The sixteen-page "Statement of Industrial Work" was repetitive and a triumph of form over content. Lists of activities of the five active local industrial departments were not accompanied by any assessment of their effectiveness at this work. While a broad range of objectives was put forward, such as an improved standard of living for workers, the passage and enforcement of industrial legislation, and the expansion of the program to cover fourteen cities, there was little suggestion as to how in practical terms all of this might be achieved. Although the Chinese YMCA had drawn so far only part of Rockefeller's allocation for industrial work and had spent only part of this amount, Nipps nonetheless put in a request for a new grant from the Rockefeller Foundation of U.S. $37,500 over a period of three years, solely for the industrial work of the YMCA. Taken as a whole, the report was a statement of intent rather than a record of accomplishment.[74]

Shortly after the report was filed, John Nipps was dismissed by the YMCA. By this time, feeling against him within the association was running high, perhaps reflecting as much as anything a general frustration at having so little to show in the industrial sphere. Sherwood Eddy wrote, "John Nipps is a straight-forward, thick-skinned, crude, impulsive, outspoken Western boy, lacking in tact, unable to sense a situation. He should never have been called here as industrial secretary."[75] He added that Nipps seemed quite unable to decide what course the YMCA ought to follow in its industrial work. David Yui, the association president, observed that Nipps was frequently busy on everything but his own job,[76] while another official criticized Nipps for spreading his "ultra-liberal" religious beliefs, which he claimed had upset many missionaries and Christian Chinese.[77] Nipps returned with his wife to the United States, where his resources were soon depleted by a long period of illness. A letter written on his behalf by prominent members of the other welfare organizations in China, praising his efforts and urging that Nipps be reinstated, failed to have any influence on the association.[78] Nipps had no further contact with the YMCA or with China.

The application of the YMCA for more money from the Rockefeller Fund was unsuccessful. In early 1929, when the YWCA and the National Christian Council had each spent their three-year allocation for industrial work, the YMCA still had $13,000 of its $30,000 grant left.[79] When Sherwood Eddy visited China in 1930 to assess the efforts of the various organizations, much of this amount remained, and it may be supposed that he found it hard to justify to Rockefeller further expenditure where the evidence of progress was so scant. Then, too, with the dismissal of Nipps the YMCA's industrial program no longer had a coordinator. Accordingly, while Rockefeller in 1931 made a final grant of two years' further assistance to both the YWCA and the National Christian Council, he declined to give any more money to the YMCA in the light of the "considerable balance left from the original application."[80] Eddy's warning of 1929 to the association, that precisely this might happen, had gone unheeded.[81] One condition under which funds had been given had been that the local or national organization should share the cost of industrial secretaries. Of the local organizations, few could be found willing to undertake this burden, particularly after 1927.[82]

The effect of the withdrawal of Rockefeller's support was compounded in due course by the impact of the depression on the business community, both in the United States and in China. Much less financial assistance was forthcoming, both to the National Committee of the YMCA in China and to the International Committee in New York. By 1933 a process of "demobilization" was well under way in the movement, and a number of secretaries had to be sent home.[83] In these circumstances the filling of the post of national industrial secretary, vacant since 1930, was not considered a priority. In the meantime, the few local industrial secretaries struggled to provide facilities for the workers in their areas. The program, in the absence of any new inspiration, continued to consist mainly of religious, educational, social, and physical activity.[84] In Shanghai, the Model Village continued to function, as did the newer center on Robison Road in the western district. In 1935 a further social center was planned for Chapei, but it seems not to have materialized. By 1937 the Chinese YMCA still lacked a national industrial secretary, when on the outbreak of war with Japan its industrial work ceased altogether.

In the meanwhile, Thomas Tchou had progressed to a position within the Nationalist government from which he was able, for a time, to influence industrial welfare matters. Under the patronage of H. H. Kung, who had himself worked for the Chinese YMCA in Japan before the First World War, in 1928 Tchou became initially Chiang Kai-shek's foreign-language secretary and then head of the Labor Department of the Ministry of Industries, for which Kung was at that time responsible.[85] Here he was given charge of the task of drawing up China's new factory law.

Initially a radical document that would have, among other measures, banned child labor under fourteen, prohibited night work for women, and imposed restrictions on the right to dismiss workers, the draft law apparently had Kung's backing. Implementation of the new act was repeatedly delayed by military emergencies, and the content watered down as a result of pressure from Chinese factory owners urged on by Chiang's rival Hu Han-min.[86] In the face of continued opposition from Chinese industrialists, who were able to point with reason to the extraterritorial protection from the law enjoyed by foreign factories, and perhaps also because H. H. Kung in due course left the Ministry of Industries to take on the Finance portfolio, the act was never enforced.

3

The YWCA

Women workers in industry faced, if possible, an even harder life than men. The challenge of trying to improve their conditions of life and work was taken up by the YWCA. Before examining the association's approach to this task, however, it is necessary to review briefly the circumstances of industrial women.

The use of women workers in Chinese industry became widespread in the 1920s and 1930s. Seeking a supply of cheap and tractable labor, factory owners in Shanghai were the first in the early 1920s to admit large numbers of women to industrial employment.[1] By 1929 one study showed that some 61 percent (173,432), of Shanghai's industrial work force were women, and their numbers were especially high in cotton spinning and weaving (76 and 77 percent), silk reeling (73 percent), cigarette-making (65 percent), and match-making (46 percent).[2] In Tientsin their acceptance was slower, but the trend was nonetheless apparent by the 1930s; while only 9 percent of cotton mill workers were women in 1929, by the time of the Japanese occupation this had risen to 39 percent, and by 1947 it was around 50 percent.[3]

Frequently women were migrants, freely or under contract, from particular villages and areas in the hinterland of major cities. Thus in Shanghai most women in the cotton industry, if they were not from Shanghai itself, came from Kiangnan—southern Kiangsu around the cities of Wusih and Changchow—or from Supei—the area of Kiangsu north of the Yangtze and west of the Grand Canal. As Honig has shown, there was a hierarchy of place of origin among workers that helped to determine their status in Shanghai. Supei women were routinely given the worst jobs to do, which in the cotton industry were reeling and roving. They worked in the dirtiest workshops and were said to take home the least pay.[4] In the cigarette and silk industries, too, Supei women were given the roughest tasks to do.

One main object of employers was, where possible, to replace male workers with women in order to lower the cost of wages. Recent work has shown the differentials in pay between men and women, confirming not only that women were consistently paid less than men for the same tasks, where they were assigned to them, but also that men tended to monopolize the best paying jobs.[5] Women were also less likely to pocket their earnings, as a great many single women had been brought from the countryside by labor contractors and still owed them their wages. Even where the contract had been fulfilled, single women might stay on with the contractors, paying a large part of their wages to them for room and board.[6]

Over and above the matter of wages and conditions of work, industrial women were felt to be more compliant, perhaps because they were particularly vulnerable to abuse of various kinds. Sexual abuse was widespread. Foremen and contractors frequently took advantage of women over whom they wielded authority to extort sexual favors. Some young women who were hired on contract to be factory workers were compelled by their contractors to become prostitutes because they could earn more in this way. In addition, women were frequently waylaid on their way to or from work, and cases of assault and rape were common. Gang members might extort compensation for some contrived injury or simply demand money with menaces. Among younger girls, kidnapping by hoodlums was not uncommon.[7]

To protect themselves from the worst of this abuse, women increasingly formed "sisterhood societies," self-help groups of women who pledged protection and assistance to one another. These would much later provide an important basis for activism among women. Where even this did not work, some women joined the gangs themselves, in this way finding refuge in the threat of revenge to anyone who bothered them.[8]

Even if it was possible to avoid all these hazards, working women still faced an onerous burden of gender-related obligations. In one typical case cited by Honig, for example, a cotton mill worker was absent from work for 193 days in a year: of these, 74 were spent caring for her husband who had TB, 45 were taken following childbirth, 36 were spent caring for a sick child, 28 caring for a sick mother-in-law, and 10 in mourning following a mother-in-law's death. Most mills had no maternity leave until after the Second World War, and many would dismiss workers who became pregnant. One contemporary observer estimated that 60 to 70 percent of babies died.[9]

Enter the YWCA

As with the YMCA, the YWCA movement had its origins in the call for a spiritual regeneration of youth in Britain in the mid-nineteenth century. The movement spread rapidly to the United States, and toward the end of the century branches of the association were established in India and Japan. In 1899 a committee was formed of foreign and Chinese Christian women to promote the organization in China. The National Committee and the first branch were established in 1905, and by 1920 no fewer than twelve "city" associations, and eighty "student" associations were in existence. In the first instance, the Chinese YWCA sought to appeal only to women of middle-class origin, but in due course its work was expanded to embrace rural and urban women of more humble circumstances.[10]

Industrial work was begun by the YWCA in China in 1921 in accordance with the recommendations accepted by the World's YWCA movement at Champery in

1920. The Champery meeting urged all national branches of the YWCA to take definite measures to promote industrial and social reform (see chapter 8). In China Grace Coppock, general secretary of the YWCA, was already seeking to procure the services of someone with expert knowledge of industrial conditions, when at the end of 1920 she met Professor J. B. Tayler of Yen Ching University, who gave her the name of Agatha Harrison of the London School of Economics (LSE). Harrison was in charge of the school's program for training welfare workers. An invitation for her to come to China to work for the YWCA was duly issued and accepted.[11]

Before taking up her position at LSE, Harrison had studied at the Froebel Institute in London and held the post of welfare officer in several major industrial concerns, managing to achieve within the limits prescribed some success in improving the condition of life of the employees in her charge.[12] One observer was later to remark, with some ambivalence, that she was "evidently a woman of ability and very strong convictions regarding the obligation of the employers to their employees."[13] She had no previous connection with the YWCA, and indeed entertained some doubts about her own attitude toward Christianity.[14]

Harrison set out for China almost immediately, traveling via the United States where the American YWCA had arranged for her to visit a number of factories and model enterprises and meet government officials, businessmen, trade unionists, and members of the association's local industrial staff.[15] She arrived in China early in May, where she found "a National Committee eager to help, and a group of keen intelligent secretaries ready to stand back of a difficult programme."[16]

After some initial reconnaissance it quickly became apparent to Harrison that conditions were much worse than anything she had anticipated. The Christian organizations as yet had little understanding of the industrial problem and no plan of action, and while some employers had asked them for help, "the kind they wanted is well known to the welfare worker, viz: willingness to give money for 'see-what-we-do-for-our-workers' kind of work . . . how anyone with any honesty could embark on such a programme when the conditions are what they are is beyond my knowledge."[17]

Determined to impress upon the leaders of the YWCA the gravity of the task they had undertaken, Harrison presented the National Committee at its meeting of June 16 with a clear choice. Either the association could embark upon a program of recreational and other activities among employed women, which would amount to work that was merely palliative, or it could put its effort into a program directed primarily toward the making of opinion with regard to labor standards, which Harrison felt to be much more fundamental. After considerable discussion the committee adopted the latter course and decided that the association would "begin at once to make a direct and accurate study of industrial conditions in typical centres to equip it with the knowledge which will enable it to serve both employers and employees in the most constructive ways and to help create the public opinion that must precede legislation."[18]

It was agreed that a Chinese association secretary, Zung Wei-tsung, would be sent to Europe to attend the International Congress of Working Women to be held in Geneva in October 1920.

The Making of Standards

During her first six months as national industrial secretary of the Chinese YWCA, Harrison spent much of her time making herself familiar with local conditions and cultivating people whom she hoped might support her in her quest for legislative reform. For part of the summer she worked with Grace Coppock at Peitaiho, pressing her cause among missionaries and preparing the first draft of a report for the Committee on the Church's Relation to Economic and Industrial Problems. The committee would present its report to the initial meeting of the National Christian Council of China the following spring. After the death in October of Coppock, who had been chairman of the committee, Harrison became its leading force.[19]

Back in Shanghai, Harrison went to see the editor of the *North China Daily News* and was able to arouse his interest in the industrial question. Correspondence about factory conditions had already begun to appear in the columns of the *News* and the weekly *North China Herald*, stimulated by publication of the report of a child labor commission set up by the Hong Kong government, and this correspondence was supplemented toward the end of the year by a series of articles on factories in Shanghai.[20]

Industrial reform had also become a subject for discussion in several bourgeois women's groups in Shanghai, and Harrison duly arranged a joint meeting of the Chinese, American, and British Women's Clubs with the National Committee of the YWCA with a view to providing them with more information and encouraging them to coordinate their activity.[21] As a result, the special joint committee formed by the women's clubs was instrumental in helping to bring about the establishment of the Shanghai Municipal Council's Child Labor Commission in 1923 (see chapter 5).

From her arrival in China, Harrison had borne the burden of the YWCA's industrial campaign almost alone, although she did have some part-time assistance from two association secretaries with no previous experience of such work—Helen Thoburn and Edith Johnston. In mid-December, however, Zung Wei-tsung returned from Europe with nearly six months of study of the problems of modern industry behind her and was henceforth able to contribute significantly to Harrison's work.[22] By December also it is clear that frequent visits to factories and conversations with managerial staff had led Harrison to conclude that she would have to direct her attention more narrowly toward the employers if she was ever to achieve any practical reforms. As she was later to observe, "The first principles of humanity and justice are being violated by the leaders of industry—many of whom come from America and England where similar actions would be penalised. If the employers can 'see' this thing and voluntarily bring about a different order, the industrial history of China may be very different from the West [*sic*]."[23]

Approaches to Employers

In the late autumn of 1921 Harrison twice obtained an interview with a prominent foreign employer to whom she refers in her notes only as "Mr. X."[24] She put to him the necessity for the "leaders of industry" to take the initiative in bringing about industrial reform, and evidently had specifically in mind measures to restrict the employment of child labor, to limit hours, and to safeguard the health of workers.[25] "Mr. X" agreed that the existing situation was wrong but maintained that foreign employers could not act to improve conditions as Chinese employers would not follow suit, and that nothing could be done until there was legislation, as competition was so keen that employers who set a different standard would go under. At a third meeting in January Mr. X said that he had consulted several other employers, who had confirmed that they would not act in the absence of legislation.[26]

At the suggestion of Mr. X, Harrison then approached the Foreign Mill Owners' Association of Shanghai with a plea for collective action to implement minimum standards, observing that in the West the existence of such standards had proved a benefit to both workers and employers.[27] She was granted the opportunity to put her case at a special meeting of the Committee of the Foreign Mill Owners' Association on January 20. On this occasion Harrison made four specific proposals to the employers: first, that they might, as an association, register their dissatisfaction with existing conditions; second, that they might appoint a committee to go into the matter thoroughly, that such a committee might be composed of English, American, and Chinese employers, some practical economists "like R. H. Tawney and Felix Frankfurter," someone to represent workers' interests, and people who had legal knowledge and would study the prevailing situation in various centers and put forward recommendations for change; third, that the employers might induce the Shanghai Municipal Council to extend the powers of their Health Department to include inspection of factories on grounds of ventilation, sanitation, and overcrowding; and fourth, that individual factories might appoint trained welfare officers who would be responsible to management for all things relating to the well-being of workers—"industrial welfare workers" of the type then to be found in many factories in Britain. Harrison suggested that if the employers would take it upon themselves to act, they would find among concerned members of the community "a body of people ready to help find a way out." "But none of the . . . suggestions appealed to them, and 'they all with one consent began to make excuse.' What one did not remember, the other did, shifting the responsibility, until one could well imagine that industry was run for philanthropic purposes to give warmth and food and shelter to men, women, and children. Listening to what was said gave the answer for all Bolshevism."[28]

The mill owners urged Harrison to appeal to the Chinese Mill Owners' Association to try to secure legislation, which Harrison well knew would be futile, and the meeting closed with no positive result.

Shortly after this abortive attempt to influence the mill owners, however, the Shanghai Rotary Club became interested in industrial reform. On February 9, the club held an open meeting to which Agatha Harrison and Mr. X, among others, were invited to speak. Subsequently, the club appointed a group of four to meet four of the reformers to discuss what could be done.[29]

It was decided that the Rotary Club would call together an international group of employers in Shanghai, who would be approached through the Chinese Mill Owners' Association and the various chambers of commerce, with a view to constituting a permanent committee of employers to consider what might be done. Rotary Club members agreed to contact Harrison when the liaison had been made. On this issue, however, business moved slowly, and while Harrison remarked in her report of September 11, 1922, that there was "a group of employers . . . willing to move forward if we have constructive plans,"[30] there is no evidence to suggest that the Rotary Club was any more successful than the YWCA had been in attempting to persuade the business community, at this stage at least, to take any initiative. So too in North China Harrison found during a trip to Peking and Tientsin in the autumn "among officials and other men of standing . . . a number who are caring profoundly about industrial matters but waiting for the initiative to be taken in some other quarter."[31]

Assistance from Abroad

The strain of battling seemingly immovable forces in Shanghai prompted Harrison to look overseas for help and support. In November 1921 she wrote to Mary Dingman, industrial secretary of the World's YWCA in London, "I am constantly subject to a fire of criticism. At each dinner I have been to the subject crops up and then to use a slang expression I have 'to go through it.' The other night I held the fort for two hours against a prominent business man here. Next week I understand I am to meet a man at dinner who says I am a menace to the public."[32]

In March 1922 Harrison wrote again to Dingman, "asking, or as I should like to put it, commandeering your help."[33] Dingman, who had been contemplating a trip to the Far East in any event, would arrive in China by the end of the year for a protracted stay.

The knowledge that she was soon to receive assistance buoyed up Harrison through the summer and autumn of 1922. She wrote to Dingman suggesting that she might approach the Home Office to discuss the possibility of introducing labor legislation in the International Settlement at Shanghai. She urged her to bring with her to China as many introductions as possible, illustrated material from the Home Officer on ventilating apparatus, fencing for machinery, sanitation facilities in factories, and copies of factory inspection reports dating back to the 1840s, "for nothing was said then to the factory inspectors that is not being repeated out here." She asked her to try to interview some of the Chinese women students in London with the idea of persuading them to train for industrial welfare work, either inside or outside the YWCA. She sought financial assistance so that other Chinese and foreigners might be sent from China to study industrial welfare in England, and she suggested that Dingman appeal to Sir John Jordan, chairman of the Boxer Indemnity Committee, to see if funds from that source might be applied to a scholarship for industrial welfare training.[34] There is no evidence to suggest that any Boxer money was made available for this purpose.

Harrison developed her argument for the creation of a skilled corps of welfare workers further in her report of September 11, 1922.[35] By this time, she had apparently been able to convince the London School of Economics to offer a tuition scholarship for one year to enable a Chinese woman to go to London to study.[36] It was Harrison's plan to try to have this scholarship offered for the next five or six years. In addition, she suggested the YWCA women might, after completing their courses in London, return to China the following summer through the United States, where they could visit factories and perhaps attend the summer school for industrial workers at Bryn Mawr. While Harrison clearly saw the necessity of training a cadre of Chinese women for this work, having an eye to the future, she also felt that what she termed the "international character of trade"—the need to deal with foreign employers—would create a steady demand for foreign welfare workers. For these women, as for their Chinese counterparts, her own experience led her to recommend a definite pattern of preparation.

> I urge that no secretary be appointed to China for industrial work unless she has had a special training. Experience of the "Industrial Girl" through clubs, etc., or a natural longing to do the work—*is not sufficient.* A thorough understanding of the history of industry in the other countries, its structure, its problems, the experiments that have been made by employers and workers, special legislation, the connection with other movements, etc., etc. [is necessary].[37]

An attempt to involve students without special training in the monitoring of industrial conditions produced no positive result. Although a special session on industry was held during the YWCA Student Workers' Conference in Shanghai and Hangchow in November 1922, it was observed that many students in mission schools were "not sufficiently aware of national movements and conditions," while many of those in government schools were "thinking in terms of a new social order."[38]

At the end of 1922 the promised help from abroad materialized. Mary Dingman, industrial secretary of the World's YWCA, arrived to begin work in China, evidently remaining there until her departure for Australia and New Zealand on July 13, 1923. During her stay Dingman traveled extensively up and down the country explaining association industrial policy at local branch meetings and sending her impressions back to the National Committee in Shanghai. Early in the year the Chinese YWCA prevailed upon the World's Committee in London to allow Dingman to return to China as temporary industrial secretary in 1924 when Agatha Harrison's tour of duty in this post would be over.[39]

Interim Results

In 1923 Harrison's efforts to bring the plight of industrial workers to public attention began to yield some fruit. In March the Peking government promulgated its provisional factory regulations, though they were never enforced. In April, more directly as a result of YWCA agitation, the Shanghai Municipal Council decided to establish a commission to investigate child labor in factories within the bounds of the International Settlement. At the National Christian Conference in May the Committee on the Relation of the Church to Economic and Industrial Problems presented its report (see chapter 4). As a result, an ongoing NCC Industrial Commission was appointed. Agatha Harrison and Zung Wei-tsung formed part of a small group that met three times a week to carry on the executive work of this commission. When the Child Labor Commission first met in June, Harrison was invited to serve on this body as well, which she did along with another YWCA secretary, the as yet unknown Soong Mei-ling, future wife of Chiang Kai-shek. In July Zung and Dingman gave a series of lectures on industrial history at a summer school arranged by the Christian organizations in Tsinanfu.[40]

Within the YWCA's Industrial Department Edith Johnston returned in the autumn from England, where she had been receiving training in industrial welfare work while on furlough, and Harriet Rietveld of the National Committee and Lily Haass of the Peking YWCA both left to undergo similar training in England and the United States, Rietveld in May and Haass in December.[41] In December Dame Adelaide Anderson arrived in China, as a result of the joint intervention of Harrison and Dr. Henry Hodgkin of the NCC, to contribute her expertise to the deliberations of the Child Labor Commission. Earlier, in August, Shin Takhing had apparently traveled to Cologne from London to address the International Congress of Working Women.[42]

The major event of 1923 in the calendar of the YWCA was the holding of the association's first national convention in Hangchow in October. At Hangchow the industrial question was presented for consideration by the delegates assembled, for the last time under Agatha Harrison's direction. The association went on record as recognizing the relationship between industrial distress and the host of other problems, social and economic, which impeded the Chinese masses from achieving the "fullness of life." In response to an appeal by the National Christian Council, it agreed to integrate its industrial campaign with that of the NCC's Industrial Commission.[43] By the year's end the best efforts of Harrison and her staff were entirely taken up with service on the commission, its subsidiary Shanghai Local Committee, and the Municipal Council's Child Labor Commission.[44]

Some time earlier, Harrison had remarked, "One of our biggest problems will be to try and go forward as part of the unified Christian force, not alone as the YWCA. It may be necessary to do the latter, but we must try the other way first."[45]

Gradually joint industrial welfare projects had absorbed more and more of the YWCA secretaries' energies, and at the time of Harrison's final departure for England in January 1924, commitment to cooperative action was complete. It would remain for others to live with the implications of this decision.

The Rockefeller Gift

In January 1924 the Christian organizations were much encouraged to learn that John D. Rockefeller, Jr., had decided to donate to them $25,000 in gold per year for three years for the promotion of industrial welfare in China. This decision had been taken by Rockefeller as a result of the intervention of Sherwood Eddy after his return from China early in 1923. Of this sum, $10,000 was to go to the YMCA, $5,000 to the YWCA, $5,000 to the NCC, and $5,000 for the purpose of investigating the desirability of setting up a permanent institute of social and economic research.[46] While the commitment on Rockefeller's part to make the money available was unequivocal, the manner of administering the funds—through the medium of the International Committee of the YMCA in New York—from the YWCA's point of view left much to be desired.[47]

From the beginning, deployment of the funds was much hampered by the unresponsive attitude of the YMCA in New York, and by the difference of opinion between the YMCA in China and the other Christian organizations over what would constitute proper use of the money, trends that augured ill for the joint approach to industrial problems to which the YWCA had so recently committed itself. While the YMCA was advised immediately of the grant in a letter from New York that arrived in February, the YWCA and the NCC had to learn of it by hearsay and were only formally advised of the terms and conditions after Harrison, by this time in the United States, was granted an interview with Rockefeller himself the following summer.[48]

In March and April representatives of the YWCA and NCC met with officials of the Chinese YMCA to discuss their interpretation of the provisions of the gift. It soon became clear that the YMCA understood the terms of the grant "in the most rigid way." This meant that the YMCA could use its money only for two new industrial secretaries from the West who would carry out practical "demonstration work," one perhaps in a specific factory, the other in a "social center." The YWCA would be obliged to use its share only for new industrial secretaries, while the NCC money could be used only for the spreading of ideas and educating opinion, and none of it toward salaries. The YWCA felt, however, that $5,000 per year was more than would be required for one industrial secretary and preferred to spend the remainder on other items of expenditure in its industrial department's budget. It specifically wished to contribute part of its grant toward the salary of a strong executive secretary for the NCC Industrial Commission.[49] The NCC itself also wanted greater flexibility in determining how its share would be spent. While Dr. Henry Hodgkin of the NCC wrote to the International Committee of the YMCA in New York in June requesting elucidation of the terms of the grant and urging greater freedom in its deployment, an appeal that Harrison would shortly repeat to Rockefeller, E. C. Jenkins of the International Committee wrote at the same time to C. W. Harvey in China confirming the YMCA's original position; the two letters crossed in the post.[50] Jenkins further expressed the view that all the participating organizations would be expected to clear all their expenditures through Harvey, who was senior secretary of the YMCA in China.

It would appear that Harrison's meeting with Rockefeller during the summer of 1924 not only clarified the terms of the grant but made it clear that Rockefeller himself intended a much greater degree of flexibility in the spending of the money than the YMCA had been willing to concede.[51] Dingman and Hodgkin both apparently conveyed the sense of this interview to Harvey, one in person and the other by letter, and asked him to demonstrate the YMCA's commitment to joint action by allowing a small amount of the sum it had been given to be put toward the salary of an NCC Industrial Secretary. It would seem that Harvey was unmoved by these arguments, however, and on August 18 he sailed for New York for discussions with the International Committee. Most of the Chinese YMCA's senior staff were now temporarily in New York, which ruled out the possibility of further discussions on joint action for several months to come.[52]

The YWCA and the NCC then went ahead and prepared their own budgets for the use of the Rockefeller money. The YWCA proposed to spend its $5,000 per year as follows: one new YWCA industrial secretary, $2,500; contribution to the salary of an executive secretary for the NCC Industrial Commission, $1,000 (the NCC put up a similar amount); traveling expenses in China, $250; toward expenses and hospitality for visiting industrial experts, $150; training of "industrial leaders" (financial assistance to students to enable them to travel abroad and study, and to colleges in China to enable them to give special courses on industrial welfare), $1,000; the production and purchase of literature on industrial subjects (to supplement that provided by the NCC), $100.[53]

Both organizations submitted their budgets to the International Committee of the YMCA in New York as required, and Dingman requested a cabled reply as she had a particular candidate in mind in London for the post of industrial secretary for the YWCA and wished to get in touch with her as soon as possible.

For five months nothing at all was heard from the YMCA despite repeated inquiries from Dingman and Hodgkin, and three telegrams. Finally, in February 1925 Hodgkin received a letter from Charles Herschleb of the YMCA in New York claiming that the problem had been caused by "the YMCA and the YWCA [having] been delaying in securing personnel and [not having] until recently been in a position to call upon the Fund." As Dingman observed, "It would almost look as if they have been unable to find the person for themselves and had kept us waiting until they were ready."[54]

Indeed, it would appear that this is precisely what happened, as YMCA correspondence shows that the association succeeded in finding its own man to go to China, G. T. Schwenning, only in the spring of 1925.[55] A review of YMCA expenditures under the Rockefeller Fund in 1930 shows that the association never gave any money toward the salary of an industrial secretary for the NCC, nor for any other joint project with the industrial sections of the NCC and the YWCA.[56] When, by April 1925, the YWCA had received a direct communication from Herschleb and it had been admitted that there was more leeway in the spending of the Rockefeller money than had at first been thought, Dingman had lost her chance to bring to China the welfare worker she had particularly wanted, as the woman had in the end been obliged to decline so uncertain an offer. While the International Committee of the YMCA continued to act as broker for the Rockefeller grant over the next five years and offered no further trouble, it is hard to dispute Dingman's conclusion that in 1924–25 the YWCA had been "abominably treated" by the committee.[57]

A Loss of Momentum

In mid-1925 the movement for the reform of child labor in Shanghai collapsed. Industrial welfare work as a whole became more difficult as events following the May Thirtieth incident served to sharpen national and class consciousness, and resistance to any kind of gradual reform, especially when initiated by foreigners, increased from both the right and the left. The YWCA had played a leading part in the child labor campaign and was now unsure as to what course to pursue in industrial work. This uncertainty was heightened by a temporary hiatus in leadership.

In June 1925 Mary Dingman, who had directed this work since Agatha Harrison's departure at the end of 1923, left China to resume her responsibilities at the World's YWCA headquarters in Europe.[58] Originally it had been proposed to call a Miss Escreet to China to replace Dingman, using part of the Rockefeller grant for this purpose. Escreet was an English welfare worker of some years' experience, and it had been hoped that if she had been on the spot in China in 1925, working for the YWCA, the Shanghai Municipal Council might have been persuaded to take her on as head of a new Industrial Section, whereupon the YWCA would have found a replacement for her.[59] The defeat of the child labor legislation and the rise of the May Thirtieth Movement, however, meant that creation of an Industrial Section by the council was now quite out of the question, while the difficulties posed by the YMCA over release of the Rockefeller money to the YWCA caused such a delay that between the autumn of 1924 and the spring of 1925 Escreet had lost interest in the job.[60]

Approaches to several other British women welfare workers apparently were no more fruitful.[61] In China itself it would appear that for the first time no suitable candidate could be found to be sent to the summer course on welfare work at the London School of Economics.[62] Of the junior YWCA staff who had come to be involved in industrial work over the past several years, some were proving to be a disappointment. Soong Mei-ling, who had served on the Child Labor Commission, was soon to marry Chiang Kai-shek and drop out of YWCA work altogether.[63] Zung Wei-tsung had turned against the child labor campaign, as she had come to see the issue of the extension of the Shanghai Municipal Council's power to legislate as evidence of an intention to encroach further on Chinese sovereignty.[64] This had soured relations between her and her foreign coworkers. In 1926 she married and participated less actively in the YWCA.[65] Shin Tak-hing, who had spent even longer than Zung in Europe studying techniques of industrial welfare, apparently failed to satisfy those who had earlier shown so much confidence in her. Late in 1925 Shin was put in charge of YWCA industrial work in Shanghai, a symptom of "a definite recognition of the fact that she will be entirely a local secretary."[66] Late in 1926 a senior official remarked that Shin "just is not in the right place. . . . I feel we must find another Chinese woman to head up the department."[67] One other young woman who had expressed interest in industrial welfare work in 1926 left to join a church mission in Changchow. As Lily Haass said of Dju Yu-bao, "There was always a bit of a reservation in her mind regarding the kind of work that we were doing since she desired a first-hand contact with workers with a strong Christian emphasis."[68] Dju, however, would subsequently return to industrial work and would in due course become one of Eleanor Hinder's assistants at the Industrial Section of the Shanghai Municipal Council. Of the staff more experienced in industrial welfare work, this left Harriet Rietveld, Lily Haass, and Edith Johnston. In 1925 Rietveld was fully occupied with the coordination of industrial welfare efforts in Chefoo, almost the only center outside Shanghai where this kind of activity continued to be promoted in the wake of the May Thirtieth rising.[69] It had been decided by the YWCA National Committee in March 1925 that Lily Haass would be loaned to the Industrial Commission of the National Christian Council upon her return from furlough in the autumn,[70] and she did in fact take up her position with the NCC in October. With the unexpected death that month of Edith Johnston,[71] however, who had been helping to carry the work of the Industrial Department at National Headquarters in Shanghai, the problem of overall direction of the association's industrial work became acute. It was at this time that the decision was made to call Eleanor Hinder to China. An Australian woman with several years' experience of industrial welfare work in her own country, Hinder would quickly assume responsibility for the YWCA's industrial efforts in China, first as a local secretary in Shanghai, and then as national industrial secretary. Ultimately it would be Hinder who, with Rewi Alley, would be put in charge of the Shanghai Municipal Council's Industrial Section upon its creation in 1932.

The Beginning of "Direct Work"

The two years that Hinder spent in Shanghai during her first period of residence in China—early 1926 to early 1928—permitted little scope for dramatic initiatives in industrial work. Foreigners in the YWCA, as elsewhere in China, were placed in the position of having to react to the sudden twisting and turning of events around them, and even those who sought to isolate themselves from the conflict between Chinese nationalism and foreign privilege were not above suspicion. One observer remarked, "The Shanghai local Association is talking of dispensing with all foreigners, which would mean the collapse of industrial work."[72]

Such projects as were undertaken in 1926 and the first half of 1927 were largely implemented under the sponsorship of the Industrial Commission of the National Christian Council, with YWCA cooperation. While Lily Haass of the YWCA was now executive secretary of this commission, her hands were tied by the growing conservatism of the NCC constituency among the churches (see chapter 8). In this climate, the emphasis in YWCA industrial work gradually shifted from efforts to mold opinion on labor standards in conjunction with other organizations to an independent program of "direct work" among industrial women and girls.

The Chapei Center

One experiment attempted as an independent initiative of the YWCA at this time was the acquisition of a house in the Chapei factory district of Shanghai as a field center for industrial work. Haass observed, "It will mean a tremendous thing to our Chinese secretaries if they can get a first hand knowledge of industrial women and their problems instead of trying to do all of their work from an office. They have clearly in mind that we are not doing any slumming in any superior way but opening the way for the development of Chinese woman leadership among the workers."[73]

A later report further emphasized that the object of the experiment was "to contribute to the leadership of the women who work in the filatures, so that they may be as intelligent as possible about the conditions under which they work."[74]

In December 1926 the house opened with Hinder, her Chinese trainee Kyong Bae-tsung, a qualified nurse, and Lily Haass—in her capacity as a YWCA worker—in residence. Popular education classes were immediately begun, though apparently for children in the first instance, and a vaccination clinic was held three nights a week with the cooperation of the Health Department of the Municipality of Shanghai and Woosung. Contact was made with forewomen from several factories, with a view to encouraging them to use what authority they possessed to improve conditions for the workers in their charge. A "forewoman's council" was envisaged, which could act as a consultative body to the YWCA workers, though during the brief existence of the Chapei center there is nothing to suggest that such a group was formally created. It was hoped in addition that Hinder would be able to reach men in "senior," presumably management, positions in the surrounding filatures by offering them English lessons, and would in this way be able to develop in them an awareness of the necessity for improved conditions of work.[75] A "ten-day program" of adult education was planned for the period when filatures would be closed for three weeks at Chinese New Year.

While the Chapei experiment may be considered as evidence of a new resolution on the part of the YWCA to establish a direct contact with working women, it may be supposed that there was a natural reluctance on the part of the latter to have very much to do with the YWCA women, except to patronize the educational and health facilities that they made available.[76] The YWCA welfare workers had occupied the Chapei center for only a few months when they were obliged to withdraw to the International Settlement by political developments in Shanghai in the spring of 1927.[77]

The First Industrial Secretaries' Conference

In August 1927 the National Christian Council held its major Conference on Christianizing Economic Relationships under the direction of Lily Haass, and immediately afterward the YWCA convened its first Industrial Secretaries Conference in Shanghai on August 29 and 30.[78] On this occasion all those who had participated in the YWCA's industrial work over the previous several years and who were still in China were brought together to share their experiences and to consider strategy. For some time there had been a growing disenchantment with the policy of "cooperation" with the other Christian agencies in the pursuit of industrial work embarked upon at the beginning of 1924. As had been observed in 1926, "It had become increasingly clear during these three years of the 'policy of co-operation' that such a policy puts not a less but a greater burden of responsibility on the YWCA. A study of local [NCC] committees shows almost without exception that work flourishes only where there is an Association person with a special interest in, and knowledge of, industrial problems."[79]

Given that the NCC seemed to function in the industrial sphere only insofar as it was led by YWCA personnel, and given the long-standing differences between the YWCA and the YMCA on the industrial question, it is perhaps not surprising that the most important resolution to come out of the August conference was a decision that the YWCA should reestablish an independent industrial program of its own as soon as possible.[80]

Among other issues apparently discussed at the conference were recruitment and training of industrial secretaries, the best disposition of available financial and human resources, and the appropriate relationship between the existing work of the association oriented toward the creation of public opinion on industrial matters and more direct work, "for and with workers."[81] In the particular circumstances of 1927, there was "a growing desire on the part of certain Chinese leaders, Miss Ting [general secretary of the Chinese YWCA] in particular, for concrete pieces of work that can be seen. The model village of the YMCA attracts her especially."[82]

At one session of the conference a Chinese secretary challenged the association to see industrial workers as "people," to "stop being a middle-class organization."[83] While the issue was not finally resolved, there was an evident shift toward direct welfare work at the conference.[84] This was accompanied by a renewed effort to get in touch with the labor movement.[85]

Information Gathering

Eleanor Hinder departed China in the early spring of 1928. Although the association's Industrial Department continued to suffer from staff changes, nevertheless, some significant industrial work was done in 1928 and 1929 as local secretaries carried on with projects initiated by Hinder and her predecessors.[86] In part, this actively concerned the gathering of information.

In 1926 the association had through its individual staff members taken an important part in a study of the cost of living of workers in Shanghai initiated by the National Christian Council. This study was subsequently taken over by the Bureau of Markets of the Nationalist Ministry of Finance and was the first of a series of such studies carried out by the Kuomintang government and the government of the Municipality of Greater Shanghai.[87] In 1929, however, the World's YWCA suggested that the various national associations might undertake "budget studies"—a comprehensive survey of income and expenditure—for working families in their areas. The Chinese YWCA felt that for the time being this would be beyond its capacity. As Lily Haass was to remark, "Budget studies are terribly involved here, since most workers seem to pool their wages in the family income. A budget study therefore means a study of the whole family income and expenditure."[88]

The association had already decided instead to embark on less complicated studies of living and working conditions that would provide "information such as cannot be obtained by more technical investigations and which would be of special help to us in deciding our own programme and policy, since it would yield much about social and moral conditions."[89] Beginning in 1928, a number of surveys were undertaken, more than in any other single period, into conditions of life and work for women workers in different industries, and the results were published in pamphlet form. Among these were *Women in Tientsin Industries* by T'ao Ling and Lydia Johnson, *Industrial Women in Wusih* by Kyong Bae-tsung, and *Women in Industry in the Chapei, Hongkew and Pootung Districts of Shanghai* by Chung Shou-ching and May Bagwell (see Bibliography). In addition, a special "Industrial Number" of the *Green Year Supplement*, the association's English-language magazine, was produced in November 1928 to try to convey to foreign readers a sense of the urgency of the need for industrial reform in China.[90] The standard of these publications was high considering their intended appeal to a general readership, and they are significant in being probably the earliest studies in any language of the lives specifically of Chinese women industrial workers.

Local Projects: Tientsin

In the spring of 1928 the YWCA embarked on an industrial program in Tientsin. Initially the two secretaries responsible, Lydia Johnson and T'ao Ling, encountered hostility, owing to "the fact that the local Chinese authorities so fear the influence of communist propaganda that anyone working in the realm of social investigation is open to suspicion. Endorsement from the Chinese Chamber of Commerce helped to allay this difficulty, however, and after some initial experience of being watched by detectives, the two secretaries have been able to pursue their investigations."[91]

A decision was taken to concentrate on providing mass education for industrial women in Tientsin, and accordingly a class was begun in Ta Wang near the British-American Tobacco Factory and another at Hsi Ku near a large match factory. While conditions in the tobacco-related industries were not the worst to be found in Tientsin, it was felt best to start with "those industrial groups whose wage and whose working hours gave a little more margin for such things as learning to read and write."[92]

Factory workers were contacted by means of distributing leaflets describing the program among the forewomen, who then passed along the word; the program had the blessing of factory managers. The two classes together appear to have had a total average enrollment for each six-month session of some fifty to sixty girls in the first two years of the operation.[93] A process of attrition naturally took place, however, as a result of combining long hours of work with evening classes, and this, along with the inherent difficulty of learning to read and write Chinese, meant that of the fifteen to twenty girls attending the first session at Ta Wang, for example, only nine passed their examinations.[94] Subject matter for the course was the *Thousand Character Text* published by the Commercial Press. Each class met for two hours in the evening, six days a week. Typically the instructor might be a junior middle school graduate, and it is interesting to note that her salary for this work, at $20 Chinese per month, compared with an average monthly wage of about $8 per month for the Hsi Ku match workers, and $12 per month for the tobacco workers of Ta Wang.[95] Of the "graduates," some apparently went on to study three nights a week subjects such as arithmetic, reading, and the "Three Principles of the People," though it is not clear that this "further study" was offered after the first year of operation.

One difficulty encountered was that of reaching the many women out-workers who worked assembling match boxes in their homes around the match factory in Hsi Ku. Quite apart from the difficulty of getting in touch with these women, the fact that they were paid on piece-work rates meant that they were even less likely than their counterparts in the factories to find the time or energy for mass education "Where every copper counts in the family budget—and one gets only three coppers for pasting 100 boxes—it is perhaps not so easy to leave one's work even for an hour in order to study."[96] The problem of out-workers was one with which the YWCA never really came to grips, with respect to mass education or anything else.

Another educational project for which the Tientsin association Industrial Department came to bear a heavy burden of responsibility was the Tientsin vocational school for women. The school had its origins in a factory for women that had existed from 1917 to 1919. Finding the school already in operation, but in need of financial assistance, the YWCA resolved to lend it support and was by 1929 subsidizing it to the extent of some $1,500 Chinese per year.

The object of the school was to "secure economic independence for young women through study and work," and this was reflected in the curriculum, which combined an elementary academic education with training for handwork. The girls in attendance at the school were from ten to twenty years in age, with the average being nearer the lower figure. The elementary work involved lessons in the party principles, "common sense," and English; the students were divided into two sections, and while one group would be doing academic work, the other group would be doing handwork. The whole teaching load was borne by two teachers, each of whom taught thirty-three hours per week and had to be responsible for four classrooms at once. A volunteer teacher came to help with the English. The school year was thirty-eight weeks, with five days a week, and six hours a day, the normal full course being four years. Some ninety-six students were in attendance in 1929.

While no tuition fees were charged, a fee of $2 per year was payable to meet incidental expenses, which must have acted as some deterrent at least to families on very marginal incomes. Also, in 1929 only 7 percent of the school's graduates went on directly to become wage earners, while the others went on either to do further study or stayed at home as "house-helpers." In a report published in 1930 the YWCA was criticized for "running an ordinary primary school with an exaggerated form of manual training" and for paying "comparatively too little attention . . . to the education of girls from poorer homes who often all need the help most of all."

This observer recommended that girls under fourteen should not be admitted in future, and that the curriculum should conform more to the norm for adult education: "Thousand characters, simple homemaking and civics should take the place of the present curriculum, because model homes for the poor classes are badly needed in this country. As to handwork, a better variety should be added to meet the needs of the young women of today."[97]

It is not clear whether the vocational school continued to function in its existing or in revised form, or whether or not the YWCA continued to support it. A similar vocational school would appear to have been started as a result of Christian initiative in Canton in 1928, but again it is not clear what responsibility the YWCA had in this initiative.[98] In Tientsin the vocational school was apparently under the supervision of the association's social service secretary, rather than that of the industrial secretary.

Once begun, industrial work continued in Tientsin until shortly after the outbreak of war with Japan in 1937. The difficulty in finding suitable staff affected work there as elsewhere, however, and in 1930 Cora Deng would observe that Lydia Johnson was "still there, but working under strain due to the lack of a trained permanent Chinese secretary to work with her."[99]

Shanghai

In Shanghai, too, direct work had begun again, taking up where the Chapei experiment had left off. It would appear that by 1929 one house in the YMCA Model Village in Pootung had been allocated to the YWCA as a base from which to conduct industrial welfare work among women of the district, with the emphasis on mass education.[100] This effectively reduced the number of "model" houses actually lived in by working families to ten. Also in 1929 the YWCA established itself firmly in the western district of Shanghai with the opening of its "centre for experiment, demonstration, and training of secretaries," under the direction of the National and Local Shanghai Industrial Departments.[101]

This center, in a part of Shanghai where "moral and social conditions among women workers are particularly bad,"[102] soon came to be the most important piece of work undertaken by the association in Shanghai. From two bases of operation, one in Ferry Road and the other in Robinson Road, the YWCA carried out an extensive program of welfare work in which the emphasis was again on education, with "popular education," presumably literacy classes, offered under the supervision of the "popular education secretary." There were also classes in arithmetic, hygiene, letter writing, Chinese history, and geography for graduates of the literacy program, and "mass education," "with larger groups of workers and their families."[103]

In addition, the association arranged talks, discussions, demonstrations, and films to promote what was termed "health education," and it provided the services of a woman doctor two evenings a month for the women of the community. A library service was made available to workers, offering books and other reading material, often with a strong Christian bias.[104] Clubs were started to bring together women interested in amateur dramatics, music, sports, and other activities, and club rooms were kept open for recreation during the workers' brief leisure hours and at times of high unemployment.

Women from the recreational clubs at each of the Shanghai YWCA industrial centers were chosen to serve on the "Joint Representative Groups" that met monthly at YWCA headquarters to discuss the preoccupations and concerns of industrial women. In the western district special discussion groups were organized to which married women could bring their particular problems, while association personnel undertook to sustain a campaign to visit women workers at home. The Industrial Department also opened a small hostel, "which serves as a demonstration in homemaking and furnishes clean comfortable living quarters for nine girls who have no family near enough to live with."[105] In all of this the YWCA welfare workers succeeded in the western district where political circumstances had caused them to fail earlier in Chapei; by moving to the district they were able for the first time to sustain direct and regular contact with working women. "The secretaries live in the centre and have a very personal touch with the girls so as to understand their problems and their ways of living. This is the only way to gain confidence from the girls."[106]

A more limited program of mass education and club work continued to be pursued by the association in rooms obtained for the purpose in the Yangtzepoo and Hongkew districts of Shanghai, though no staff was in residence at these centers. By October 1930 the YWCA Industrial Department claimed to be "reaching" some 300 women workers through mass education classes in the various districts of Shanghai, and 150 more through organized club work.[107]

Wusih

Another new project undertaken by the YWCA was the opening of an industrial department and center in the city of Wusih in 1929, subsequent to the completion of a survey of conditions there by Kyong Bae-tsung. The principal industries in Wusih were cotton and silk, which employed a large number of women workers, making the city of particular interest to the YWCA. As Wusih was not a treaty port, most of the capital invested there was Chinese, and the foreign community was quite small. The new Industrial Department soon acquired a house in the factory district, and, despite the fact that there was no established branch of the YWCA in the city to give it support, it began to promote mass education and health work among Wusih's working women.[108] The initial response of employers to the program was found to be "cordial."

From the beginning the association's work in Wusih ran into difficulties. In the spring of 1929 Kyong Bae-tsung, who it had been intended would direct the work, contracted typhoid fever and was unable to work at all for several months. Upon her recovery, Kyong resigned from the YWCA in order to be married. A suggestion that May Bagwell, an American industrial secretary working in Shanghai, should go to Wusih to help with the work appears never to have been taken up. Work continued in 1930 through the medium of relatively untried stop-gap appointments, but it lacked effective leadership. Cora Deng was to remark shortly after taking office, with respect to Wusih, "Our trouble is lack of personnel. We don't have enough trained Chinese secretaries, and it doesn't seem to be possible to put a western secretary in that city, which is so thoroughly native."[109]

Despite the staffing problem, there seemed to be a generally shared optimism about the possibilities for successful welfare work in Wusih. In 1929 Lily Haass expressed her feeling that Wusih was "the most thrilling thing"[110] among the various industrial welfare projects that the YWCA had undertaken. A year later, Cora Deng was equally enthusiastic: "You know this is the most indigenous industrial city in whole China [sic] and it is the city chosen by the National Government for experiments on industrial hygiene, public health, as well as adult education. So it has the hope of having some very important things to come out in the near future."[111]

Implicit in this view, it may be suspected, is the growing assumption that where foreign capital was less in evidence, and was not protected by extraterritorial privilege, the likelihood that industrial reform would succeed was much greater (see chapter 8). It is ironic that Wusih was the shortest-lived of all the association industrial centers, the YWCA terminating its industrial work there in 1934.[112]

Government Programs

Occasionally YWCA industrial staff were called upon to assist various levels of government. Cooperation with government agencies sometimes took the form of the provision of experienced industrial secretaries to help Chinese municipal authorities, particularly after 1927, to implement their "welfare" programs, where these existed. It would appear that in 1927 Kyong Bae-tsung and possibly other association personnel were asked to participate in a study of the working conditions of the city's women and children to be carried out by the Labor Department of the new Shanghai municipal government.[113] In December 1928 Grace Li, of the association's industrial staff in Tientsin, was asked to organize a program in popular education for the Department of Education of the municipal government of Tientsin.[114] Furthermore, the YWCA continued to actively promote the passage of legislation to regulate hours and conditions in factories, particularly with respect to women, though there is little evidence to suggest that such legislation was ever enforced.

It may be observed that the attitude of the association toward cooperation with government was somewhat equivocal and tended to fluctuate according to the prevailing estimation of the government's integrity. In the years immediately after the establishment of the Nationalist government in 1927, and of new provincial and municipal governments, the expectation that there could be fruitful cooperation was at its height. This hope was to be dashed by the passage of the repressive new Trade Union Law in 1929.[115]

Summing up the functions of the YWCA Industrial Department in 1930, May Bagwell, speaking from her experience in Shanghai, saw its role on the one hand as that of an interpreter of the needs of industrial workers to the broader community, and on the other hand as that of an agency engaged in the promotion of direct educational, health, and welfare work among industrial women. Indeed, the latter reinforced the former. In pursuit of the first objective, the association sought to inform itself and to inform others through studying the field and collecting information by means of visiting factories, meeting workers at their homes and discussing their needs with them, through arranging trips to factories and tenements for concerned individuals in positions of influence, through the maintenance of an Industrial Committee of interested individuals to act as liaison with the community, and through cooperation with government bureaus and other social agencies, often Christian in inspiration, occupied with the plight of working people. The association had acted to disseminate the information it had gathered "so that people who have had little touch with industry and industrial women have been helped to understand something of the problems which industrial women face in Shanghai."[116]

As far as the "direct work" is concerned, something of the spirit of this is caught in a passage from a report by Eleanor Hinder early in 1928:

> How usual the words sound!—"Obtain direct touch." But how unusual the things involved for the Chinese YWCA secretaries! Crossing the Whangpoo River to an industrial section of the city, often by a hand-propelled ferry, because there is no regular steamer conveyance that Chinese women may take: teaching a class of 22 women, tobacco workers there who, possessed by an inordinate desire to read, had insinuated themselves into a men's night school—teaching for an hour for the sake of ten minutes of "discussion time" with them: taking advantage of a prolonged strike to organise instead an all day school—five hours one day accomplishing as much as could be done in two weeks, hour by hour, at night, when wearied by all day work, (this though untold winter misery is following the enforced unemployment) taking advantage of the fortnightly holiday of another factory to take the women workers for a picnic, penetrating into "li's" or alleys and establishing schools or clubrooms, because women workers will not stir more than half a block from their houses at night. . . . This activity in time of lawlessness and crime demands from these Chinese girls a courage which is real. Not to any great extent have educated girls in China "taken off the gloves," in social work, and there are elements of physical danger in this work which call for the use of the term "bravery" in carrying it out.[117]

So much had been achieved by the end of the decade.

Cultivating Leaders

The beginning of a new decade in 1930 brought new and for the first time Chinese leadership to the industrial program of the YWCA. Cora Deng Yu-chih had apparently joined the association sometime in the mid-1920s and had initially undergone training as a secretary in the "Student Department" before developing an interest in and an affinity for industrial welfare work. Deng came quite early to the attention of Lily Haass, the veteran industrial secretary at this time working for the NCC.[118] Despite her misgivings about her capacity to assume an increasing responsibility for leadership in industrial work, Deng was prevailed upon to try and was in the autumn of 1929 sent off to England to spend a year in preparation at the London School of Economics.[119]

Upon her return to China in 1930 as national industrial secretary, Deng inherited an association industrial program that was essentially paternalistic, and which was particularly concerned with bringing literacy to as many working women as possible. Subtly and almost imperceptibly the orientation of the program would change under her direction so that it would come to embrace much more of an effort to understand economic problems and the function of women workers within the system of production. Inevitably, in due course the system itself was brought into question, and it is possible to discern a rising political consciousness on the part of Cora Deng and some of her coworkers as the decade wore on.

Financial Problems

One of the first difficulties Deng had to contend with was the winding down of Rockefeller support for the voluntary associations' industrial work. Throughout the period from 1926 onward, the industrial welfare activity of the YWCA had been sustained with the financial assistance of the Rockefeller Foundation, which had agreed to give the association $5,000 gold per year for three years for this purpose. By the spring of 1929, however, this grant had been exhausted. As a result of the intercession of Sherwood Eddy with Rockefeller, the YWCA and the NCC were each in May of that year given a further $5,000,[120] and it would appear that a considerable part of this sum in the case of the YWCA went to fund the "demonstration work" in the new centers opened that year by the association in the western district of Shanghai.[121] In 1930 Sherwood Eddy visited China to observe the progress made in welfare work, and as a consequence of his subsequent report to Rockefeller, the YWCA and the NCC again received sums of money for this work, for the YWCA $4,000 for the coming year, and $2,000 for the year after, to be regarded as a "final commitment." It would appear that in the straitened circumstances of the depression the foundation was unwilling to go on funding welfare work in far-off China, though the action to terminate assistance was represented as consistent with Rockefeller's normal policy. "Such a decision does not involve any decrease in interest in the problem or any criticism, but is made because of his belief that as the work continues, it should be financed increasingly from other sources more directly concerned and related to the problem."[122]

Before this final grant was made, the YWCA had hoped to appeal to the Rockefeller Foundation jointly with the NCC and the YMCA for separate funds to set up a Workers' Education Institute in Shanghai, "to be administered independently with its own staff who are responsible to a board which is to be set up by the respective organisations plus individuals in the community who are interested in the cause." The YMCA evidently could not be persuaded to support the proposal, however, and as no funds were forthcoming for it the project was stillborn.[123] This experience tended to reinforce the commitment of the YWCA, and Cora Deng in particular, to making industrial work as far as possible self-sustaining and locally directed.

Feeling the Way

In the light of these financial difficulties, Deng was obliged at first to proceed with caution. In her initial plans for her work, she proposed to spend part of her time in Wusih, where the absence of personnel had hampered the Industrial Department's progress, and the rest of her time in Shanghai managing the overall program and working on a number of projects that would broaden its theoretical scope. In particular Deng wanted to work up a reading course for the industrial secretaries, complete a "discussion book" on "women and money" for publication, and begin a series on other "economic and labour problems" that would rely heavily on pictorial representation so as to encourage the interest and understanding of working women. "The first series is on the fact that China is not producing enough and needs to produce more. Rice and wheat will be chosen for this purpose. I shall make a comparison as to how much we have produced and how much imported in the last three years by graph presentation. Then try to find the causes, such as civil war effect [sic], lack of forestry, bad communication, inefficient tools, internal tax, etc., by pictures, figures, graphs, and maps. And of course give suggestions as to how we can help the situation. The next series will be on industrial products, showing the elements bringing the industrial revolution and the problems connected with it."[124]

In 1930 the Second Industrial Secretaries' Conference was held by the YWCA, under the supervision of Lily Haass. Repeating the precedent established in 1927, the conference brought together for several days all of the association's industrial staff for a discussion of the department's problems and priorities. This conference also helped to focus the attention of staff in a different way and was, as Cora Deng remarked, "a piece of educational work on economic and labour problems for ourselves as secretaries."[125]

The following year a limited initiative was taken toward a more active consultation of working women with respect to their needs and the resolution of them, when the association held its first weekend conference of industrial girls and women at Nanziang near Shanghai. The conference was attended by ten young industrial women from Shanghai, one from Wusih, and six industrial secretaries.[126] Discussions were held on three themes: how to improve standards of work through trade unionism, "employer goodwill," and government action; how to improve one's health; and how to increase the membership of industrial women in the YWCA.[127] "It was the feeling of the group that improvement of their conditions would only come in two ways: through the effort of labour unions and through legislation such as proposed in the new Factory Law."[128]

The group resolved to urge the YWCA to press the Nanking government to enforce its Factory Law "without further delay."[129] More interesting is the recognition by the working women that unions were their best hope for improved conditions, even at a time of strict government supervision of unions. The YWCA had supported in principle the extension of trade unionism since the beginning of its industrial work, but still needed to get to grips with this commitment in practice (see chapter 8). At a meeting of over a hundred women workers at the Shanghai YWCA in connection with May Day shortly afterward, dramatic representations and discussions of industrial issues were organized by the working women themselves, leading Cora Deng to observe, "Working women are conscious of their own problems and are thinking on some ways to remedy them."[130]

Cultivating Leaders

In January 1933 the YWCA held its Third Conference of Industrial Secretaries. Extending over six days, the conference appears to have been broader in scope than its predecessors, and to have involved a number of outside speakers. At this conference, it may be argued, the association moved a step forward toward recognition of class struggle as the means of fundamentally improving workers' conditions and committed itself to developing "a self-directed workers' movement," though it is by no means clear that the association as a whole or even all of the industrial staff saw the implications of this decision.

In popular education, the object was no longer only to achieve literacy among working women and a capacity for self-expression, but more explicitly to enable them to improve their livelihood, and to see the value of raising the whole status of working people as opposed to trying individually to get out of the working class. The need was, then, "to prepare them to assume responsibility for the affairs of their group and community; to develop their abilities so they may function in organisations working for the advancement of their group."[131]

In the lower-level literacy classes, this was to be achieved by using course material directly rooted in the daily experience of working women. Discussion would be encouraged at every opportunity, what was termed "leading on," to help the women to become more confident and articulate and consciously to define their own aims. At a more advanced level, graduates of the literacy program were to be offered courses on "industrial problems," trade unionism, economics, labor legislation, and public speaking. Every effort was to be made to organize and schedule classes in such a way that some of the difficulties that had in the past impeded larger numbers of women from attending courses would be overcome.[132]

In "club work," with industrial women who had actually become members of the YWCA, recreational projects were to be arranged that would again serve to develop confidence and the solidarity of the group. In the production of a short play about an episode in working-class life, for example, a number of issues would be raised that would give rise to discussion. The following is an illustration of what might now be called "consciousness raising."

Analysis of how this play leads on to other interests—
Play "Before Lunch," by T'ien Han

Girls too tired to practise after night work.	Plan to consider how others may know of evil of night work.
Play about employers or employers' objectives.	Gives rise to discussion whether aims and interests of employers and workers are the same.
The play is fun.	Want to give another.
Respect was gained by admiration of others for play.	Discuss how further to increase the respect for workers.
Members absent.	Sense of responsibility brought by group.
Quarrel.	Can workers get together?

The leader should be alive to pick up "leading on" threads; there are many if leader is aware of them.[133]

Club girls were to be encouraged to debate current events, and subjects such as child labor, night work, hours of work, old and new forms of family organization, and education for women workers.

In pursuing its industrial program, the YWCA had for some time maintained an advisory committee of experts—economists, sociologists, educators, doctors, and others—who had also performed a liaison function with the general community. In 1933 it was decided for the first time that workers should also be members of the committee, and that "if they are not ready yet to participate with profit, effort should be made to prepare them as quickly as possible" in order that they could take an increasing share of responsibility. It was further observed that the Industrial Committee ought to consider not only budgets and the like, but ought to concern itself with "all kinds of publicity," to undertake special studies, and to discuss the "larger issues" of policy. In reaching out to the community, new emphasis was put on the need to bring about an understanding of labor unionism and the class struggle, and to "change attitudes towards workers and their problems," aims that were not perhaps wholly compatible. It was hoped that the association could establish better contact with labor union leaders, and could arrange meetings at which workers could express their grievances.[134]

Finally, it was proposed at the Industrial Secretaries' Conference that there should be an "Industrial Assembly" convened in the autumn to coincide with the Third National Convention of the YWCA, the object of which would be "to develop group consciousness among industrial girls, and to get a further understanding of industrial problems and their part in the solution of them."[135] In planning the assembly, working women were to be consulted in advance, and it was hoped that the delegates themselves would take the initiative in presenting reports on working conditions and related matters, and putting forward ideas for ameliorating them.

The Third National Convention was held over several days in August, and the first "National Assembly of Industrial Girls" met every morning for the course of the convention from 6:15 to 7:45. In addition to industrial secretaries, twenty-three working women were present, representing Shanghai, Tientsin, Wusih, and Chefoo, and drawn from six industries in which mainly women were employed—cotton, silk, cigarettes, hosiery-knitting, hair nets, and lace-making. While it is difficult to determine the extent to which the assembly was self-directed, it is reported that the delegates took an active part in the discussions, which centered around the problems of factory legislation, trade unionism, workers' education, and "changing the present economic system." "The girls all expressed quite freely their ideas and they all feel that the fundamental way out is for workers to strive for their own emancipation through workers' education and by organising themselves."[136]

Industrial issues were also considered as part of the overall program of the convention. The working women participated in the general debate, and it is reported that "their poise won admiration and their opinions and presentation of facts have won respect from nearly all the delegations." The convention decided that "Livelihood" would be a major emphasis of the association henceforth, and that both rural and industrial work would be pushed for the next five years.[137]

Taken as a whole, the period from 1930 to the outbreak of the Japanese war in 1937 witnessed a change in the thinking behind YWCA industrial work such that it was no longer simply welfare work for industrial women, but more often work with them. A remarkable article by Cora Deng in the *China Christian Yearbook* of 1935 on "Labour Problems" shows how far her own political understanding and radical sympathies had progressed—both a cause and an effect of grass-roots involvement with working women.[138] It is interesting to speculate on what the consequences of this new consciousness might have been, both for Deng and for the YWCA's industrial program, if the beginning of hostilities with Japan had not set the association's Industrial Department off on a new course. Through the YWCA's efforts a seed had been sown; as Honig has observed it would remain to mature and ripen in the postwar period, contributing materially to the radicalization of industrial women in the run-up to the revolution.[139]

As the nature of YWCA industrial work changed, so also it is possible to observe a gradual increase in the extent of the work, despite financial stringency. Projects in mass education, health, club, and demonstration work begun before the tenure of Cora Deng were continued and expanded on, until just before the outbreak of war the association was reported to be conducting work among industrial women in six cities—Shanghai, Tientsin, Chefoo, Taiyuan, Tsinan, and Hankow, operating nine separate groups or centers in these places.[140] By this time the industrial staff numbered four "national" secretaries and six local secretaries.[141] In administering the program, Deng was ably assisted by Lily Haass, who had returned to the association from the National Christian Council in 1929. Eleanor Hinder appears to have once again worked for the Industrial Department briefly after returning to China from

Australia in 1930,[142] but in 1932 left to join the new Factory Inspection Department of the Shanghai Municipal Council as its first director.

Among the branches, there were some improvements to the services offered,[143] although with respect to the objective enunciated in 1933 of having working women serve on each of the advisory Industrial Committees, while Chefoo managed to achieve a committee made up only of such women, Shanghai had a mixed committee of professionals and workers, and Tientsin and Taiyuan were said to have had exclusively bourgeois women. It would seem that progress was not always easy, particularly outside Shanghai. Industrial work was discontinued permanently in Wusih in 1934 evidently for lack of financial support and local interest.[144] The industrial programs in both Tientsin and Chefoo, however, dormant for a time in the 1930s for the same reason, reemerged a few months later.[145]

4

The National Christian
Council of China

At the end of the First World War, spurred on by evidence of the growing complexity of industrial society, and, it may be supposed, by the increasing strength of organized labor, various churches and Christian organizations began to take a new interest in the problems of workers. At its Lambeth Conference in 1921, the Church of England agreed to use its influence "to remove inhuman or oppressive conditions of labour in all parts of the world, especially among the weaker races." The same year the Protestant Church of America, affirming that the "entire social order" must be Christianized, called for the reorganization of society "on the basis of service rather than profit."[1] In 1924 major conferences were held by church coordinating bodies in Britain and the United States that dealt in part with industrial problems.[2]

The church in China could not remain aloof from this new concern with industry. Although at this time few missionaries had any direct knowledge of the subject, there were some who had troubled to inform themselves. Among these were J. B. Tayler, the British Christian chemist turned economist who had taught for some years at Peking University, and the prominent Quaker missionary Henry Hodgkin, who returned to China in 1920 after a ten-year absence. Tayler had been responsible for the appointment of Agatha Harrison, the YWCA's industrial welfare worker, and would reappear to head the NCC's industrial program in the 1930s. Hodgkin was concerned with the broad range of mission work but was especially struck by the challenge offered by modern history. "At the present time quite a considerable number of the men who control large industries in China are Christians. These men are anxious to do the right thing by their employees, but they do not know what to do and lack direction. Any help just now will be peculiarly useful, and may serve to direct development for years to come."[3]

In 1920 there was still no permanent coordinating body for Protestant missionary activity in China, though a China Continuation Committee (CCC) met every year to carry on the work of the World Missionary Conference, held in Edinburgh in 1910. At its meeting in the spring of 1921, the CCC decided to hold the following year a major National Christian Conference at which the future tasks of the church would be discussed. At the instigation of Grace Coppock of the YWCA, a subcommittee was created to prepare a report for the conference on the Church's Relation to Economic and Industrial Problems; Coppock was made its chairman.[4]

The Church Takes a Stand

At the National Christian Conference in Shanghai in May 1922, the report of the committee was finally presented. The industrial issue was contentious, and conservative missionaries had almost forced its abandonment when the CCC had met again in the autumn of 1921. The project had been dealt another blow in October when Grace Coppock had suddenly died; the chair had passed jointly to Zung Wei-tsung of the YWCA and C. F. Remer of St. John's University. In April 1922 the World's Student Christian Federation, meeting in Peking, had taken up the question and adopted a series of far-reaching resolutions on economic matters, the implications of which may not have been fully apparent to the delegates. Apart from this, though, there is little to suggest that the work of the committee, primarily that of amassing and compiling information, had aroused much enthusiasm by the time of the May meeting.[5]

The report dealt in turn with each of the three main categories of productive labor—agriculture, handicraft work, and modern industry. With respect to agriculture, the report noted the uncertainty and hardship of rural life in China, which it put down to technical deficiencies rather than to social causes. It recommended the training of missionaries in agricultural knowledge, a program of agricultural education for schools and colleges, and an investigation of the suitability of cooperative credit societies to China.[6]

With respect to handicraft industry, the report acknowledged the importance of this form of economic activity in traditional Chinese society but noted that a decline was taking place in certain handicrafts, particularly textiles, in the face of competition from machines. It expressed the hope that "the Christian Church will make its influence felt toward the conserving of those handicrafts that contribute to Chinese art and toward the building up of an art that will be both Chinese and Christian.[7]

The report went on to suggest that the church might promote improved methods in handicraft industry through the staging of exhibitions and the spread of information, and through the encouragement of cooperation among those in various handicraft industries. In particular, cooperation was needed in securing markets at home and abroad, in purchasing raw materials, in arranging credit on better terms, and to enable production to be carried on a larger scale. The report noted the problems inherent in domestic industry, usually practiced by women and girls, and in the apprenticeship system, which it found in many cases amounted simply to a form of child labor.[8]

The main substance of the report dealt, however, with modern industry, and it is with respect to this that the most important recommendations were made. In general, the report found that all the mistakes made during the process of industrialization in the West had been repeated in China, but that the result was "aggravated by the greater ignorance and poverty of the workers." The report observed that wealth was becoming concentrated in a few hands while "the masses are left as poor as before, but with the added handicap of not owning their own tools." A working day of from fourteen to sixteen hours was common, the use of high-powered machinery and certain dangerous processes of manufacture entailed grave risks, child labor was prevalent, and women suffered both from night work and from working too close to childbirth. The breakdown of the Chinese family system in these circumstances dramatically impaired the possibility for a better home life, which was "one of the deepest concerns of the Christian Church."[9]

The report finally observed, "Conflict between labour and capital has not yet developed in any very acute form, but there are many signs that labour is beginning to be restless and to seek organisation. Unless the obvious mistakes are avoided, it is likely to adopt some of the more reckless measures of the labour movements of the West but with infinitely more serious results due to ignorance."[10]

Believing that the existing situation in industry constituted a challenge that the church must accept, the committee, in its report, put forward the following specific recommendations:

1. That the church hasten to equip itself with all possible knowledge on the development of modern industry in China, and on the experience of the West upon which we should draw for meeting the situation here.
2. That the church, recognising the need for a labor standard for China, endorse the setting, as a goal, of the standard adopted at the First International Conference of the League of Nations dealing with:

   Hours of work
   Unemployment
   Employment of women before and after childbirth
   Night work for women and children
   Safeguarding the health of workers
   Child labour.

3. That in the view of the difficulty of immediate application of the League of Nations standard to the industrial situation in China, the following standard be adopted and promoted by the church for application now:

   a. No employment of children under twelve full years of age.
   b. One day's rest in seven.
   c. The safeguarding of the health of workers, eg limiting working hours, improvement of sanitary conditions, installation of safety devices.[11]

The provisions of part three were subsequently referred to as the "threefold labour standard."

The report further urged that the church use all the means in its power to secure the recognition of "fundamental Christian principles" in the economic sphere, and that the NCC appoint an ongoing Council on Economic and Industrial Problems with a permanent secretary with a view to gathering more information and promoting better measures of social welfare. It asked that the universities be encouraged to develop programs in social science, and Christian institutions to add trained social workers to their staffs so that "social work" could be accorded the emphasis already given to medicine, education, and evangelism.[12]

At the presentation of the report Agatha Harrison of the YWCA and C. C. Nieh, a "Christian industrialist," spoke in support of it. Discussion followed, both at a plenary session of the conference and at a separate session later at which some sixty people were in attendance. While Harrison appealed to the consciences of delegates, Nieh appealed more directly to their pockets, and to those of the leading industrialists, making the point that "that which improves the conditions of the labourers improves the factory, the industrial situation, and the outlook, and anything which improves factory work for the operators should also improve it for the labourers."[13]

The discussion sessions were unremarkable, except for a spirited call for reformed motives in industry from M. T. Tchou of the YMCA. The "threefold labour standard" advocated by the Committee on the Church's Relation to Economic and Industrial Problems was accepted by delegates as a minimum standard in one of the few resolutions to be adopted by the conference as a whole. The committee was mandated to continue its work. C. F. Remer's warning that in the West "it has not been the church, but labour itself, that has won labour standards . . . in the West labour considers the church conservative" went unheeded.[14]

The NCC Industrial Commission

The Committee on the Church's Relation to Economic and Industrial Problems met biweekly from the autumn of 1922 until the next assembly of the National Christian Council in May 1923. The committee operated under the interim direction of Thomas Tchou of the YMCA, Zung Wei-tsung of the YWCA, and Dr. Frank Rawlinson of the NCC.[15] As the committee's objectives became better known, expressions of support came from several quarters.[16] By early 1923 endorsements for the "labour standard" had come from the National, Shanghai, Tientsin, and Peking boards of the YWCA, the Tientsin and Chefoo boards of the YMCA, the Kiangsu Synod of the Episcopal Church, and the Chinese Chambers of Commerce of Chefoo and Peking. At a meeting of the Shanghai Missionary Association in November 1922 it was suggested that the standard ought to be applied in determining mission contracts. A decision to do this in respect of its own contracts had already been taken by the YWCA.

The visit to China of Sherwood Eddy toward the end of 1922 at the invitation of the YMCA, and his speaking and study tour of some twenty cities, did much to publicize the need for the proposed "threefold labour standard" (see chapter 2). In December the committee organized a two-day conference in Shanghai at which church and other Christian delegates met to hear Eddy, and to plan for "industrial work" in the months ahead. As a result, local committees were formed in a number of cities to investigate industrial conditions, and these groups were visited during the winter by members of the central committee in Shanghai.[17] Study groups were apparently organized in Canton, Changsha, Chefoo, Hangchow, Hankow, Nanking,

Peking, Tientsin, Tsinan, and Wuchang, as well as in Shanghai, though some of them may have been short-lived. The committee began to publish pamphlet material about industrial questions, which it distributed in response to requests for information.[18]

At the May 1923 meeting of what was now the National Christian Council, the committee was put on a permanent footing and was subsequently known as the Industrial Commission of the NCC, though no request was yet made for a permanent staff.[19] Henry Hodgkin was invited to join the commission. While for the most part delegates gave voice for a second time to the aspirations that had been expressed a year earlier, a series of discussions did give rise to a more precise definition of the commission's functions. These were to be:

1. The promotion of an educational campaign with particular reference to theological students, pastors, and other Christian leaders.
2. To secure demonstrations of the application of Christian industrial principles by having the staff render assistance, when invited, to local centres on some definite problems.
3. Study and research.
4. To draw up detailed programmes for local use; these programmes to emphasise the direct application by Christians of Christian principles to industrial conditions with which they are connected, or for which they are responsible.
5. To act as a central clearing house on industrial questions."[20]

Pains were taken to emphasize the need for information to be gathered through systematic study.

The commission adjourned for the summer but began meeting again in the autumn of 1923. At this time a "Cabinet" was created as a standing committee within the Industrial Commission. Composed of Thomas Tchou, Henry Hodgkin, Dr. Frank Rawlinson, Agatha Harrison, Zung Wei-tsung, Mary Dingman, and Gideon Chen, the Cabinet met three times a week throughout the winter to promote the work of the Commission.[21] Hodgkin became its secretary, and in due course Gideon Chen was employed by the NCC as the commission's assistant secretary, its first full-time officer.[22] Early in the new year the Cabinet resolved to hold, at Thomas Tchou's suggestion, a series of local, regional, and national conferences on the church and industry in 1924, 1925, and 1926. It was also agreed that a news bulletin would be published from time to time, and the first issue, entitled *Christian Industry*, appeared in March 1924.[23] This contained news of further visits by members of the Cabinet to local centers, and of the tour of China in connection with the investigations of the Shanghai Municipal Council's Child Labor Commission by Dame Adelaide Anderson, former chief lady inspector of factories in Britain.

In its report of May 1924 to the now annual conference of the National Christian Council, the Industrial Commission reviewed progress and set forth its plans. There was much repetitious expression of goodwill.[24] Nonetheless, there had been certain steps forward during the year. The list of items published by the commission had grown considerably as its members contributed short tracts on various aspects of industrial life or translated the work of others. In particular, an "Industrial Reconstruction" series was begun, in one issue of which a plan of action was put forward for a local center beginning "industrial work."[25] According to this plan it was proposed that a local committee should isolate and study one or two outstanding problems, seek the cooperation of the church and "Christian employers" in publicizing their findings, and agitate for reform of conditions through "the public press . . . special literature . . . public meetings . . . use of the pulpit, through posters, approach to leading citizens, etc."[26] The commission's program for publication of treatises on industrial matters offered an outlet for the dissemination of information uncovered in studies to which the new interest in industry had given rise in various parts of China.[27]

Most of the items in the Industrial Reconstruction Series appear to have been quite ephemeral in nature, and all copies of a number of them seem to have disappeared without trace. While it may be supposed that some of these items were published in Chinese as well as in English, there is no clear indication of this, suggesting that the principal readership was still conceived at this time to be among the foreign mission and business community. The assumption that reform would be undertaken voluntarily because of a sense of shame on the part of the employer is a common thread running through much Christian thinking on industrial matters in the early 1920s. The pamphlets also proposed as methods of work the holding of study conferences on particular problems; conferences of employers and employed; conferences of teachers, pastors, and similar groups; the establishment of a "social center" as a focal point for investigation and welfare work; and the undertaking of specific experiments such as starting a small-scale industry, perhaps on a cooperative basis.

Among other developments, the commission was able to report that it had organized special courses for students of "industrial work" to be given at the East China University Summer School in 1924 at St. John's University in Shanghai.[28] Repeating the precedent established by the YWCA at Tsinan the previous year, the most important courses were given in English and Mandarin. Admission was reserved to those with at least a middle school diploma, men or women, and preference given to individuals who intended to become actively involved in ameliorative work. Central to the program were courses in elementary economics, industrial history, special industrial problems, and social theories "such as State Socialism, Guild Socialism, Communism, etc."[29]

Looking to the future, the commission envisaged an expanded industrial program consequent upon the engagement of Gideon Chen on a full-time basis, and on receipt of the Rockefeller Foundation's gift of $5,000 gold a year for three years, news of which had just reached the NCC. For the coming year a budget of $4,500 Chinese was proposed by the commission and apparently granted, a sum substantially in excess of the $1,296.14 spent over the financial year 1923–24. Indeed, this latter amount fell far short of the budget provision made by the NCC for industrial work, and it is perhaps revealing that the report should observe in explanation, "The expenses of the Commission have been much less than was anticipated, owing mainly to the fact that the work has been only gradually developed and has not yet by any means reached its maximum."[30]

If the record of the Industrial Commission itself left something to be desired, a number of projects to which it had given encouragement were progressing more smoothly. In Shanghai, the Child Labor Commission, appointed by the Municipal Council of the International Settlement at the instigation of the Christian reformers, had been meeting since June 1923 to gather evidence. The report of the commission would be presented to the council in the autumn of 1924, and members of the NCC Industrial Commission would be active in the campaign to promote acceptance of its recommendations for the limitation of child labor in the spring of 1925 (see chapter 5).

The use of white phosphorous in the manufacture of matches was another industrial evil to which reformers turned their attention in 1924. Such use of white phosphorous had been banned in many Western countries since 1908 because of the appalling disease "phossy-jaw" in which it resulted. In the spring of 1924, therefore, the Industrial Commission resolved to engage a medical expert to study the effects of the continued use of this phosphorous in China, and in this they had the endorsement of the China Medical Missionary Association.[31]

Dr. G. T. Maitland began his study on September 1, visiting hospitals and factories to collect data,[32] and when the International Labour Office official Pierre Henry came to China shortly afterward, Maitland accompanied him on his tour of regions in the north and east.[33] When his salary from the Industrial Commission ran out, Maitland stayed on at his own expense in order to be able to present his findings to the conference of the China Medical Missionary Association in Hong Kong on January 20, 1925.[34] He also published his findings in an article, "The Use of White Phosphorous in Match-making," in the *China Journal of Arts and Science*.[35] Reprints of the article were distributed widely by the NCC Industrial Commission, and a text in English and Chinese was prepared for middle school students.

In response to this agitation, the Peking government promulgated an ordinance forbidding the manufacture of white phosphorous matches after January 1, 1925, and their sale after July 1, though there was no provision for enforcement of the regulation, and thus it may be supposed that little notice was paid to it.[36] Efforts to have the authorities of the International Settlement adopt the standard, encouraged by Pierre Henry, appear to have met with no result.[37]

The Shanghai Committee

Of the local groups brought into existence by the Industrial Commission, by far the most important was the Shanghai Committee on the Church and Industry, which had been established in January 1923 in the first flush of enthusiasm after Sherwood Eddy's visit. While it was intended that this committee should be a separate and distinct entity, there was inevitably a good deal of overlap in both its personnel and activity with the Industrial Departments of the YMCA and the YWCA, and with the national Industrial Commission of the NCC.[38] In 1924 Edith Johnston reported that the committee was actively engaged in research into occupational diseases, the possibility of a "part-work, part-education" scheme for children, and wages and the cost of living in Shanghai. It was also petitioning the Kiangsu and Chekiang provincial governments for enactment of labor legislation and was "trying to get in touch with the various Labour Unions that are springing up and to understand them, and to see how we can cooperate and help."[39]

From the autumn of 1924 the attention of the Shanghai committee members was focused on the campaign to restrict child labor. Anticipating victory in this campaign at the Ratepayers meeting on April 15, the local committee had prepared to hold the first industrial conference in Shanghai for two and a half years from May 8 to May 11, 1925. Despite the unexpected defeat of the campaign, the conference duly went ahead. Topics taken up included "New Motives for Old in Business and Industry," "The Old Chinese Civilisation and the New Order," and "Our Task in Shanghai." The sessions, in Cantonese, Mandarin, and Shanghainese, were said to have been attended by social workers, students, pastors, and "certain labour leaders."[40]

The conference had in part been intended to serve as a model for those that the NCC had hoped to promote in other local and regional centers. In the wake of the May Thirtieth massacre, however, and probably also because of the uncertainty attendant upon the progress of the Northern Expedition, there was no further attempt to hold a gathering of this nature until the major Conference on the Christianizing of Economic Relations over two years later.

Ironically, the Shanghai committee did try to investigate the causes of the strike against the Japanese cotton mill that gave rise to the May Thirtieth incident, with respect to which Mary Dingman observed at the end of February 1925, "Happily that seems to be about over, but I am sure there is much to be learned from it if only we can get accurate information."[41]

The belief that strikes were fueled by acute economic deprivation led the committee in 1926 to pursue more actively its research into the cost of living in Shanghai, at a time when most of its other work had been allowed to lapse. When a preliminary survey had been completed, the project was taken over by the Bureau of Markets of the Nanking government's Ministry of Finance.[42] Subsequently, other, similar studies were undertaken by the authorities of the Municipality of Greater Shanghai.

The loss of initiative in the cost-of-living study dealt a further blow to the Shanghai Industrial Committee, and in early 1927 Eleanor Hinder described it as being "nearly dead": "it ran round in circles. There was no activity in the programme, and hence little life—the thing resolved itself into just two or three people at the end."[43] A successor organization, the Shanghai International Industrial Service League, was active briefly in 1927 arranging forums on labor standards and factory visits for concerned members of the general public, but this too seems to have passed into oblivion within a year or so.[44]

The Institute of Social and Economic Research

One other parallel development encouraged by the Industrial Commission of the National Christian Council in the mid-1920s was the attempt to establish and find funds for a proper Institute of Social and Economic Research that would bring professional expertise and resources to bear in a systematic investigation of conditions of life and labor in China. The need for a permanent body of this kind had been expressed as early as 1922 by three of the committees reporting to the first National Christian Conference[45] and had subsequently been urged by the China Christian Educational Commission[46] and at the Conference of Christian Colleges and Universities in Nanking in 1924.[47]

The institute was brought a step nearer realization in January 1924 when Rockefeller, at the time of his pledges to the other Christian organizations, promised $5,000 gold to send an expert to China "to make a preliminary survey with a view to determining whether such an institute is necessary and desirable."[48] The idea of a preliminary reconnaissance was taken up by the Institute of Social and Religious Research in New York, which agreed over the summer in correspondence with the NCC Industrial Commission to help organize a committee to carry out the task.[49] Both Rockefeller and the institute in New York were concerned that there should be significant Chinese participation in the project. J. B. Tayler of Yenching University was appointed chairman of the Reconnaissance Committee, to be joined later by Dr. Royal Meeker from the United States and several other members recruited locally. The committee scheduled its first meeting in Shanghai for January 5, 1925.[50]

What the Reconnaissance Committee did during the year or so of its existence is a matter of speculation, as no coherent record of its activity appears to have survived. It may be inferred, however, that it traveled about the country gathering evidence as to the effect of wages and the cost of living on strikes, of occupational diseases on the health of workers, and other material that would serve to justify the creation of a permanent institute to carry out an ongoing study of these phenomena.[51] It must be supposed that the recommendation of the Reconnaissance Committee was positive, as a new Institute of Economic and Social Research had been set up by mid-1926 with its headquarters in Peking. Given the rise in patriotic feeling in the wake of the May Thirtieth incident, and as J. B. Tayler had in any event been granted only a year of leave from Yenching University, the institute was placed under the direction of the Chinese economist, L. K. Tao.[52] In the autumn of 1926 the institute undertook jointly with the Shanghai Industrial Committee the preliminary cost-of-living study in Shanghai mentioned above, with a view to embarking on a more comprehensive study the following year in order to "get an index figure as a basis for fixing wages."[53]

It was claimed, however, that the new institute's freedom of action was limited by its lack of long-term financial support, despite the considerable initial boost given it by Rockefeller, and a new commitment for some measure of assistance made in 1926 by the China Foundation.[54] When two appeals for support to the British Boxer Indemnity Commission evidently yielded no tangible result, the institute appears to have been merged fully into the China Foundation as its Department of Social Research.[55] As noted above, the cost-of-living study in Shanghai was taken over by an agency of the Nanking government in 1927.

Departures

Throughout this period, there had been some changes of leadership within the Industrial Commission of the NCC. The departure of the commission's secretary, Henry Hodgkin, in May 1925 and that of its assistant secretary, Gideon Chen, and one of its most active contributing members, Mary Dingman, in June coincided with the collapse of the campaign for limitation of child labor, and heralded a less optimistic time for the Christian reformers of industry. All three went to England—Hodgkin on furlough, Chen for what proved to be two years of study, and Dingman to return to her post as industrial secretary of the World's YWCA in London.[56] In November William Paton, chairman of the commission, also left to go on furlough.[57] Hodgkin's place was taken by Lily Haass, whose secondment to the NCC for an undefined period was approved by the YWCA in March 1925.[58] A new staff member, T. P. Meng, replaced Gideon Chen, taking the title of associate secretary in September, while Dr. Frank Rawlinson became chairman of the commission on the resignation of William Paton.[59]

Struggle for Consensus

The Rockefeller Foundation had in 1924 granted $5,000 gold a year for three years to the National Christian Council "to be used in promoting right ideas and ideals among the churches, with reference to their relation to men, women, and children in industry."[60] This money began to be available shortly after Haass had joined the NCC, providing for her salary and that of her assistant, an expanded program of publication, and other incidental expenses. This shot in the arm had not come at the most opportune time, however, and Haass in the autumn of 1925 complained of her sense of isolation: "Here in the office it is not easy to learn just where we stand. Too many of you disappeared all at once."[61]

While the Industrial Commission was convened from time to time, there is no indication that it met with anything like the frequency of three times a week of its old Industrial Cabinet, now disbanded. Nonetheless, Haass went ahead with the formulation of a new strategy for the commission. This, she began to feel, should have two dimensions to it. On one hand, the commission should be concerned with "spiritualising the labour movement . . . through education in the broader sense, particularly citizenship training classes and discussion groups," and on the other it should be concerned with the problems of hand industries, which were "still the largest aspect of labour problems in China."[62] Increasingly, Haass dwelt on the latter dimension, as she felt that a campaign to improve conditions in handicraft industry could embrace many Christian field workers who had not previously accepted any responsibility for the state of affairs in industry. "City after city reports that they have no industrial problem meaning in the sense of modern industry, to which we have mainly directed our attention. We are going to begin then by having a *church* rather than a city-wide committee face the problem of its immediate district, which in most cases will mean handicraft industry, and try to meet the needs they discover exist there."[63]

It was proposed to hold "experimentation conferences" in 1926 in Nanking, Hangchow, and possibly Soochow. The bulletin *Christian Industry* was no longer to concentrate on Western industrial thinking and experiments, but was to be reshaped so that it would "appeal to the average pastor and Christian worker." "Reports of what has actually been done for apprentices and in part-time education, incidents and outlines for sermon use, expression on the part of pastors themselves as to what they think of it all—these are to be its main aspects."[64]

Haass observed that it was a little like "primary work after college," but in the circumstances she saw no other way of moving ahead. At the annual meeting of the National Christian Council in October 1926, the first for over two years, the name of the Industrial Commission was changed to the Committee on Christianizing Economic Relations as a reflection of its broader preoccupations. Its work was defined "more in terms of the promotion of inquiry through conferences, study outlines, etc." while it was felt that the YM and YWCA would be called upon specifically for the implementation of projects.[65]

In December 1926 Lily Haass was dealt a major blow by the loss of her associate secretary, her most important staff member. The reasons for his departure are of interest, as they are symptomatic of a growing sentiment among the younger part of the Chinese Christian community. Haass wrote:

> Just now I feel as though the waters would drown me. Mr Meng, the young man who has been working with me, has just, after a visit to Canton to help in a survey there, handed in his resignation on the grounds that Christianity is a failure, cannot meet the real needs of China, and other alternatives must be sought—i.e., revolution. It is a part of the movement sweeping from the South—the movement that is the most hopeful thing on the horizon for checking militarism. It is being successful, as Christianity is not. It is also bringing, in its left wing, a belief in the supremacy of material forces, and a denial of spiritual forces. Mr Meng is a product of Christianity in China at its best: his family were persecuted in Boxer days, he is a graduate of Yenching. I cannot comfort myself with the belief that he has not understood Christianity nor that he has not [had] a chance to see the social passion in it. What crushes me is the fact that we don't seem to be able to share the spiritual experience that rises up at such a time and says "I know that my Redeemer liveth."[66]

The Conference on Christianizing Economic Relations

For much of the time after Meng's resignation, Lily Haass labored alone in preparation for the first National Conference on Christianizing Economic Relations, scheduled for August 1927.[67] The conference, held under the auspices of the National Christian Council, took place in Shanghai August 18–28, 1927. An event of major importance in the history of Christian industrial reform efforts in China, it was intended to bring about a bold step forward in Christian thinking on economic problems: "It did not attempt to express a complete social theory or doctrinaire solutions, but its frank recognition of the evils of large property holding, and its advocacy of the limitation of large landholdings, its questioning of the sources and use of income and the division of profits, and its acceptance of the ideal, 'From each according to his ability, to each according to his needs,' mark tendencies far-reaching in their results."[68] If these ideals were not subsequently translated into reality, this must in part have been because the issues taken up meant different things to different people, and because the Christian forces in China were, if anything, growing not more socially oriented, but less so.

The conference, conducted completely in Chinese, was attended by nearly sixty delegates, most of whom were by now familiar figures in the movement for industrial reform.[69] The program clearly marked a departure from Haass's recent concentration on land industry and provided for consideration of the whole range of problems of workers in modern industry, of rural economic problems, and of the relation of Christianity to social progress. Papers of varying length were given under these three broad headings and were usually followed by discussion. The conference was punctuated by religious exercises, and by addresses by invited speakers, most of whom concentrated on a theoretical exposition of the duty and the opportunity afforded to Christianity in the economic sphere.[70]

With respect to modern industry, short papers were given on industrial conditions in Canton and on the labor movement, both in Wuhan and generally, but the most informative and precise presentations were given on industrial conditions in Wusih and Changchow (by Dju Yu-bao) and in Shanghai (by Eleanor Hinder). Hinder particularly, recalling past resolutions on economic matters adopted by the NCC, urged the conference to reach a consensus and state its position on the important economic questions of the day. These were, in her view, the length of the working day and the working week, the continued use of child labor, the custom of permitting labor contractors to act as intermediaries between workers and employers, the use of the specious "bonus system" in industry, which often led workers to put in even more hours of labor than they were already obliged to give in the hope of a small reward, the proposed "cost-of-living study" of the government's Bureau of Markets, and the rise of the labor movement and the relation of Christian groups to it. Many of these points were taken up in the ensuing discussion and came to be embodied as resolutions at the end of the conference. However, the suggestions made by some participants that both workers and employers were "ready for a longer working day" or that given a weekly rest day workers would occupy themselves "in gambling and other undesirable ways" show that it was an uphill struggle. Significantly, it was found necessary to observe, "Coercive measures, granting relief from work for one half-day, on condition that workers attend church services, were not likely to have good results."[71]

On the rural side, papers were offered on "rural economic problems"—especially credit, marketing, and farm tenancy—the peasant movement in Kwangtung, and farmers' unions in Chekiang and Kiangsu. Surprisingly, despite earlier signs of a new interest in handicrafts, it would seem that the problems of handicraft industry were hardly considered at the conference. During discussion it became apparent that while some delegates favored communal ownership of land, others felt that the existing family-sized unit was "the most efficient."[72]

The distribution of profits between landlord and tenant was held by a majority of those present to be "a technical matter on which they could not express an opinion," while some were at pains to point out "the tenant's responsibility for the fullest production." The church was urged to take steps to promote credit cooperatives, eligibility for membership in which would depend normally on judgment of character, but might sometimes rely on material possessions. During discussion of farmers' unions, the opinion was expressed that "in some parts of the country the membership had a large percent of troublemakers, and in others a large percent of good farmers."[73]

With respect to "Christianity and Economic Problems," a paper was given by C. Y. Hsu in which the writer sought to call attention to communism as the chief threat to Christianity. "Communists urge revolution, while Christianity would change society by peaceful methods. We have seen the results of the use of violence as a means of changing the social order in Russia." In the course of discussion, the merits and demerits of private property were argued, those in favor emphasizing the incentive it was alleged to provide, and those who, if not opposed, had reservations, deploring the social evils that its accumulation often produced. For modern industry, profit sharing and workers' councils to provide for participation in management were suggested as means of alleviating the worst excesses.[74]

In the case of both industry and agriculture, "findings committees" were appointed whose task it was to embody the consensus of the conference as expressed in discussion in a series of specific resolutions. With respect to modern industry the conference endorsed the following principles:

- Freedom of association for all workers.
- A minimum wage.
- Progress toward the eight-hour day.
- One day's rest in seven.
- No child labour for children under twelve.
- Special protection for women workers.
- Formation of shop committees and arbitration boards.[75]

Toward the end of achieving these standards, a variety of means were suggested, most of which had been employed before. They included the training of more industrial welfare workers, the provision of courses in labor problems, the promotion of workers' education, special study projects, campaigning for legislation, and encouraging employers to improve conditions. Delegates were also urged to "join in the patriotic movements for freedom and justice to the workers."[76]

Resolutions on rural economic problems dealt mainly with farm tenancy and cooperatives. In particular, the conference called for government limitation of large landholdings, a formula for the reduction of rent where crop yields fell below normal, experiments with marketing cooperatives, and the establishment of rural cooperative credit and savings societies supported by a fund to be administered by the Committee on Christianizing Economic Relations. The conference also recommended the introduction of better seeds, fertilizers, and other technical improvements. In order that the church could play a role in bringing about these changes, it was suggested that training should be offered to rural clergy through correspondence courses, summer schools, and similar means, and that the committee should sponsor an investigation of farm tenancy. The church should do all it could to cooperate with the constructive measures of farmers' unions.[77]

On the subject of "Christianity and Economic Problems," conference resolutions deplored the concentration of wealth in the hands of a few and urged Christians to practice philanthropy and moderation in their personal lives. While income derived "from personal services, and from capital invested in constructive enterprise" was regarded as legitimate, income "whose source is speculation and monopoly" was not to be so regarded. Christians were encouraged to "study how economic co-operation can take the place of economic competition, and at the same time promote the incentive to work, invention, and progress." As has been noted, the conference endorsed the ideal "from each according to his ability, to each according to his need," invoking the traditional sanction of the need for harmony in society, which it was suggested the realization of this ideal would achieve.[78]

While these "findings" appear to have been approved by the conference the day before its closure, it is not clear whether the views embodied in them represent a consensus or only a majority of those present. Certainly there was scope for differing interpretations of what had been achieved, even among those most closely involved with the conference. While Lily Haass felt that the conclusions reached were "a distinct advance in thinking" and wondered "what will happen when their full import dawns on some people," Henry Hodgkin was pleased that "the whole drift of it was away from the extremes which have been so popular during the last year or two." "There was a clear visualising of a future in which economic relations would match more nearly with Christian principles, but at the same time a great disinclination to rush into hasty experiments, and an unwillingness to regard the revolutionary method as the only way of achieving the results."[79]

The contradiction between these two views, and between the industrial "activists," on one hand, and the much more numerous and largely disinterested Christian constituency, on the other, would in the event prove decisive.

One Step Forward . . .

As if the Shanghai conference had exhausted both the creative resources of its organizers and the sympathy of the public, little would be accomplished by the Committee on Christianizing Economic Relations over the next two and a half years. While several new items had been added to the list of publications for distribution,[80] and the occasional local meeting or study project was attempted, it would appear that the committee took no new initiatives of any note between 1927 and 1930. Indeed, the scope for industrial welfare work, at a time of growing political repression, was increasingly limited.

By February 1928 Gideon Chen had rejoined the committee as assistant to Lily Haass after an absence of nearly three years, but in February 1929 he offered his resignation again on the grounds that "the labour is fruitless, and the movement is not progressing."[81] He complained to Mary Dingman that the Kuomintang harassed the labor movement, and also that "[a] tendency toward individual salvation and spiritual revival in a narrow sense has been popular among the churches. It makes industrial work tremendously difficult to push.[82]

Chen's resignation became effective in June, and he went to Yenching University to assist J. B. Tayler with the training of welfare workers."[83] Chen's assessment of the prospects for industrial work under the NCC was confirmed by Haass. She observed that the reorganization of the council due to take place at its annual meeting in May 1929 to make it more representative was also likely to make it "very much more conservative."

> It looks as though the chief emphasis of the future were to be on the lines of a five-year evangelistic campaign. All of this, as you may judge, does not create a very bright outlook for our kind of work. Perhaps it is necessary for the Chinese church, discouraged and weak as it is, to have the impetus that would come from that kind of a campaign, but I cannot but wish that we had put our energy into getting deeper content in the Christian message such as would meet the political and social demands of the time, rather than continuing to create more Christians of the same kind that we have."[84]

By the autumn of 1929, Haass herself had left the NCC to go on furlough and then to return to the Industrial Department of the YWCA. A replacement for Gideon Chen, a returned student named William Wang,[85] does not appear to have stayed long with the NCC, and with the departure of Lily Haass the Committee on Christianizing Economic Relations became dormant for a time, with no one at all to direct it in the last few months of the decade.[86] As a final act, Gideon Chen and Lily Haass had prepared in Chinese a long-awaited "Industrial Handbook for Social Workers." "It contains in brief form much of the information that people have been looking for and is so up-to-date and so reliable, having in it all our pooled knowledge, and the information that we have acquired in these recent years that I think there is nothing else quite in the same class."[87]

New Directions

Early in 1930 the National Christian Council, with no active members on its Committee for Christianizing Economic Relations, approached J. B. Tayler to make plans for the future of the committee, and to be responsible for a specific investigation into rural industries. Tayler accepted, and in carrying out this task he was to be assisted by Gideon Chen. From the beginning it was clear that the appointment was to be a temporary one, perhaps as much at Tayler's insistence as by any wish of the NCC, for he had been close to Lily Haass and her work for long enough to appreciate the difficulties she had faced and was aware that the NCC now consisted "largely of the older generation of pastors who, in China, are not as socially minded as the group which has hitherto dominated the Council."[88]

By mid-April Tayler had formulated in outline the committee's program for the next four years and had it approved by the Administrative Council of the NCC. The committee's responsibility during the "five-year movement" to which the NCC was committed was to be the "social interpretation of Christian stewardship." This was understood to mean "evangelism among the industrial classes," the production and distribution of literature both for working people and interested Christians, the promotion of social study circles in the churches, and an investigation of the position of apprentices.[89] In addition to having these ongoing responsibilities, Tayler felt that the committee should undertake two major projects, the first to bring several foreign experts to China for a period of teaching and study, and the second to go ahead with research into small-scale industry.

Foreign Experts and Rural Industry

The idea of bringing European or American expertise to China as a means of publicizing and promoting industrial reform was not new; Sherwood Eddy, Dame Adelaide Anderson, and others had visited China for varying lengths of time in the 1920s, and a distinguished speakers series had been planned by the YMCA in 1924, though it had not achieved fruition.[90] In this case, Tayler wanted to bring Mary Van Kleeck of the Russell Sage Foundation, vice-chair of the International Congress of Working Women, to China for an extended period, and two or three men like Seebohm Rowntree from England, or the "Christian employers" Dennison and Hapgood from the United States for shorter visits.[91] Another name subsequently suggested to Tayler was that of Angus Watson, a manufacturer from Newcastle-upon-Tyne.[92]

The object was to find those people who could contribute the skills needed for "industrial welfare as we understand it in England, or in employment management as they interpret it in America"[93] with a view to determining how this experience could be applied in China. One possibility was that some of these experts might collaborate with the China Institute of Scientific Management recently established by H. H. Kung's Ministry of Industry and Commerce.[94] "My hope is that we should conclude with a large conference on this subject at which some prominent government officials, leading business men, social workers and so on, would be brought together to discuss the possibilities in China with these experts, and that an Institute for the promotion of such activities should be set up as the result of that conference."[95]

In promoting the second project, the study of rural and small-scale industry, Tayler was looking for a way of helping farmers, especially those in North China whose hardships were increased by uncertain rainfall and long winters, by finding the most appropriate subsidiary industries that could be developed locally as a means of supplementing their income. The implications of this approach were far-reaching. "A few of us are feeling that the technical improvement of small-scale industry, and the bulking and standardisation of its products through co-operative marketing arrangements very much on the lines followed in regard to agriculture, is a better method of developing industry in China than the introduction of large, joint-stock corporations, except in cases in which technical considerations make large-scale units necessary."[96]

Tayler had himself already completed a study of the Hopei pottery industry, where he felt worthwhile improvements could be made, and had sanctioned a study on behalf of the NCC of the possibilities in the woolen industry in Northwest China. He was convinced that durable woolen clothing could be manufactured there as cheaply as the wadded cotton garments worn by most of the population. A model for the "efficient federation of small-scale units," he believed, might sooner be found in continental Europe or in India than in England or the United States where modern industry was most advanced. He hoped for practical assistance from the Industrial and Social Department soon to be created by the American-based International Missionary Council,[97] but little help would be forthcoming from this source.[98]

For the remainder of the year, Tayler was occupied principally with the preparations for the Conference on the People's Livelihood, to be held under the auspices of the Committee on Christianizing Economic Relations in February 1931, and with his attempt to bring to China R. H. Tawney, the noted English economist. Tayler first heard in May that Tawney had expressed a desire to spend some time in China during a sabbatical leave that he was about to be offered by the London School of Economics.[99] Tayler wrote to Tawney, extending him a formal invitation to come to China under the sponsorship of the National Christian Council, but a condition of the proposal was that Tawney spend one term teaching two courses at Hsing Hua University, probably because Tayler was compelled to seek the support of the university in meeting Tawney's expenses.[100] Apparently this was not the most attractive offer put to Tawney, and by July it was clear that he was coming to China under the auspices of the Institute of Pacific Relations.[101] Nonetheless, Tayler was able to secure a part at least of Tawney's time in China, as well as his services as the keynote speaker at the Conference on the People's Livelihood.

The Conference on the People's Livelihood

The Conference on the People's Livelihood took place in Shanghai February 21–28, 1931. Appropriately enough for a gathering that was in many ways more orthodox and conservative than its predecessor of 1927, the conference was opened by H. H. Kung, the Kuomintang minister of industries, who called for the application of scientific method in harnessing the natural resources of China and the "innate industrial capacity" of its people. In both agriculture and industry, "productive efficiency . . . is altogether too low. Its improvement is fundamentally necessary to the raising of wages and standard of living."[102]

Kung's message, and that of many other speakers, was that through scientific management and the passage of legislation, China's economic and social ills could be overcome. In Eleanor Hinder's view, the conference represented a "notable advance" on that of 1927, a progression from "hopes" to "scientifically based experiments."[103] While it is true that the state of knowledge had advanced, however, and the information presented was much more comprehensive and precise than had been the case earlier, so too was there less questioning of the existing social order.

The conference attracted a broader membership than that of 1927, drawing in "representative employers and labour leaders, forewomen and promoters of co-operative societies, welfare workers and government officials, with social workers and those from academic institutions,"[104] an undetermined number, though probably again in the region of fifty to sixty. Among those attending were Cora Deng, May Bagwell, and Eleanor Hinder of the YWCA, Philip Cheng of the YMCA, Tayler, and Gideon Chen of Yenching University, as well as a number of well-known writers on economic affairs including Chen Ta of Hsing Hua University, H. D. Fong of Nankai University, M. T. Tchou, now of the Ministry of Industries, and J. D. H. Lamb (Lin Tung-hai) of Yenching, among others.[105] Each day delegates assembled to hear papers and hold discussions around one of six themes: the "economic needs of the people"; "workers' education"; "small-scale industry and cooperation"; "large-scale industry"; "government policy and legislation" with reference to industrial standards and organized labor; and "Christianity and the People's Livelihood."[106]

Of the papers presented, several are of particular interest. In a paper entitled "The People's Livelihood as Revealed by Family Budget Studies," H. D. Lamson attempted to correlate the findings of a number of researchers with respect to the percentage of income spent on different items by families engaged in various occupations in different cities. Owing to the proliferation of statistical surveys over the previous five years, such a project was now possible, and certain conclusions could be drawn from it, though perhaps the most useful was the realization that "[t]here is a great lack of uniformity in the methods of gathering data and of classifying material, in the China studies quoted, and of drawing conclusions, so that in only a few studies can any one particular item of interest be followed for comparison. Standardisation of technique, terminology, and units of importance, are needed."[107]

Reviewing the progress of the union movement in his paper "Chinese Labour Since 1927," Chen Ta deplored the abuse of liberty by the unions, which, as he saw it, had led to their suppression after 1927 by the Kuomintang, and called the more recent tendency of strikes to be concerned with bread and butter issues a "hopeful sign," asserting that "[t]he chief aim of the union should be the improvement of the economic and social conditions of the workers, not their participation in political activities." He urged that further study be undertaken of wages and conditions, accident prevention, and unemployment, and wanted the Kuomintang's recent industrial legislation to be enforced, but expressed the view that at the root of China's problems was an oversupply of labor. Ultimately he felt this excess could be absorbed by widespread industrialization, but in the meantime a comprehensive system of birth control would help to ease the pressure.[108]

The Kuomintang's new Labor Union Law, Factory Law, and Factory Inspection Law were the subject of a discussion by M. T. Tchou, the former industrial secretary of the YMCA, now working for the government. Faced with the problem of regulating the "multifarious, often irregular activities" of the labor unions, Tchou argued, the Kuomintang had begun in 1926 to expel Communist members and to reorganize the unions.[109] The new Labor Union Law was part of a gradual process of restoring freedom of association to labor.

The Factory Law provided for "some of the most fundamental reforms advocated by social reformers," dealing as it did with hours and conditions of work, labor by women and children, apprenticeship, welfare safety and health, conditions for dismissal, and other subjects. Tchou regarded the provision for the institution of factory councils as "of unusual significance." The councils were to be composed of equal numbers representing employers and workers, and were intended to "act as a clearing house for a good deal of the misunderstanding which has often resulted in the taking of extreme measures by one party or the other."[110]

The Factory Inspection Law passed the responsibility for inspection to local authorities, though the training of inspectors was to be undertaken by the national government. Overall, Tchou foresaw a trend toward central administration and enforcement of labor laws and emphasized the need for "officials of a high grade of moral character" in the inspectorate. "Men and women qualified to serve are not only to have the technical preparations that are indispensable, but must be devoted to their cause and be willing to sacrifice for it."[111]

Perhaps not surprisingly for a conference that was semiofficial in character, there was little contribution from working people themselves. In two cases, welfare workers reported on conversations they had with working people, the most interesting being an interview reported by May Bagwell of the YWCA with two women, one "a labour leader" and the other a woman with seven years' experience as an ordinary worker in cotton mills, and six years as a forewoman.

> Both women interviewed were decidedly conscious of belonging to the workers' group and of the opposed interests of workers and management.
> Both women expressed the belief that it was the aim of the government to control the labour unions and that the local organs were used on the side of capital and against labour.
> . . . they felt that the labour union law was aimed at doing away with the labour unions as the unions would have no power if the law were enforced.[112]

Another woman worker, referring to industrial welfare work in Wusih, "was not at all in favor of the 'benevolent despotism' of the Wusih scheme, and felt that if the conditions of the workers were to be improved it had to be done by the workers themselves."[113] These points were not picked up, however, and delegates appear to have remained largely indifferent to the views of working people.

There was some discussion of agricultural problems during the conference, and of cooperative experiments in credit and marketing for agriculture, but Tayler seems to have been alone in proposing that the cooperative principle should be applied to the development of small-scale industry, thereby providing farmers with an alternative source of income, and in some measure bridging the gap between city and countryside. This manner of approach would be "healthier," Tayler maintained, and would permit the application of modern science and modern methods of organization to China's economic life, while avoiding "undue reliance on the urbanisation of industry." Essentially a small-scale industrial cooperative would require a federation of a number of small producers within a given area, and provision for credit and expert guidance and for the cooperative supply of raw materials and equipment. Collective marketing arrangements and collective provision of electric power would also be needed.[114]

What Tayler was suggesting, as another put it, was implementation of "Kropotkin's three principles"—"decentralisation of industry, combination of agriculture with industry in industrial villages, and complete education in the form of combined brainwork and manual work." "The whole crux of the situation lies in this, that such a method of development necessitates educative work among the rank and file of industry. While this is its main difficulty, it is on the other hand its great advantage, because the education which is required to bring men to follow such a cooperative plan is an education that links economic activity with the fuller life of the community, and which has high social and cultural values. It breaks down the opposition which is now only too apparent between the cultural and economic life."[115]

On the final day of the conference delegates assembled to approve the "findings' put together by the organizers, a cautious summation of the main points brought out during the week. Deploring the lack of education among workers, and their consequent lack of "ambition to better themselves," the conference urged the Committee on Christianizing Economic Relations to promote the establishment of a "Workers' Institute" in Shanghai and the initiation of programs in workers' education generally, to provide an education "which develops the personality of the worker, trains him for citizenship in a modern state, and furnishes the vocational training and guidance that are now lacking." Housing conditions and the "unbalanced" diet of workers were a cause of anxiety, as were "acute moral problems created by overcrowded conditions"; the exploitation of workers by moneylenders, and their abuse by the agents of secret societies and labor contractors, needed attention, as did the excessive hours of work still prevalent, the evils of night work, unhealthy conditions, and the perils of apprenticeship. Delegates recommended, however, only that workers be assisted "to make a better use of their leisure," that friendly societies should be formed for mutual insurance and protection, and that the owners of smaller industries should be encouraged to better the conditions in their workshops. They noted "with satisfaction the tendency to better working conditions in modern industry,"[116] though on what grounds it is hard to see.

The conference recommended that further study be made of safety provision and accident compensation in factories and mines, and of the possibilities for profit-sharing and the possible constitution and duties of "works councils" in industry. Further study was also recommended to determine what action might be taken to promote birth control among workers. The conference endorsed the application of the cooperative principle in the "scientific development" of agriculture and small-scale industry, and called for further research into cooperatives and the creation of a "special institute for experiment and training in connection with the improvement of local industries." Delegates expressed approval of the government's new Factory Law and Factory Inspection Law and called for their early enforcement, while also encouraging the government to pursue negotiations with the foreign powers "with a view to overcoming hindrances to the enforcement of the Law associated with the practice of the system of extra-territoriality." For the future, it was recommended that the Committee on Christianizing Economic Relations organize local and regional conferences to follow up the proceedings in Shanghai, that the committee plan for a regular biennial national conference on economic matters, and generally take steps to "lead the churches to a fuller understanding of Christian concern with economic relations."[117]

The recommendations from the conference were considered at the Biennial Meeting of the National Christian Council in Hangchow in April 1931. While the council recorded that it "notes with interest and satisfaction" the work of the February conference, it also made clear that it "accepts responsibility only for those findings and recommendations of this Conference which came before it and were adopted at the biennial meeting." The council approved the plans of its Committee on Christianizing Economic Relations for the study and promotion of rural and other small-scale industries, the study and promotion of cooperatives, of industrial welfare, personnel management, training for labor for participation in control of matters affecting their welfare, and the Factory Law. Plans for workers' education were also approved. The council proposed that the committee emphasize in the immediate future the preparation of appropriate literature for the churches, the organization of local groups, and the undertaking of certain carefully chosen pieces of demonstration work both in the city and in the countryside. The council suggested that the committee seek the cooperation of the universities in its work.[118]

If the council's distillation of the findings of the February conference appears severe, the contrast with the findings of the 1927 conference is even more marked. Gone are the calls for a minimum wage, for freedom of association for workers, for the limitation of large landholdings and other similarly progressive innovations; gone is the appeal for a society in which each would receive according to his need. With the Conference on the People's Livelihood it became apparent that a decisive shift in attitude toward economic problems had taken place within the National Christian Council, a shift that would prove irreversible.

Sharing the Burden

In mid-1931 J. B. Tayler was to leave China for Europe to pursue his study of the technique and organization of small-scale industries on behalf of the Committee on Christianizing Economic Relations (CCER). In the months leading up to his departure he spent much of his time endeavoring to promote devolution of the responsibility for study and experiment in economic matters on to the universities, as the best method of ensuring some continuity in research. He had earlier expressed his conviction that "[t]he Committee will probably have to carry the responsibility for work in the fields it takes up during the experimental stage, but if, as hoped, these experiments are successful, they should give rise to permanent organisations."[119]

Among the projects Tayler envisaged were the creation of an Institute of Rural Industry, associated with a university, which would have a textile expert, a mechanical engineer, and an industrial chemist on its staff. Men trained in the promotion of cooperative experiments could be attached to the universities, at least one to have a special knowledge of agriculture, and another to be experienced in rural industry. One expert could teach industrial welfare; another, personnel management. If these arrangements could be made, this would "leave to the secretariat of the CCER the work of coordination, promotion and literature."[120] In this way, the tasks of the secretary could be kept within bounds, and the position would be less difficult to fill.

By the time Tayler left China in July, some progress had been made. Nankai University in Tientsin had agreed in principle to undertake studies of half a dozen rural industries over a period of three years, while Mr. Sam Dean of the North China School of Engineering Practice in Peking was to develop new implements and equipment suited to the needs of rural industry, and to train people in their use.[121] The proposed Institute of Rural Industry had not, however, materialized.

Several new cooperatives were under consideration for Shantung, though no one had yet been found with an expert knowledge of cooperative work in rural industry. Two universities, apparently Yenching and Shanghai, were actively considering joint action to provide training for students in industrial welfare and personnel management.[122] Much of this depended on the discovery of external sources of funding, however, and the prospects for this at the time of Tayler's departure were not particularly favorable.[123] Meanwhile, a few more enterprising missionaries struggled with their own local experiments[124] and in Shanghai Chen Ta of Hsing Hua University completed a study for the CCER on the applicability of the Factory Act.[125]

Tayler spent the remainder of the summer in Europe gathering information about successful small-scale industrial enterprises, mainly it would seem in France and Switzerland.[126] Later he proceeded to London, where on September 21 he organized, with H. T. Silcock and William Sewell of the United Committee for Christian Universities of China, a meeting to discuss Chinese rural and industrial problems. To this were invited some two dozen missionaries, academics, social workers, and others who had some personal contact with China. The consensus of those present was, as Tayler had expressed it, that the universities "must do more in the way of research, in the study of actual situations, and in trying to find solutions," and Tayler, Silcock, Sewell, and Agatha Harrison were asked to draw up plans for a permanent committee that could act as liaison between university and other social workers in the field and the public at home in Britain. These four subsequently proposed a committee to be responsible to the Standing Committee of the Conference of Missionary Societies, one of the functions of which would be to secure support, financial and otherwise, for projects undertaken abroad.[127] Unfortunately, it would appear that this committee was never constituted.

Toward the end of the year, Tayler returned to China, and early in the spring of 1932 he started out on a trip to Shansi via Shantung and Hopei. Here he found that a certain amount had been achieved in isolated cases, but that on the whole the three provinces were "ripe for work." Mr. Sam Dean in Peking was "hopeful of being freer in the future than he has been in the past," while staff at Nankai University were now talking not of six studies, but of two, funds permitting, with the possibility of others later. Tayler's hopes that institutions other than the CCER would take on part of the burden of involvement with rural industry had not borne fruit during his absence in Europe. In his report on his trip, Tayler recommended that the CCER should establish a special subcommittee to lay plans for a practical program to develop rural industries in Hopei, Shansi, and Shantung.[128]

The North China Industrial Service Union

Such a committee came into being a few months later with the formation of the North China Industrial Service Union, created with the purpose of "coordinating and extending the work of industrial research and promotion that is already being done by a number of Universities and other agencies in North China."[129] At a meeting on September 17, 1932, representatives of the interested universities discussed their work and plans and chose Tayler as secretary of the group, who would "pending fuller organisation . . . assume executive responsibilities."[130] Committees were set up on Mineral Industries, Textile and Other Industries, and Economic Research and Industrial Organization.

In the year following its founding, the Industrial Service Union was able under Tayler's direction to stimulate new research into the weaving and knitting of wool, the production of cotton goods, and the smelting of iron, all for village use. While the objective of the union remained "to organise and federate local groups for their common interest in such matters as credit, supply and marketing, securing trade information and so on,"[131] the initial emphasis was placed on study and experiment. Probably typical is the following account of efforts to improve the woolen industry:

> The first thing was to devise simple, inexpensive equipment capable of manufacture by the village carpenter or smithy. This was undertaken by the engineering staff of the North China School of Engineering Practice, who carried on their experiments in a workshop equipped like a village carpenter's and blacksmith's shop. They produced simple hand-cards, treadle-cards and carding machines much like those used in England a century ago, and hand-mules based on the Welsh type; and it is found that, working on these in their homes, the villagers can earn more than a factory wage.
>
> Next the Union began to concentrate on the study of wool supplies, the demand for woollen goods in North China and the organisation of the local production centres.[132]

In the future, it was hoped to investigate the potential of village pottery, woodworking, leatherworking, papermaking, and the chemical trades, though the union would have to proceed as funds permitted. These plans apparently did not reach fruition either. In 1934 Tayler evidently resigned his responsibilities as secretary of the Industrial Service Union.[133] No further mention is made of the union after that year, and it must be assumed that it too passed into oblivion like so many committees before it, though some interest in supplementary industries was kept alive in the universities. Tayler himself remained an enthusiastic supporter of the cooperative ideal for rural industry and in 1936 initiated a study at Yenching of the economic position of one hundred rural families in Hopei as a means of promoting his cause.[134]

The Church and Its Environment

While North China Industrial Service Union had been formed "with the encouragement" of the National Christian Council,[135] it does not appear to have been responsible to it, and about the time that he became secretary of the union Tayler seems to have ceased to occupy his position as secretary of the NCC's Committee on Christianizing Economic Relations.[136] The new post was undoubtedly an honorary one, and Tayler combined it with a return to his research work at Yenching, with which institution he retained an affiliation throughout his years in China. With the CCER once again without a coordinator, and the NCC apparently not in any hurry to find a replacement for Tayler, the committee's work was allowed to lapse. A survey of its publications in 1934 shows that most of them dated from the 1920s.[137] With the exception of the question of the church and its rural environment, the NCC took little further interest in economic matters.

This loss of interest was in part at least a consequence of the difficulty at a time of recession of finding money to finance research into rural industry and put the results into practice on any significant scale. This problem had hampered Tayler in his efforts since he had first taken responsibility for the NCC's program in 1930. Although the CCER had been granted two final sums of $4,000 and $2,000 gold by the Rockefeller Foundation for the years 1931–32,[138] and some of this may in due course have found its way to the Industrial Service Union, other demands on this money must have meant that not much of it was available for the development of rural industries. In 1930 Tayler had sought assistance from the new Department of Social and Industrial Research of the International Missionary Council in Geneva, without success.[139] In 1931 he made a more direct approach to the Institute of Social and Religious Research in New York, again in vain. In Britain Tayler appealed for support through Henry Hodgkin and other "old China hands," but to no avail.[140]

When, in 1933, the Rockefeller Foundation apparently agreed to provide some further funding,[141] it was too little and too late to resuscitate the program, and Tayler was already looking for a new challenge.[142] In 1934 he was appointed a member of the British Boxer Indemnity Commission, and while retaining his post at Yenching he would spend the next several years traveling in the interior for the commission advising on plans for aid to education.[143]

Ironically, the head of the International Missionary Council's Department of Social and Industrial Research, whom Tayler had approached in 1930, came to China for a tour in 1936. J. Merle Davis spent eight weeks in China, almost exclusively in major cities, and visited thirteen institutions of higher learning—five of them theological seminaries. His aim was "[t]o secure the opinion of a few picked Church and Mission leaders, and faculty members of the Christian colleges, in regard to the chief problems of the Church in relation to its environment; to find what studies have been made, or are now in progress, in the field of these problems; to determine the questions of major concern among the problems suggested, and to decide upon those which would probably yield the most profitable results."[144]

In fact, the only study that Davis agreed to finance was one into "The Chinese Rural Church in Relation to Its Environment," to be undertaken by a member of Nanking Theological Seminary. Indeed, it was proposed to hold a World Christian Conference in Hangchow in 1938 on the theme of "The Church and Its Environment," and Davis was surprised to find that at Yenching some faculty "challenged the validity or usefulness of centring the discussions of the Conference upon 'The Church.'"[145] On the other hand, a "few of the most thoughtful Chinese leaders" expressed concern that the conference might "deal with problems that have validity for the West but which would bear an atmosphere of unreality for Asiatic Christians." "This feeling, that the economic and social problems of the church are of secondary importance to the issues of war, political and national integrity, Communism, etc, was a very common obstacle that I met in talking with Christians wherever I went."[146]

In 1937 Davis paid a return visit to China, and managed to secure the agreement of certain faculty members in the Sociology Department at Yenching to carry out a program of field research on the rural environment of the church.[147] At a separate interview, J. B. Tayler once again pressed Davis to use his good offices to secure financial support for three or four experimental industrial cooperatives,[148] though with what effect cannot be told as within a month of the interview China had become engulfed in war with Japan.

5

The Shanghai Municipal Council

So far, this discussion has been confined to the efforts of the two main Christian social service agencies to promote industrial reform, and those of the organized church in China. There was also, however, a major secular institution involved, in the form of the Shanghai Municipal Council of the International Settlement.

The council was originally established to govern the settlement following the merger of the British and American concession areas in 1863. Its mandate in the nineteenth century largely concerned the provision of attributes of municipal civilization in the West, such as street lighting, parks, sewers, and public order. To the extent that Shanghai had become, by the end of the First World War, a complex modern city with all the social problems of twentieth-century Western society, as well as many of its own, it should not be surprising that pressure grew in some quarters for the Municipal Council to address these new social evils. The first of these, crying out for intervention, was the widespread employment of children in Shanghai's factories.

The 1920s: The Shanghai Child Labor Commission

The Problem of Child Labor

The employment of women and children had for some years been a salient feature of the operation of both Chinese and foreign factories in Shanghai. In itself, the phenomenon of whole families working was not at all new to China; it had long been known in handicraft industry and in agriculture. The strain and unsuitability of the work for women and children was far greater in modern industry than it was in the more traditional occupations, however, and the excessive hours and hazardous conditions posed a necessity for regulation that, though it had begun to be met in Europe some half a century previously, had not been faced in China by 1920.

The evidence as to the extent of the employment of children in modern industry in Shanghai in the 1920s is inadequate and conflicting. For example, in the government white paper *Labour Conditions in China*, a British consular official found that in 1925 some 4,800 (approximately 17 percent) of the 28,000 workers in British-owned factories in Shanghai were children under twelve.[1] In two British-American plants some 550 of the 6,000 workers (roughly 9 percent) were under twelve. In Japanese factories the figure was 5 percent; in Chinese factories, 13 percent; and in all factories, foreign and Chinese, the average was 14 percent, according to the same source. In some foreign concerns, notably the five French factories, children constituted almost 50 percent of the work force.

A further set of figures, taken by Jean Chesneaux from an independent contemporary source, shows that for the silk industry in the same period there were in Shanghai thirty-nine Chinese factories employing 3,566 children under twelve, representing 15.9 percent of total labor employed, while there were twenty-seven foreign factories employing 9,930 children under twelve, representing 41 percent of the total labor employed.[2] These figures comprised a child labor force of a remarkable 44 percent in British-owned factories (nine factories, 3,021 children), 28.1 percent in American factories (seven factories, 1,250 children), 47.7 percent in French factories (five factories, 2,599 children), and 48.4 percent in Italian factories (six factories, 3,060 children). In the cotton industry, there were said to be in Shanghai eighteen Chinese mills whose 3,615 children constituted 9.3 percent of total employees, and twenty-four British and Japanese mills whose 4,305 children were 8 percent of the labor force. In nine other factories performing various functions related to the textile industry, 5.3 percent (140) of the workers were children.

While these two sets of figures cannot be made to correspond with any degree of precision, it will nonetheless be clear that a considerable number of children were employed in the mills and factories of Shanghai. The two sources are in accord on the substantial preponderance of girls over boys employed in industrial undertakings, and the figures cited by Chesneaux show this same disproportion existing between women and men, especially in textiles.[3]

A more comprehensive picture is given by the survey of the Bureau of Social Affairs of Greater Shanghai, published in 1929. According to this source there were 27,482 children working in industry in Shanghai at that time, by far the greatest number in silk reeling (12,453), followed by cotton spinning (3,548), machinery manufacture (3,300), printing (3,252), glass-making (1,455), and cigarette manufacture (1,259).[4] Hershatter found that in Tientsin in the early 1920s, more than a quarter of all millhands were children, including many who were termed apprentices. Typically children could be found in every department of a mill, though particularly where dexterity was required; boys usually worked with men, and girls with women. They were employed because, as one contemporary observer put it, they were "cheap, young, pretty honest, and didn't try to shirk."[5]

That Chinese workers were willing to see their women and children go into the factories in such great numbers, it would sometimes be argued, was a reflection of the strength of patriarchal Confucian values among people who had left the countryside at most only a generation or so before; according to this theory, women and children had always worked, and it was their duty to do so to advance the position of the family. Yet children were not put to work in traditional China simply because it taught them a sense of responsibility, but primarily because of their contribution to the common income—for the value of their labor. So it was too in Shanghai in the twentieth century.

Only fragmentary information is available for this early period as to the average income and cost of living for a working-class family in Shanghai, but figures thrown up during public discussion of the proposed child labor legislation and other measures advocated by reformers in the early 1920s will give some idea of the subsistence level of existence endured by most working people. According to the *China Year Book,* the average monthly wage of the ordinary unskilled worker in Shanghai in 1921 had been approximately $10.50, and of a skilled worker $28.00, while women and children would have earned about $6.00 per month.[6] A writer for the *North China Herald* estimated that by 1926 the unskilled worker would be paid $15.00 per month, and so the other wages might be projected accordingly. It was also suggested that the absolute minimum subsistence wage for one person in 1926 was $12.00 per month, for a husband and wife $15.00, and for a family of four, $21.00.[7]

A Chinese correspondent submitted his own calculations to the *North China Herald* in April 1925 to show that at that time a family of six—mother and father, two children, and two grandparents—would spend at least $34.76 per month in order to subsist, and that this would require all six members of the family to be working.[8] Although the *International Labour Review* was to assert in 1929 that in general wages in Shanghai had kept pace with the rise in the cost of living in the 1920s, figures cited by Jean Chesneaux show that the price of rice, the staple of the working person's diet, had almost doubled in Shanghai between 1919 and 1925.[9] If this is compared to the less than 50 percent increase in wages between 1921 and 1926 noted above, it is possible to conclude that the standard of living of the Shanghai working family may even have declined somewhat in this period, and that where the father was unskilled and there were any children at all, the mother would have to work, and most probably the children as well, if the family was even to stay alive. This contention is supported by testimony, never published, to the Shanghai Child Labor Commission, to which witness after witness stated that the income of the children was essential to the survival of the family.[10]

The Child Labor Commission and Its Report

Formation of the Commission

It was in response to this situation that a major campaign was conducted between 1922 and 1925 to limit the use of child labor in factories in the International Settlement of Shanghai. This campaign is of particular interest on several counts. It remains the best documented of any project of industrial reform undertaken in the early period, offering not only, in the Report of the Child Labor Commission of 1924, a vivid insight into the life and labor of working-class children in Shanghai, but also, in unpublished minutes recording the proceedings of the commission, one of the earliest comprehensive surveys of factory life as a whole. The appointment of the Child Labor Commission by the Shanghai Municipal Council represents the first practical initiative taken by any administration in China on industrial welfare matters, leaving aside the Peking government's unenforced factory legislation of 1923. Finally, the defeat of the attempt to regulate the hours and working conditions of children in the aftermath of the May Thirtieth incident of 1925 serves to illustrate the difficulties attending any effort by outsiders to achieve progress of this kind at a time of rising Chinese nationalism.

The movement for the reform of child labor in Shanghai was in fact first given impetus by the appointment in 1921 of a commission to inquire into the extent and nature of child labor in Hong Kong. It may be supposed that this commission in turn had been established in response to the creation of the International Labour Organization in 1919, and the adoption by that body of various labor standards, among others those with respect to the employment of children. The activity in Hong Kong aroused considerable interest in Shanghai and prompted a run of correspondence in the *North China Daily News* in September 1921 under the heading "The Children of Martha and Mary."[11] The problem was already under review by the YWCA, and the association now decided to approach certain women's organizations with a view to seeing what could be done about it. On November 2 a Joint Committee of Women's Clubs was formed from representatives of the American, British, and Japanese Women's Clubs, the Shanghai Women's Club, and the Shanghai YWCA. The object of this committee was to promote interest in the conditions under which children labored in Shanghai, and to work toward alleviating those conditions.[12]

In the following year, members of the Joint Committee were able to visit shops and factories and gain a first-hand impression of children at work, but when they came to seek support from prominent employers for legislation to restrict the use of child labor they met with the first of a long series of complications. Foreign mill owners would support legislation only if it were to be applied both inside and outside the International Settlement. Chinese mill owners responded similarly,[13] and in any event they would not act until the Peking government's Provisional Factory Regulations, proposed for 1923, had been promulgated. The Shanghai Municipal Council would take no initiative at this stage without the approval of both Chinese and foreign employers.[14]

After much frustration, the Joint Committee addressed a formal letter to the Shanghai Municipal Council on March 1, 1923, outlining a minimum program calling for the abolition of night work for children under twelve, the provision of part-time schools, and the extension of the power of the Municipal Health Department to include supervision of ventilation, sanitation, and safety in factories. The letter made reference also to the call by the National Christian Council some time earlier for the abolition of all employment of children under twelve. In its reply of April 5, the council agreed to appoint a commission similar to that which had existed in Hong Kong to investigate the whole question of child labor in the International Settlement, and invited the Joint Committee to nominate prospective candidates for it.[15] The commission was duly constituted and held its first meeting in late June 1923.

Composition and Approach

The composition of the Child Labor Commission was clearly weighted in favor of the business community, with five of its ten members drawn from among executives of the major manufacturing interests in Shanghai. Its chairman was a lawyer, while the other four members were women—two from the YWCA, another the wife of a prominent missionary, and one a doctor with experience of treating factory workers. Several commissioners were compelled to drop out for various reasons as the investigation progressed, only one of whom was replaced. In the autumn of 1923 Dame Adelaide Anderson, former chief lady inspector of factories in the United Kingdom, was invited to serve on the commission and took up her seat in December. The commission was mandated by the Municipal Council "to enquire into the conditions of child labour in Shanghai and vicinity, and to make recommendations to the Council as to what regulations, if any, should be applied to child labour in the foreign settlement of Shanghai, having regard to practical considerations and local conditions generally."[16]

The commission was instructed to explore the possibility of cooperation with the Chinese authorities in Peking with a view to developing the Peking government's existing factory legislation so that it might be applied by the council in the settlement.

At their first meeting, members of the commission decided that their principal method of approach would be to summon witnesses whom it was thought could give expert testimony about the nature, extent, and implications of the use of child labor. Over the next twelve months, therefore, the commission held thirty-three meetings, usually of about two hours duration, to which some thirty-six witnesses were summoned. Of these witnesses, surviving evidence enables thirty to be identified: eleven were prominent lawyers (of whom two were actually commission members), four were senior police officials, five were doctors or other medical personnel, four were employees of the YMCA or YWCA, two were labor contractors, one was a compradore for a silk filature, one an architect, one the editor of a Nationalist newspaper, and only one—a woman—was a worker, this despite the fact that the YWCA's Agatha Harrison had pointed out at the first meeting that "it would be possible to get some of the workers to give very articulate evidence."[17]

The commission also reviewed evidence submitted in writing with respect to the numbers of children employed (according to the police), current Chinese factory legislation, current and past British factory legislation, and the policy of individual companies with regard to the employment of children and workers' welfare.[18] In addition, members of the commission made several tours of inspection of representative factories in all the major industrial districts of Shanghai, both in the daytime and at night, and developed a standard form of enquiry used to measure conditions in one factory against those in another.[19]

Testimony

All of the witnesses questioned by the Child Labor Commission were asked about hours and conditions of labor for children in Shanghai factories; this information was incorporated in the findings of the commission. Most were also asked for their view of the practicability of implementing legislation to curtail child labor, and on this matter it is quite significant that even the protagonists of reform among their number could see very substantial difficulties in the way of any change in the existing policy of complete laissez-faire.

The obstacles in the way of reform envisaged by witnesses fell broadly into three categories. There were the objections that it was felt would be raised by the workers themselves, the objections registered by employers, and the practical difficulties in the way of enforcement of any legislation to limit the use of child labor.

Among the objections likely to be raised by workers, the one given greatest emphasis was that rooted in the low level of adult wages. This point was made by no fewer than seven witnesses, none of whom seemed to think it likely that employers would raise adult wages in order to compensate for the loss by the family of the earnings of the children.[20] In these circumstances parents were obliged to, and did, insist that their children go to work. Another reason for parents' likely resistance to legislation, put forward by five witnesses, would be that their children would have no one to look after them and nowhere to go while adults were working if they too were not allowed into the factories.[21] Two other witnesses feared that legislation to restrict child labor would interfere with "general practice" or established custom in China, according to which children had always worked at an early age.[22] One witness thought adults would find children's work in silk filatures too tedious,[23] while another felt adults performing processes in the filatures previously performed by children would object to the strict discipline necessary to the smooth running of production.[24]   Finally, seven witnesses thought it very likely that any attempt to introduce legislation to ban child labor would lead to strikes by adult workers and social disorder on the part of their children,[25] who, so long as they were in the factories, were "less likely to become criminals."[26] Of all these objections, only the primary economic one was put forward by the single worker testifying before the commission, and she felt that most working people would be willing to make sacrifices to keep their children out of the mills.[27]

Of the objections voiced on behalf of employers, the principal concerned the possible financial cost to them of the elimination of children from their factories. Three witnesses felt that factories might be compelled to pay higher wages for jobs performed by children because adults could command higher wages, because they would need more money to support their children who were not working, or indeed simply to attract the labor;[28] one of these witnesses went so far as to observe that his company had to close down one of its mills in Hong Kong because of increased labor costs attendant upon the passage of labor legislation.[29] Another witness felt that legislation to ban child labor solely in the International Settlement might drive much adult labor to the areas of Chinese jurisdiction, thereby forcing up the cost of adult labor generally within the settlement.[30] Two witnesses were worried that employers would simply not be able to find the adult labor to compensate for the loss of the children in their factories,[31] one calculating that, allowing for some migration of adults along with their children to areas outside the settlement, certain factories would face the loss of approximately 40 percent of their labor force.[32] Other arguments concerned the efficiency with which children were supposed to perform their work, two witnesses noting that children under twelve picked things up more quickly than older workers,[33] and another witness observing that adult women might hurt their backs bending down to brush the silk cocoons if they took over this process from children in the filatures.[34] Responding to the suggestion that the abolition of child labor might in the long run produce more alert and efficient adult workers as had happened in the West, one prominent witness remarked, "In this respect Chinese workers could not be compared with Western. He was afraid any efforts to make the Oriental work at high pressure would be fruitless."[35]

One final problem was raised with respect to night work, from which it was felt it would be difficult to exclude children at the risk of impeding the smooth functioning of the two-shift system.[36]

Several practical difficulties were also seen to stand in the way of actual implementation of any reform. The principal of these was the need to obtain the cooperation of the Chinese authorities in order to try to have similar legislation enforced both inside and outside the International Settlement so as to minimize both the cost and dislocation to employers and to reduce the likelihood of wholesale migration of labor.[37] It was recognized that the absence of any strong central authority in China militated against any such uniform enforcement of new regulations. A number of witnesses pointed out that there was no way of accurately telling the age of Chinese children who presented themselves for employment, as there was no system of birth registration in China.[38] Usually height and weight were the criteria used to judge a child's age where any attempt was made to bar very young children from a mill, but one witness suggested that in future children seeking employment might be obliged to carry a certificate as proof of age, which one commission member thought might carry a photograph and fingerprints.[39] A witness from the YWCA pointed out that many child workers were in fact outworkers, whose labor, by virtue of being carried on at home, was very difficult to control.[40] Another witness, the editor of a Nationalist newspaper, warned that any attempt on the part of foreigners to impose factory inspection on Chinese employers was likely to meet with a hostile reaction.[41]

In spite of all these objections, few witnesses when confronted directly took a position expressly opposed to any limitation on child labor, and some even thought that reform would be a good thing.[42] Most employers contrived both to register strenuous objections and to say that child labor was not necessary to the continued success of their enterprises.[43]

Two witnesses, from the Municipal Police, "did not think there was any great evil" in the employment of children in Shanghai factories.[44] The deputy commissioner of police for the International Settlement felt that the difficulties in the way of provision of any form of factory inspection would be insuperable, and that the Municipal Council had neither the mandate nor the power to enact and enforce labor legislation. In his view there was no Chinese opinion in favor of it, and no chance of cooperation with authorities outside the settlement on the question. The enactment of legislation to restrict the use of child labor inside the settlement would impose "a restriction upon legitimate business and for that reason he would say it would be unfair."[45] The deputy commissioner and his director of criminal intelligence admitted, however, that they had "no particular knowledge at first hand of the extent or conditions of child labour in Shanghai."[46]

A number of witnesses were asked whether they thought workers' children would be better off in the mills or on the streets. Although the mandate of the commission did not proscribe discussion of other alternatives, it evidently did not seem possible that serious consideration should be given to the provision of schools for children, so they would have somewhere to go, and where their future prospects might be enhanced. Dame Adelaide Anderson's observation that "education and child labour prohibition went side by side" apparently passed without notice.[47]

Findings and Recommendations

The commission finally drew up its report and presented it to the Municipal Council, complete with recommendations, on July 9, 1924. The main body of the report dealt with testimony and observation as to the actual conditions in which children worked in Shanghai, and a review of this evidence is appropriate here.

In general, it was observed that while Chinese children living in rural surroundings were on the whole relatively healthy, their counterparts in Shanghai endured an existence that was adverse in the extreme to their bodily and mental well-being. In particular, they suffered frequently from industrial accidents because of the long hours and monotony of their work, and they tended to be highly susceptible to tuberculosis brought about by the often very humid conditions of work in the factory buildings. Crowded living arrangements and extreme poverty were also blamed for the city children's poor physique.

Concerning itself with child labor in the larger "mills, factories, and similar places of industry," the commission found that common to all these enterprises was the fact that children usually started work in them as soon as they could be of any economic value to the employer. The commission estimated that many of the children it saw at work were very probably no more than five or six years old. Night work was more the rule than the exception, two shifts of twelve hours generally being worked in the day, with never more than an hour off for a meal. Children were compelled to work the same hours as adults, in order to keep up with the pace of manufacture. In most factories, work stopped for one shift every week to enable maintenance to be carried out on the machinery. In addition, some concerns encouraged their employees to take a day off each week, without much success, however, as workers often could not afford the loss of salary. These interruptions, and the holiday at the Chinese New Year, formed the only respite from the otherwise continuous cycle of work and sleep. Sanitary provisions were found to be primitive, while the often high level of dust and inadequate ventilation were also criticized.

Apart from the British-American Tobacco factories, the largest and most important factories in Shanghai were the cotton mills, to which many of these criticisms were found to apply. The commission noted that children employed by the mills were chiefly to be seen in the spinning departments, where they had to stand at their work throughout their entire shift. Many of those working were estimated to be only six or seven years old. Day and night, mothers would bring with them to the mills their children who were as yet too young to work, and leave them in baskets to try to sleep in close proximity to the fast-moving machinery. It was determined that those children who were supposed to be at work frequently succumbed to fatigue and either tried to find a quiet corner in which to pass the remainder of their shift, hoping to avoid discovery, or else dozed off at their machines, usually with disastrous results.

The commission concluded that the children's work could be done just as well by adults, and that as there appeared to be no shortage of labor in the cotton industry there was no reason why children should not be debarred from employment in the cotton mills of Shanghai.

Turning to silk filatures, the commission found that nearly all the employees in these concerns were either women or young girls. The task of the children was to brush the cocoons and remove the waste material from them so they would be ready for the reelers who reeled the silk thread. One child was normally employed for every two adults in the total process. The peeling of the cocoons was usually carried on over cauldrons of nearly boiling water with which the children's fingers regularly came into contact, leaving them rough and swollen. It was not uncommon for workers to faint from the humidity, especially in hot weather. As in the cotton mills, the work was invariably performed standing up, many of the children going through the motion of alternately bending and straightening their knees in rapid succession in order to ease the strain. Night work was found to be unusual in the silk industry, the normal working day being twelve hours. One problem peculiar to this industry concerned the fulfillment of quotas. Adults were given a certain number of cocoons, and from them were obliged to produce a certain quantity of silk. If they had too little to show they were fined, and they often took their revenge on the children working under them.

The commission concluded that the employment of children under the conditions they observed in the silk industry was indefensible. "In the main they present a pitiable sight. Their physical condition is poor, and their faces are devoid of any expression of happiness or well-being. They appear to be miserable, both physically and mentally."[48]

The commission found that the work could just as well be done by adults, though certain machinery might have to be reconstructed because of the difference in height. Some shortage of labor was reported in the silk industry. It was suggested that the silk mills in Shanghai might adopt a procedure employed by one successful Chinese filature in Hangchow and in use in Japan, whereby the boiling room, tended by boys of sixteen or over, was kept separate from the reeling room and cocoons were cooled before they were peeled.

In cigarette and tobacco factories, the commission found conditions of employment for children to be substantially better than in the cotton and silk industries. Year-round employment was not customary, night work was not frequent, and the children put in a nine- or ten-hour day and were able to sit at their work, which was "light in nature." The situation in match factories was quite different, however. Members of the commission visited several match factories in the vicinity of Shanghai and saw children as young as five years of age performing with "incredible rapidity" chores such as boxing matches and making up parcels of boxes, for wages only half those paid to children in other industries. Here again, babies and children not old enough even to box matches slept or played on the floor while their mothers worked.

In some factories it was discovered that white phosphorous was used in the manufacture of the matches, with cases of phosphorous poisoning having been observed to result. Although most governments in Western Europe had banned the manufacture or importation of white phosphorous matches in 1908, they continued to be produced in China into the late 1920s. The making of matchboxes was carried on outside the factories and was normally farmed out to women and their young children to be done at home.

The risk of fire was obviously very great in match factories, yet the commission noted that not even the most simple precautions were observed, such as the provision of fire screens between child workers. Indeed, the lack of precautions against the outbreak of fire was a general criticism made of all factories visited. Old buildings were not governed at all by the Municipal Fire Safety Regulations, while new factories were required only to submit their plans for approval at the drawing-board stage. Inspections were carried out periodically and recommendations made for fire prevention, but little notice was usually taken because they did not carry the force of law. Many older buildings were considered unsafe, and time after time the commission observed that fire exits were locked or made inaccessible by new supplies of material stacked in front of the doors.

In addition to cotton mills and silk filatures, cigarette and match factories, the commission also discussed in its report the engineering and ship-building trades, printing works, laundries, and the building trade, with varying amounts of evidence to hand for each. Foreign ownership was represented less in these endeavors, however, and the employment of children in them seems to have been less evident, and of less concern to the commission.

The commission gave explicit recognition to the many obstacles in the way of reform of child labor noted in testimony before it, but nonetheless put forward a strong recommendation in favor of reform, urging the Municipal Council to seek power to make and enforce regulations as follows:

- to prohibit the employment in factories and industrial undertakings of children under ten years of age, rising to twelve years of age within four years
- to prohibit the employment of children under fourteen for more than twelve hours out of twenty-four, one hour of rest to be provided in twelve
- not to prohibit the employment of children at night, although this was consid-

ered to be a serious evil, but to provide for further consideration of this question at the end of a period of four years

- to provide for a compulsory twenty-four-hour rest period every fourteen days for children under fourteen
- to prohibit the employment of all children under fourteen in dangerous places, at unguarded machinery, or at work likely to seriously injure body or health
- to require a test of age of young people wishing employment, either by height or height and weight, or by the judgment of a sitting magistrate in the case of any prosecution

The Commission went on to clarify the scope of its recommendations, providing

- that 'factory' be defined so as to include; premises where ten or more persons were engaged in manual work
- that "industrial undertaking" be defined so as to include out-of-door occupations such as building, construction work, and transport, but not agriculture
- that regulations should allow for fines or imprisonment for child labour offenses
- that the Council should establish an adequate staff of trained men and women for carrying out duties of inspection.[49]

As the Municipal Council was not a sovereign government in the ordinary sense, it was recognized that it could not simply extend its power by enacting legislation to regulate industrial conditions in the International Settlement. Rather, it would be necessary for it to acquire the power through formal adoption of a new bylaw, which would require the approval of a majority of ratepayers in the settlement convened in special meeting, as well as ratification by the consuls and ministers of all the foreign powers having treaty relations with China. Ratification posed no problem, and the issue would really be for the ratepayers to decide.

The council expressed its broad approval of the commission's report in the *Municipal Gazette* of October 23, 1924, and at its meeting on January 21, 1925, it formally adopted the commission's recommendations and instructed its legal adviser to frame a bylaw incorporating them for presentation to the next annual meeting of ratepayers.[50] The date fixed for this meeting was April 15, 1925.

The Campaign for Legislation

The announcement of a date for the holding of a referendum of ratepayers on child labor legislation gave the reform lobby a focal point for their activity, but in fact a sustained effort had been made to keep the child labor issue before the public throughout the time that the commission had been in session. Much had been made of the presence in China of Dame Adelaide Anderson during the first ten months of 1924, and her experience, coupled with her membership in the commission, gave her the prestige necessary to command support for reform. Anderson visited factories and addressed meetings in Shanghai, Wuchang, Xuling, and Peking, and she delivered a series of lectures on factory law and administration at Peking University.[51] She also had interviews with officials of the Labor Department and the Ministry of Agriculture and Commerce of the Peking government. In Kiangsu she met the civil governor, who promised to implement child labor legislation in his province. The advent of civil war in Kiangsu in 1924, however, relieved the governor of the necessity of matching his words with action. He spoke to employers, urging them to introduce reforms in advance of legislation, and on May Day he participated in a "large gathering of labour groups" in Shanghai at which resolutions in favor of the abolition of employment of children under twelve and the adoption of the eight-hour day were carried unanimously. In June 1924 Anderson remarked that "although the conditions . . . are generally speaking very terrible, the outlook is hopeful."[52]

The original publication of the Child Labor Commission's Report in July 1924, when many of the foreign residents of Shanghai were away on holiday, meant that it did not immediately arouse the response that some had anticipated, and indeed to the dismay of reformers this hiatus in public interest persisted throughout the autumn.[53] After the council's endorsement in principle of the report near the end of October, however, there was a resurgence of interest further stimulated by the activity of the reform lobby, and this reached a climax in March and early April 1925. From overseas, expressions of concern and support for the proposed legislation were sent from nine countries, by organizations and individuals as diverse as the French Women's Union for the League of Nations, the Tata Steel Company in India, officials of the American Department of Labor—Women's Bureau, and Alice Masaryk, daughter of the president of Czechoslovakia.[54] The International Labour Organization in Geneva also followed the progress of the campaign.[55]

In Britain articles in support of reform appeared in the *Times*, the *Manchester Guardian*, and the *New Statesman*, and in the United States in the *New York Sun*.[56] Speeches were made in several cities in Britain and elsewhere by returned members of the Child Labor Commission, notably Agatha Harrison, whose lecture tour in Great Britain was apparently sponsored by the Industrial Law Bureau.[57] In early February 1925, a special meeting was held in London at which Dame Adelaide Anderson addressed a gathering of MPs, trade unionists, welfare workers, missionaries, and others on the subject of the commission's work.[58] As a result of a meeting with Agatha Harrison, the executive of the Manchester Chamber of Commerce was persuaded also in February to cable its British counterpart in Shanghai: "Child labour, our China Executive having carefully considered report, hope you will be able to very strongly urge Council adopt at an early date their Commission's recommendations."[59]

In China itself, the issue was discussed by the Ratepayers' Association, the Theosophical Society, the Jewish Club, the Japanese Club, and the various national women's clubs,[60] while officials of the Joint Committee of Women's Clubs saw to it that a series of articles favorable to reform appeared in the major foreign newspapers in Shanghai.[61] The British consul general, John Pratt, acting apparently on the instructions of the foreign secretary, canvassed the opinion of all the important manufacturers in the city; his letter brought forth a favorable response to the proposed legislation from seven British, six Chinese, six Japanese, and five American concerns.[62]

In addition, public endorsements of the new bylaw were forthcoming from the

Shanghai General Chamber of Commerce, the British Chamber of Commerce, and the American Chamber of Commerce, but not from the all-important Chinese General Chamber of Commerce, which, while claiming to approve in principle of child labor regulation, opposed its application by the Municipal Council on terms which would be different from those provided for in the Peking government's Provisional Factory Act of 1923.[63] That government now announced its intention of promulgating a more permanent set of factory regulations, with provision for inspection. In the last weeks of the campaign, some sixty letters about child labor were published in the *North China Daily News and Herald* in Shanghai. These letters formed a distillation of local views upon the subject. By the late spring of 1925 it was possible to believe that there was "a strong and widely diffused movement, national in scope to press for and secure both legislation and voluntary reform."[64]

Defeat and Disarray

The Special Meetings

On the afternoon of April 15, 1925, the Shanghai Municipal Council convened the special meeting of ratepayers to consider proposed new bylaws, not only concerning the restriction of child labor, but also to introduce an increase in wharfage dues and measures of press control on Chinese newspapers published in the International Settlement. "The annual meeting . . . passed off quietly. The total number of voters present was only 399, these representing 622 votes. This was far short of the number required to form a quorum to deal with the special resolutions regarding child labour and the printed matter Bye-law, a total of 914 being necessary for such a purpose, . . . in consequence these could not be brought up for consideration." That the child labor bylaw should not even have been discussed at the meeting stunned and consternated many who had worked for its acceptance. "That it should seem as if Shanghai did not care, as if it could not be bothered, as if perhaps the attraction, of a fine day and a game of golf were too much to be resisted even for a matter of profound humanity and vital importance, this is indeed tragic."[65] In an editorial three weeks later, the *North China Herald* emphasized the opposition to reform that had existed among the Chinese and suggested that foreigners had a "duty to show them the way."[66]

A second attempt to have the new bylaw considered was given impetus by the British consul, who appealed for support to the leading merchants and manufacturers in Shanghai. A letter was forwarded to the council calling for another special meeting of ratepayers to be held early in June, and signed by seventy-six of the settlement's most prominent residents, of whom it was remarked "not one . . . is a woman or a missionary,"[67] although an opponent of reform subsequently claimed that forty-one of these had not taken the trouble to appear at the first meeting.[68] On May 8 the consul addressed a gathering on the subject at his home, and a house-to-house canvass of ratepayers was organized, apparently by the Joint Committee of Women's Organisations.[69] Overtures to the council to have the second meeting deal only with the question of child labor and not with wharfage dues or press censorship were unsuccessful.[70]

The second special meeting was held on June 2. In the interim, however, there occurred on May 30 the shooting of workers by the Municipal Police in the Nanking Road, later to be known as the May Thirtieth incident, which plunged much of China into turmoil the likes of which it had not seen since 1919. Despite the fact that the council sent out messengers on the morning of June 2 to urge people not to come to the meeting for fear of their safety, the increased canvassing and personal involvement of prominent individuals succeeded in raising the number of ratepayers present to 514, and the number of votes represented to 725.[71] This was still 177 votes short of the required quorum, however, and the meeting adjourned after fifteen minutes. Shanghai was now under a state of emergency, and for all intents and purposes the child labor issue was dead.

Postmortem

There was no shortage of explanations as to why the child labor campaign had failed. It was suggested that the tedious nature of council meetings, which involved the reading of reports and the registering of formal votes, had discouraged attendance.[72] It was pointed out that a quorum—one-third of ratepayers present or represented—had not been achieved at any annual meeting over the previous nine years,[73] one observer commenting that only a rise in rates or taxes or the imposition of prohibition would be likely to bring out the numbers required for a vote in special meeting.[74] It was felt that the conduct of the campaign principally by women might have put off some ratepayers.[75] Another problem had been the disposition of Japanese voters, of whom it was estimated that four-fifths spoke no English at all. The Municipal Council had been requested, but had refused, to provide simultaneous translation into Japanese for the meetings, arguing that this would set a precedent. In fact, many Japanese received letters in May from Chinese friends, urging them to abstain from attending the second meeting as part of a coordinated campaign to oppose the introduction of the measures on wharfage dues and press censorship.[76] As a result, the Japanese were apparently absent en bloc from the meeting of June 2.[77] One observer estimated that while 50 percent of British ratepayers attended this meeting, there was only nominal representation from other nationalities in Shanghai.[78]

The *China Year Book*, analyzing the defeat in its annual review of developments in China, chose to emphasize the opposition to reform that it claimed had grown up among Chinese employers. It is significant that Chinese residing in the International Settlement were not permitted at this time to vote in the elections or special meetings of the Municipal Council, although wealthy Chinese contributed substantially through their rates and taxes to the budget of the council, and the privilege of voting was extended to almost all other nationalities.[79] Chinese opposition almost certainly stemmed in part from the juxtaposition of the child labor bylaw with those designed to raise wharfage dues and to control the Chinese press. It may also be supposed that, like their foreign counterparts, Chinese employers were disinclined to replace the children in their factories with more expensive adults.

On May 29, thirty leading Chinese organizations and businesses issued a statement through the Chinese General Chamber of Commerce denouncing the wharfage and press resolutions, and giving only qualified support to the principle represented in the resolution on child labor.[80]

The manifesto expressed the view that it was more humane to let the children work than to force them into starvation, and that if the council intended to put the reform into effect it ought to provide a food allowance and free schooling for every child deprived of work. All in all national pride, practical objections, and self-interest may have combined to determine Chinese opposition to the child labor legislation, and it is not possible to agree wholly with Augusta Wagner's observation, made some years later, that "[i]n the exacerbated state of nationalism, the issue became the right of the foreign Council to make any regulation which would extend foreign power and give greater control over Chinese lives."[81] What is significant is that Chinese opposition may have discouraged some foreign voters who might otherwise have turned out to support the child labor bylaw.

Editorial comment and correspondence in the local English-language press serves to underline the ambivalence of the foreign community in the weeks preceding the two meetings. The leading British newspaper in Shanghai, the *North China Daily News*—in its weekly form the *North China Herald*—followed the progress of the campaign in its columns and gave support to it in a series of editorials. In its last editorial on the subject before the April meeting, however, it appealed to voters solely on grounds of self-interest: "Putting aside all considerations of morality or humanity, we cannot afford to alienate the sympathies of people at home, whose attention has been widely attracted to Shanghai in this matter. The time may come when we shall need that sympathy very much—are we likely to get much of it if all that the man in the street remembers about Shanghai is that it is the place where they work children of six years old for anything up to fifteen hours in the mills and filatures?"[82]

When two meetings had failed to achieve a quorum, and the events of May Thirtieth had intervened, the *Herald* seemed quite willing to accept the collapse of the child labor campaign, pronouncing it a "defeat with honour."[83] It concerned itself no further with the question, and in an editorial two years later it remarked that "only the most profound ignorance of conditions here could betray even the most superficial thinker onto believing that any foreign firm that employs Chinese thereby exploits them."[84]

Correspondence in the *Herald* on the child labor question in the spring of 1925 was similarly ambivalent. Undeniably, a proportion of letters to the paper favored reform, though some of these were written by individuals who had either served on the commission or been closely involved with it. Among these, a number sought to emphasize the responsibility of foreigners in the matter, as the purveyors of modern industry to China,[85] while others pointed out that the proposed reforms were mild in comparison with legislation existing in England and America and were the least that could be expected if "Bolshevism is to be destroyed and war is to be no more."[86] More shrewdly, it was suggested that the legislation might curtail the drift of large families to the cities.[87]

On the other hand, many letters were written as well by opponents of reform, led by an individual who signed himself "Shanghailander," whom the British consul described as suffering from "a kind of itch which compels him to write to the newspapers on every conceivable topic and every conceivable occasion."[88] The burden of the opposition argument was that the legislation would bring the need for a Poor Law, and compulsory education, and possibly even the dole.[89] This would, it was argued, impose an insupportable strain on "financially broken Shanghai."[90] It was envisaged that closure of the factories to children would drive thousands of them into prostitution, while the reformers, safely back in England, would be able to shirk their responsibilities.[91] What was considered to be the "absurd level" of welfare in England in 1925 was roundly condemned.[92] Some correspondents were genuinely concerned that the pace of reform might be too rapid. Although there were in all nearly sixty letters to the *Herald*, it is clear that while attracting attention, the child labor issue had by no means elicited universal sympathy among the foreign population in Shanghai, a state of affairs that was to some extent hidden from the reformers by their own enthusiasm for the rightness of their cause.

In Britain the child labor campaign had attracted considerable interest, with support forthcoming from the *Times,* the *Manchester Guardian,* and, most passionately, the *New Statesman.*[93] In June the General Council of the Trades Union Congress (TUC) and the National Executive of the Labour party jointly passed a resolution urging implementation of the Child Labor Commission's recommendations in all the treaty ports of China, along with a British initiative to end extraterritoriality.[94] A debate on the prevailing situation in China, of which discussion of the child labor question formed a prominent part, took place in Parliament on June 13, 17, and 18. In the course of this, opposition MPs linked the current unrest in China to the "naked exploitation" of all forms of cheap labor, although one former resident of Shanghai assured the House that women and children came out of the mills in Shanghai each day "happy and laughing."[95] The government committed itself to doing everything possible to ameliorate conditions of labor in China,[96] but rejected a suggestion that a TUC delegation should be sent there to investigate.

No further progress was made with legislation to restrict the use of child labor in the International Settlement, although some reports exist of improvements made on a voluntary basis. The *China Weekly Review* observed in 1928 that as far as working conditions were concerned, many enterprises appeared by then to be "managed along Western lines."[97] The *International Labour Review* was led to remark in 1932 that "child labour in the ordinary sense (under 14) had disappeared from foreign enterprises," while the adoption during the 1930s of the central boiling system for cocoons in a number of silk filatures freed children from the worst evils of work in that industry.[98] On the other hand, the Joint Committee of Women's Clubs in their submission to Justice Richard Feetham during the course of his review of the status of Shanghai in 1931 stated their belief that "conditions in the factories, in the

Settlement and its vicinity, as regards child labour have practically undergone no change since the commission reported in 1924."[99]

More recent studies confirm that in the longer term, while progress was not linear, the trend was toward a substantial reduction in the number of children employed in industry. For Shanghai, Honig cites a decrease in children employed in mills and factories from 9 percent of the overall industrial working population in 1929 to only 2 percent in 1946, while Hershatter observes that in the mills of Tientsin child workers under sixteen declined from a quarter in the early 1920s to 14 percent by 1929, and only 3 percent by 1933.[100]

The child labor campaign could by no means be counted as a total failure. The appointment of the Child Labor Commission, and the support given to its recommendations by the Municipal Council, represented the first practical intervention by any organ of government in China in the matter of labor standards, did much to establish public acceptance of the principle of such intervention, and effectively paved the way for the creation of the Industrial Section of the Municipal Council in the 1930s.

The child labor episode served to highlight certain areas of particular difficulty in the application of labor legislation, such as the need to respect the sensitivities of Chinese nationalism, and the attention that must be given to the whole question of multiple jurisdictions. Finally, it showed that the argument of self-interest invariably carried the greatest weight with employers, in inducing them to carry out reforms regardless of the existing state of legislation. In all these important respects, the Industrial Section's piecemeal and functional approach of the 1930s drew on the lessons of the child labor campaign.

The 1930s: The Industrial Section of
the Shanghai Municipal Council

As early as 1925, an official of the YWCA had raised the possibility that the Shanghai Municipal Council might be persuaded to engage as a permanent member of staff an industrial welfare worker whose task would be to monitor conditions, with respect to the health and safety of workers in factories in the International Settlement. In the wake of the May Thirtieth incident and the collapse of the campaign for child labor legislation, the prospect that any such appointment would be made receded for a time, and the issue was not raised again for some years.

The promulgation of factory legislation by the Kuomintang government between 1929 and 1931, however, renewed interest in the question of industrial standards in the settlement and helped to persuade the council that some further initiative toward intervention in this area would be appropriate. Certainly the scope was there, for a council survey in 1935 revealed that there were by then 3,421 factories and workshops in the settlement employing 170,704 workers, a sizable proportion of China's industrial work force as a whole.[101]

Critical to the application of any factory legislation in Shanghai would be the resolution of the conflicting jurisdictional claims of the Chinese and settlement authorities. In 1931 the ILO sent a delegation to China to try to effect a compromise between the Chinese government and the Shanghai Municipal Council on the application of the Kuomintang's factory legislation in territory under the council's control. On the recommendation of this delegation, the council took a decision to appoint an officer with special responsibility for factory inspection and enforcement of the Nanking factory legislation within the International Settlement. Although other aspects of the agreement reached with the Kuomintang government broke down early in 1932, the council went ahead with the creation of its "Industrial Section," which was formally inaugurated at the end of 1932 with a staff of four, a loose mandate to concern itself with industrial health and safety, and wholly undefined legal powers.[102] Eleanor Hinder, late of the YWCA's Industrial Department, was made its first head, while the New Zealander Rewi Alley, who had served for five years with the council's Fire Department, became chief factory inspector.

In the ten years from 1932 to 1942, the section sought to minister to the needs of the settlement's industrial workers, concentrating in the initial period up to the outbreak of war in 1937 on the implementation of measures to bring about improved conditions for health and safety in the factories, branching out during the first three years of the war emergency to encompass a concern for a wide variety of social matters affecting the working population, and culminating in the establishment of the "Industrial and Social Division" of the council in October 1940. If a considerable work of amelioration was achieved, it was accomplished largely without resort to legal sanction, and in such a way that the complicated question of jurisdiction could be circumvented. In the years up to the outbreak of war with Japan, however, efforts were made simultaneously to resolve the dispute over jurisdiction in order, as it was thought, to pave the way for factory legislation in the settlement. It will be appropriate, therefore, to consider the dynamics of this question first, before proceeding to an account of other aspects of the section's work.

The Question of Jurisdiction

The view had frequently been expressed by the Peking, and later the Nanking government at the International Labor Conferences in Geneva and on other occasions that Chinese labor laws should be applicable in the foreign concessions and settlements as elsewhere in China, and that they should be enforced by agents of the Chinese government.[103] In the 1920s, however, the foreign powers had consistently rejected this demand, as its satisfaction, they claimed, would compromise the administrative integrity of the various concessions and would represent a partial abrogation of the treaty privileges conferred on the foreigners through the system of extraterritoriality.

The British position was clearly set out in the White Paper of 1924, *Labour Conditions in China*, in which any interference with the extraterritorial rights of British factory owners was declared inadmissible, while it was suggested that in concessions under British jurisdiction regulations might be applied by means of bylaws, though some mechanism to allow for control of Chinese factories in the concessions, and foreign factories outside them, would be necessary. A guarantee of the enforcement of labor legislation by the Chinese authorities elsewhere in China was held to be essential, so that British factories would not suffer from competition from factories operating under fewer constraints.[104]

The creation of the Chinese municipality in Shanghai in 1927, and the passage of the Nanking government's Factory Act finally in 1931, lent a greater urgency to the need to reconcile somehow the conflicting positions on this question of China and the foreign powers. Three attempts were made in the 1930s to resolve the problem. Dame Adelaide Anderson and M. Camille Pone were sent by the ILO in 1931 to try to negotiate a compromise, and they produced a plan that would have provided for Chinese-trained factory inspectors reporting both to the Chinese government and to the authorities of the International Settlement and French Concession to apply regulations in the two concessions the same in all respects as those applied outside.[105] Enforcement was to be the task of the appropriate courts in the concessions. Although the agreement had been reached as a result of talks conducted at a very high level,[106] it broke down shortly after the departure of the ILO mission for Europe.

The second series of negotiations began in May 1933, after the council's Industrial Section had been created with Eleanor Hinder at its head. During the course of these discussions between the secretary general of the Municipality of Greater Shanghai and his counterpart of the Municipal Council, the Chinese side put forward a proposal for a joint factory inspectorate for all of Shanghai, which would be responsible both to the authorities of the settlement and to the Chinese municipality. The Shanghai Municipal Council found this proposal unacceptable, and rejected the suggestion that it should share its authority in the settlement. It advanced in return a plan for separate inspectorates applying similar legislation, which was equally unacceptable to the Chinese. The negotiations broke down in October.

Immediately prior to these discussions in March and April 1933, a considerable agitation had broken out in the Chinese community over the council's efforts to introduce an amendment to its bylaws that would permit licensing, and therefore control, of industrial premises. The council argued that such premises had not been dealt with at the last revision of the bylaws in 1898 because at that time there had been almost no modern industry in Shanghai. In 1933, however, it was logical that factories should be added to the list of premises requiring licensing and inspection before they could operate.

Eleanor Hinder, who recognized that cooperation between the Chinese and settlement authorities would be essential to the success of any program of enforcement for factory legislation, apparently spent her first two months in office trying to dissuade the council from taking unilateral action, but without success.[107] A special meeting of ratepayers was convened, which in this case managed to achieve a quorum, to approve the amendment to licensing regulations, and the bylaw as amended was formally adopted by the council on April 19. Ratification was soon forthcoming from the appropriate consular and diplomatic bodies.

In fact this was a pyrrhic victory. Enforcement of the bylaw would have been of necessity through the First Special District Court in the case of Chinese factory owners, and the cooperation of that agency was unlikely to be forthcoming. For the next several years the right to license factory premises was not invoked, and the Industrial Section would rely on persuasion rather than the threat of legal sanction to bring about those changes which it was able to achieve.[108]

No further progress was made on the jurisdiction question for the next three years, Hinder noting in 1935 that the local representative of the ILO, Chen Hai-fong, who had expressed interest in the problem, had insufficient weight to bring the council and the municipality together again.[109] In 1936, however, a final attempt was made to reconcile their differences, this time in the wake of the Nanking government's decision to apply the provisions of its factory legislation in stages (see chapter 1). On this occasion the council and the Chinese authorities actually reached an accord on the manner of implementation of factory inspection. The council was to apply, under authority delegated to it by the Chinese government, those portions of the Factory Act and related legislation that were applied in territory under Chinese jurisdiction. The council's inspectors were to be chosen in equal numbers by the council and by the Chinese government, and they were to report to the council, which would in turn report from time to time to the Chinese authorities. Cases of infringement of the regulations were to be referred to "the Courts." The agreement was to run initially for three years.[110]

The proposal was then sent to the consular body in Shanghai for approval. In July it was returned, rejected. The consuls' judgment was that the agreement seemed to allow for the application of Chinese law to factories, owned by foreign nationals enjoying extraterritorial privileges, and therefore was inadmissible. The consular body recommended again that the Chinese could apply the terms of the Factory Act to their own factories, while the Municipal Council could apply its own similar legislation to other factories.[111] There was apparently no longer any way out of this impasse, and with the coming of the war the following year no further effort was made to solve the problem.

The Council's Industrial Program: The Early Years

As head of the council's Industrial Section, Eleanor Hinder was in close touch with the state of negotiations over jurisdiction. After a time she became convinced that whatever could be achieved in the settlement in the way of amelioration of industrial conditions would be accomplished through persuasion rather than the threat of legal sanctions. "Almost, I think, I shall regret the time when we are able to move with mandatory powers. Chinese people are essentially reasonable, and if one can get one's views understood there is just as much likelihood of obtaining compliance by persuasion as by any exercise of legal power."[112] The urgency of the situation was apparent, and efforts to monitor and where possible to reform conditions were begun forthwith.

In February 1933, scarcely a month after Hinder had returned to Shanghai to occupy her new post, an explosion occurred in a rubber shoe factory in the settlement that killed eighty-one people. Even by the standards of Shanghai this was a disaster of some magnitude. The explosion had apparently been caused by ignition of the petrol mixture given off during the process of vulcanizing the rubber shoes in large vats, and had resulted in the walls of the factory being blown outward and the roof collapsing, trapping three hundred women on the upper floor in a mass of burning debris.[113] An investigation subsequently initiated by Hinder revealed that there was imminent danger of a similar catastrophe occurring in any one of the twenty-seven rubber factories in the settlement.[114]

The Beginnings of Intervention on Safety and Health

Although the controversy over the licensing question in the spring and summer of 1933 determined that the Industrial Section proceed with care in attempting to bring about safer conditions of work, steps were taken nevertheless in 1933 to begin the collection of data on industrial accidents. In the first year only those accidents coming to the attention of the police, fire, and ambulance service were incorporated into the section's findings, but in 1934 and subsequently hospitals in the settlement, and factory managers, were encouraged to provide the section with details of industrial accidents. A more complete, though still by no means comprehensive, picture was thereby made available. This information on the frequency of different kinds of accidents revealed no consistent pattern, but did enable the section's staff to determine in what circumstances a misadventure was more likely to occur, and to begin a campaign of education and persuasion to make the occurrence less likely.[115] In this endeavor, the section came to enjoy the cooperation of certain insurance companies whose management increasingly sought to impose safety requirements on factories whose owners insured with them.[116]

One increasingly common cause of death and injury was the faulty construction or operation of boilers and other pressure vessels, many of the more recent of which had been manufactured in China with little knowledge of the standard of materials necessary for their safe operation. Not infrequently factory managers would render the safety valves of pressure vessels inoperative in order that the manufacturing process could be carried on with what they regarded as greater efficiency. In 1934, therefore, the Industrial Section induced the Municipal Council to outline the requirements for safe practice in the use of boilers and pressure vessels, and an enumeration of boilers in the settlement was carried out, and testing for safety begun, with a view to implementing in due course a regular annual inspection.[117] In many cases testing was conducted by foreign engineers who had a special expertise in the inspection of boilers recognized in their country of origin, there being as yet an insufficient number of Chinese engineers who were qualified in this respect.

In March 1936 the commissioner of public works, with the advice and support of the Industrial Section, recommended to the council that it adopt "Rules Governing Vessels and Systems, under Pressure," and these regulations were in fact enforced from October 1. These provided for the licensing of all pressure vessels, both new and existing, after it had been determined that design, manufacture, and installation had been carried out under qualified supervision.[118] In 1937 the Industrial Section offered its first experimental course for boiler attendants, drawn from the tobacco, dyeing and weaving, printing, rubber, metal, hosiery, hat, and chemical industries, giving instruction in the safe operation of boilers, while the same year a judgment was rendered by the First Special District Court under the "Law Governing Penalties for Police Offenses" resulting in a fine for the owner of a rubber shoe factory who was found to have endangered public safety by obstructing the flow of steam through the safety valve of a boiler in his plant.[119]

Hazardous processes and the handling of dangerous substances were also an early cause for concern on the part of the Industrial Section. In particular, the careless handling of materials in celluloid plants and gas mantle factories had not uncommonly resulted in serious fires, as had the use of acetylene generators in welding shops.[120] The section's inspectors, finding in the premises they visited practices that put employees at risk, would urge the owners to attend a meeting at the section's headquarters where the problem would be discussed and solutions put forward. It is claimed that it was possible to achieve much progress by this method and to defuse the owners' resistance to change.[121]

Similarly, owners of chrome plating and metal polishing shops were encouraged to install exhaust systems in their shops, to remove poisonous fumes from the vicinity of workers.[122] In 1936 and 1937 the Industrial Section, in conjunction with the Henry Lester Institute in Shanghai, published studies of lead poisoning in the printing industry, the effects of the handling of lead and antimony in a variety of other processes, and of acid poisoning in the chrome and metal plating industry (see chapter 1). These studies were intended to point the way to reform.

A systematic survey of factories and workshops in the settlement was initiated by the commissioner of public works in 1934, completed in June 1935, which revealed, inter alia, information about poisonous effluents into drains and creeks. Little seems to have been done about this aspect of pollution, though the three officials responsible for the survey were transferred to the staff of the Industrial Section.[123]

Another matter of concern was the standard of electrical apparatus and wiring in use in settlement factories, which was suspected to be the cause of an undetermined number of fires. In spite of frequent comment on electrical hazards by inspectors on their rounds, little progress was reported in this sphere by the end of 1937.[124]

More hopeful was the situation with respect to guards on machinery. By the close of 1935 it was reported that a significant rapport had been established with the owners of textile plants and other factories making extensive use of power machinery, and that many such plants were experimenting with machine guards under the direction of the Industrial Section. Key to a more general acceptance of guards was a recognition that they could, if necessary, be manufactured and fitted easily and cheaply, and the section's initiatives went some way toward convincing owners of this. Accidents on power presses were also very common, and the section purchased its own press to demonstrate the function of an automatic guard in preventing injuries on this piece of machinery. Attempts were made to persuade workers to wear clothing more suitable to the factory environment than the traditional Chinese loose pajamas, but apparently to no avail, probably because of the cost that would have been involved in replacing them.[125]

Among the other projects undertaken by the section in this early period was the study promoted jointly by the section and the Lester Institute in 1937 into the diet of workers, as a result of which it was found that the use of un-dehusked rice in factory lunches could, without any additional cost, virtually eliminate beri-beri and other nutrition deficiency diseases.[126] A further experiment on these lines would be carried out in 1940.

The council's Public Health Department, in collaboration with the section, in 1937 devised a cheap latrine that could be installed in the most proprietary workshop, while it also carried out a campaign against bed-bugs, which played a large part in causing industrial fatigue, and began that year to insist on the whitewashing and cleaning of industrial premises at the Chinese New Year.[127]

One area in which the Industrial Section met with little success was in its attempt to convince workshop proprietors occupying converted dwellings to move to more suitable premises; it encouraged one private experiment in 1934, however, which saw the construction of thirty-one workshops with columns and beams of reinforced concrete, stairs leading directly outside, modern toilets, and steel windows.[128]

In 1933 the Municipal Council appointed a commission to inquire into the state of the ricksha business in Shanghai, and Eleanor Hinder was invited to join the commission as a member. Apparently at Hinder's instigation, the commission decided to carry out a limited survey of income and expenditure among the pullers, the first such study among a specific group of workers in the settlement, and Hinder's former colleague at the YWCA, Dju Yu-bao, was engaged as one of the investigators.[129] Despite the fact that the Ricksha Commission's report resulted in control of the tariff for which the puller hired the vehicle from its owner, and in creation of a Pullers' Mutual Aid Association to provide educational, hospital, and other welfare facilities for pullers, the number of pullers was so large that it was Hinder's conclusion in 1941 that the authorities had not succeeded in "ameliorating the puller's lot to any material extent."[130]

Among other matters, the Industrial Section in 1936 began to monitor the fluctuation in economic conditions more closely, and it conducted jointly with the Institute of Pacific Relations a study of the standard of living among municipal and utility workers in Shanghai. The same year it expressed for the first time an interest in effecting regulation of dormitory accommodation for women workers, and terms of apprenticeship for young boys, though little practical action was yet taken in either case.[131] Thus the principal concern of the section in the four years or so of its operation before the Japanese war was the health and safety of workers.

In promoting better conditions in the factories, extensive use was made of techniques that would demonstrate the need for reform, such as the mounting of exhibits in photographic, poster, and model form. From time to time leaflets were distributed to owners and working people outlining the provisions of the Chinese Factory Act with respect to health and safety and the rights of apprentices, among other matters.[132] An active collaboration was pursued with the Bureau of Social Affairs of the Municipality of Greater Shanghai, and with officials of the National Factory Inspection Bureau of the Ministry of Industries in Nanking, and after a time Eleanor Hinder reported that the monthly magazine of the Factory Safety Association, promoted by the Bureau of Social Affairs, drew frequently on information supplied by the council's Industrial Section.[133] The Industrial Section was invited to contribute to the "National Safety First Exhibition" organized by the Kuomintang government in Nanking in January 1936, and it participated in similar exhibitions in Wusih, Hankow, and Shanghai in 1937.[134]

6

Wartime Work

In August 1937 war broke out between China and Japan, and a period of conflict and civil strife began that would continue intermittently until the Communist victory in 1949. In Shanghai, many factories outside the settlement areas closed, cutting off the normal livelihood of thousands of workers. Many streamed into the International Settlement and French Concession in search of a haven from the fighting, as they had done during the Japanese bombardment of 1932. The need to house and feed these people became an immediate concern of settlement authorities.

By the end of 1937 there were 190 temporary refugee camps in the settlement, run by the Municipal Council and by charities, accommodating some 95,000 refugees.[1] Some of these camps were located in public buildings like theaters, schools, banks, and restaurants. Others were in vacant houses, one of which is said to have accommodated two thousand people. Still others were in mat sheds on the roads outside the settlement.[2] Refugees were provided with basic sustenance, but in most of the camps they were in effect interned, severely restricted in their movements. Conditions were often unsanitary in the extreme, and deaths from cholera and other forms of illness were frequent.

Not all those fleeing the hostilities passed through the camps. A few were able to find work in the settlement and could pay the inflated prices now demanded for private accommodation. Many more returned to their villages once the worst of the fighting was over, attempting to escape the shortages of food, fuel, and other supplies. For some, however, whose grasp on life was already tenuous, the disruption caused by the war proved too much to endure. Driven to eat garbage and live out in the open, they succumbed; in 1938, 101,000 corpses were collected from the streets of Shanghai, twenty times the number in 1935, before the war had begun.[3] The situation was the same, or worse, in other Chinese cities.[4]

For Shanghai, the most difficult period was the autumn and winter of 1937; by the spring of 1938 some degree of normality had been restored, and, aided by the neutrality of the International Settlement, the city began to experience a final brief economic resurgence before the Japanese takeover in December 1941. Numbers in the refugee camps dwindled as people left for the countryside or were able once again to find employment.[5]

After mid-1937, therefore, industrial welfare work in the form that it had previously taken became in many areas impossible, and in others much more difficult. Yet new opportunities arose as a different set of demands was placed on those engaged in it. In particular, the Industrial Section of the Shanghai Municipal Council was obliged to become involved in many new types of activity, while the Chinese Industrial Cooperative Movement and the YWCA sought to minister to the needs of people displaced by the war emergency, while at the same time contributing to the war effort.

The SMC Industrial Section

The Second Phase

In the period that effectively began with the outbreak of war between China and Japan in July 1937, the Industrial Section expanded its area of responsibility to embrace a concern for many aspects of the welfare of the urban population, artificially swollen by the new emergency, in addition to its established preoccupation with industrial health and safety. This new work encompassed a concern for refugees, the housing problem, the provision of technical training, and the gathering of statistics. It was consolidated through the formation in October 1940 of the Industrial and Social Division, with separate sections for the promotion of health and safety, technical training, mediation in industrial disputes, the collection of statistics, welfare, and the protection of children. In December 1941 the Japanese occupied the International Settlement. By and large, the long-standing foreign involvement with industrial welfare work in the International Settlement came to an end with the repatriation of foreign civilian refugees from Shanghai in August 1942.

Of particular interest are the Industrial Section's initiatives in the gathering of economic data on working people, the provision of mediation in industrial disputes, and the protection of children.

The Gathering of Economic Data

Upon the collapse of the Nationalist resistance to the Japanese in Shanghai at the end of 1937, many officials of the Chinese municipal government fled inland to Hankow and Chungking, and the Bureau of Social Affairs ceased to function. This posed the prospect of the discontinuation of the flow of information about wages and the cost of living for working people in Shanghai, which had been regularly amassed and published by the bureau since 1930. Whatever had been the shortcomings of these data,[6] it was felt to be undesirable that, at a time of acute inflation and fluctuation in the level of employment because of the war, the Industrial Section should be deprived of any statistical indication of the people's livelihood. Accordingly T. Y. Tsha, who had directed the study for the Chinese municipal government, was engaged jointly by the Industrial Section and the Chinese Statistical Society to carry on his work.[7]

As a result, information as to the cost of living based on an index showing the increase in price of fifty-eight commodities and data on the earnings of workers calculated from wages paid and hours worked in a wide variety of occupations were available until after the Japanese occupation in 1941, though the survey of wages excluded those paid by foreign factories in the settlement.[8] In chapter 1 I briefly discussed the overall trend of earnings and the cost of living. The Industrial Section claimed in 1940 that some firms had come to rely on the cost of living index and on the weekly commodity retail price reports in adjusting wages and providing special inflation bonuses for their workers.[9]

Mediation in Industrial Disputes

It is reported that in 1938, following the withdrawal of the Bureau of Social Affairs, workers began to apply to the Industrial Section for mediation in their disputes with their employers. A mediation service had previously been available through the bureau. In 1938 seven disputes were referred, principally by workers in the tobacco and printing industries, of which in two cases the section was able to effect a compromise sufficiently satisfactory that the workers accepted it.[10] Although the precise nature of the grievance in these two cases is not clear, most disputes at this time revolved about questions of dismissal, short-time working, and reduction of pay attendant upon the destruction of industry caused by hostilities with Japan. In 1939 the section was called upon to mediate in fifty-nine disputes, in twelve of which it was able to prevent strike action from taking place, though no indication is given of the overall number of cases in which the section's intervention resulted in a satisfactory resolution of differences. In this year the conflict was chiefly over wages, because of the steep rise in the cost of living since the previous year. The section began to urge upon workers and management the conclusion of collective agreements to which the Industrial Section was a party, and seven such agreements were signed in 1939. In 1940 the section mediated in one-hundred-and-eleven disputes, the majority of which originated in wage questions, and was able to forestall strike action in fifty-six cases. Collective agreements signed during the year numbered twenty-six, and not only provided for the scale of wages and hours of work but also specified certain fringe benefits and required the prior mediation of the Industrial Section before any industrial dispute could result in a strike or lockout.[11]

As mediation in industrial disputes was an entirely new activity for the Industrial Section, and one that might be the subject of some controversy, the section found it necessary in its 1939 report to the council to justify its intervention in this sphere: "The city is still overcrowded, and for the sake of its general peace and safety disputes should not be allowed to become exacerbated, to continue unnecessarily, or to spread to other industries. Difficulties in operation of plants are already so great that losses from stoppages of work should be reduced to a minimum. Where thousands are still a charge on the charity of the city, workers with work to do should not be permitted to lose their power to earn."[12]

The first step of section officials in attempting mediation was always to establish the pattern of wage progress in a factory to see how it compared with the rise in the cost of living,[13] and it was claimed that where a stoppage had taken place no pressure was brought to bear to "induce workers to resume before they were satisfied that they had obtained the best possible adjustment of their claims."[14] It is apparent, however, that the section's view that workers should not be coerced was not shared by the Municipal Police, by whom an increasing number of disputes were referred for "mediation."[15] It is significant that the section should choose to warn the council in 1940 that "[u]ntil workers may express themselves without fear of loss of employment, it cannot be said that full freedom of workers to act collectively exists."[16]

The Protection of Children

In February 1937 the head of the Industrial Section was made concurrently "Protector of Mui Tsai" in the International Settlement and charged with the responsibility of investigating the extent to which the domestic service performed by these girls constituted a form of slavery. Expansion in this sphere led in due course to a more active concern for other young people exploited in employment or otherwise victimized.

In September 1937 the Industrial Section appointed its first social worker, who proceeded to investigate so far as possible the conditions of employment of *mui tsai* and the existing provision among charitable organizations for disposition of those cases that were brought before the courts. In fact, it was subsequently recognized that it was only really possible to explore cases of abuse brought by the police before the courts, as the First Special District Court was disinclined to view the selling or receiving of young girls into domestic service as constituting in itself an offense.[17]

The investigation into the plight of *mui tsai* raised questions about other aspects of juvenile employment. In 1937 the Engineering Society of China initiated an inquiry into apprenticeship in machine shops; while no published report appears to have been produced, it did result in due course in a scheme according to which engineering establishments offering training that conformed to standards outlined by the society could voluntarily register their apprentices with the Industrial Section.[18] In 1938 the Industrial Section itself carried out a study into the situation of twenty-seven girls under labor contract, temporarily unemployed and housed in a refugee camp; the previous year the section had managed to persuade one major British employer to abandon altogether the use of intermediaries in the hiring of labor.[19] No attempt would be made to proscribe the labor contract system, but these soundings helped to convince the Industrial Section that girls under contract were in need of constant supervision if they were not to be subject to mistreatment.

In the course of 1938 the report on *mui tsai* was completed, and the findings were adopted by the council on December 16. The report recommended the creation of a Child Protection Section appended to the Industrial Section, in recognition of the fact that there were several categories of young people at risk, and that *mui tsai* were only a part of the problem. The report found that "exploited young persons" were:

1. Those in domestic environment—*mui tsai* or *pei' nu*: adopted daughters, daughters-in-law-in-raising, maid servants.
2. Those who are beggars, lost, homeless, abandoned, abducted, who are on the streets and some of whom come to police attention.
3. Those in "amusement" occupations, "girl guides," dancing partners, some of whom are in the control of contractors, girls in houses of prostitution.
4. Those who are employed in industry—girls under labour contract in textile mills and boys, so-called apprentices, who are unpaid workers in small-scale industry.[20]

Ironically, of these four groups it was decided that *mui tsai*, hidden as they were in domestic employment, were the least susceptible to assistance, and the section therefore postponed action on them until conditions were more favorable except in cases of abuse that came to its attention. Upon creation of the Child Protection Section, however, ameliorative work began with the other three groups. The section hired two more social workers, and the services of another were donated by the Shanghai Community Church; henceforth two social workers would attend to juvenile beggars and delinquents, and one each to girls in amusement occupations and young people in industry.[21]

Abandoned or delinquent children coming into the hands of the police were often referred directly to one of the charitable institutions caring for juveniles in Shanghai; where charges were pressed in juvenile cases, representations made by a social worker would often have the same result. The section's social workers attempted to establish a close liaison with children in the institutions, to prepare them where possible for reintegration into society. To this end, many were taught to be hawkers, shoe-menders, street barbers, and the like, and given limited financial assistance with which to establish themselves. Efforts to place delinquent children in industrial employment were only moderately successful.[22] Concern for girls in the "amusement" occupations was principally expressed as assistance to those who had suffered abuse, or to those brought in by the police. The section made a study in 1940 of 68 girls convicted for prostitution, and another of 244 dancing girls. While the condition of the dancing girls was considered to be relatively satisfactory, the nature and extent of prostitution in Shanghai was found to be a cause for grave concern.[23]

On behalf of children in industry, an attempt was made in 1939 to have an experimental "Young Workers' Employment Contract" accepted throughout one industry, that producing miniature lamp bulbs. The contract required that management assume responsibility for paying a young worker a definite wage approved by the section, in addition to providing food and lodging. Hours of work were laid down, and employers were obliged to keep young workers who had no resources even when business was slack. While it had been the intention of the section to regulate ever more closely the employment of juvenile workers in industry, there is little evidence to suggest that even this rather mild form of intervention became widespread. As in the case of other young people, the section seems to have concentrated its energy more on instances of abuse that came to its attention than on taking out the evil by its roots. In all, the section handled 677 cases of disadvantaged children in 1939, and a further 676 cases in 1940.[24]

Other Matters

Other initiatives taken by the Industrial Section in the second phase of its activity related to attempts to improve workers' housing and diet, the provision of technical training, and the ongoing promotion of health and safety in industry.

After decades of the uncontrolled growth of slum housing in Shanghai, the decision of the Municipal Council in 1936, reinforced at a meeting of ratepayers, to appoint a committee to investigate accommodation in the International Settlement was welcomed by many as a major step forward. The resultant Housing Committee lost no time in carrying out its mandate, and its report and recommendations had been submitted to council and adopted with some modifications by the end of June 1937. Among other things, the committee recommended that alterations to buildings should come under close supervision and that partitioning to provide "dovecote" accommodation for workers and conversion of unsuitable housing for industrial purposes be discouraged. It urged the council to encourage the construction of new dwellings in which a single family would occupy a single room, and also the construction of small buildings to be used solely as industrial premises.

It proposed that the provision of "lofts" in future dwellings, into which still more people were usually crammed, should be banned. The report recommended that an ongoing committee should consider means of reducing rent and improving hygiene. Further study was also suggested of possibilities with respect to subsidized public housing, reduced rate assessment for existing housing, cooperation with the Chinese authorities in housing questions, the provision of cheaper and better transportation, and increased wages. It proposed that "excessive population influx" into the settlement be discouraged.[25]

While the report was adopted by the council, its only mandatory provision, that lofts be banned, was rejected on the grounds that poor families were better placed in lofts than they would be on the street. A standing committee was appointed that included the commissioners of health and public works, and Eleanor Hinder from the Industrial Section to advise on the economic and social recommendations.[26] In August, however, hostilities intervened, and no part of the Housing Committee's report was ever put into practice.

Upon the outbreak of war, as noted above, the most urgent necessity facing the settlement authorities was the provision of food and shelter for working people whose homes had been destroyed in fighting that had encroached on settlement territory in places, and for the many thousands of refugees from the Chinese municipality and beyond. Where possible, new jobs needed to be found for those whose livelihood had been forfeited through destruction or closure of their place of work. The council and the various charitable agencies cooperated in the administration of a number of large refugee camps, and in this work the Industrial Section actively participated.

By 1938 there had been a sufficient return to more normal conditions for the section to undertake a study of the accommodation of sixty textile workers, which revealed a dramatic increase in overcrowding as well as in rent paid. The same year a study of "truck" was begun—the extent to which workers were paid in other than a money wage, for example through the provision of food and housing—though there is no indication that this study was ever completed. By 1940 the rise in rents attendant upon the shortage of housing had become an acute problem; although principal tenants were protected by law from the more exceptional demands of their landlords, subtenants were afforded no similar protection from principal tenants.[27] The Industrial Section studied the situation in 1940. Although the council adopted a bylaw on overcrowding in April 1941, the necessary complementary legislation on terms for subletting was not put forward, and no action was taken. Only after the Japanese occupation had taken place did the newly reconstituted council forbid the summary eviction of subtenants, require a license to sublet, and control all rents.[28]

Throughout the war years the section had from time to time expressed distaste for the growing tendency on the part of factory management to house workers in dormitories, officials of the section arguing that this reduced still further the freedom of working people. Apart from offering a six-week discussion course to thirty-six dormitory matrons in 1940 on the subject of how to improve conditions of dormitory life, however, no other initiative was taken on this question.

Because of the wartime emergency, no new research into the diet of workers was undertaken between 1937 and 1940. In the latter year, the section conducted jointly with the Henry Lester Institute of Medical Research a study of the diet and physical condition of 500 women and 200 men working in a textile mill. Recommendations were made for an improved diet and the installation of air conditioning to reduce the incidence of dietary deficiency disease, labor turnover, and absenteeism. Other factories were encouraged to improve the diet of their workers, and some began to provide facilities to enable workers to cook properly the rice they brought with them. Where a *pao fan-ti*, or rice contractor, was responsible for providing a factory with food, efforts were made to contact him in order to explain how the most nutritious food could be supplied for the least money.[29] A promotional film designed to illustrate precisely this was in the process of being made at the time of the outbreak of the Pacific War in December 1941.[30]

In the sphere of technical training, the Industrial Section began in 1939 to build on its earlier experience of offering evening instruction to boiler attendants. That year, a further 243 attendants were given twenty-four hours of instruction in the safe operation of boilers, while the following year another 113 completed a similar course. In 1939, 148 fitters completed a sixty-eight-hour course designed to provide them with a theoretical training to reinforce their existing practical knowledge; their classes were attended by 30 *lao kwei*, more experienced workers who substituted for qualified engineering foremen in many factories. In 1940, 182 fitters and mechanics from machinery manufacturing workshops attended a similar course. The same year, 112 men took a twenty-four-hour course in the safe operation of power presses. The section also attempted to educate the owners of plant and machinery in the principles of safe practice; over the two years, special meetings were convened for the owners of small lamp bulb factories, tanneries, boiler yards, metal polishing shops, cellulose spray paint shops, and plants using power presses, among others.[31]

Although facilities for regular postsecondary school technical education existed in Shanghai by 1940,[32] no opportunity was available to rank-and-file workers with practical technical experience to gain a theoretical understanding of their work other than the ad hoc classes described above. It was therefore decided that a permanent facility for rank-and-file technical education was needed, and in the autumn of 1941 the Industrial Section opened two evening technical schools for adult workers, beginning with mechanics and fitters. Electricians were admitted the following year. The entrance requirements were three years' apprenticeship in the appropriate trade and a passing mark in an examination pitched approximately at the level of completion of primary school. The course was to be of three years' duration; eighty-five students were in attendance at the end of the first year of operation of the schools.[33] It was anticipated that in due course the night primary schools already operated by the council for several years would become feeders for the technical schools.

In the realm of industrial health and safety, after 1937 the section continued with the work it had begun earlier, monitoring accidents and advising and persuading owners of the need for precautionary measures, though without the assistance of Rewi Alley, who left shortly after the outbreak of war to work for Indusco. The section came no nearer to winning acceptance for the principle that the law should require factory owners to pay compensation for death or injury to workers; the Chinese government was neither willing nor able to apply this part of its factory legislation to Chinese firms, while foreign firms sheltered themselves under extraterritorial privilege. The novel suggestion that the Compensation Act of the District of Columbia should apply to American factories in China was neither accepted nor rejected in any finite way (see introduction to this volume). The practice remained for owners to pay some compensation in case of death, but seldom in case of injury. In 1939 the section achieved a small victory when the First Special District Court accepted jurisdiction in one case involving fire risk in industrial premises and two more involving danger from pressure vessels, under provisions of the Law Governing Penalties for Police Offenses.[34] Although the matter would never really be put to the test, the possibility of legal sanctions to reinforce Industrial Section regulations seemed less remote.

YWCA Wartime Work

The sudden outbreak of war between China and Japan in the summer of 1937 took the YWCA movement by surprise, despite the growth of hostility between the two powers. It would seem that here, as elsewhere, the Christian will to peace and accommodation of differences had served to blind the association to the political realities. There is little evidence to suggest that the YWCA had foreseen the immense burden that a commitment to the mass of working people would place on its resources in a time of all-out war, or that it had planned for it in any way, though the association's response under the circumstances showed initiative and courage.

The association's industrial work during the war years had three dimensions to it. In the first place, there was a continuation of the mass education, health, and club work already well established, though now in much reduced circumstances and subject to the physical limitations imposed by the war. Second, the YWCA undertook responsibility for a new range of activities the need for which had been created by the war; these included job creation programs to counter unemployment, the care of refugees, and other relief work among needy families. Third, inspired by the example of the National Christian Council and the Chinese Industrial Cooperative Movement, the YWCA Industrial Department began to sponsor the creation of industrial cooperatives for women.

The Existing Program

On August 13, 1937, the Japanese bombardment of Shanghai began, and as an immediate consequence of this three of the four industrial centers operated by the YWCA there were forced to close.[35] In the remaining center, and in other quarters hastily organized, the Industrial Department did its best to cope with the enormous influx of refugees, and in due course it was able to recommence some of its normal work. Some of the special war emergency work undertaken by the association is outlined below. While it was possible to sustain operations in Shanghai because of the relative immunity of the International Settlement and therefore of the YWCA headquarters from Japanese pressure, the steady advance of Japanese troops in China brought the cessation of industrial work in other cities.

By mid-1938 the association had abandoned its industrial program in Tsinan and Taiyuan, while in Hankow the whole of the YWCA staff were evacuated just before the Japanese occupation. In two cities, Chefoo and Tientsin, the industrial program was pursued for a time after the Japanese had come to be in control, though it is unlikely that the occupation authorities had much sympathy for the association's brand of welfare. In Chefoo work ceased in 1939, while it seems to have disappeared in Tientsin by 1940.[36] On the other hand, as YWCA personnel moved inland with the flow of refugees, so the concept of industrial welfare work reached into areas where it would otherwise most likely not have penetrated. An industrial program had been started in Kunming by 1939,[37] while cooperative experiments were begun in other smaller towns shortly afterward (see below).

By 1940, of all the cities originally having an industrial program, only Shanghai remained, and here there were 701 working women enrolled in classes, and a further 1,283 participating in club activities.[38] On a visit to Shanghai early in 1941, Ruth Woodsmall of the World's YWCA observed of this surviving project, "it was good to find again in the midst of such changed conditions, this centre full of vigorous, and self-respecting young factory workers, so eagerly taking advantage of the social and educational opportunities offered by the YWCA." However, Woodsmall added,

"In connection with the industrial work, it is interesting to note the change in nomenclature. The term 'industrial' is no longer used because this might invite suspicion. 'Social Service' has been substituted."[39]

In December 1941 the outbreak of general war in the Pacific and the Japanese occupation of the International Settlement meant that there was no further possibility of foreigners participating in industrial work in Shanghai. Few records have survived of the work undertaken during the occupation, but it would appear that Shanghai maintained at least a skeleton industrial program throughout the war.[40]

Emergency Measures

As has been noted, the war emergency led the YWCA Industrial Department to undertake work of an extraordinary nature in an attempt to ease the suffering among working people, particularly women. In the earliest phase of the war, this distress was perhaps most acute in Shanghai where the density of the population and the proximity of Japanese artillery made for appalling devastation and loss of life. As Shanghai YWCA Industrial Club girls noted in a letter to their counterparts in the United States, "Our homes are being destroyed; our people are slaughtered; we are living under constant horror and terror of cannon fire, machine gunning and air raids. Some of us have not yet found our family members who became separated from us while escaping from the war zones."[41]

As an immediate response to this situation, the YWCA in the first days of the conflict set up a refugee center at its general headquarters in the International Settlement and assisted the other Christian organizations in establishing and operating another, larger, camp for refugees in the Continental Bank Building, also within the settlement. Here food and shelter were provided for the many working people streaming into the settlement from Chapei, Woosung, and other areas of fighting. On the initiative of the YWCA, a system of "vocational registration" was adopted in these two camps so that the association would have a record of the particular skills and experience of each refugee, many thousands of whom had lost their jobs in mills and factories closed or gutted during the Japanese bombardment. This idea was taken up by a body known as the Citizens' Emergency Committee, which set up a central Vocational Guidance Committee to gather similar information throughout the approximately fifty refugee camps in the city.[42] The object of the registration procedure was to try to use the information obtained to find new jobs for the refugees, and thereby to raise morale.

With Shanghai experiencing a period of economic stagnation so long as the production and exchange of goods continued to be threatened by the fighting, it was difficult to find managers willing to take on additional labor. Even where a limited number of jobs was made available, other problems arose. Eleanor Hinder gives the example of the woman from the western district whose husband prevented her from taking work in a cotton mill in Yangtzepoo for fear of losing her.[43] More generally, Industrial Department personnel found a strong sense of inertia prevailing among women traumatized by the disruption of their daily lives and by personal loss.

In many cases, it was discovered that "deeply ingrained employment methods form almost insuperable obstacles," inhibiting a quick response to the unemployment crisis.

> There were the fourteen little girls who are in the control of a contractor, who has paid a sum to their parents in the country in return for permission to exploit their little labour. A mill refused to employ them, saying that the contractor would turn up sooner or later and take them again. Then again, these refugee workers have been introduced to management, who has accepted them—obviously the only channel for the association workers to use. But habit gives the foremen the privilege of introducing new workers, and they pay him for the job they get! It is natural to find then that many workers have found difficulty with foremen, and have had to leave.[44]

Nonetheless, the YWCA did achieve some success in placing jobless women workers. According to one report, in the first few months of the emergency several hundred women had been found factory work by Cora Deng and her assistant, Helen Chung, most of these individually, but in some cases in groups of from 16 to 60.[45]

As time passed, camp organizers began to appreciate the importance of keeping the refugees busy while waiting for placement or a passage to the countryside, and so set about involving the residents in the maintenance of the camps and in the learning of new handicraft skills. One camp, that on Yu Yuen Road for unemployed women established in December 1937, was described as being like "a big old Chinese family," where tasks such as cooking, cleaning, gate-keeping, teaching, and nursing were divided up according to the interests of the women.[46] When these tasks were complete, the refugees were encouraged to attend classes in the cutting and sewing of garments, the making of paper flowers, embroidery, appliqué, hemstitching, the making of toys and shoes, and knitting. Nearly $2,000 was made from the sale of items produced in this way during the first few weeks, of which 60 percent went as wages and the rest to help pay for food and materials.[47] In time, workers in this camp came to concentrate on the making of garments, shoes, and on knitting, for which work they would be paid $3 to $4 per month.

There was a growing turnover in the camps, particularly as conditions in Shanghai became more settled in the spring of 1938. Refugees either were assisted to join relatives in the countryside or returned to the factories, or in some cases were able to find work using their new handicraft or other skills outside the camps. In all, the YWCA had taken care of some two thousand people, the great majority working women, in its three camps. By the spring of 1938 only one camp remained, where 180 women were still in residence.[48]

Apart from doing "employment" and relief work among the refugees, the Industrial Department of the Shanghai YWCA gave support and encouragement to working women who were already members of the association, and who took it upon themselves to offer their services to the community during the emergency. Some of them wrote of their activities in October 1937:

We have organized a "Women Workers' Service Corps" here in Shanghai. It does the following kinds of work: organising the people who live in a "li"; first aid corps; sewing groups; wall newspaper committees; committees for collecting contributions; teaching children's classes; helping in health and educational work in the refugee camps; getting assistants for nursing soldiers; laundry squads in the Red Cross military hospitals.[49]

Outside Shanghai, the service rendered to refugees took a pattern similar to that already established—the provision of food and shelter, followed by handicraft training and some mass education, and finally an attempt to find employment for the women—though as the war moved inland association personnel were increasingly dealing no longer with industrial workers, but rather with peasants displaced from their land by the ravages of battle. In Sian, for example, the YWCA found many refugees from Honan living in caves and undertook to help them by opening a clinic and starting a spinning project to provide employment. As spinning was by convention a low-paid occupation with wages calculated by piece-work, however, the project ran into difficulty. The women found that they would take three or four days to spin a pound of cotton, which would not bring in enough to pay even for a day's food. The YWCA ultimately decided to overpay the spinners to make it more worth their while to spin than to beg. In this way, 150 families were provided with a steady income.[50]

YWCA Industrial Cooperatives

In light of such difficulties, it is not surprising that the YWCA had for some time been searching for a formula for assistance to working women that would be more nearly self-sustaining. As the focus of the association's attention came to move farther and farther away from the treaty ports, the pattern that came to have the most appeal was that of the "Industrial Cooperative."

The significance of the cooperative experiments should not be underestimated. The cooperatives provided for job training, a guaranteed livelihood, and self-sufficiency within a miniature "planned" economy, while expanding the political consciousness of workers and developing their capacity for responsibility. This was achieved as a result of collective effort with a community, while at the same time the nature of the work, employing raw materials that were cheap and available, and introducing industry to remote areas where hitherto there had been no real substitute for agriculture as a livelihood, served to bridge the gap that had existed between city and countryside. The novelty and ingenuity of the cooperatives as a solution to a number of different problems is by no means less because they were generated as an expedient during the war emergency. They were the last major project undertaken by the industrial reformers in China before the Communists came to power in 1949, only to embody many of the principles to be found in the co-ops in their own cooperative experiments, and subsequently in the communes.

The Chinese Industrial Cooperative (CIC) Movement was begun in August 1938 on the initiative of Rewi Alley and others with the objective of providing immediate relief and work for refugees, while at the same time mobilizing as many people as possible for production geared to the war effort (see chapter 4). By April 1939 the CIC had decided to open a Women's Department, and just prior to this, in March, the YWCA committed itself to the pursuit of the cooperative ideal.[51] The distinction between the CIC program and that of the association was deemed important by the organizers: "It was the policy to cooperate with the Chinese Industrial Co-operative Movement in the way of requesting advice and technical help when needed, but to operate the co-operatives independently so that the YWCA could have its own experiment."[52] Two YWCA secretaries were sent to the CIC headquarters for training in the organization of cooperatives.[53]

By September 1939 the YWCA had started its own first industrial cooperative among refugee women in Chengtu. This co-op, variously described as a tailoring cooperative or a sewing cooperative, brought together sixteen women who, with the aid of a YWCA secretary, borrowed capital from the CIC Movement, rented space from the Chengtu YWCA, and secured a contract to make student uniforms. Within three months, capital was paid up and the project considered a success.[54] Other co-ops followed, until at the height of the movement in 1943 the YWCA had under its sponsorship a total of six cooperatives. Apart from the sewing co-op mentioned, there was also a weaving co-op in Chengtu, an umbrella-making co-op in Kweiyang, a shoemaking co-op in Chungking, a cotton-spinning and weaving co-op in Wusu, and a wool spinning co-op in Penghsien.[55] Proposed cooperative projects under YWCA auspices for Kunming and several other interior cities appear not to have been realized.[56]

The cooperatives under YWCA supervision fell into two categories. On one hand there were those, like the Chungking shoe-making co-op, in which the members lived and ate together in addition to carrying on their production in common. On the other, there were those like the Penghsien wool spinning co-op, in which the members lived and ate at home and only came together to work.[57] A third form of cooperative, described in 1943 as still in the process of being worked out, was that in which members would not only live and eat at home, but also work at home. It was suggested that the outworkers who fashioned the soles at home for the shoe co-op, and who in fact outnumbered the co-op members, could be organized into a co-op of their own instead of being only wage earners paid on piece rate. Again, it was hoped that the number of outworkers participating in the Penghsien wool spinning co-op could be increased. It was felt that this form of cooperative, embracing those women who because they were old or had to attend to household duties could not get away regularly to a central place of work, but who could put in a few hours of labor at home each day, would be particularly suited to China's women.[58] It would appear, however, that the YWCA never reached the point of developing a cooperative exclusively of outworkers.

Common to all the association cooperative experiments was a period of training for co-op members, varying in length from a few weeks to four months.[59] During this time, a skilled worker would be brought in by the YWCA to train the prospective co-op members for their chosen work, whether it be spinning wool, making umbrellas or some other task, while qualified association personnel would also come to instruct the women for part of each day in literacy, arithmetic, hygiene, and the running of a cooperative.[60] The latter was deemed particularly important, as only when the women themselves were able to assume responsibility for running all of their own affairs was the cooperative considered a success. In the case of the Chengtu sewing co-op, which was probably typical, there was a Board of Managers of five, chosen from among the sixteen women members. This board met once a week for a business meeting and once a week with the whole co-op membership for an evaluation meeting at which subjects such as "ways and means," terms of contracts, and conditions of work might be discussed.[61] Action on points raised was left to the Board of Managers, however, and they also had the responsibility for ensuring a supply of raw materials, negotiating contracts, and finding new markets. As with the CIC cooperatives, a cardinal principle was that raw materials should be close by, cheap, and readily available; indeed, these considerations, coupled with an assessment of the potential market, largely determined the nature of the product.[62]

It would appear that some among the YWCA staff saw participation in the cooperatives as "citizenship training" for the women, preparation for democracy in the bourgeois sense.[63] Undoubtedly, however, the effect of the experiment on those who took part was much more far-reaching than this, as even the following rather casual observation will show:

> Two years ago these girls would come to the secretaries and say to them, "Please, the YWCA take it over and be the employer and we shall gladly come to be employees, for it is too much responsibility or too difficult to run the business of a co-op." But now, these same girls have noticeably stopped saying such things but have also become the zealous propagandists in winning people to their convictions. In spite of such difficulties in getting both the capital loan and raw materials, none of these girls shrunk from the least bit of responsibility and hardships. The co-operatives are theirs now, and they are proud of being both the owners and the workers in the co-operative movement.[64]

Throughout their existence, the cooperatives generally and the YWCA cooperatives in particular were faced with a number of problems. These were broadly technical or financial in nature. On the technical side, the dispersal of YWCA personnel during the war meant that there was an inadequate staff trained in industrial matters to deal with the cooperative program.[65]

Furthermore, because of the disruption of normal communications it may be supposed that it was not always possible for the experience gained in one co-op to profit those engaged in trying to create another co-op elsewhere.[66] In setting up a co-op there was always the necessity for the YWCA worker to find raw materials and a market, define a product, raise some capital, and find a worker willing to come, sometimes from a considerable distance, to teach the women the skills necessary to make the product. Even when this was done, there was sometimes a reluctance to accept the co-op idea, particularly among older women.[67] It is also the case that when the last YWCA cooperative was established at Penghsien in 1943, the training program for prospective members lasted four months,[68] in recognition perhaps that a longer period of preparation for self-sufficiency was necessary than had at first been thought.

On the financial side, the major difficulty was always to secure enough capital to enable a supply of the appropriate raw material to be obtained, any necessary tools to be purchased, and possibly to pay both the craft worker and the trainees a small wage during the period of preparation. In the first case, that of the Chengtu sewing co-op, founded in 1939, a capital loan was forthcoming from the Chinese Industrial Cooperative Movement, with each of the participating women putting in a few dollars herself.[69] In the case of the Kweiyang umbrella co-op, founded in 1941, the CIC Movement provided only a third of the required capital, while the YWCA furnished two-thirds.[70] When the Penghsien wool spinning co-op was created in 1943 it was evidently able to secure a capital loan only from the YWCA.[71] Money to pay for the training program in this case was raised by the village fathers and by local officials; extra capital to finance the cooperative once it was a going concern was apparently secured by the issue of shares.[72]

The decline of the Chinese Industrial Cooperative Movement, which may be seen at least in part as a function of its loss of favor in the eyes of the Kuomintang, was a cause for lament among those trying to promote cooperatives in the YWCA. As was observed in the association's annual report on the cooperatives in 1943, "Unless the newly re-organised CIC Promotion Committee will give more aid and financial help for the newly organized co-ops there will be need of the YWCA . . . to provide more technical help as well as financial backing to the individual co-ops that have been organised under the local YWCA auspices."[73] In the event no more help was forthcoming, and it is to the credit of the YWCA that it was able to maintain its cooperative experiment at its existing level for the duration of the war. After 1943, described as a "bad year" for the cooperative movement,[74] no new association cooperatives were formed. At the end of the war, four of the six YWCA co-ops were closed "for various reasons," probably largely financial at a time of dislocation and uncertainty; these were both the weaving and the sewing co-ops in Chengtu, the umbrella coop in Kweiyang, and the cotton spinning and weaving co-op of Wusu. Only two co-ops continued to function, at least until 1947—the Chungking shoe co-op and the wool spinning co-op in Penghsien—and these were kept open for "experimental purposes."[75]

Taken as a whole, the YWCA industrial program during the war represented a continuation of the main strands of work established in peacetime, subject to the compromises imposed by the emergency, as well as development of the new types of work described. This program had been pursued under the direction of Cora Deng and Lily Haass in Shanghai until the spring of 1939, when the former left China for an extended visit to the United States and Europe.[76] Thereafter, it may be supposed that Lily Haass bore much of the responsibility alone until the outbreak of general warfare in the Pacific would have made her position untenable late in 1941.[77] As the main focus of YWCA activity among working women shifted inland, the burden of directing this work passed largely to secretaries in the various local associations, who are for the most part unidentifiable.

For her part, Cora Deng arrived in Geneva on May 31, 1939, after a working tour of the United States, and settled down to a period of study at the International Labour Office.[78] Here, it is likely that she attended seminars on industrial legislation, factory inspection, workers' education, and other subjects, and exchanged information with ILO officials about labor conditions in China.[79] Deng also was able to confer with her association colleagues at the Geneva headquarters of the World's YWCA on industrial and social strategy.[80] Hitler's invasion of Poland apparently cut short Deng's period of study in Geneva, but on the outbreak of war she did not return immediately to China but rather traveled to the United States once more. There she spent some time in New York, completing a master's thesis for New York University in 1941 entitled "The Economic Status of Women in Industry in China, with Special Reference to a Group in Shanghai," for which she drew on her own extensive research and field work. Sometime after this, Deng returned to China, though it is not at all clear that she resumed responsibility for the YWCA's industrial work either in the latter part of the war or in the postwar period. She played a prominent part in the "three-anti" campaign, which took place among the Chinese Christian community in the early 1950s, and continued to live in Shanghai well into the 1980s.[81]

1945–1949

At the end of the Pacific War, the YWCA attempted to rebuild its industrial program. Work was begun in Shanghai and Tientsin and was initiated for the first time in Canton. Mass education, introduced by the association into the interior during the war, was carried on in Chungking, Chengtu, Kunming, and Nanking, though in these cities the constituency was more frequently among handicraft workers. In 1947 the association planned to rehabilitate industrial work in Hankow, Wuchang, Chefoo and Tsinan, and to develop a program in Mukden as soon as possible.[82]

In its tone, however, the new industrial program represented a departure from the more progressive analysis of the mid-1930s, and its objectives were couched in the language of moderation. They were described in the following terms:

1. Education for democracy among industrial women and girls.
2. To help girls learn to meet their own problems; the YWCA does not run "services" for industrial women but tries to help them help themselves.
3. Education of leaders—the population in cities is too large to hope to reach all the girls and women with a club program classes [sic]; hence an effort is made to train leaders among the girls.
4. To help industrial women to learn to take part as active citizens in community life by participating in club activities, learning to think for themselves, planning together, expressing their ideas in public, etc.[83]

The emphasis on the training of "leaders" was different in spirit from this aspect of the program as it had been developing under Cora Deng. A "Labour Welfare Experimenting Station" set up in Shanghai as a joint project of the national and local YWCA Industrial Departments seems primarily to have been concerned with the production of new textbooks for the literacy classes, and with encouraging the revival of reading, drama, and singing as appropriate activities for working women. At a Teachers' Training Institute held in Shanghai in the summer of 1947, courses were offered in history, philosophy, "YWCA methods," industrial work, and education, but "a consideration of the Christian religion occupied quite an important part of the Institute program, because Christianity is the foundation for character building in the club program of the YWCA."[84]

This conservative industrial program had no time to take root, however; the victory of the Communists in 1949 rendered all attempts at gradual reform obsolete. Cora Deng and many others like her remained in China to help build a new society in which many of the social evils that had been ubiquitous for so many years would in due course cease to exist.

The Chinese Industrial Cooperative Movement

The history of the Chinese industrial cooperatives is a subject in itself and has been dealt with more fully elsewhere.[85] It is necessary here only to recall the broad outlines of the Industrial Cooperative movement, and to place the movement in its proper context as the last major piece of "industrial welfare" work undertaken in China before the revolution.

On the outbreak of war with Japan, the rapid occupation of much of the east coast of China brought with it two important consequences: first, much of the modern industrial capacity that might have supplied China's war effort was soon destroyed, in enemy hands, or, if in the treaty ports, cut off from the areas under Chinese control in the interior; second, there was a significant flow of refugees inland, many of whom were peasants, but some of whom brought with them into the interior handicraft skills or a knowledge of modern industry. There were, therefore, a need for both finished goods and human resources available in the form of refugees desperate for employment of one kind or another. It was the genius of those who administered the industrial cooperatives that they were able to organize the resources to meet the need and to guarantee credit, supplies, and markets within the framework of a cooperative system.

Scope of the Movement

During the winter and spring of 1937–38 a small group held meetings in Shanghai to discuss what might be done to solve some of the urgent problems created by the war emergency. The proposal for a network of industrial cooperatives seems to have originated with Rewi Alley, and with Edgar Snow and his wife Nym Wales,[86] though it is clear that J. B. Tayler had been urging experiment on these lines since the beginning of the decade. This time, the idea was taken up by prominent Chinese and by other foreigners, and then put to the government, by now in Hankow, apparently through the good offices of the British ambassador, Sir Archibald Clark

Kerr.[87] The government decided to act on the proposal, and in August 1938 the Chinese Industrial Cooperative Association was established as an official body responsible directly to the Executive Yuan, whose President was H. H. Kung.[88]

In the beginning, the organizers of the movement hoped to create some 10,000 industrial cooperatives in its first full operating year, May 1939 to May 1940, and a further 20,000 cooperatives in the next year to May 1941.[89] These targets were not reached, and by May 1940 there were in fact 1,810 cooperatives, though they contained "24,000 members in sixteen provinces spread from Lanchow in the north-west to the outskirts of Canton in the southeast."[90] This shortfall was not for want of effort on the part of the organizers, many of whom worked extremely long hours under very difficult conditions to promote the spread of the movement, but rather was due in large part to the scarcity of capital.

Initially, the government had promised capital support of $5 million Chinese for the movement and had agreed also to pay the association's promotional expenses.[91] A report on the movement written early in its history, however, shows that with 800 cooperatives established, the rate of capital investment was such that $15 million, and not $5 million, would be required for the first 10,000.[92] While the proportion of local capital invested naturally increased as the co-ops became successful and members plowed back their profits into them, the restricted initial availability of capital would certainly have been a constraint on growth. Many societies apparently sought loans from the banks to improve their position. Nonetheless, the performance of those societies that had been formed was impressive: the total value of production by all the co-ops was said by May 1940 to be $7 million per month.[93]

A second sum of $5 million was given to the association by the government in 1940, but this was to be used to promote marketing and supply agencies that were being set up by existing federations of cooperatives.[94] While new co-ops continued to be created, it is apparent that expansion proceeded at a slower pace after 1940, and the movement became more dependent on financial assistance from overseas channeled through the International Committee for Indusco in Hong Kong, and later in New York. In 1943 the Chinese Industrial Cooperative Association became the Association for the Advancement of Chinese Industrial Cooperatives, and some administrative reorganization occurred. While this was done "to make it clear to everyone that Indusco itself was only a promotional agency and that its job was the creation of a genuine co-operative movement of federated societies,"[95] it was symptomatic of a gradual official disengagement from the movement, a consequence of growing fear on the part of some members of the government that there were revolutionary implications that had not been foreseen.

Structure and Function

That the Industrial Cooperative Movement was destined to do more than fill an immediate need for supplies and provide a livelihood for refugees is apparent from the manner of its organization, which was designed "to ensure that the maximum amount of responsibility for production was borne by the maximum number of people"; the movement was committed to an education much broader than offered to ordinary people hitherto, which would "ensure that the utmost was made of the creative potential in the Chinese peasant and refugee worker." It challenged the existing pattern of economic development in China in the twentieth century, which had served to further widen the gap between city and countryside. Rewi Alley has remarked, "Seeing the failure of centralised coastal industry to bring anything but famine to the interior, and misery to industrial workers on the coast [it was intended] to start a movement that would carry on into post war years and assist in the necessary integration of the agricultural and the pastoral with the industrial."[96]

The initiative in the formation of an industrial cooperative in a given area was usually taken by a trained association organizer, who would go into a district and try "to bring together groups of workers who were prepared to follow Indusco's lead and manage their societies in accordance with the model rules, which embodied the rules necessary for co-operative administration." The cooperatives usually contained between seven and thirty members, the average being about fifteen, and the particular function of each depended upon the skills of the participants and the organizer's assessment of local needs and the resources available to meet them.[97]

The activities undertaken were diverse. They included small-scale mining and iron smelting, the production of machine tools and equipment for light industries, bamboo paper-making, tanning, soap-making and candle-making, dyeing, the making of leather goods, fur-dressing and fur garment-making, brick-making and tile-making, the manufacture of pottery and glass, flour-milling, rice-hulling, oil pressing and ginning, and in textiles weaving and the manufacture of garments and other items in both wool and cotton. More than half of the co-ops were concerned with the production of textiles in one form or another, and in North China especially much effort was put into fulfilling a series of orders for blankets for the army.[98] There were also transport cooperatives and "labor" co-ops that contracted out their labor.[99]

Each co-op chose a manager, either from among its own members or, if no one suitable was available, a candidate put forward by the organizer. The manager oversaw the technical functions of the co-op from day to day and was usually a member of the Board of Directors, whose responsibility was to ensure that business was conducted "efficiently and cooperatively" and "subject to the general principles and policies laid down by the General Meeting." The chairman of the Board of Directors represented the cooperative in its dealings with outsiders. There was additionally a Supervisory Committee, whose job it was to make sure that the accounts were properly audited, and which generally kept watch over the work of the Board of Directors. Each of these bodies was elected by, and responsible to, the General Meeting of all the cooperative members, which had supreme authority. The General Meeting was convened when necessary to approve the admission of new members, occasionally to expel members, to fix salaries and wages to be paid, and at the end of the year to divide up the profits.[100]

This last function was of considerable importance to the cooperative life of the society. Every member held at least some shares in his society, and when the annual interest on these had been deducted, along with an allowance for depreciation on equipment, the remainder of the year's surplus was divided according to a scale fixed by association headquarters. Of the net profit, 20 percent went to the co-op's Reserve Fund, 10 percent to the Common Good Fund to provide for educational and welfare facilities, 10 percent to directors and hired staff who did not share in the bonus on wages, 10 percent to the local Industrial Cooperative Development Fund or to the local federation, and the remaining 50 percent to members and nonmember workers as a bonus on wages. Of this last amount, two-fifths was to be taken in shares by members, or paid by nonmembers to the Industrial Cooperative Development Fund. Throughout the year workers received wages similar to or slightly higher than those prevailing in local industries, and the principle of equal pay for equal work was observed between members and nonmembers. Each co-op was permitted to hire a limited number of nonmember workers to assist with production, usually on a temporary basis.[101]

As individual units, the cooperatives remained vulnerable, both materially and psychologically. As J. B. Tayler was to remark, "The greatest single step in the developing of the co-operatives is to unite them locally in federations. If this is done successfully it makes them realise that they belong to something bigger than their own society."[102]

The federations were formed either by industry or by locality, and as they grew in both scope and confidence it was intended that they take over from association organizers most promotional work, the arranging of credit, inspection, audit, experiment, and training, and from their member cooperatives the negotiation of supplies and markets.[103] By the end of 1943, however, it would appear that most technical assistance was still provided by staff from association headquarters.[104] It was further hoped that provincial, regional, and national federations might develop, but these seem not to have materialized because of the increasing "difficulties, delays, and expense of travel" in China in the last years of the war.

Education and Training

The preparation of a new generation of skilled and capable workers was an essential part of Industrial Cooperative Movement activity. Central to this educational effort was the network of "Bailie schools" established wherever there were cooperatives. These schools, which had their origin in the experimental work of Joseph Bailie at his Institute of Technical Training in the early 1930s, took promising apprentices, members of cooperative families, and other young men and gave them two years of technical and scientific training with a view to making them technicians, foremen, and local leaders in the cooperative movement. The program combined practical work and academic study with group activity. It was "meant to open the boys' minds to understand the bases and trends of modern industrial development and at the same time to accustom them, through team activities and by sharing in responsibility for the conduct of the kitchen and general ordering and discipline of school life, to the co-operative way of doing things."[105]

The Bailie schools, promoted particularly by Rewi Alley, continued to operate for some time after the war. While the Bailie schools were preparing a new generation of cooperators, existing cooperative members also had to be catered to. Where necessary, vocational training was given when a cooperative was first set up to enable men and women to learn the arts of spinning and weaving and other processes of manufacture, often using new techniques brought in from outside.[106] Evening classes were arranged over a period of two or three weeks for several neighboring cooperatives if it was felt necessary to elaborate on aspects of cooperative practice, or to explain scientific principles underlying part of the members' work.[107] Special evening classes were sometimes provided to enable members to pursue a technical subject more systematically. For all of this training, as well as for the instruction of committee men and ministering to the needs of groups like juvenile workers and women, the association organizers, and later to some extent the federations, were responsible.

It was essential, therefore, that the organizers themselves be well trained. In the early days experience in the field was the main teacher for movement officials, but by the end of 1940 a program of courses had been developed that was of three months' duration and was offered at each of the association's regional headquarters. Candidates usually had a middle school education. After completing the program and working in the field for a time, organizers were often brought together again for a two- or three-week refresher course.[108]

In the autumn of 1940 the universities, beginning with the University of Nanking at Chengtu, began to offer higher training courses for Indusco organizers, apparently of six months' or twelve months' duration.[109] It had been thought that it might be possible to organize a full-fledged "CIC Institute" as a focal point for research into technical innovation for small-scale industry, and for organizational training, but this hope was apparently not realized, probably for lack of funds. At a lower level, every depot of Indusco reinforced the educational work of local organizers by offering classes to prospective accountants, directors, supervisors and managers.[110] Weekly conferences and discussions were held at many depots, and some may have experimented with correspondence courses.[111]

Practical Problems

The Industrial Cooperative Movement was not without its problems. The difficulty encountered in finding capital funds for the cooperative has been noted. Particularly as inflation came to have a firm grip on the Chinese economy after 1940, expansion of the network was quite significantly disturbed, and emphasis was placed on the formation of federations of existing co-ops, and on the development of ancillary services. Attempts by some staff to start noncooperative businesses as a means of financing promotional expenses of the co-ops "entirely failed in their purpose."[112]

Again, there was a tendency to neglect the educational features of the movement, on which experience had shown its success ultimately depended. Workers might go through the motions of cooperative management of their enterprise while in fact showing little initiative because they had not yet come to think of it as theirs. Managers who had gained their training in small private industries often continued to show evidence of the "*laopan* psychology" and treated their workers as inferiors. As a cooperative's production usually met an urgent local need, there was sometimes a conspiracy of silence about its less tangible deficiencies. In the long run, however, progressive education and involvement of the co-op members paid off, and it was found that "the truly co-operative is also the stablest and least vulnerable."[113]

Furthermore, it is apparent that there were both deviations from official policy by some members of association staff, and opposition to the movement from individuals outside it who disliked the direction in which it was going.[114] It may be supposed that as with any significant movement there were some who sought to use it to enhance their personal power and prestige. Also, apart from fulfilling its immediate function of meeting wartime needs, the Industrial Cooperative Movement constituted a new and relatively independent force in the economic life of China whose postwar impact was impossible to predict, and it could have been expected that it should arouse the suspicion and even the hostility of industrialists and others whose interests were tied to the existing economic and social order. This suspicion was in time shared by the government, whose commitment to the movement wavered and virtually ceased in the later years of the war. J. B. Tayler noted in 1945 that "work was much easier and more successful in those provinces in which the authorities were favourably disposed."[115]

Writing during the war of the possibilities and limitations of the industrial cooperatives, Tayler concluded that their continued success depended on three things: "first, technical development so that small-scale processes can be improved sufficiently to compete in the interior with the products of large-scale industries . . . ; second, federation, which will give them the advantages of large-scale purchase and of large-scale marketing facilities; third, sound finance." He further warned that "[w]hile the co-operative movement is non-political and when started right can carry on by itself without government aid, it does need satisfactory enabling legislation and freedom to operate. Any compulsory system or attempt to bring it under state regimentation will mean its death as a movement, although its shell may continue as an expensive government bureaucracy."[116]

Rewi Alley, writing in 1943, expressed the view that postwar success was assured if "(a) the movement side is permitted; (b) co-operative loans are available; (c) technical advance is made, and cooperative training is carried on; [and] (d) machinery for the village co-op is made available from abroad for copying and for use." In particular, Alley felt that there was room for expansion in the development of small-scale mining, and for the extension of Indusco into areas it had not yet penetrated, such as Kansu and Sinkiang, the region around the Burma Road, and, after the war, Manchuria. Cooperative work might also have been initiated among the tribal and other minority people of China. Alley also urged that industrial cooperatives be established and supported behind Japanese lines in territory controlled by Communist guerrillas, in order to "assist them to maintain themselves, and to turn the flow of essential raw material away from the Japanese."[117]

The Co-ops in Perspective

Summing up his experience of the Chinese Industrial Cooperative Movement and other cooperative ventures, J. B. Tayler wrote toward the end of the war that cooperatives were "more ethical and therefore more Christian than capitalistic enterprises." This was so because they "eliminate the practice of a few profiting from the many, . . . organise collective economic action but retain the principle that the individual is the chief ethical end, . . . inspire individual initiative but direct it into serving the larger group, . . . [and] require education of members in the very nature of the case because of their democratic principle of operation. . . . Contrast this with the trend of modern industry towards autocracy, an enlightened autocracy perhaps, but emphatically not a manifestation of control from below."[118]

The Industrial Cooperative Movement must be seen in the context of the whole industrial welfare effort of the previous two decades. It was an emanation of this effort in that it was originally conceived and nurtured by individuals who had gained their experience trying to cope with the enormous social consequences of the coming of modern capitalist industry to China—Rewi Alley in the SMC Industrial Section, Tayler in the NCC Industrial Commission, Cora Deng and Eleanor Hinder and others in the YWCA—and also because it built on the accumulated experience of two decades, was in a definite sense a culmination of the effort put forth, and represented a groping toward a solution that more nearly approximated what was needed in China. Indeed although cooperatives were not communes, in scope or in structure, they were closer to them in spirit than were the squalid factories of the treaty ports with which industrial welfare work had begun in China in the early 1920s. The cooperative experiment had opened the way to a new mode of industrial production, and therefore of modernization for China, according to which the distinctions between city and countryside, master and servant, might gradually disappear. Whether such a transition could continue to be achieved gradually or peacefully is a question that cannot be considered here.

7

China and the International
Labour Organization

At the Washington Conference of 1919, the major powers established the International Labour Organization under the League of Nations to monitor and promote improvement of labor standards throughout the world. In practice, the organization proved for many years to be Eurocentric in its approach to labor issues, and it frequently neglected to promote better standards for labor in countries that were far away from Europe and about which its officials knew little. Indeed, it had been recognized that in the case of those territories where "climatic conditions, the imperfect development of industrial organizations, or other special circumstances make the industrial conditions substantially different,"[1] it would be necessary to modify the expectation that specific objectives could be quickly realized, in terms of either uniform standards of labor legislation or ratification and application of the Draft Conventions of the ILO.

In China, significant obstacles stood in the way of enforcement of modern industrial legislation, principally the vastness of the country, the absence of tariff autonomy, the existence of foreign settlements with extraterritorial privileges, and the absence of any previous experience of factory inspection.[2] For this reason, although China was nominally a member of the ILO from its inception, there was little pressure on the Peking government in the early years to induce it to comply with the standards being worked out in Geneva. Most modern factories in China were in territory outside either the jurisdiction or the effective control of that government, and the ILO seemed satisfied for the short term at least with official statements of intent, made formal by the enactment of the Provisional Factory Regulations of 1923 (see below).

By the mid-1920s this attitude had begun to change. There was a growing apprehension in Europe over the effect that an influx of goods made with cheap labor in the East might have on existing European patterns of manufacture and trade. The implications of this for employment in Britain were made much of in Parliament in 1925 by advocates of the reform of child labor in Shanghai, a campaign that the ILO watched with interest. The organization became increasingly anxious at the rapid growth of radical trade union activity in China after the summer of 1925, reflecting the concern of its principal member governments. It was no longer felt to be satisfactory that the ILO should have only second-hand information about labor conditions in China, and accordingly the organization set about rectifying this situation in two ways: it began to send officials to China on short fact-finding missions, and occasionally to offer advice to the local authorities on questions pertaining to labor legislation. In 1930 it established in China a local office of the ILO to gather information and to promote the objectives of the organization.[3]

Special Missions

Pierre Henry

The first ILO official to arrive in China was Pierre Henry, who landed in Shanghai in September 1924 with a broad mandate to explore industrial conditions, and in particular to see what progress had been made by the campaign to restrict the use of child labor in Shanghai factories. A middle-level bureaucrat within the ILO, with little if any experience outside Europe, Henry was surprised to find that the organization was not regarded with universal favor in China; indeed, the head of the Labor Department of the Canton government went so far as to say that in his view it was at the beck and call of the imperial powers, and that its influence in the country could only be for ill.[4]

Henry spent three months in China, visiting Shanghai, Tsingtao, Chefoo, Tientsin, Peking, Nanking, Chungking, Canton, and Hong Kong. In each center he met representative local employers, officials, academics, and other dignitaries, and he toured both traditional and modern factories.[5] In planning and executing his itinerary, he owed much to the assistance of the YM and YWCA, whose executives seemed able to effect introductions to the highest levels of government with comparative ease. At the other end of the social scale, Henry apparently made contact with the workers themselves on only one occasion, when he was invited to speak to a gathering of workers at a Nanyang Brothers tobacco factory. Here Henry found that he was in a difficult position as the emissary of an organization that claimed to represent workers' interests. Faced with the sanguine declarations of other speakers with whom he shared a platform, Henry hastened to make it clear to his audience that while the ILO could assist them with information about labor conditions in other countries, it could in no circumstances contemplate giving its support to revolution.[6]

In his report to Geneva, Henry submitted an account of the actual conditions he had witnessed which was professional and without bias,[7] but in interpreting this material his tendency to identify with the interests and explanations of the factory owners becomes apparent. He found it took "four Chinese to do the work of one white," confirming claims made to him by employers in this respect. Although wages were low, he found there was a certain natural justice in the fact that in the silk industry four Chinese workers would earn between them almost as much per week as a single worker would be paid in England for similar work. He was persuaded that industry as a whole in the treaty ports was only marginally profitable and could only be kept going because factories paid little or no tax, transport costs were low, and the Chinese market was content with a coarser grade of product. Not unexpectedly, Henry reported that there was no effective legislation governing conditions of labor in China. He echoed the belief universally shared among foreigners resident there that in general conditions were better in modern factories and that salaries were uniformly higher in foreign-owned enterprises, a view never documented in any comprehensive way. In spite of this, workers in modern industry seemed to be less happy than their counterparts in the older establishments: "les ouvriers les plus joyeux qu'il m'avait été donné de rencontrer étaient ceux des usines les plus miserables d'aspect intérieur et extérieur. Il me semble que dans un atelier propre, bien éclairé, même si c'est un de ses compatriots qui le dirige, l'ouvrier chinois se trouve en dehors de son élément. Je m'excuse de la brutalité de cette supposition mais je ne crois pas devoir la passer sous silence." This preference for the older style of workshop Henry attributed to the fact that a less rigorous discipline was usually in force, and that relations with the employer were often more cordial. In a modern factory, Henry reasoned, whether or not the old traditions of paternalism had been retained, an employer was obliged to exact more return because of the financial sacrifice he had made; in this connection it was necessary to educate workers, though their attitude could be expected to change only slowly.

In one passage above all in his report, Henry conveys his impression of the mentality of Chinese workers and at the same time dispels any doubt about his own position:

> Enfin, un Asiatique n'est en général pas accessible aux sentiments de reconnaissance. Ceci vient en partie de l'influence de Confucius. . . . Un ouvrier chinois de Pékin ne pourra donc acceuillir qu'avec méfiance toute tentative faite par son employeur ou par toute autre personne pour améliorer son sort, s'ils n'appartient pas à sa famille ou ne sonts pas originaires de sa province natale. Ceci est vrai 'a fortiori' en ce qui concerne les étrangers. Cet ouvrier croira a un marché qui lui est offert, même si l'on n'exige rien en retour, et tâchera d'en tirer le maximum d'avantages possible, sans aucune consideration pour les sentiments qui ont inspiré l'acte de générosité, ou en parfaite ignorance de ceux-ci. Un patron—qu'il soit chinois ou européen—qui commetrait la faiblesse de donner un secours à un de ses ouvriers momentanément dans la gêne, non seulement l'aurait à sa charge, lui et sa famille, toute sa vie durant, mais encore serait obligé de fermer son usine devant les reclamations des autres ouvriers demandant un traitement analogue.

Henry goes on to ask rhetorically if there was any "duty of humanity" toward Chinese workers, whether their hopes and expectations ought to be raised when there was so little chance of their being fulfilled, and admits having left China without having reached any definite conclusion. If, however, Chinese labor were ever to become by its cheapness a threat to Western labor, then Henry took the view that there ought to be no further hesitation over a decision to intervene. His report finally recommended the gradual introduction of certain improvements in Chinese industry, such as the elimination of women and children from night work, reduction of hours, an increase in wages, and better safety precautions, but it held out little hope that any of these could be achieved without an end to the existing political turmoil in China.[8]

Six months after Henry left China, circumstances conspired to defeat the campaign for legislation to control child labor in Shanghai. In the last half of 1925 and throughout 1926, Henry made repeated attempts to have the ILO send him back to China, and he even sought in vain to obtain funds from the Rockefeller Foundation to enable him to go.[9] Apparently he felt that if he were present he might be able to push the movement to protect child labor forward. Reformers in Shanghai tried to discourage him, however, pointing out that in light of the prevailing strength of national sentiment, a second visit would be inopportune. It would seem that by December 1926 the ILO had definitely decided not to allow Henry to return to China.[10]

William Caldwell and Albert Thomas

In 1927 the ILO official William Caldwell passed through the Far East on his way to Australia and New Zealand, and in July he attended the second conference of the Institute of Pacific Relations in Honolulu, where he hoped among other things to learn something of the progress of organized labor in China. Caldwell recorded, however, that "there seemed to be practically no one present who was really familiar with the Chinese workers' movement or their actual working conditions."[11] His schedule did not permit him to stay in China and undertake an investigation himself.

In late 1928 Albert Thomas, the director of the ILO, himself embarked on a tour of the principal countries of the Far East, during which he twice visited China, in November–December 1928 and in early January 1929, spending a total of just over three weeks there. The scope for investigation in such a short time was necessarily very limited, and Thomas's itinerary took him only to Shanghai, Nanking, and Peking, but it is clear that his perception of what he saw was more acute than that of Henry.

Thomas noted with disapproval the juxtaposition of extreme wealth and extreme poverty in Shanghai. He was disturbed also by the almost complete disappearance of the independent labor movement brought about by the Kuomintang under the pretext of the need to extirpate Communists, and he took it upon himself to warn government officials that harmony between labor and capital achieved at the expense of the proscription of the labor movement was no harmony at all. Thomas was not without his contradictions, however, and his aloofness must have been trying to those who sought to make his brief stay in China as complete an experience as possible. "J'apprends avec quelque surprise que l'on a voulu me réunir confusement non seulement les experts, mais aussi les ouvriers et les patrons. . . . C'est devenu une sorte de réunion publique au lieu de la réunion de travail que j'attendais."[12] On no other occasion was a director of the ILO to tread on Chinese soil.

Camille Pone and Adelaide Anderson

In 1931 the ILO sponsored a mission to China that looked for once as if it might bear some fruit. This was the mission of Camille Pone, an ILO expert in labor legislation, and Dame Adelaide Anderson, former chief lady inspector of factories in the United Kingdom. Two years earlier the Kuomintang had made public its proposed new set of factory laws, and the invitation now came to the organization directly from H. H. Kung to send a mission to advise on the implementation of factory inspection.[13] In the interim, the ILO had established its branch office in China. It was expected that Pone and Anderson would stay in China for some months.

The Factory Inspection Act, which was to have become effective on October 31, 1931, provided that each province and municipality should establish with its own resources a factory inspectorate, and that while there would be initially no central inspectorate, the Nanking government would be responsible for the training and appointment of inspectors. By the time the ILO mission arrived in China in the autumn of 1931, a plan had already been drawn up for a three-month study course for potential inspectors, to be given by officials who had some training abroad.[14] Subject matter ranged from accident prevention and industrial hygiene to statistics and the principles of Sun Yat-sen. It was agreed that Pone and Anderson should investigate industrial conditions at first hand before recommending what other steps should be taken to implement inspection. They would concern themselves in particular with Shanghai, where the dispute over jurisdiction with respect to proposed factory inspection between the Chinese authorities of the Municipality of Greater Shanghai and the foreign Municipal Council of the International Settlement was approaching an impasse.

Further study of the Factory Law and the Factory Inspection Law convinced the two experts that the legislation attempted to solve at a stroke problems that had not been overcome elsewhere except by a slow process of evolution. The experience of visiting Chinese factories, in Anderson's case for the second time, confirmed the mission's impression that it would only be possible to proceed "à une application progressive, par degrés, des différentes catégories de dispositions de la loi."[15] They therefore recommended that Chinese factory inspectors should begin by taking measures to induce limited compliance with the law, specifically suggesting that they get in touch with managers in their districts to give them employee registers and acquaint them with the law, that they endeavor to promote health and safety in the factories, and that they investigate all industrial accidents and see that children were removed from dangerous work. Later, they could begin to enforce the provisions for a weekly day of rest, breaks from work, and holidays, and start collecting information which would be of use when the other sections of the Factory Act came to be implemented. For the time being, the exclusion of children from the factories was not considered a practical proposition.[16] With respect to jurisdiction over factory inspection in Shanghai, Pone and Anderson were quick to realize the need for a uniform application of the law in all parts of the city, and they expressed the hope that this could ultimately be achieved by means of a single service of inspection and machinery of enforcement. In the meanwhile, however, they were able shortly before leaving China to effect a compromise between the Chinese and foreign authorities, according to which Chinese-trained inspectors under the control of the central government at Nanking would operate in the International Settlement and the French Concession, reporting regularly both to the authorities of the foreign concessions and to the Chinese government, but referring any cases for legal enforcement in the foreign concessions to the authorities of those concessions.[17] It was hoped that the threat of legal sanctions would be enough to induce compliance with the law before any referral was necessary. In Chinese territory, the law would be enforced in the normal way.

Unfortunately the agreement over Shanghai broke down not long after the ILO mission had left China, and the shadow of this failure was thrown across the path of the application of all factory law. When the ILO inquired in 1933 as to when some of the provisions of the Factory Act might be implemented, the minister for industries, K. P. Chen, blamed the obstinacy of the foreigners at Shanghai for the lack of progress. "Selon lui, s'il n'y avait pas cette controverse avec les autorités des concessions les choses seraient beaucoup plus avancées."[18] Nor is it possible, taking the longer view, to agree with the contemporary observer Augusta Wagner that the Pone/Anderson mission made a positive contribution to the progress of factory inspection in China simply by insisting on the principle of gradual enforcement. Wagner concedes that the "Program for the Enforcement of Factory Inspection," introduced by the government in 1934 to provide for application of the Factory Act in five stages, which she offers as evidence of the influence of the ILO mission, did not bring about implementation of the earliest stages of enforcement by the outbreak of the Sino-Japanese War in 1937.[19]

François Maurette, Mack Eastman, and Alfred Butler

In the middle and late 1930s, several more special missions to China by ILO officials based in Geneva were either undertaken or proposed. In 1934 Francois Maurette, an assistant director of the ILO, spent three weeks in China in March during a mission to China and Japan to advise on primary and professional education. Although the mission was not strictly speaking on behalf of the ILO, it was planned that Maurette should take the opportunity to meet people concerned with labor questions. To his disappointment, he found that no progress had been made on the issue of factory inspection since the visit of Pone and Anderson three years earlier, and he expressed himself in agreement with other experts in calling for gradual progress.[20] Maurette was also mandated to explore discreetly the operation of the ILO's branch in China and the resignation of its head, C. S. Chan, later in the year may not have been unconnected with his visit.

In the summer of 1936 another official from Geneva, Mack Eastman, spent three months in China and Japan. Although no record remains of his itinerary, it would seem that Eastman's main objective in going to China was to promote the implementation of factory inspection.[21] In 1937 preparations had reached an advanced stage for a visit to China by the director of the ILO, Alfred Butler. It was proposed that Butler should spend three weeks in China visiting factories and meeting government officials, employers, and workers' groups. In particular it was hoped that he might be able to break the deadlock over factory inspection in the International Settlement in Shanghai.[22] The outbreak of hostilities with Japan in the summer intervened, however, and the trip did not take place.[23] There were to be no further special missions to China before the outbreak of general war in Europe, when operations were so disrupted that the ILO was obliged to move its headquarters from Geneva to Montreal for the duration.

The ILO in China

The China Bureau under C. S. Chan, 1930–34

In the 1920s the possibility was raised from time to time in Geneva that the ILO might establish an office in China to facilitate the passage of information about labor conditions and standards in both directions. Such an office had been opened in Japan in 1923, and the prospects for a similar branch in China were undoubtedly discussed by Pierre Henry during his visit there in 1924. The issue was brought up again in 1926, although those most informed about industrial conditions in China felt at that time that the creation of a voluntary organization, similar to the Association for Labour Legislation in Britain, would be an initiative more suited to China's needs, particularly in light of the probable hostility of the labor movement toward the ILO.[24] After further consideration and a resolution of the immediate political uncertainty, a "China bureau" of the ILO was inaugurated in the summer of 1930 under the direction of the French-educated former diplomat, C. S. Chan. The bureau had its headquarters at Nanking and a branch office in Shanghai.

Chan saw the functions of the China bureau as threefold: the gathering of information, maintenance of ongoing relations with organizations and individuals, and dissemination of information about the ILO and about labor standards, or what he termed "propaganda" work. On the first score, the promotion of "intelligence gathering," Chan claimed in a review at the end of his period of tenure in 1934 to have had a certain, albeit limited, success. In the beginning, major obstacles had stood in the way of this work, in particular the scarcity of government statistics and the reluctance of the press to discuss labor questions because of "le cauchemar des menaces communistes," but in time the proliferation of enquiries, both official and private, into such questions as conditions, wages, and the cost of living had rendered the task easier, and monthly reports had been submitted to Geneva conforming to a prescribed pattern from the summer of 1933. A press-cutting service was also initiated by the China bureau, to record anything of value in the Chinese press. From time to time it would seem that the bureau attempted to collate the results of research undertaken by other agencies, and "special reports" would then be presented to Geneva, each on a certain theme. Two such reports submitted in 1933 dealt with "the cost of living of Chinese workers" and "salaries and the length of work," while two others in preparation at the time of Chan's departure in 1934 dealt with "labor disputes" and "handicrafts." It had always been the hope of officials at headquarters that the China bureau would itself ultimately be able to coordinate the main efforts at scientific research into labor conditions in China, and on this Chan had to admit that little progress had been made. "La question mérite d'etre examinée. Mais pour y trouver une solution satisfaisante, il faudrait des éléments de travail et des conditions de succès que je n'ai pas à discuter ici." In fact Chan had failed to take the initiative on this matter, and it was in the event even less likely to be taken by Chan's successor.

It was in the area of relations with other institutions and individuals that Chan felt the greatest gains had been made during his term of office. If his report is to be believed, "excellent" relations had by 1934 been established with government departments, which regularly sought the advice of the China bureau—the Labor Department of the Ministry of Industries even on one occasion having urged the bureau to intercede on its behalf with superior organs of government, with employers, whom it had helped to organize an institute for scientific management and with whom it had collaborated on a study of the applicability of the Factory Act, with workers, who had "warmly welcomed" its intervention, with students, private welfare agencies, diplomats, journalists, and others. Speaking at one university, Chan was apparently able so to impress his audience with his account of the work of the ILO that, from having been initially hostile to him, they later implored him to become dean of their Faculty of Social Studies. Among all these groups, Chan claimed, the China bureau had made firm friends, while the number of people who regarded the ILO as an agent of Western imperialism had significantly decreased.

On the basis of this success, it was maintained, the job of disseminating information became easier. As of October 1931 the China bureau published a monthly bulletin in Chinese," "International Labour Information," from 1934 "International Labour," which contained news, articles, and translations of ILO and other documents, and which circulated chiefly among government agencies and academic institutions. The production of this bulletin was claimed to take up much of the time of Chan and his staff, but was felt to be the surest method of making the objectives of the organization better known. It was supplemented from time to time by other published items in Chinese, such as "The ILO and Its Relations with China," a propaganda brochure produced in 1930 and revised in 1934, and a compendium of the Conventions and Recommendations of the ILO to date, also released in 1934. Further items were to appear later. Chan also regarded public lectures as an important propaganda technique, as will be apparent from the incident noted above, and was especially concerned to win over the intellectual youth to the cause of labor reform.[25]

Not surprisingly, Chan's review of his period in office does not consider at any length those factors that rendered the work of the China bureau less effective. That the bureau in gathering information relied so heavily on government surveys and even more casual sources rather than on first-hand investigation meant that the reports it sent back to Geneva were often patently inaccurate, incomplete, and internally inconsistent. These deficiencies were not lost on officials at Geneva, who sometimes seemed to despair of getting any reliable information from their branch in China. Typically, with respect to a report entitled "Summary of an Official Enquiry on Working and Living Conditions and on the Situation of Industry in China," submitted December 22, 1930, officials in Geneva noted that no information was given on the method of inquiry that gave rise to the statistics, and that in some cases the figures appeared "paradoxical." Terms such as "average family," and "average income" were not defined.[26]

Furthermore, it would appear that this lack of accurate statistical evidence was not in any large measure compensated for by experience gained from direct contact with the labor movement; such contact was of necessity limited and became if anything more so. Chan noted that it was necessary to be "prudent" and "circumspect" in the conduct of relations with the unions because the Kuomintang was jealous of its control over the labor movement, some unions were illegal, and some professional union leaders were concerned only with personal advancement.[27]

The existing state of the labor movement in China, he conceded, left much to be desired. Nor was there apparently any impetus from Geneva on this score, with no less a person than the director, Albert Thomas, having dismissed in 1930 Chan's suggestion that he act as intermediary for correspondence between European and Chinese labor unions as "une conception . . . assez singulière."[28]

During his four years as head of the China bureau, Chan suffered from indifferent health. He became ill in the course of a routine visit to Geneva and was away from his post in China for the first ten months of 1932.[29] His place was taken temporarily by Jennings Wong, who became acting director of the China bureau, a post he held concurrently for several months with that of commissioner of finance for Nanking Municipality, causing at least one observer to complain that the bureau lacked effective leadership.[30] There was little improvement in Chan's health upon his return to China, and although he stayed at his post for almost another two years, he was obliged to resign for health reasons in late 1934. Chan returned in due course to Geneva, where he worked for the ILO in a less responsible capacity.

The China Bureau under H. F. Cheng, 1934–39

When it became obvious in 1934 that it would be necessary to find a new director for its China bureau, officials in Geneva began to cast around for possible candidates. In due course, the man chosen for the job was H. F. Cheng. While there is no indication of this in general correspondence between Geneva and the China bureau, it is apparent from confidential material at Geneva that Cheng was in fact a nominee of the Nationalist government.[31] He had previously been for some time chief of the Factory Inspection Section of the Labor Department of the Ministry of Industries.[32] The undue influence that the government had in his appointment did not augur well for the independence of the organization in carrying out its work in China.

Shortly after his inauguration, Cheng wrote to his superiors in Geneva that he saw his most important task as increasing the prestige and influence of the ILO in China. To do this it would be necessary to "establish close relations with Government authorities and leaders of industrial, social, and intellectual organizations and . . . to adopt all the possible and effective means of propaganda such as broadcasting, delivery of speeches, issuing of news and holding of memorial meetings."[33] The building up of the China bureau as a research center on labor problems was, Cheng felt, not a task for the immediate future.

Upon his appointment in the autumn of 1934, Cheng embarked on a round of interviews with national and local government officials in Nanking and Shanghai, with employers and their organizations, and with representatives of such trade unions as could be found. Cheng notes that the employers in Shanghai, both Chinese and foreign, were particularly cooperative. "They are very friendly to me, and promised to render any service whenever I deem to demand from them [sic]."[34] The employers expressed support for a "policy of tri-partite cooperation in the improvement of the workers' situation."[35] Of some fifty interviews Cheng claims to have arranged at this time, only four were with people ostensibly representative of workers' interests. These were with officials of the Shanghai General Federation of Trade Unions, the Preparatory Bureau of the Chinese National Seamen's Union, the National Postal Employees' Federation, and the National Postal Workers' Federation.[36]

In the early stages of his tenure as its director, Cheng seems to have moved the center of operations of the bureau from Nanking to Shanghai, retaining the branch in Nanking as a subsidiary office. Between 1934 and the outbreak of war with Japan in 1937, however, Cheng left Shanghai on several occasions to "investigate" conditions in other industrial centers. In October–November 1935 he spent three weeks in Hankow and Changsha, and in December ten days in Chingkiang and Wusih.[37] In June–July 1936 he visited the Hui Nan Coal Mine and the city of Anking in Anhwei for a similar period, and in November of that year he made a four-day trip to Nantung in Kiangsu.[38] Subsequently, Cheng appears not to have ventured beyond Shanghai and Nanking, and after the beginning of hostilities in 1937, not outside Shanghai. An appeal he made to Geneva in 1939 for funds to enable him to go to Chungking seems to have been turned down.[39]

On the occasion of each of these trips, Cheng sent back to Geneva a report of his findings. These reports dealt in a summary way with a wide variety of areas, in none of which Cheng seemed to have any particular expertise—conditions of labor, wages, hours of work, unemployment, industrial conflicts, trade unions, employment agencies, rickshaw coolies, dockers, housing, employers' organizations, factory inspection, welfare, and education, among others. Each report also mentioned individuals with whom there had been "relations established" or interviews.[40] As Cheng seems to have been most concerned to establish relations with employers and government officials, his reports inevitably tended to reflect their point of view.

Where statistics were included, they were usually taken from surveys compiled by the Ministry of Industries or by the local government in the area being inspected. As these surveys no longer exhibited the most obvious inconsistencies and other deficiencies of their earlier counterparts, this information seems to have been welcomed by officials in Geneva as a more accurate indication of the true state of affairs in Chinese industry than had been the reports submitted by C. S. Chan. Unfortunately, however, although the reports were now consistent, they were also probably consistently erroneous. Two independent observers, Augusta Wagner and D. K. Lieu, were both critical of statistics published throughout this period by the Ministry of Industries, not only with respect to hours and wages, but also with respect to such basic items as the extent of capitalization of an industry, the number of factories, and the number of workers employed.[41]

Sometimes Cheng would interpret the material he had collected, observing, for example, that the level of wages seemed gradually to be dropping while hours worked were tending to increase.[42] More typical, however, would be the comment "Working conditions in Wusih factories are very good. Most of the large factories undertake to provide welfare for their workers."[43]

On one occasion Cheng records having been told by a factory inspector in Wuchang that conditions in factories there were "not satisfactory," while in both Anking and Changsha he met inspectors who were obliged to attend to "other duties," and had either very little time or no time at all to give to factory inspection.[44] In Changsha, Cheng reasoned, this did not pose a significant problem, for "as most of the factories are operated by the Government, which usually provides with a [sic] better working conditions, the inspection in private undertakings which are not only less in number but also employ only a few hundred workers, is thus comparatively simple."[45]

There is little reference in Cheng's reports to organized labor, and no suggestion that he made any effort to get in touch with it, however difficult that may have been. In his report on Hankow, Cheng noted that the Dockers' Union there had suffered from "communist penetration and many other troubles" and had not functioned "normally" until 1933. He noted that Chiang Kai-shek had forbidden the collection of union dues in Hankow, and also in Honan, Hupeh, Anhwei, Kiangsi, and Fukien under the pretext of the emergency created by the campaign against the Communists. He observed that in Anhwei, most unions elected the "well-to-do" workers as their officers in order to reduce expenses to a minimum.[46] He remitted to Geneva a statement by the Wusih Chamber of Commerce attributing workers' opposition to redundancy to ignorance,[47] and another by the municipal government of Hankow maintaining that the recent decrease in industrial militancy was owing to workers' "contentment" with their lot in difficult economic times. It is hard to avoid concluding that Cheng agreed with an official of that government when he observed, "The labour movement in Hankow is now on the right track. On the contrary, one can also say that there is no labour movement here. As trade unions are not permitted to collect membership fees they are thus put into an inactive state."[48]

If Cheng had ever given any indication that there might be explanations of what he saw other than those advanced by the employers and officials whom he met, if he had penned any qualifying remarks or criticisms of their reports, it might be possible to believe that he was forwarding them to Geneva to enable officials there to form a more complete picture of conditions and attitudes prevailing in China. That he did not do so must confirm the suspicions of political bias that his background and the manner of his appointment invite. It is the more remarkable, therefore, that Cheng should on more than one occasion complain that he had been mistaken for a representative of the Nanking government.[49]

At the end of 1936 K. S. Chen, who had been in charge of the subsidiary banking branch of the China bureau, died, and early in 1937 that branch was closed, leaving only the office at Shanghai. There Cheng remained during the first eighteen months of the war with Japan. In 1938 he wrote enigmatically to Geneva that the Chinese labor moment would "undergo a radical change after the war. . . . there are many things I like to tell you [sic]. But I think it would be wise for me to keep silent for a while."[50] When his request to transfer to Chungking was turned down, Cheng wrote his last letter to Geneva in March 1939.[51] It must be assumed that soon after this the ILO's China bureau ceased to function altogether.

China at the ILO

So far the focus of this discussion has been ILO activity in China, but brief mention must be made of the other side of this equation, Chinese representation in Geneva during the two decades under consideration. Throughout this period, Chinese representation at the ILO headquarters in Geneva was intermittent and, for much of the time, ill qualified. From 1919 to 1929 the only Chinese delegates to the ILO were diplomats sent from the legation in Berne to be present during the annual International Labour Conference. In 1929 and subsequently, except for 1932 when the Japanese emergency was said to prevent it, nominally "complete" delegations representing the interests of the government, employers, and workers attended the conference, as required by the regulations of the organization. Thomas Tchou, formerly of the YMCA's Industrial Department, led the first of these three-part delegations in 1929 and again represented China alone in 1932.

The supposedly "balanced" nature of these delegations was belied, however, by the delegates' unvarying unanimity of view on all the questions before them. One observer was led to remark,

> The information on Chinese conditions on which the so-called workers' and employers' representatives as well as the government representatives favoured the conferences ran along parallel lines. It consisted on the one hand of a catalogue of the achievements of the Government in enacting labour legislation and on the other hand of charges that the evil industrial conditions and the non-enforcement of labour legislation were due to the iniquities of foreign factory owners, extraterritorial privileges and unequal treaties.[52]

There was evidently some disapproval in Geneva of the Chinese practice of having the Kuomintang choose the worker delegates to the conference, but the practice continued for as long as China was represented.[53] It is apparent that even some of the worker delegates themselves may have become restless under the close scrutiny of the Kuomintang by the late 1930s.[54]

The other dimension to participation in the proceedings at Geneva is the matter of ratification and application of ILO conventions, which some would take to be the true measure of China's membership in the organization, and of the influence which the ILO came to have over China.

When the ILO was created in 1919 it was proposed that China should be required to adhere initially only to the principle of factory legislation, and should report at subsequent conferences on how it would go about putting the principle into practice.[55] It was suggested that China might begin by applying a ten-hour day (eight in the case of children under fifteen), six-day week, to workers in all factories employing over one hundred. The Peking government procrastinated, but after some pressure eventually produced in 1923 its Provisional Factory Regulations. These were never enforced.[56] They were followed in 1929 by the industrial legislation of the Nanking government, implementation of which was supposed to have commenced in 1931, but most provisions of which were also never enforced.[57]

Between 1919 and the outbreak of war with Japan in 1937, China nonetheless ratified twelve draft conventions of the ILO, of which ten were ratified between 1934 and 1936. Augusta Wagner, whose study of labor legislation in China remains the standard work for the period, argues that successive Chinese governments' complete disregard of the need for serious action on labor conditions is even apparent in the choice of draft conventions that China chose to ratify. These were:

ILO No.   7   Minimum Age (Sea)
      15   Minimum Age (Trimmers and Stokers)
      16   Medical Examination for Young Persons (Sea)

      27   Marking of Weight (Packages Transported by Vessels)
      32   Protection Against Accidents (Dockers)(Revised)

      19   Equality of Treatment (Accident Compensation)
      22   Seamen's Articles of Agreement
      23   Repatriation of Seamen

      45   Underground Work (Women)
      11   Right of Association (Agriculture)
      14   Weekly Rest (Industry)
      26   Minimum Wage Fixing Machinery

Wagner points out that the application of 7, 15, and 16 would be anomalous in light of the fact that children working in industry were not protected. The employment of children at sea was not a problem of great magnitude in China, and where the convention might afford protection to Chinese children working on foreign vessels it might also offer Chinese shipowners some competitive advantage. The cost of compliance with 27 and 32 could almost certainly be passed on to foreign shipowners, while 19, 22, and 23 also prescribed measures of protection for Chinese sailors and others working abroad at no cost to the Chinese government. Convention 19 provided for equality of treatment with respect to accident compensation only in countries where legislation on compensation already existed; it would be no benefit, for example, to foreigners working in China. There was little point to 45, as almost no women were employed underground in China. The right of association in agriculture provided by 11 was flagrantly violated from the day it was ratified. It was repeatedly stated that 14, which provided a weekly day of rest, was not a practical possibility in the foreseeable future, despite its having been ratified, while 26, requiring the establishment of machinery to fix minimum wages for casual labor, including outworkers, had proved virtually impossible to enforce even where there was long experience of labor legislation. Wagner concluded that by and large the Chinese government chose to ratify those conventions that would cause it the least trouble, and did this only to cater to world opinion.[58]

The relationship between China and the ILO in the 1920s and 1930s has been examined above in its various dimensions—the special missions to China by officials based in Geneva to seek information and give advice, the ILO's presence in China from 1930 through its branch office, and China's participation in proceedings of the ILO at Geneva. How may this relationship be characterized overall?

In a rare comment on the ILO by a Chinese observer working in the field, Lowe Chuan-hua, a former industrial secretary with the YMCA, wrote in the *China Critic* in 1930 that the policies of the organization were determined by the strong capitalist powers and were of no benefit to workers in weaker countries. The organization, he said, sought primarily to offset the influence of the Third International. It had taken no stand on extraterritorial privilege in China and had failed to secure even minimum standards of protection for Chinese workers.[59] These criticisms might well have been applied with equal force a decade later, at the end of the period of ILO involvement in China. The accusation of bias would seem to be supported particularly by the political nature of the appointment of H. F. Cheng as head of the ILO's Chinese branch in 1934, and by the fact that neither Cheng nor his predecessor in the post, nor indeed any of the ILO officials who came on short visits to China, made any serious effort to get in touch with the workers themselves, whose welfare was, after all, the object of the whole exercise.

Quite apart from partisanship, the ILO's involvement with China seemed to be marked by low expectations on all sides. Staff at headquarters in Geneva showed few signs of genuine interest in conditions in China, and the special missions sent there were too infrequent and of too short a duration to establish any continuity of contact with workers in the field. Neither of the two directors of the ILO's Chinese office were trained for the task, and both consistently misinformed their headquarters about the true nature of conditions on which they were obliged to report. No adequate procedures were laid down for the gathering of statistics, with the result that a full documentary inquiry on China called for at the International Labor Conference of 1925 had hardly been begun when it was canceled because of the war in 1938, this despite the fact that similar reports had been completed for India, Japan, and Indo-China.[60] Above all, there was no clear articulation of what the ILO was about in China, so that lassitude and drift were the order of the day.

For its part, the Chinese government by the 1930s had lost any reforming zeal it might once have had. Menaced by the Japanese on its borders and by the Communists within them, and angered by the continued presence of foreign concessions on Chinese soil, it was unlikely to give any but the most cursory acknowledgment to the activities of the ILO. Any pressure exerted on it on labor questions from outside the country would almost certainly have been counterproductive. Any momentum for change would have to be generated from within.

8

Between Capital and Labor

At the heart of the movement for industrial reform in China was a belief that welfare workers in industry could constitute a neutral buffer between capital and labor. This chapter will explore whether or not such a role was truly open to reformers, and the extent to which they could transcend the paternalism that characterized so much welfare work.

Relations with Employers

From the outset, the YMCA maintained a very close relationship with employers, initially entering factories to begin welfare work specifically at their invitation. In 1920 YMCA officials had begun their industrial welfare program by offering literacy classes, Bible study, and entertainment actually on the premises of seven factories in Shanghai. The rationale for this and similar initiatives is given in the annual report of the Chinese YMCA for 1921. While labor organizations based on the old guild system were "constructive and promising," others were arising, "so radical as to give cause for alarm."[1]

YMCA officials attempted to develop personal contact with employers and met them from time to time to discuss their plans. The spirit of this liaison is caught in the record of one such meeting:

> WOO: Mr. Brockman has brought to us a plan of putting the YMCA in between the labourer and the capitalist. They know about these strikes in the West; pretty soon they will wonder why they are not doing the same; there is hope that the YMCA can add to their knowledge and let them understand that they cannot take the place of capital.
>
> WANG: I promote a man, raise him to a dollar a day; then he says, I am a different man. . . . I see then that I have practically trained other people's weapons to kill me.
>
> WOO: The YMCA will help to create circumstances so that such things will not happen in your place.[2]

It would appear that prominent employers supported the YMCA's industrial program through contributions of both cash and buildings in which to carry out the work.[3] Business was also well represented on the association's National Executive Committee, which had the responsibility of supervising the broad lines of work, and on the various industrial committees, which exercised a similar supervisory function over the work of Industrial Departments in local centers.[4] Money for the support of the YMCA program as a whole came regularly from the International Committee of the Association in New York—indeed without these funds the YMCA operation in China could hardly have existed—and this imposed planning constraints on the association's administration in China.[5]

The fact was that much of the American YMCA's support was drawn from among the business community too, whose enthusiasm for experiments in industrial welfare was slow to develop. John D. Rockefeller, whose extraordinary wealth set him free from common anxiety about success or failure in business, was the exception that proved the rule. Thus, both in the United States and in China, the YMCA and certain elements of the business community, if their interests were not completely the same, certainly cooperated closely in the development of the association's industrial program. It is therefore less surprising that when the threat of working-class militancy that had spawned the experiment seemed to have passed, toward the end of the 1920s, the Chinese YMCA's interest in industrial welfare declined, and the program became in effect a dead letter.

The YWCA pursued a course in its relations with employers significantly different from that followed by its male equivalent. A preliminary survey of factory conditions in and about Shanghai led the YWCA's first industrial secretary, Agatha Harrison, to the conclusion that the association should "refuse to embark on what is called an 'industrial program' of work OUTSIDE the factory as long as such conditions prevail INSIDE."[6] The association gave its energy instead to a campaign intended to create a climate of opinion favorable to the passage of industrial legislation. An important part of this campaign was the attempt to persuade factory owners to undertake reforms voluntarily within their factories. It had been hoped that a more thorough recognition of the need for reform in industry might be achieved in China than had thus far been achieved in the West, for "it is easier for people to see the evils of child labour than it is the evils of taking money from firms that are denying to their workers real democracy in industry. It is easier to see the evils of the twelve hour day than it is to see that perhaps our whole industry, which is organised for profits rather than service, is un-Christian."[7]

Harrison's struggle to enlist the support of employers for labor standards left her, as she once remarked, "literally battered."[8] She and her successor, Mary Dingman, were obliged to negotiate with men who resented their interference both for its own sake and because they were women. They had to cajole and push the employers forward very much against their will, while appearing in public to present a common front with them in support of reform. In doing this, they sought to emphasize not the "efficiency motive," which might have had some appeal, but the need for a just and Christian society, a concept as alien to the mill owner as it must have been to his laborer.[9]

That all this effort should result in little voluntary improvement and, in practical terms, no legislated reform at all, even to restrict the use of child labor in the

International Settlement, must have been both a bitter experience and a lesson. The YWCA subsequently made no further serious overtures to employers. When the association began its own "direct" work among industrial women in 1926, it took care never to carry on its program in premises owned or donated by management.[10] At the time of the uprising in Shanghai in 1927 YWCA industrial secretaries saw the disturbances in a new and different light. Lily Haass wrote, "Perhaps in Europe and America the YWCA does not question the capitalistic order; here in China we must—God be praised! People may question the work of the Left Wing, but they *are* stirring up thinking in this respect in a way that the Christian Church never has."[11]

By 1933 any hope that capitalism in China might reform itself of its own accord was eroded completely. It was the consensus of delegates to the association's Third Industrial Secretaries Conference that year that "employers will not try to achieve industrial democracy. In many cases too, they do not desire workers' education, and approve of us only because they think we are harmless. . . . [A]s to how much time should be spent in making contacts with employers . . . on the whole it was agreed that men's groups would be able to accomplish more than the YWCA in this field."[12]

While the YMCA in its industrial work collaborated with employers, and the YWCA came into sharp conflict with them, the National Christian Council seems never in practice to have come close enough to the confrontation of opposed interests of labor and capital to have done one or the other. Several employers did serve on the committee that prepared the original report on conditions in industry presented to the National Christian Conference in 1922 (see chapter 4) and the NCC accepted that the concept of the brotherhood of man excluded "the selfish exploitation of labour by employers and by capitalists."[13] However, a review of the activity of the council's Industrial Commission suggests that subsequent to 1922 no employers sat on the commission, and that it had very little direct contact with employers at all. This is the more remarkable when it is realized that the whole point of the commission's campaign for legislated change, and of the publicity material that was the commission's main output in the early years, was to influence the thinking not only of Christian clergy but also of the employers. The object was to encourage them to introduce those voluntary reforms that, it was felt, must precede legislation.

The Industrial Commission did not come to grips with the fact that employers were little moved by the moral argument for reform; therefore, it never progressed beyond the moral argument.[14] The more radical proposals at the NCC's 1927 Conference on Christianizing Economic Relations, which called for an end to the unequal distribution of wealth and for cooperation to replace competition,[15] almost certainly represented the thinking of one woman, Lily Haass. Haass by that time stood alone in the Industrial Commission, and in due course herself left the commission because of the NCC's unwillingness to take a stand, or even recognize that there was a stand to be taken. The successor to Lily Haass, J. B. Tayler, shifted the attention of the commission, by now virtually a one-person operation, to small-scale industrial cooperatives, but when the council proved uninterested in promoting deeper research in this field either, Tayler withdrew and the commission ceased to function.

The National Christian Council's underlying attitude toward employers was one of mild censure; it was not funded by the direct experience that might have made it change. At the 1927 conference it was observed that among Chinese workers "it is known that the Church, as an organisation, depends upon financial support, and it is felt that in a crisis, the Church would stand with the capitalist."[16]

Relations with Labor

Contacts between the YMCA and organized labor were limited. Charles Shedd in Wuhan noted that he was "digging in to get contact with labour groups" in 1922.[17] Thomas Tchou addressed a mass gathering of 1,400 workers in Chefoo in 1923 and expressed in 1924 a strong desire to begin work in cooperation with unions in Canton to help "build up the moral and intellectual foundation on which all healthy movements must rest."[18] Surviving records give no indication, however, that there were any joint projects or even that there was any significant dialogue with any part of the labor movement. Workers were, with justification, suspicious of an organization that seemed so closely identified with employers.

This sentiment is revealed during two confrontations between workers and a local YMCA industrial secretary. On the occasion of a strike in 1925 at a cotton mill in Chengchow, where the association had begun industrial work some years earlier, "one of the first things the strikers did was to come over to the 'Y' and demand possession saying that it had been built for them and it was theirs." The secretary was able by quick thinking to avert occupation of the building, but subsequently representatives of the local Labor Federation demanded use of the building, which was within the grounds of the mill, for a provincial labor conference. The YMCA secretary agreed, but not without having first secretly consulted the mill owners to obtain their approval. The workers then insisted that the secretary address the conference on "the attitude of the YMCA toward the Labour Unions." Reluctantly he did so, "for . . . the fat was in the fire and the Y's future was at stake." According to the secretary, the YMCA was "nonpartisan" and, provided that the labor movement was not "dominated from Moscow," and "if the unions are good," then the association could help them, "especially in character education."[19] On this occasion, the fifty-five delegates seem to have been satisfied with the explanation, but more generally organized labor probably regarded the YMCA with indifference or hostility.

Compounding the problem was a division within the association between those staff members, generally younger men, who were prepared to accept and if possible work with the labor movement, up to a point, and the older foreign staff members, who had little patience with the unions. In the former category were John Nipps, who saw the unions as a natural response to "an un-Christian system,"[20] Thomas Tchou, who sought to emphasize the Chinese—as opposed to Russian—origins of the labor movement, and Y. L. Lee of Canton, who writing in 1928 observed that the movement had in the previous two years "done more good than harm to the workers."[21] These views may be contrasted with those of E. E. Barnett, who wrote in May 1927 that "[u]ndoubtedly . . . large sections of the labour movement have fallen into the hands of extremists," and E. H. Lockwood, who wrote that until the coup against the Communists in Canton in December 1927, "labour leaders, drunk with new power, had employers at their mercy."[22] As the younger men active in industrial work either left or were dismissed from the association, the hope for any real contact between the YMCA and the unions was accordingly diminished.

For the YWCA, its commitment to labor grew as its disenchantment with employers increased. In principle, the association's industrial workers had always supported the idea that working people should be free to organize themselves, a principle endorsed by the World's Committee of the Association at Champery in 1920. In practice, however, Agatha Harrison's decision to press ahead with the campaign for legislation meant that little effort was made in the early years to identify or get in touch with any of the labor unions, despite the fact that at one point in connection with the child labor campaign it was suggested that this might be helpful.[23] Only after the collapse of the campaign in 1925 was this question pursued, Lily Haass having returned from furlough in the autumn, giving expression to "a stronger conviction . . . that one of our immediate tasks is to get in touch with labour. I see no other way of spiritualising the labour movement, as it were, than by first-hand contact with it."[24]

In the event, Haass was soon to begin her period of service with the NCC, and the matter was left to Eleanor Hinder to follow up on her arrival in China early in 1926. Hinder claimed to have obtained "first touch with the workers' organisations" in March of that year. She had brought with her "credentials," probably a letter of testimonial, from the labor movement in her native Australia, and she was "delighted to have one of the leaders say . . . that 'the only workers who had seen fit to hold out a helping hand to the workers of China had been the Russians; did the Australians mean to help?' "[25] Whom she met on this occasion and what took place remains a mystery, but whatever dialogue there was must have been extremely tentative. Hinder remarks elsewhere that the labor movement was "difficult enough to find," but she was apparently put in touch with some prominent union members through the good offices of Colonel l'Estrange Malone, the former British Independent Labour Party M.P., who visited China in the spring of 1926.[26] No record remains of these contacts either.

Hinder was, of course, especially concerned to meet women who might be, at present or in the future, active in the unions, and it was this that prompted her in due course to take a room in one of Shanghai's factory districts and begin offering English to industrial girls, in company with an interpreter. After an hour or so of English, Hinder would turn to a discussion of factory life, of its implications for women, and of the responsibilities it imposed upon them. Most of the women were not union members, but rather forewomen in one of the tobacco factories, upon whom Hinder sought to impress a sense of duty toward their fellows. "I don't know how far my theory will work that I can make possible trade union secretaries of the future out of forewomen; but it is certain that it will have to be from the ranks of the people who have had the real experience that the women leaders will have to come."[27]

Although Hinder appears to have had no definite strategy with regard to the unions, she was nonetheless much more favorably disposed toward the labor movement at this time than were officials in the YMCA, and she was prepared to act on her convictions. Her experiment with the English lessons lasted at most only a few months, but it evidently helped to provoke a reexamination of attitudes toward the unions within the association as a whole.[28]

The union movement at this turbulent time was not by any means homogeneous, and Hinder was ambivalent in her approach to the division between the so-called moderates and extremists. She deplored the policy of repression and harassment pursued toward the unions in 1926 by the Chinese authorities in Shanghai and by the Shanghai Municipal Council, arguing that such policies led to "the more extreme types of thinking in the minds of the leaders; meeting no tolerance and understanding, they exhibit none."[29]

A practical consequence of this repression, Hinder found, was that it was difficult to discover just where the labor movement stood on efforts at reform and regulation. For example, union members had, unsolicited, written offering to cooperate with the National Christian Council's Cost of Living Enquiry undertaken in 1926, but "by the time a messenger could carry answer to the communication to the address from which the letter was sent, the headquarters was sealed by the Chinese police."[30] By the autumn of 1926 the world in Shanghai had, in the words of Lily Haass, "turned upside down," and all contact with union members involved grave risks. "Labour leaders are living in hiding, and if you could have heard, as I did not long ago, M. T. Tchou's story of how these men from time to time disappear you would understand how we cannot take any steps that will endanger their lives further. Much as we desire to know these men we are not pushing the matter at the present time."[31]

On the other hand, Hinder, while recognizing the harassment to which unions were subject, seemed to wish in her own work with women to endorse only their economic objectives. "So far it seems that labour is largely organised for political purposes, and our effort to stand by women in relation to their employment, and without any relation to politics will not be welcome, possibly."[32]

If the YWCA could contribute to the emergence of an "intelligent leadership" among working women, then the women would be better equipped to organize and to judge for themselves the consequences of any action they might take in future, political or otherwise.[33] This is not to say that Hinder opposed political action or cooperation in some measure with groups that advocated it—indeed, at the height of the turmoil in Shanghai in April 1927 she said she would have no objection to dealing with the General Labor Union, "however 'left' it might be"[34]—but rather that she did not wish to involve the YWCA directly in overt political initiatives. "In the final issue the struggle belongs to labour: but there may be contributing agencies."[35] Reinforcing Hinder's natural caution was the fact that the National Board of the Chinese YWCA apparently only approved its Industrial Department's approaches to women's labor unions early in 1927.[36]

While some contact seems to have been established with union leaders, probably both men and women, during the short-lived occupation of the house in Chapei in the winter of 1926–27 and further exchanges took place spasmodically throughout 1927,[37] the erosion of the independence of the unions and their reorganization under the Kuomintang must in time have severely curtailed the opportunities for contact. Early in 1928 Hinder published in the missionary journal *Chinese Recorder* an article about the growth of the labor movement which, though by no means pro-Communist, noted, in retrospect, "a sense of vitality and vigour and willingness to suffer on the part of the proponents of the radical cause."[38] Not in the article, but in the manuscript original, Hinder expressed her fear that a new "reign of repression" was coming to Shanghai, only slightly better than that known under the regime of Sun Chuan-fang.[39]

Shortly thereafter Hinder left China, and when she returned over two years later she passed relatively quickly from the YWCA to her new post with the Shanghai Municipal Council. In 1929 the Nanking government passed its new Labour Union Law, of which Lily Haass observed, "Even the conservative foreign papers feel that the draft goes too far . . . it is exceedingly disappointing . . ."[40] thus setting the final seal on the destruction of the unions as an independent force.

At the 1933 Conference of Industrial Secretaries, under the supervision of Cora Deng, YWCA industrial welfare workers reviewed the relation of the association to the trade unions. It was recognized that existing trade unions were "controlled by the Tang Pu," and for this reason, and because association officials could not themselves directly become members of unions, it was decided that the YWCA should not actively organize unions itself.[41] It could, however, educate working women about trade unionism, give counsel to their leaders, and offer training in group experience that would help women to participate in organizing their own unions, and it resolved to do so.[42]

As the impact of the depression on China gave employers an excuse to dismiss many workers and reduce the wages of others, the number of strikes in Shanghai and elsewhere rose after 1931, despite the fact that workers in many cases had no union. The memory of what had been achieved in the 1920s had not been entirely lost, and, as Cora Deng observed in 1935, "Workers have shown their willingness to suffer, and their ability to organise. Given a chance, a spontaneous movement of workers will emerge as quickly as bamboo sprouts. Meantime the suppressed energy has been gathering momentum and acquiring ideology underground, which may well startle the world when a change takes place."[43]

By the mid-1930s, the Industrial Department of the YWCA under Cora Deng's leadership had come to perceive the contradiction in the proposition on the basis of which the department had originally begun its work in 1921, that the interests of capital and labor might be reconciled through the intermediary of a Christian organization. This position had been arrived at as a result of the cumulative experience and disillusionment of a succession of industrial secretaries. That it was an exceptional position for Christian workers to take is tacitly recognized in the admission at the 1933 Industrial Secretaries' Conference that YWCA industrial policy would "inevitably arouse antagonisms" and that the various executive boards "do not always have a favourable attitude toward unions." It was accepted that it would be necessary to reach out to explain the work within the association as a whole, particularly "the question of class struggle as the method of changing the economic system, since there are those who feel the change is to be accomplished by joint struggle."[44]

It must be supposed that Cora Deng did not seriously expect wholehearted endorsement of her program from association members, many of whom would probably have regarded her efforts to prepare working women for trade unionism as wholly unacceptable. That she was able to pursue this program may be attributed to several factors. First, although the membership of the association as a whole was largely drawn from among the daughters of the well-to-do, and the National Executive Committee included women such as Mrs. C. C. Chen and Mrs. Fong Sec,[45] the wives of prominent business leaders, the actual intervention in, or even knowledge of, the day-to-day operations of the Industrial Department by the Executive Committee and other members seems always to have been quite limited, and indeed to have become more so after the departure of the more publicity-conscious foreign staff of the 1920s. The Industrial Department was therefore able to develop an independence in its everyday work that was partly a function of the specialized nature of the knowledge its secretaries needed to acquire, and partly a function of diminishing interest on the part of outsiders.

Again the department's work was given legitimacy in the eye of the broader association membership by the existence of an Industrial Advisory Committee within the World's Committee of the YWCA in London, and later in Geneva. The endorsement by this committee as early as 1920 of the right of workers to organize, and of definite industrial standards, must have made these innovations seem less radical to Chinese YWCA members, most of whom must have wished to appear modern in their thinking on these matters, despite their anxieties about what these changes might mean for the stability of Chinese society.

Moreover, YWCA industrial work does not appear to have depended for funds, as did that of the YMCA, principally on one donor agency abroad, which then insisted upon close supervision of the work. Neither did the association accept gifts of cash or buildings from employers to assist it to carry out its program. Instead, with the one exception of the grant from the Rockefeller Foundation, funds for the work seem to have been generated within the association, both through the provision of people or cash by other national branches—in the United States, Britain, or Australia—and through an allocation from the Chinese YWCA's regular annual budget.[46] The fact that this money must have come originally from contributions of people who were middle class, or even wealthy, seems to have had little impact on the nature of the work for which it was used. Contributions to the various national branches of the YWCA seem normally to have gone first into a common pot, so the allocation made to an Industrial Department was sufficiently remote from its source to guarantee the department a certain freedom of action.

More generally, it was undoubtedly the case that many of the problems confronting women transcended class and national boundaries, and invited the sympathy of all women. The particular vulnerability of women workers was partly a function of the vulnerability of women in general. The particular dangers confronting little girls in the cotton mills and silk filatures were in part a consequence of the fact that traditional societies almost everywhere assigned the manufacture of textiles to women, and this custom had passed into the modern age in China as elsewhere. The abuse and manipulation that working women often suffered in China was treatment not confined to women of one nationality or one class. YWCA industrial reformers generally recognized this, and that recognition enabled them much more readily to summon up a conviction and a commitment that their male counterparts often lacked. It also gave them a freedom to advocate more radical solutions.

The National Christian Council showed great caution in its approach to the labor movement. No endorsement was given at the 1922 conference to freedom for working people to organize, and indeed the NCC Industrial Commission went about its business for the next several years as if labor unions simply did not exist. It declined to consider their potential role in improving conditions. Only when the events of the mid-1920s thrust the problem of relations with the unions unavoidably in front of the NCC did the council reluctantly decide that "[i]n view of the emergence of self-conscious labour groups we believe the time has come for both the national Industrial Committee and local committees to attempt to make such methods of service to them as will further the cause of justice and brotherhood,"[47] a development of which Lily Haas remarked, "I am not imagining, of course, that this expresses the general attitude of the NCC."[48]

At the 1927 conference the labor movement was again discussed, but it was noted that as most church members were bourgeois, they had few natural contacts with workers. The latter, looking to the past, had little reason to trust that the church would take much interest in their plight. The conference did formally endorse in its "findings" the principle of freedom of association for working people, but with the eclipse of the unions' independence under Chiang Kai-shek, and against the background of the growing conservatism of the NCC's constituency, this gesture must seem hollow.[49] With the exception of a paper given by Ch'en Ta, unions were hardly mentioned at the 1931 Conference on the People's Livelihood, delegates observing only that the repressive new Labor Union Law might "fetter the liberty of workers."[50]

Beyond Paternalism

Like all forms of philanthropy, the industrial welfare movement was essentially paternalistic. The object of each of the agencies involved was to help working people move toward lives of greater dignity, in the case of the Christian agencies, both spiritual and material. Yet a prerequisite of dignity must surely be independence, not only of the economic pressures operating within society, but also of the help of philanthropic agencies.

With the consciousness of workers rising through bitter experience, and through such education as could be obtained, the recognition among them of the need for independence and self-directed struggle could be expected to grow. From the workers' point of view there was the contradiction between the means—help offered from above—and the end—independence and dignity. For the Christian agencies there was the dilemma that, to the extent that they truly succeeded in helping workers, they were likely to lose control over them.

The YMCA did not recognize this dilemma. Its "direct" work with factory hands was one-dimensional, consisting largely of literacy classes, Bible study, and one or two practical projects such as the Model Village. The work never really developed to the point at which more fundamental questions would be asked, and YMCA leadership would be in jeopardy. The NCC in its industrial work concentrated its attention very largely on people of influence. Its work, therefore, though still "on behalf" of working people, was for the most part at one remove from them. Only the YWCA, in the third phase of its industrial work under Cora Deng, came to realize that if working people were truly to grow in stature, they had to be helped to stand on their own feet. Ultimately, this meant "letting go," and the attendant possibility that the YWCA would become superfluous.

In the broader context, much Christian industrial work in China was an extension of a concern for the poor long professed by the church in Europe and elsewhere. Times had changed, however. In the words of Zung Weit-sung, "It is true that the Church is ever ready to do any kind of charitable work, but the cry of these exploited poor is, 'We want no charity we want justice.' "[51]

To what extent, then, did industrial reformers learn from experience, transcend this paternalism, and modify the original premises of their work? Two instances stand out. The first is the conversion of the industrial staff of the YWCA from a belief in the possibility of voluntary reform from above in industry, reinforced by legislation, to a belief in the need for collective struggle from below to achieve a complete transformation of the economic system, and a full realization of the dignity of working people. This dramatic reversal did not come about suddenly but had its roots in the experience of YWCA secretaries in the turbulent two years between the May Thirtieth incident in 1925 and Chiang Kai-shek's campaigns against the Communists in 1927.

During this time, the association's industrial staff saw foreigners in Shanghai refuse to approve the Municipal Council's child labor legislation and succumb to extremes of jingoist hysteria and racial prejudice as troops of the Northern Expedition approached the International Settlement.[52] They vested their hopes for legislated reform in the promise of a government of all the progressive forces in the United Front, only to have these hopes dashed with Chiang's first anti-Communist coup in April 1927.[53] Toward the end of that year they witnessed the beginning of the regimentation of unions under Kuomintang control and the growth of the compact between government and business.

This train of events brought profound disillusionment to Eleanor Hinder, at that time chief industrial secretary of the YWCA, and undoubtedly contributed to her decision to resign and return to Australia in the early spring of 1922. This disappointment was shared by other members of the association's Industrial Department[54] and was almost certainly felt in other departments, in one of which—the Student Department—Cora Deng was a young trainee secretary. In 1929 promulgation of Nanking's Factory Acts was accompanied by passage of trade union legislation that finally set the seal on the destruction of the unions as an independent force.

By the end of the decade, therefore, all the channels through which the YWCA had hoped to promote gradual reform—the foreign ratepayers of Shanghai, the employers, the new government—had been effectively closed off. When Cora Deng returned from Europe in 1930 to assume leadership of the Industrial Department, the cumulative experience and wisdom of the department left no choice but to strike out in a totally new direction, which Deng, after a brief period in which she came to grips with her new job, did in fact do. This shift in industrial policy to a campaign to raise class consciousness and cultivate women for participation in collective struggle, dating from the Industrial Secretaries Conference in January 1933, was of fundamental importance. Although the scope of the program implemented as a result was quite limited, the work was perhaps the most useful the YWCA Industrial Department could do under the circumstances.

The second case in which the approach was altered through practical involvement was the realization on the part of J. B. Tayler that he could apply the experience of cooperative organization that he had gained in the agricultural sphere while working for the China Committee on Famine Relief, along with certain "modern" techniques of manufacture, to the creation of rural industrial cooperatives.

Tayler had long taken an interest in urban industrial reform, had been in part responsible for Agatha Harrison's being brought to China, and had piloted the Reconnaissance Committee funded by the Rockefeller Foundation out of whose investigations ultimately emerged the Cost of Living Study of 1926–27, among other projects. Tayler knew therefore at first hand of the problems of the urban industrial worker and appreciated the enormous difficulties involved in ameliorating these conditions in the crowded and competitive environment of the treaty port cities. He also knew of the poverty of rural families whose sole means of subsistence was agriculture, and who in times of economic crisis even more acute than usual flocked to the cities in search of work, making matters there still worse.

While it could not be said that Tayler shared completely the disillusionment of YWCA staff with employers and government in the late 1920s, he had come by the end of the decade to feel the need for a totally new strategy that would provide an alternative to the growing dichotomy between city and countryside. This strategy is first clearly articulated in the paper on industrial cooperatives that he presented to the Conference on the People's Livelihood in 1931. While over the next several years he was able to raise enough money and practical help to promote only two or three experimental industrial co-ops, Tayler went on thinking and writing about cooperatives, and when the war came he was called on to act as an adviser to the large-scale Industrial Cooperative Movement.

Tayler apparently did not expect the cooperative principle in industry to displace capitalism, though if it had been cultivated and developed at the pace apparent early in the war, and if it had met no opposition, it might have done so in time.[55] Rather he felt that individual cooperatives and federations of which they were a part should grow up side by side with capitalist industrial enterprise and be able to compete with it. His feeling that cooperation could constitute a middle way between capitalism and communism, and might in time supplant both, seems to belong to his thinking on this subject after the war.

The real genius of Tayler's insight of 1931 lies in two points. First, he proposed to introduce industry, albeit simple industry, into the hinterland, and second, he proposed to do this through cooperatives. In both of these he foreshadowed not only the industrial cooperatives but also in some measure developments in China after 1949. Both these concepts were potentially quite revolutionary in their implications, for the diffusion of industry in the countryside was key to a more equal distribution of wealth between city and country, reduction of the pressure on the cities, and the consequent improvement of the conditions of life and labor in them, while the education for participation in important decisions essential to the practice of the cooperative principle would in time, perhaps, spawn a more critical work force able to take the destiny of its class and its nation into its own hands.

It is not unlikely that the Kuomintang came during the war to see the implications of the rural Industrial Cooperative Movement. The movement's demise is only an indication that Tayler's co-ops could not have been realized on any significant scale so long as the power in China remained in the hands of militarists, capitalists, and the landowning class.

Conclusion

Broadly speaking, the pursuit of industrial welfare might be expected to involve the amelioration of all those conditions that combine to determine the well-being of the industrial worker and his family. Any consideration of industrial welfare in China ought then to take into account the origins and skill level of workers, the extent of urban-rural mobility, hiring practices involved in apprenticeship, the labor contract system, and the letting of outwork, the employment of women and children, hours, days of rest, and holidays, rates of pay, the cost of living, the measure of unemployment, factors affecting workers' health and safety, the quality of housing available, the accessibility of education, the provision, if any, of welfare facilities by the employers, and the existence and enforcement of legislation to govern conditions of labor. Any organization concerned with the welfare of labor might also be expected to get in touch with the organizations of labor, to ascertain what working people themselves were doing to improve their lot.

Of the agencies that have been the focus of this study, the YMCA, the YWCA, the Industrial Commission of the National Christian Council, the ILO, and the Industrial Section of the Shanghai Municipal Council, it would appear that none showed any interest in the pattern of movement between the countryside and the city and the factors that gave rise to it, nor in the skill level of workers, which was partly a function of this mobility. With respect to hiring practices, both apprenticeship and the contract labor system came in for sharp criticism during the deliberations of the Child Labor Commission in 1924. Nothing positive emerged from this criticism, however, though in 1940 the Engineering Society of China in conjunction with the Industrial Section of the Shanghai Municipal Council began to implement a program for registration and training for bona fide apprentices. No real effort seems to have been made to discourage employers from hiring through labor contractors, while the conditions of employment of outworkers seem to have been completely neglected. Although the use of children in industry attracted much attention in Shanghai in the early 1920s, after the failure of the Municipal Council to enact legislation to limit the employment of children in factories this issue was no longer a principal concern of the reform lobby. The particular difficulties faced by women industrial workers were, however, an ongoing preoccupation of the YWCA, which throughout the period under consideration sought to gather detailed information about the conditions women had to endure, and to help them in a practical way wherever possible.

Data on hours of work, rates of pay, and the cost of living for industrial workers were collected with varying degrees of precision by each of the agencies considered here. This information gathering on the part of the YMCA was carried on chiefly under the auspices of Thomas Tchou in the early 1920s, and with his departure from the association it was effectively discontinued. Both the YMCA and the YWCA, which continued to gather data into the 1930s, concentrated on hours and rates of pay in different industries and regions, and it would only be on the initiative of the National Christian Council's Industrial Commission, albeit under YWCA leadership, that the first attempt to make a coherent estimate of the cost of living for workers was undertaken in 1926. This survey was taken over by the Social Affairs Bureau of the municipal government of Greater Shanghai in 1927 and was the basis for other surveys undertaken subsequently by the bureau, and by the Industrial Section of the Shanghai Municipal Council after the outbreak of war with Japan.

The council's Industrial Section began to collect comprehensive information on hours, rates of pay, and the cost of living in the area under its control in the late 1930s. No original surveys were undertaken by the China Bureau of the ILO, though some data were gathered rather haphazardly by visiting officials from the organization's headquarters in Geneva. Generally, information sent back to Geneva by the China Bureau was lifted wholesale from other, often government, sources and was apt to be unreliable. Unfortunately, such energy as was invested in the gathering of information about the livelihood of industrial workers yielded little of the fruit of practical improvement in their lives. In the vast majority of cases, it is generally conceded that hours of work were no shorter, and real wages very little higher, in early 1937 than they had been in the early 1920s, when at least the growing labor movement held out the prospect of some improvement. With the coming of the war, rising prices forced a drastic reduction in the standard of living of working people.

Another problem that appears largely to have eluded the consciousness of students of industrial welfare was unemployment. Among the projects undertaken by reformers, it is not possible to find a single survey devoted to an analysis of the extent or effects of unemployment, and it was not until the influx of refugees into the International Settlement in Shanghai posed a serious administrative problem for the authorities that the council's Industrial Section attempted to estimate the number of unemployed in the settlement, and, along with officials of the YWCA, to find work for some of them. Nor, of course, was there any regular welfare provision for the unemployed.

With respect to the health and safety of industrial workers, the record is somewhat different. Although little attention was paid to health and safety questions by the YMCA, except briefly under Thomas Tchou, the YWCA and the NCC Industrial Commission were from the beginning concerned to point out to employers conditions or practices in their factories that threatened the health or safety of working people. The NCC commissioned the study into phosphorous poisoning in match factories in 1924, which was instrumental in causing the abandonment of the most poisonous type of phosphorous by many manufacturers of matches. The Child Labor Commission in its report commented repeatedly on those aspects of factory work that damaged the health of children, with the result that certain practices, for example with respect to the boiling and peeling of silk cocoons, were changed.

The YWCA in its "direct" work with factory women after 1926 almost always provided the facilities of a clinic and the services of a doctor, in addition to carrying on its other work of education and group training. Vaccination against smallpox and other diseases was also frequently available. The most urgent concern of the Shanghai Municipal Council's Industrial Section upon its formation in 1932 was to induce employers to act to remove some of the hazards rife in industrial employment. Staff of the section paid regular visits of inspection to factories in the settlement to assess health and safety precautions, while wherever possible reports were taken and statistics kept on the incidence of industrial accidents. Several special studies were commissioned, with respect to processes in manufacture particularly hazardous to the health of workers, and with respect to the diet of workers.

In the area of housing for working people, Thomas Tchou's study of 1926 on Shanghai stands out. His Model Village project was a logical and constructive response to the situation that his research had revealed. It is unfortunate that upon his resignation from the YMCA, association officials should have sought to use the village for rather narrow ends. That the village should be reproduced on a much larger scale in the mid-1930s by the Municipality of Greater Shanghai is some testimony to the worth of the original project. The Shanghai Municipal Council commissioned rather belatedly in 1936 its own report on workers' housing in the settlement, which exposed conditions of overcrowding soon to be made much worse by the war. Its Industrial and Social Division in 1941 influenced the council to enact legislation to provide for control of rent for tenants and subtenants, which was subsequently enforced with some success. Efforts by the Industrial Section to discourage the spread of dormitory accommodation, however, were unrewarded.

The aspect of "direct" social work for which the Christian agencies were perhaps best known in China was the provision of adult education. This was the mainstay of YMCA involvement with working people, both in the cities and, after the inception of James Yen's "Mass Education Movement" in 1923, in the countryside as well. The YMCA's adult education program consisted largely of literacy classes offering instruction in the one thousand basic characters, as well as classes in such subjects as elementary mathematics, civics, and, of course, Christian scripture. Much emphasis was placed on the need to achieve a "moral uplift" among the working classes, and this rather narrow view of the purpose of education, and indeed of all contact with working people, survived Thomas Tchou's attempt to broaden the horizons of the association in its industrial work.

The YWCA also offered literacy classes to working women, beginning in 1926, as well as courses in arithmetic, history, geography, and other subjects to graduates of the literacy program. After Cora Deng came to direct the association's Industrial Department, the literacy campaign was infused with new color as secretaries sought to introduce reference to the day-to-day problems of working women into their classes. At a more advanced level, courses were offered in such subjects as trade unionism, labor legislation, and economics. It is apparent, therefore, that in the 1930s the YWCA Industrial Department came to see adult education not only as an end in itself but as a means of cultivating a more sophisticated political awareness among working women. For the YWCA, as for the YMCA, the fact that human and financial resources were so limited in comparison with the size of the problem meant that only a very small proportion of those who stood to gain from popular education could possibly be reached.

Much of the earlier activity of reformers was directed toward the "forming of opinion" among employers with respect to the need for improved working conditions and the provision of welfare facilities of various kinds for their employees. Working conditions improved negligibly, if at all, during the period under review. It is also apparent, however, that the Christian reform lobby materially failed to alter the extent to which welfare facilities, such as literacy classes, health care, accident compensation, and pension schemes, were provided by individual firms. Those companies that by the standard of the time might have been considered more advanced in their attitude toward welfare, such as the Commercial Press, Naigai Wata Kaisha, and the British-American Tobacco Company, appear to have demonstrated some commitment to the principle of welfare quite independently of the entreaties of the reform lobby, probably because they had found that the concession of a few benefits was repaid through the loyalty of the work force. The great majority of employers did not provide their workers with any significant benefits in addition to their pay, and as a body they remained unmoved by the arguments for reform, and in many cases probably unapproached.

The resistance that the reformers met among employers prompted some of them quite early to press for legislation to regulate conditions of work, particularly with reference to the employment of children, a weekly day of rest, and hours of work. Agitation in support of these objectives on the part of officials of the YWCA and the NCC probably contributed in some measure to the decision of the Peking government in 1923 to promulgate its Provisional Factory Regulations, though the growing militancy of the labor unions may have played a larger part. Similarly, the Kuomintang legislation of 1929–31 may have been influenced by the thinking of Christian reformers, though it is equally likely that in enacting the regulations the government was principally concerned with its reputation nationally and internationally, and for this reason felt obliged to keep a commitment first made before the death of Sun Yat-sen. It must also be recalled that the regulations were passed in company with the new Labor Union Law of 1929–31, which gave legitimacy to the drastic curtailment of the power and independence of trade unions. What is most significant about the record with respect to factory legislation, however, is that in all cases almost no effort was made to enforce it, that excuses were made and reasons found for interminable delay.

Most employers and government officials shared an allegiance to the logic of laissez-faire, against which agitation for reform, whether voluntary or legislated, ran as a contrary current. A few of the more perceptive reformers recognized this in due course, and changed their tactics accordingly. Notable among these were Cora Deng, Rewi Alley, and perhaps unconsciously J. B. Tayler. The most enduring contributions to the welfare of working people may in the long run have been made by Cora Deng of the YWCA, who, after years of neglect of the labor unions on the part of Christian reformers, sought to train women for trade union activity, and by J. B. Tayler, who sought to promote rural industrial cooperatives on a model that would in some measure be the inspiration for the ingenious network of industrial cooperatives built up by Rewi Alley and others during the war. In both cases, the endeavor was to encourage the collective initiative of working people, rather than to provide palliatives or lobby for concessions from above. This progress beyond paternalism sets their efforts apart from all other industrial work.

Appendixes

Appendix 1A

The Usual Range of Adult Wages in Certain Chinese Industries, 1931–1932

	Number of Establishments	Total Workers	Usual Wage per Day in Chinese Dollars	Sex of Workers
Cotton spinning	16 ⎫	44,146	$0.50 to $0.60	male and female
Cotton weaving	39 ⎭		0.50 to 0.80	male and female
Knitting	9	2,464	0.65 to 1.00	male and female
Silk filatures	4	1,400	0.40 to 0.70	female
Silk weaving	10	945	0.70 to 1.00	male and female
Rug weaving	28	5,170	0.44 to 0.67	male
Engineering	6	2,170	0.55 to 2.00	male
Iron works	4	4,560	0.55 to 2.00	male
Rice mills	2	150	0.70 to 1.00	male
Egg produce	2	650	0.70 to 0.90	male
Rubber goods	2	860	⎧ 0.78 to 0.93	female
			⎩ 1.55 to 1.75	male
Firecracker	2	450	0.60 to 0.90	male
Flashlight	2	320	⎧ 0.23 to 0.35	female
			⎩ 0.78 to 1.16	male
			per month	
Flour mills	13	1,925	$20.00 to $40.00	male
Match factories	12	6,104	11.00 to 22.00	male
Oil mills	8	1,210	18.00 to 30.00	male
Leather	4	177	16.00 to 31.00	male
Dyeing	5	235	10.00 to 30.00	male
Total	168	72,936		

Source: Dorothy J. Orchard, "Man Power in China," pp. 18–20. Orchard says: "This summary covers establishments in thirty-four centers stretching from Harbin in Manchuria to Canton in South China. Some 282 industrial establishments from small handicraft workshops to large modern factories were visited, and of this number, wage data are here presented for 168 establishments employing 72,936 workers."

Appendix 1B

Average Monthly Earnings of Workers in Shanghai, 1930–1940

	1930		1931		1932	
Relative Position	Industries	Earnings per Month	Industries	Earnings per Month	Industries	Earnings per Month
1	Printing	$41.720	Printing	$40.696	Shipbuilding	$43.518
2	Shipbuilding	35.930	Shipbuilding	40.672	Silk Weaving	32.705
3	Machinery	26.364	Machinery	27.497	Printing	28.343
4	Silk Weaving	23.507	Silk Weaving	23.207	Machinery	27.672
5	Oil Pressing	21.808	Enamelling	21.586	Underwear Knitting	19.902
6	Enamelling	21.764	Paper Making	21.449	Paper Making	19.512
7	Hosiery Knitting	19.256	Under Knitting	20.168	Hosiery Knitting	17.901
8	Flour	18.658	Oil Pressing	19.311	Oil Pressing	17.219
9	Under Knitting	18.123	Flour	16.024	Cotton Weaving	15.806
10	Paper Making	17.160	Wool Weaving	15.692	Enamelling	15.515
11	Cotton Weaving	15.160	Tobacco	15.439	Wool Weaving	14.589
12	Tobacco	14.878	Hosiery Knitting	14.058	Flour	14.497
13	Wool Weaving	13.232	Cotton Weaving	13.464	Tobacco	14.129
14	Cotton Spinning	10.868	Cotton Spinning	11.091	Match Making	12.615
15	Match Making	10.685	Silk Reeling	9.860	Cotton Spinning	11.393
16	Silk Reeling	8.833	Match Making	9.517	Silk Reeling	7.935
	1933		1934		1935	
1	Shipbuilding	$47.633	Shipbuilding	$43.049	Shipbuilding	$40.189
2	Printing	32.609	Printing	29.487	Printing	29.245
3	Silk Weaving	27.759	Machinery	24.253	Machinery	23.085
4	Machinery	24.581	Silk Weaving	23.357	Paper Making	20.843
5	Underwear Knitting	20.034	Enamelling	19.957	Enamelling	18.546
6	Oil Pressing	18.683	Underwear Knitting	18.291	Oil Pressing	18.291
7	Enamelling	17.386	Wool Weaving	17.539	Underwear Knitting	17.675
8	Flour	17.119	Flour	17.441	Silk Weaving	17.370
9	Wool Weaving	15.845	Paper Making	17.410	Flour	16.711
10	Paper Making	15.840	Oil Pressing	15.711	Hosiery Knitting	14.639
11	Cotton Weaving	14.329	Tobacco	15.605	Tobacco	14.598
12	Tobacco	14.309	Cotton Weaving	15.539	Wool Weaving	14.371
13	Hosiery Knitting	13.674	Hosiery Knitting	12.009	Cotton Weaving	12.852
14	Cotton Spinning	10.719	Cotton Spinning	11.005	Cotton Spinning	9.648
15	Match Making	9.771	Match Making	7.918	Match Making	7.917
16	Silk Reeling	8.498	Silk Reeling	6.310	Silk Reeling	6.561

Appendix 1.B *continued*

Relative Position	1936 Industries	1936 Earnings per Month	1937 Industries	1937 Earnings per Month	1938 Industries	1938 Earnings per Month
1	Shipbuilding	$40.025	Printing	$30.229	Printing	$31.383
2	Printing	36.167	Silk Weaving	21.484	Machinery	22.169
3	Machinery	26.078	Machinery	18.319	Oil Pressing	18.163
4	Underwear Knitting	19.887	Oil Pressing	18.163	Silk Weaving	17.904
5	Enamelling	19.038	Flour	16.627	Cotton Weaving	16.809
6	Silk Weaving	18.660	Wool Weaving	14.845	Paper Making	16.730
7	Flour	16.588	Cotton Weaving	13.542	Flour	16.627
8	Paper Making	16.178	Enamelling	12.306	Enamelling	16.345
9	Wool Weaving	15.845	Underwear Knitting	12.115	Wool Weaving	16.261
10	Oil Pressing	15.724	Hosiery Knitting	11.803	Underwear Knitting	13.764
11	Cotton Weaving	15.483	Paper Making	11.120	Cotton Spinning	13.301
12	Tobacco	11.680	Tobacco	10.868	Hosiery Knitting	12.729
13	Hosiery Knitting	13.635	Cotton Spinning	9.324	Tobacco	11.367
14	Match Making	11.718	Silk Reeling	1.898	Silk Reeling	6.766
15	Cotton Spinning	10.054				
16	Silk Reeling	8.253				

Relative Position	1939 Industries	1939 Earnings per Month	1940 Industries	1940 Earnings per Month
1	Printing	$36.289	Printing	$65.446
2	Machinery	24.870	Flour	45.676
3	Paper Making	23.352	Machinery	45.200
4	Silk Weaving	22.196	Cotton Weaving	42.530
5	Flour	21.885	Wool Weaving	42.453
6	Underwear Knitting	21.763	Oil Pressing	39.873
7	Cotton Weaving	21.315	Paper Making	39.313
8	Wool Weaving	19.910	Enamelling	38.580
9	Enamelling	19.408	Cotton Spinning	37.083
10	Oil Pressing	18.980	Hosiery Knitting	32.839
11	Cotton Spinning	16.917	Silk Weaving	31.918
12	Hosiery Knitting	12.442	Underwear Knitting	23.565
13	Tobacco	11.117	Tobacco	22.553
14	Silk Reeling	10.900	Match Making	22.491
15	Match Making	7.935	Silk Reeling	17.924

Source: Annual Report of the Shanghai Municipal Council, 1940.

Appendix 1C

Indices of Actual Earnings, Cost of Living, and Real Wages, 1930–1940

Indices	1930	1931	1932	1933	1934	
Actual earnings	106.95	107.34	106.06	103.21	98.10	
Cost of living	111.19	108.36	102.37	92.51	92.68	
Real wages	96.19	99.06	103.12	111.57	105.85	

Indices	1935	1936	1937	1938	1939	1940
Actual earnings	90.49	100.00	84.83	92.38	119.09	242.47
Cost of living	93.99	100.00	118.15	152.90	203.25	439.22
Real wages	96.28	100.00	71.80	60.42	58.59	55.33

Source: Annual Report of the Shanghai Municipal Council, 1940, p. 76.

Regional Differences in Factory Wages, 1933
(in yuan)

Sector	Average	Shanghai	Other
Matches	123	234	110
Cotton yarn	166	204	142
Cotton cloth	110	145	91
Silk yarn	45	48	44
Silk cloth	243	291	179
Flour milling	225	260	208
Cigarettes	176	181	57
All industry	163	178	151

Source: Thomas Rawski, *Economic Growth in Prewar China*, p. 82.

Peking Provisional Factory Regulations, 1923

Provisional Factory General Regulations. Promulgated by Ministerial Order No. 223 of the Ministry of Agriculture and Commerce on March 29, 1923

Article 1

These regulations are applicable to the following factories:

1. Factories which have on ordinary time more than 100 workers.
2. Factories in which the work is dangerous in character and injurious to health.

Factories for which these regulations are not applicable shall be specified by separate Ministerial orders.

Article 2

These regulations shall be likewise applicable to any foreign factory established in Chinese territory, which is of the same character as described in the provision of the preceding article.

Article 3

A factory owner shall be prohibited from employing boys under 10 and girls under 12 years of age.

Article 4

Boys under 17 and girls under 18 shall be termed juvenile workers.

Article 5

Juvenile workers shall be employed only on light work.

Article 6

Excluding the time of rest, the working hours for juvenile workers shall not exceed eight hours a day and for adult workers, ten hours a day.

Article 7

A factory owner shall be prohibited from employing juvenile workers in any kind of work between the hours of 8 PM and 4 AM.

Article 8

Adult workers shall be given at least two days rest per month and juvenile workers three days rest per month.

But in case of serious accident or emergencies, the provisions contained in the proceeding paragraph may be temporarily suspended. The administrative authorities concerned shall be notified of the same within three days.

Article 9

Any worker shall be given one or more rest periods per day. The rest period or periods referred to in the preceding paragraph shall be not less than one hour a day.

Article 10

In case a special factory should adopt a system of day and night shifts, the working schedules shall be so arranged that the hours of the workers may be interchanged at least once every ten days.

Article 11

Wages shall be paid in money of legal tender and unless with their consent they shall not be paid in kind.

Article 12

Wages shall be paid regularly and at least once a month.

Article 13

In case the working hours should be prolonged because of special conditions, a special increase of wages shall be made.

Article 14

A factory owner shall be prohibited from deducting in advance a sum of money from the wages of any employee as a security for compensation for breach of contract or any other damage.

Article 15

If a scheme should be adopted whereby a part of the employee's wages is deducted as his savings or for any other benefit of the employee, the latter's consent to such deduction must be obtained, and the proposed scheme must be submitted to the administrative authorities concerned for approval.

Article 16

In case an employee should leave the factory or die, the factory owner shall pay in full the wages due to the employee or to the deceased's family together with all his savings.

Article 17

A factory owner shall, in accordance with the conditions of the factory, draw up regulations providing for compensation for the family of a deceased employee as well as regulations providing for rewards and pension of the employee. Such regulations shall be submitted to the administrative authorities concerned for approval.

Article 18

A factory owner shall at the expense of the factory, provide supplementary and suitable education for juvenile workers or uneducated employees.

The time spent in supplementary education, as referred to in the foregoing paragraph, shall be at least ten hours a week for a juvenile worker and six hours for an uneducated employee.

Article 19

A factory owner shall at his discretion, limit or suspend the work of an employee when such employee is injured or sick. If such injury or sickness is caused through work in the factory, the factory owner shall bear all medical expenses and shall not be permitted to make any deduction from the wages which the employee should receive while he is injured or sick.

Article 20

A female worker shall be given five weeks rest before and after a confinement and a suitable sum of money shall be given to assist such female worker.

Article 21

A juvenile or female worker shall not be required to clean, oil, examine, repair, fix or change a belt or rope, or to engage in any other dangerous work, when a machine is in motion, nor shall such worker be employed at the dangerous parts of the machine for the transmission of power.

Article 22

A juvenile worker shall not be required to handle poisonous, violent or explosive materials, or any other harmful materials.

Article 23

A juvenile worker shall not be required to work in a place which is unsanitary or dangerous, or in any place infested with dust, powder or any poisonous gases.

Article 24

A factory shall provide necessary and suitable equipment for the purpose of preserving the health of its employees and preventing any dangers that may arise.

Inspectors may be appointed from time to time by the administrative authorities concerned to investigate the condition of the factory.

Article 25

When the administrative authorities concerned consider that a factory, its auxiliary buildings or its equipment may easily be a cause of danger, or endanger the health of its employees or the public welfare, the factory owner shall immediately make necessary and suitable alterations in accordance with the order of the said authorities.

When the said authorities deem it necessary to intervene in any matter referred to in the foregoing paragraph, they may order to suspend the operation of the whole plant or a part of it.

Article 26

A factory owner may appoint a suitable person or persons to act as the factory superintendent to manage all the affairs of the factory.

The appointment of such superintendent shall be submitted to the administrative authorities concerned for record.

Article 27

A factory superintendent shall on behalf of the factory owner bear all the responsibilities specified in these regulations.

Article 28

These regulations shall take effect from the day of promulgation.

    N.B.: This translation is made to facilitate the understanding of these regulations. The Chinese text shall be authoritative in case of doubt.

Factory Act of the Nanking Government, 1931

1. FACTORY LAW

Chapter 1: General Provisions

Article 1

This Law shall apply to all factories where power generators are used and where in ordinary times thirty or more labourers are employed.

Article 2

When used in this Law, unless the regulations otherwise indicate, the term "Proper Authorities" means the municipal government in municipalities and the district government in the districts (hsien).

Article 3

Factories shall keep a labourers' register, record fully the following particulars concerning each labourer, and file such information with the Proper Authorities:

1. Name, sex, age, native place and address;
2. Date of entry into the factory;
3. The kind of work, hours and remuneration;
4. Physical condition;
5. The rewards and penalties received in the factory;
6. The kinds of illness suffered by the labourer and the causes thereof.

Article 4

Once every six months factories shall submit to the Proper Authorities a report, containing the following particulars:

1. Changes made in the labourers' register;
2. Illness suffered by the labourers, treatment and results;
3. Accidents and measures taken for relief thereof;
4. The dismissal of labourers and reasons therefor.

Chapter 2: Child and Female Labour

Article 5

No person, male or female, who has not completed his or her fourteenth year shall be employed in any factory as a labourer.

Boys or girls above the age of twelve and below the age of fourteen who are already in employment prior to the promulgation of this Law may, with the consent of the Proper Authorities, have the age limit extended when this Law is put into effect.

Article 6

Males or females above the age of fourteen but who have not completed their sixteenth year shall be deemed child labourers and are permitted to perform light or easy work only.

Article 7

Child and female labourers shall not be employed in the following work:

1. In handling explosive, inflammatory or poisonous articles;
2. In places which are exposed to dust or poisonous odours and gas;
3. In fixing, cleaning, oiling, inspecting, or repairing moving machines, power transmitting equipment, or risky parts thereof, or in adjusting belts and ropes;
4. In connecting highly charged electric wires;
5. In handling molten metals or the residue thereof;
6. In handling furnaces or boilers; or
7. Other work that is immoral or of a dangerous character.

Chapter 3: Working Hours

Article 8

In principle the number of working hours for adult labourers shall be eight per day; but may be extended to ten per day in cases of necessity due to varying local conditions or the nature of the work.

Article 9

All factories that use the system of day and night shifts shall so arrange their working schedules that the shifts for the labourers may be interchanged at least once a week.

Article 10

Notwithstanding the provisions of Article 8 a factory may, in case of force majeure and with the consent of the labourer union, extend the working day, but the total number of working hours shall not exceed twelve per day, and the overtime work shall not exceed forty-six hours per month for any labourer.

Article 11

The regular working day for child labourers shall, under no circumstances, exceed eight hours.

Article 12

Child labourers shall not work between the hours of eight o'clock in the evening and six o'clock the following morning.

Article 13

Female labourers shall not work between the hours of ten o'clock in the evening and six o'clock the following morning.

Chapter 4: Rest and Holidays

Article 14

Any labourer who works continuously for a period of five hours shall have half an hour's rest.

Article 15

All labourers shall have one day of regular holiday in every seven days.

Article 16

All factories shall cease work on holidays designated by the laws or orders of the National Government.

Article 17

All labourers who work continuously for a fixed period shall be allowed a special holiday which shall be based on the following scale:

1. All labourers who have worked continuously for more than one year but less than three years, shall be allowed a holiday period of seven days each year;
2. All labourers who have worked continuously for more than three years but less than five years, shall be allowed a holiday period of ten days per year;
3. All labourers who have worked continuously for more than five years but less than ten years, shall be allowed a holiday period of fourteen days a year;
4. All labourers who have worked continuously for more than ten years shall have an additional day for each additional year added to his holiday period, but the total number of rest days shall not exceed thirty.

Article 18

All labourers shall be paid their regular wages for the holidays and rest periods provided in Articles 15, 16 and 17.

In cases where the labourers do not wish to enjoy the special holiday to which they are entitled, their wages for the said period shall be doubled.

Article 19

Where military establishments or public utility workers are concerned, the Proper Authorities may refuse to grant holiday periods whenever they deem such action necessary.

Chapter 5: Wages

Article 20

Minimum wages of the labourers shall be determined in accordance with the living conditions prevalent in the various localities in which the factories are established.

Article 21

Wages shall be paid to the labourers in full legal tender of the localities where the factories are situated.

Article 22

Regular wages based either on the time-rate or the piece-rate shall be paid to the workers at least twice a month. Wages shall be paid on fixed dates.

Article 23

Whenever an extension of working hours is made in accordance with Article 10 or

Article 19, the labourers' wages shall be increased from one-third to two-thirds of their regular wages calculated on an hourly basis.

Article 24

Male and female labourers of the same occupation and of equal efficiency shall receive equal wages.

Article 25

Factories shall not deduct in advance the wages of the labourers as security for penalties for breach of contract or as indemnity for damages.

Chapter 6: Termination of Working Contracts

Article 26

Contracts entered into for a stipulated period of time may upon expiration be renewed only by mutual agreement.

Article 27

In cases where the contract has no stipulation as to its term, the factory may cancel the same only by serving on the labourers a notice in advance. The time allowed by the notice shall be based upon the following scale, but this provision shall not apply to contracts which have stipulations concerning the manner of termination:

1. Ten days' advance notice to labourers who have worked in the factory for more than three months but less than one year
2. Twenty days' advance notice to labourers who have worked for more than one year but less than three years;
3. Thirty days' advance notice to labourers who have worked for more than three years.

Article 28

Labourers who have received notices of dismissal may ask for a leave of absence in order to apply for other jobs, but said leave of absence shall not exceed two working days a week. Wages during the said period shall be paid to said labourers.

Article 29

Factories which terminate the working contract in conformity with the provisions of Article 27 shall pay the labourers, in addition to their regular wages, half of the wages due for the period of notification as stipulated in the said Article. Failing to comply with the provisions of Article 27, the factories which desire summary termination of the working contract, shall pay to the labourers the entire wages for the period of notification as stipulated in the said Article.

Article 30

Factories may terminate the employment agreements with their labourers under any one of the following conditions, but must serve previous notices on them in accordance with the provisions of Article 27:

1. When a factory totally or partially suspends operations;
2. When a factory either through natural disasters or the force of unforeseen circumstances, is obliged to suspend operations for a period of over one month;
3. When a labourer is incapable of performing his work.

Article 31

Factories may terminate the employment agreements with their labourers without serving on them any previous notice under any one of the following conditions:

1. When a labourer repeatedly violates the factory's regulations;
2. When a labourer fails to reports for work without good cause for over three consecutive days or for over six days within one month.

Article 32

Labourers may terminate their working contracts by serving on the factories a notice of one week, in case said contracts have no stipulation as to the term thereof.

Article 33

Under any one of the following conditions the labourers may terminate their contracts with the factories without serving on the latter any previous notice:

1. When a factory violates the terms of the working contract or any important provisions of the Government's labour laws:
2. When a factory fails to pay the wages at the proper time without just cause.
3. When a factory maltreats the labourers.

Article 34

Disputes arising from the interpretations and applications of paragraph 3 of Article

30, paragraph 1 of Article 31 and Article 33 may be referred to the Factory Council for settlement.

Article 35

Upon termination of the working contract, the labourers may request the factory to issue them certificates of work, but this stipulation shall not be applicable in cases where the labourers summarily terminate their contract without conforming with the provisions of Article 32, or in cases where the contracts are terminated in accordance with any one of the conditions mentioned in Article 31. The certificates of work shall contain the following particulars:

1. The labourers' name in full, sex, age, native-place and address;
2. The kind of work engaged in by the labourer;
3. The period of time during which the labourer was employed by the factory and his record.

Chapter 7: Labourers' Welfare

Article 36

All factories shall provide supplementary education for the child labourers and apprentices, and shall be responsible for all the expenses incurred thereof. Such supplementary education shall not be less than ten hours a week. For other labourers who have no opportunity for education, the factories shall also establish within their means educational facilities. The time for conducting the above-mentioned education shall be arranged outside of the working hours.

Article 37

Female labourers shall be given leave with full wages before and after child-birth, amounting altogether to eight weeks in duration.

Article 38

Factories shall within the means of possibility assist the labourers in establishing workers' savings and co-operative societies, etc.

Article 39

Factories shall within the means of possibility erect workers' houses and promote proper amusements for their labourers.

Article 40

At the end of each fiscal year, after due appropriations have been made for divi-

dends and reserve funds, the factory shall give those labourers who have no demerits during the year, either a reward or a share of the remaining profits.

Chapter 8: Safety and Sanitation

Article 41

All factories shall take the following safety precautions:

1. Safety precautions against risk of personal injury to the labourers;
2. Safety precautions regarding the structure of the factory;
3. Precautions regarding the proper installation of machines;
4. Precautions for the prevention of fire and floods.

Article 42

All factories shall have the following sanitary provisions:

1. Provisions for good ventilation;
2. Provisions for pure drinks;
3. Provisions for lavatories and toilet facilities;
4. Provisions for light;
5. Provisions for poison prevention.

Article 43

All factories shall give their labourers safety education.

Article 44

Whenever the safety or sanitary provisions of a factory are found inadequate, the
Proper Authorities may require improvement within a definite period of time, and in
case of necessity may also forbid the use of any part of the factory.

Chapter 9: Labourers' Compensation and Pensions

Article 45

Pending the enforcement of Workers' Insurance Law, the factory shall pay to the
labourers who are injured or killed in the performance of their duty all medical
expenses and a sum based on the following scale. If, however, the capital of the
factory is less than fifty thousand dollars, the factory may petition the Proper Authorities to reduce the sums to be paid.

1. For labourers temporarily incapacitated, the factory shall, besides bearing the
   medical expenses, pay them each day a sum amounting to two-thirds of their
   regular wage for a period of not more than six months. Upon the expiration of

this said period, the factory may reduce the amount of compensation to half of the labourers' average wage for a period of not more than one year;

2. For workers permanently disabled in the performance of their duty, the factory shall pay a sum commensurate with the extent of the disablement. Such compensation, however, shall under no circumstances exceed three years' regular wages, or be less than one years' wages;

3. For labourers killed in the course of their employment, the factory shall, besides paying a sum of fifty dollars as funeral expenses, pay to the legal heirs, a sum of three hundred dollars, plus two years' regular wages. The regular wage mentioned above shall be based upon the laborers' average wage during the last three months of their employment. Funeral expenses and pensions shall be paid at one and the same time, but compensation for injuries or sickness or disablement may be paid at regular intervals.

Article 46

Pensions provided for in the previous Article shall be paid to the wife or husband of the deceased labourer. Should the deceased leave no wife or husband the pension, unless otherwise provided in the will of the deceased, shall be paid in accordance with the following order:

1. Children
2. Parents
3. Grandchildren
4. Brothers and Sisters

Article 47

Whenever a labourer urgently needs money on occasions of marriage or death, he may request the factory to advance him a sum not exceeding one month's wages, or the whole or a part of his savings.

Article 48

Should any accident occur resulting in the death or grave injury to a labourer, the factory shall, within five days, report its occurrence and the consequent measures taken to the Proper Authorities.

Chapter 10: Factory Council

Article 49

The Factory Council shall be composed of an equal number of representatives from both the factory and the labourers.

The factory representatives on the Factory Council shall be selected from those who are familiar with the conditions of the factory and the conditions of the labourers.

The election of labourers' representatives shall be reported to and supervised by the representatives of the Proper Authorities.

Article 50

The duties of the Factory Council shall be as follows:

1. To study the improvement of working efficiency;
2. To improve the relations between the factory and the labourers, and to settle disputes between them;
3. To co-operate in carrying out the collective agreement, the working contract and the regulations of the factory;
4. To co-operate in discussing methods of extending the working day;
5. To improve the safety and sanitary conditions of the factory;
6. To submit proposals for the improvement of factory conditions;
7. To plan welfare enterprises for the labourers.

Article 51

Matters referred to in the previous Article and concerning one workshop only shall first be referred to the representatives of the workshop in question and the factory for settlement. Should the representatives fail to effect a solution or should the matter concern two or more workshops, then the dispute shall be submitted to the Factory Council for settlement. Should the Council fail to effect a solution, then the dispute shall be settled in accordance with the Law for the Settlement of Disputes Between Capital and Labour.

Article 52

Labourers above sixteen years of age shall have the right to vote for the labourers' representatives on the Factory Council.

Article 53

Labourers who are of Chinese nationality, above twenty years of age and have worked in the factory for more than six months shall have the right to be elected as labourers' representatives.

Article 54

The number of representatives for either the factory or the labourers shall be limited to from three to nine.

Article 55

The chairman of the Factory Council shall be elected alternatively by the factory representatives and the labourers' representatives. The Factory Council shall have one regular meeting each month but in case of necessity may call special meetings. The quorum of the Factory meetings shall consist of a majority of the total representatives elected by the labourers and by the factory, and the decisions of the Factory Council shall become effective on a vote of two-thirds of the members present.

Chapter 11: Apprentices

Article 56

Factories taking apprentices shall first conclude contracts with them or their legal representatives. The contract shall be made in triplicate, one copy for each of the contracting parties and one to be submitted to the Proper Authorities for registration. The contract shall contain the following articles:

1. The name, sex, age, native place and address of the apprentice;
2. The kind of trade the apprentice is to follow;
3. The date on which the contract is made and its duration;
4. Mutual obligations. Should the apprentice be required to pay tuition, the amount and time for payment shall be stipulated. Where the contract of apprenticeship provides remuneration for the apprentice's service, the amount and time of payment shall likewise be stipulated. The above contract shall not restrict the apprentice's freedom to work upon the expiration of the apprenticeship.

Article 57

Neither male nor female persons below the age of thirteen shall be engaged as apprentices, excepting those who were already engaged as apprentices prior to the enforcement of this Law.

Article 58

The hours of training for apprentices shall be governed by the provisions of Chapter 3 of this Law.

Article 59

Except for purposes of practice, apprentices shall not be engaged in any of the occupations enumerated in Article 7.

Article 60

Apprentices shall be diligent, obedient and loyal towards the officers and masters of the factory.

Article 61

During the whole term of apprenticeship, the apprentices shall be supplied with board, lodging and medical care by the factory, in addition to a proper allowance for incidentals each month. The amount of this allowance shall be fixed by the Proper Authorities in accordance with the economic conditions of the locality and the standing of the factory, and with the approval of the Ministry of Industry.

Article 62

Except in cases of great necessity, no apprentices shall leave the factory during the period of apprenticeship; otherwise the apprentice or his legal representative shall refund the board, lodging and medical expenses incurred by the factory during the period of apprenticeship already served.

Article 63

The total number of apprentices taken by a factory shall not exceed one-third of its regular workers.

Article 64

Should a factory take more apprentices than it can adequately train, the Proper Authorities may order a partial reduction, and also set a limit to the number of apprentices the factory may thereafter take.

Article 65

During the period of apprenticeship the factory shall to the best of its ability train the apprentices for the trade specified in the contract of apprenticeship.

Article 66

In addition to the provision of Article 31, the factory may terminate the contract of apprenticeship under any one of the following conditions:

1. When the apprentice revolts against proper instructions;
2. When the apprentice commits theft and fails to repent, in spite of repeated admonitions.

Article 67

In addition to the provisions of Article 33, the apprentice or his legal representative may terminate the contract of apprenticeship under any one of the following conditions:

1. When the factory is incapable of performing its obligations stipulated in the contract;
2. When a factory becomes dangerous to the life and health of the apprentice or harmful to his character.

Chapter 12: Penalties

Article 68

Factories, violating the provisions of Article 7, 11, 12 and 13, shall be fined a sum of not less than one hundred and not more than five hundred dollars for each offence.

Article 69

Factories, violating the provision of Articles 5, 8, 9, 10, 37, and 63, shall be fined a sum of not less than fifty and not more than three hundred dollars for each offence.

Article 70

Factories, violating the provisions of Article 45, shall be fined a sum of not less than fifty and not more than two hundred dollars for each offence.

Article 71

Factories, violating the provisions of Articles 3, 4, 14, 15, 16, 17, 18, 19, and 36, shall be fined a sum of not more than one hundred dollars for each offence.

Article 72

When a factory foreman, due to disloyal conduct or negligence, causes thereby an accident or the extension thereof, he shall be punished with imprisonment for the period of not more than one year, or with a fine of not more than five hundred dollars.

Article 73

Any labourer who obstructs the operation of the factory or destroys the tools or equipment of the factory by violence, shall be punished in accordance with Law.

Article 74

A labourer who by duress compels other workers to strike, shall be dealt with in accordance with Law.

Chapter 13: Addenda

Article 75

The complication or alteration of factory regulations shall be submitted to the Proper Authorities for approval and promulgation.

Article 76

Regulations for the enforcement of this Law shall be issued separately.

Article 77

This Law shall come into force on and from the day of promulgation.

Appendix 3

Shanghai Child Labor Commission Enquiry Form, with Sample Responses, 1923–1924

1. Name of mill, factory, or workshop, address, and district	— Shanghai Cotton Manufacturing Co., Yangtzeppo Road.
2. Nature of work carried on there.	— cotton
3. Nature of premises.	— good
a. age and conditions:	— good
b. light and air:	— light good, air dust laden
c. space:	— adequate
d. temperature:	— hot in spinning room
e. sanitary conveniences	— leading out of work rooms, bad odor pervaded that part of room near lavatory — low wooden partitions — very bad air; appalling stench.
f. suitability for occupations, particularly as regards employment of young persons	— as in no. 2 — sympathetic management
g. further remarks:	— dining room provided, part-time school in factory for children, special fire appliances provided — medical treatment provided in the factory — supervisor engagement and dismissal — no contract system
4. Employment of children.	
a. approximate age of youngest child:	— 12, Chinese count
b. hours of labor:	— 12, with break of 15 minutes for meals — no night work for children under 13 — one day's rest in seven
c. night work:	— yes, but none for those under 13
d. nature of work done by children under 12/over 12:	— as in other cotton mills
e. apparent physical condition of children under 12/over 12:	— only fair
f. any objections to particular employment of children	— same as no. 1 mill

Appendix 3 *continued*,

g. any suggested improvements in
condition:

— same as 1: limiting age of children, prohibition of night work, removal of fluff from air, better ventilation, strict attention paid to sanitary accommodation. One day's rest in seven, limitation of working hours

Suggested general improvement regarding age of children, night work, ventilation in certain rooms, and sanitation.,

Source: Child Labor Commission, ''Enquiry Form,'' with comments in margins, in the archives of the Library at Friends' Meeting House, London, Agatha Harrison Papers, Temporary Box 50-B.,

Notes

Introduction

1. See, e.g., Shirley Garrett, *Social Reformers in Urban China: The Chinese YMCA, 1895–1926.*

2. Cited in Charles Hayford, *To the People: James Yen and Village China*, p. xi.

3. See World's Committee of the YMCA, *Industrial and Labour Problems* (Geneva, 1931), p. 16, in the archives of the library of the World's YMCA, Geneva, Box X314.119.5.

4. See World's YWCA, *World's YWCA: Industrial and Economic Questionnaire in Preparation for the World's Committee Meeting of 1928* (London, 1928), in the archives of the World's YWCA, Geneva (W), p. 1.

5. Ibid., p. 5, Appendix A, "Extract from Recommendations Adopted by the World's YWCA Committee Meeting, Champery, 1920."

6. Ibid. The draft conventions were: (a) establishing an eight-hour day or forty-eight-hour week in industry; (b) prohibiting night work by women of all ages; (c) prohibiting night work by male persons under eighteen (except in a very few continuous processes, in which only boys of sixteen years and upwards could be employed); (d) fixing the minimum age for admission of children to industrial employment at fourteen; (e) prohibiting employment of women during six weeks after childbirth, and granting them permission to leave work under medical certificate that their confinement would probably take place within six weeks (benefit sufficient for full and healthy maintenance of mother and child being provided either out of public funds or by means of a system of insurance, free attendance of doctor or midwife being an additional benefit); and (f) setting up free public employment agencies.

The recommendations were: (a) prevention of unemployment; (b) reciprocity of treatment of foreign workers; (c) international action for the prevention of anthrax; (d) international agreement for the protection of women and children from lead poisoning; (e) creation of government health services; and (f) application of the Berne Convention, 1906, prohibiting the use of white phosphorus in the manufacture of matches.

7. "Classeur 1/132, Reports from 1936–1940, Sections: Social and Industrial Section," manuscript, in the archives of the World's YWCA, Geneva, p. 2.

8. "Report of the Third Conference of Industrial Secretaries, YWCA of China, held at Shanghai, Jan. 19–25, 1933," manuscript, at National Headquarters, YWCA of the US, New York (D).

9. Hayford, *To the People*, pp. xi–xii, thus describes the belief in liberal and democratic values intermixed with Protestant Christianity and faith in business methods that Americans hoped to convey to China in the twentieth century.

10. See below, chapter 3.

11. See "Christianity and Industrial Problems," manuscript, in file entitled "Jerusalem Conference, 1928," World Council of Churches, Geneva (24).

12. While foreigners sometimes provided advice and assistance to the Mass Education Movement and to the Tinghsien project, as Hayford has shown the degree of success that these programs achieved was largely due to James Yen's persistence and that of his Chinese staff, as well as to patronage from key influential Chinese. See Hayford, *To the People.*

13. It will be argued in chapter 8 that this greater sympathy was in part because the YWCA officials came from several different countries, notably from Australia, Britain, and the United States, a well as China, and because many of the problems confronting women transcended class and national boundaries.

14. See, for example, the resolutions on the national question passed at the two major missionary conferences on economic questions: *Report of the Conference on Christianizing Economic Relations,* held under the auspices of the National Christian Council of China, Shanghai, August 18–28, 1927, NCC Shanghai, 1927, p. 117, World Council of Churches, Geneva (X); and *Papers, Abstracts and Extracts from Papers Contributed as a Basis of a Discussion to the Conference on the People's Livelihood, Shanghai, February 21–28, 1931,* p. 107, World Council of Churches, Geneva (X).

15. Among these men were well-known Y personalities, including E. E. Barnett, Fletcher Brockman, and William Lockwood.

16. See letter by Fletcher Brockman "for the Brockman family *only,*" n.d., in folder Jan.–Feb. 1927 in the archives of YMCA Historical Library, New York.

17. A discussion in 1926 between U.S. Minister McMurray and E. E. Barnett of the YMCA elicited the advice that in the event Chinese soldiers were quartered on YMCA property, the matter should be referred to the nearest U.S. consul: "In such an event the consul would lodge a protest which would serve later as a basis on which to make claims if serious damage should result from the occupancy of the house by soldiers. . . . By protesting at all such infringements on the rights of foreign property in different parts of the country, the United States authorities in China would show that they were not indifferent to interference made with American interests." Letter E. E. Barnett to Fletcher Brockman, Sept. 22, 1926, archives of YMCA Historical Library, New York (R15). It was recognized that the likelihood of any compensation being exacted for damages was small.

18. A comprehensive account of the legal position of foreigners in China at this time is contained in Richard Rigby, *The May Thirtieth Movement.* See especially the introduction and chapter 5.

19. Ibid., p. 21.

20. Nanking's direct supervision of Greater Shanghai, motivated no doubt in part by a desire to control developments there, inevitably gave a strong focus to any conflict that might arise there between Chinese and foreign interests.

21. For a discussion of these cases, see Eleanor Hinder, *Life and Labour in Shanghai,* pp. 8–9, n. 5. The proposition was that "the Congressional will manifest in the District of Columbia Compensation Act" might thus be enforced on American citizens operating factories in China.

22. There were similar difficulties over the possible enforcement of the Chinese labor laws by the Second Special District Court in the French Concession.

23. See Feetham, *Report of Mr. Justice Feetham to the Shanghai Municipal Council, 1931,* for a comprehensive review of the status of the settlement from the foreign perspective. With respect to this question as it affected enforcement of labor legislation see Augusta Wagner, *Labour Legislation in China,* pp. 15–65, and Hinder, *Life and Labour in Shanghai,* pp. 6–11.

Chapter 1

1. Albert Feuerwerker, "Economic Trends in the Late Ch'ing Empire, 1870–1911," in *The Cambridge History of China,* ed. J. K. Fairbank and Kwang-ching Liu, p. 29.

2. Lloyd Eastman, *Family, Fields and Ancestors: Constancy and Change in China's Social and Economic History*, p. 76.

3. "Minutes of the Child Labour Commission of Shanghai," manuscript, 1923–24, testimony of McNicol, in library archives at Friends' Meeting House, London (hereafter referred to as Friends' House, London), Agatha Harrison Papers, Temporary Box 50-B.

4. Augusta Wagner, *Labour Legislation in China*, p. 11.

5. Ibid.

6. Ibid., pp. 11–12.

7. See D. K. Lieu, *The Growth and Industrialisation of Shanghai*, pp. 346–58, table C-VI, and Wagner, *Labour Legislation in China*, p. 12; also Ho Han-wen, *Chung-kuo kuomin ching-chi kai-k'uang* (Outline of the Chinese national economy), pp. 7–8.

8. See, e.g., Gail Hershatter, *The Workers of Tianjin 1900–1949*, chap. 3.

9. Thomas G. Rawski, *Economic Growth in Prewar China*, p. 78.

10. See, e.g., the discussion of this problem in Wagner, *Labour Legislation in China*, pp. 4–11, and in Nym Wales, *The Chinese Labour Movement*, pp. 152–55.

11. According to Franklin Ho and H. D. Fong, directors of the Nankai University Committee on Social and Economic Research, the inadequacy of the early figures was a result of disruption caused by civil war and the failure to assess the level of mechanization in the factories being surveyed or to fix the definition of a factory, "inexperience" and "inertia" on the part of those gathering data, miscalculations, and misprints. See Franklin Ho and H. D. Fong, *The Extent and Effects of Industrialization in China*, p. 8. Many of the same criticisms could be made of data gathered in the 1930s. See D. K. Lieu, *The Growth and Industrialization of Shanghai*, pp. 61–64. A recent assessment of China's industrial growth by Chinese historians also recognizes the inadequacy of early statistical information. See comments in Ch'en Chen et al., *Chung-kuo chin-tai kung-yeh-shih tzu-liao* (Source material for the history of China's modern industry), 1:54, n. 4, and 57, n. 2.

12. The British White Paper, *Labour Conditions in China*, Cmd. 2442, published in 1925, which contained a considerable amount of information compiled by British consular officers on the scope and value of British enterprise in China, was the exception to the more general practice of discretion in such matters. This document was produced in response to a growing concern in Britain about labor militancy in China, and to the exposure of conditions of life and labor there by the lobby seeking to restrict the use of child labor in Shanghai.

13. See below, chapter 6.

14. Statistics from the Annual Reports of the Ministry of Agriculture and Commerce, 1914–1920, are reproduced in Ho and Fong, *Extent and Effects of Industrialization*, pp. 9–12.

15. Wagner, *Labour Legislation in China*, p. 11. According to the Factory Act of 1931, a "factory" was an industrial establishment that used power machinery and employed thirty people or more.

16. Rawski, *Economic Growth in Prewar China*, pp. 9, 65, and 87–88, citing Ta-chung Liu and Kung-chia Yeh, *The Economy of the Chinese Mainland: National Income and Economic Development, 1933–1959*, table F–1.

17. Richard C. Bush, *The Politics of Cotton Textiles in Kuomintang China, 1927–1937*, p. 31.

18. Ho and Fong, *Extent and Effects of Industrialization*, p. 13. In the *China Year Book* it was maintained that this was a result not only of the war, which had reduced the extent of competition from outside China, but also of the revision of tariffs effective in 1919, which had imposed higher import duties on cotton yarn. See the *China Year Book* (1938), p. 539. Yen Chung-p'ing, in his recent study of the growth of the cotton industry in China, places its progress at this time in the context of the erosion of British commercial supremacy in the Far East and elsewhere. See Yen Chung-p'ing, *Chung-kuo mien-fong-chih shih-kao* (Draft history of the cotton-spinning industry in China, 1289–1937), p. 162.

19. Rawski, *Economic Growth in Prewar China*, p. 71.

20. Ho and Fong, *Extent and Effects of Industrialization*, p. 17.

21. *Chung-kuo sha-ch'ang i-lan piao* (Complete list of cotton mills in China) (Shanghai:

Chinese Cotton Mill Owners' Association, 1937), cited in Wagner, *Labour Legislation in China*, p. 11.

22. Cited in Rawski, *Economic Growth in Prewar China*, p. 88.

23. From Shanghaishi mianfangzhi gongye tongye gonghui, *Zhongguo mianfang tongji shiliao*, cited in Emily Honig, *Sisters and Strangers: Women in the Shanghai Cotton Mills, 1919–1949*, table 2, p. 30.

24. See, for example, Kyong Bae-tsung, *Industrial Women in Wusih* (Shanghai: YWCA, 1929), in library archives of National Headquarters, YWCA of the United States, New York (hereafter referred to as YWCA, New York), Box B. This study reveals that 82 percent of the 9,539 operatives in four cotton mills in Wusih were women. For an indication of the precise designation of files at the YWCA, New York, see the bibliography.

25. Ho and Fong, *Extent and Effects of Industrialization*, pp. 17–18.

26. Kyong, *Industrial Women in Wusih*, p. 2.

27. This figure is obtained if the average number of workers per filature in Shanghai and Wusih is taken to apply to filatures throughout China. This assumption would seem not unreasonable, for although some filatures may have been smaller than those in Shanghai and Wusih, those in Kwangtung are supposed to have been larger. See Ho and Fong, *Extent and Effects of Industrialization*, pp. 19–20.

28. Liu and Yeh, cited in Rawski, *Economic Growth in Prewar China*, p. 88.

29. Ho and Fong, *Extent and Effects of Industrialization*, p. 20.

30. Sherman Cochran, *Big Business in China: Sino-Foreign Rivalry in the Cigarette Industry, 1890–1930*, p. 202.

31. *China Year Book*, 1938, p. 545.

32. Liu and Yeh, cited in Rawski, *Economic Growth in Prewar China*, p. 88.

33. Ibid. A comprehensive account of the history of the Nanyang Brothers Tobacco Company is contained in the commentary to *Nan-yang hsiung-ti yen-ts'ao kung-ssu shih-liao* (Source material for the history of the Nanyang Brothers Tobacco Co.) (Shanghai: Chung-kuo k'o-hsueh-yuan Shang-hai ching-chi yen-chiu-so, 1958.) This study, as well as giving prominence to social matters and labor struggles, recounts the competition that developed between the company and the British-American Tobacco Company for influence with the Nationalist government. A brief account of the history of the BAT Company is given in "Tsung ying-mei yen kung-ssu kan ti-kuo-chu-i ti ching-chi chin-lae" (Imperialist penetration of China as seen in the case of the British-American Tobacco Company).

34. Liu and Yeh, cited in Rawski, *Economic Growth in Prewar China*, p. 548. According to a report of the Nanking government's Bureau of Information in 1928, cited in Ho and Fong, *Extent and Effects of Industrialization*, p. 24, there were at that time 189 match factories in China.

35. Liu and Yeh, cited in Rawski, *Economic Growth in Prewar China*, p. 88.

36. *China Year Book*, 1938, p. 548.

37. Liu and Yeh, cited in Rawski, *Economic Growth in Prewar China*, p. 88.

38. *China Year Book*, 1938, p. 542.

39. Eastman, *Family, Fields and Ancestors*, pp. 177–78.

40. Rawski, *Economic Growth in Prewar China*, p. 71.

41. Testimony of R. J. McNicol, "Minutes of the Child Labor Commission of Shanghai" (unpublished manuscript located among the Agatha Harrison Papers).

42. The present work does not discuss labor militancy or the role of trade unions in any detail. In addition to earlier work by Jean Chesneaux and Nym Wales on this subject, there is now also substantial reference to the labor movement in the work of Emily Honig, Gail Hershatter, and others. See bibliography.

43. See Parks M. Coble, Jr., *The Shanghai Capitalists and the Nationalist Government 1927–1937*, and Bush, *The Politics of Cotton Textiles*. Lloyd Eastman, in *The Abortive Revolution: China under Nationalist Rule 1927–1937*, takes a more extreme view of the divergence of interests between the Kuomintang government and Chinese capitalists. Joseph

Fewsmith, on the other hand, in *Party, State, and Local Elites in Republican China: Merchant Organizations and Politics in Shanghai, 1890–1930*, sees the party, the Kuomintang, ultimately squeezed out by a "corporatist" identity of interests between government and Chinese big business (p. 163), a view that seems not inconsistent with that of David Strand, in his *Rickshaw Beijing: City People and Politics in the 1920's*, who observes of 1920s Peking that the police and Chamber of Commerce were the "two most important order-keeping bodies in the city" (p. xiv).

44. Bush, *The Politics of Cotton Textiles*, pp. 165–75.

45. Coble, *The Shanghai Capitalists*, p. 141.

46. Rawski, *Economic Growth in Prewar China*, p. 173.

47. Coble, pp. 147, 152.

48. *China Year Book*, 1938, pp. 541, 539.

49. Rawski, *Economic Growth in Prewar China*, pp. 174–75.

50. The efforts of the Shanghai Municipal Council's Industrial Section to cope with the problems created by the emergency are considered in chapter 6.

51. Rawski, *Economic Growth in Prewar China*, pp. 71, 95–96, 110–11, 353–59.

52. See C. F. Remer, *Foreign Investment in China*, pp. 70, 86, 289, 400, 499–500, 603. Remer had been involved in the 1920s in the early Christian initiatives to disseminate information about working conditions in Chinese industry. He appears to treat the BAT Co. as British for the purpose of his study. Chinese historians have more recently reviewed the former foreign economic presence in their country. In Ch'en Chen et al., *Chung-kuo chin-tai kung-yeh-shih tzu-liao*, vol. 2, source material is assembled to show in some detail the nature and extent of foreign investment in China, by origin of capital invested.

53. Eastman, *Family, Fields and Ancestors*, p. 171.

54. Rawski, *Economic Growth in Prewar China*, pp. 74 and 87.

55. Cochran, *Big Business in China*, p. 213.

56. Cochran looks at four key areas in his study: investment of capital, management-labor relations, relations between business and government, and procurement of raw materials.

57. See the work of Hou Chi-ming and of Robert F. Dernberger, cited in ibid., p. 4. See also Eastman, *Family, Fields and Ancestors*, p. 171.

58. Strikes against the BAT Company occurred thirty-one times between 1918 and 1930, and only five times against Nanyang Brothers in the same period. See Cochran, *Big Business in China*, p. 208.

59. Rawski, *Economic Growth in Prewar China*, p. 92.

60. See the comments of ILO official Pierre Henry in chapter 7.

61. Strand, *Rickshaw Beijing*, p. 30, notes many more rickshaw men in Peking in winter.

62. Jean Chesneaux, *The Chinese Labour Movement, 1919–1927*, p. 451. The terms Chiangpei, used by Chesneaux, and Supei (Subei in Pinyin), preferred by Honig, are interchangeable.

63. See Hershatter, *The Workers of Tianjin*, pp. 17, 49, 59. See also Honig, *Sisters and Strangers*, chap. 3.

64. Eastman, *Family, Fields and Ancestors*, p. 209.

65. Chesneaux, *The Chinese Labour Movement*, p. 54.

66. Strand, *Rickshaw Beijing*, p. 163.

67. Chesneaux, *The Chinese Labour Movement*, p. 56. Chesneaux maintains that in Shanghai the use of apprenticeship was restricted to small enterprises such as dye works, canneries, and some printing works, but testimony before the Child Labor Commission in Shanghai in 1923 suggests that its use in the city was more common, notable in shipbuilding, construction, and rug factories. See "Minutes of the Child Labour Commission of Shanghai" (unpublished manuscript located among the Agatha Harrison Papers), testimony of Skinner, Chen, and Hille.

68. Hershatter, *The Workers of Tianjin*, p. 52. Hershatter devotes chapter 4 of her book to a discussion of contract labor.

69. Honig, *Sisters and Strangers*, p. 119, notes that some mills in Shanghai in the 1920s hired female labor under the apprentice system.

70. Chesneaux, *The Chinese Labour Movement*, p. 56. The issue of apprenticeship is taken up by Lowe Ch'uan-hua, both in his *Facing Labour Issues in China*, pp. 23–27, and in his *Chin-jih Chung-kuo lao-tung wen-ti*, pp. 226–32. The former was published in London in 1934, and the latter in Shanghai in 1933; while substantially similar, their texts vary in detail. It is significant that Lowe should feel unable to put such a strong case against apprenticeship in the Chinese version as in the English edition of his book.

71. See, for example, Hershatter, *The Workers of Tianjin*, p. 53, and Eastman, *Family, Fields and Ancestors*, p. 207.

72. Hershatter, *The Workers of Tianjin*, pp. 53, 103.

73. Chesneaux, *The Chinese Labour Movement*, pp. 59–61.

74. Wagner, *Labour Legislation in China*, pp. 37, 38.

75. Ibid.

76. "Report of the Child Labour Commission," part 1, in *Shanghai Municipal Gazette*, July 19, Friends' House, London, Temporary Box 50-B. It is perhaps surprising that Communist and other militant observers did not make more of the issue of the employment of children under contract and in other ways. Probably typical, however, is the attitude of Li Ta-chao expressed in a letter to *Chung-kuo kung-jen* at the time of the campaign against child labor in 1925. Li took the view that any attempt at gradual reform of child labor was futile, and that the issue could only be resolved through mass struggle on the part of the trade unions. See Li Ta-chao, "Shang-hai te t'ung-kung wen-ti," April 1925, in *Li Ta-chao hsuan-chi* (Collected Works of Li Ta-chao) (Peking: People's Publishers, 1962), pp. 516–22.

77. Honig, *Sisters and Strangers*, pp. 96, 117.

78. Ibid., pp. 121–31.

79. For example: Bureau of Social Affairs, City Government of Greater Shanghai, *Wage Rates in Shanghai* (Shang-hai shih chih kung-tzu li) (1935) (English and Chinese); D. K. Lieu, *The Growth and Industrialization of Shanghai*, especially appendix B, pp. 306–14; T. Y. Tsha, "A Study of Wage Rates in Shanghai, 1930–1934," in *Nankai Social and Economic Quarterly* 88, 3 (October 1935); Dorothy Orchard, "Man Power in China," *Political Science Quarterly* 50 and 51 (December 1935 and March 1936). The study that gave rise to a more general interest in this problem was Bureau of Social Affairs, City Government of Greater Shanghai, *The Index Numbers of Earnings of Factory Labourers in Greater Shanghai, July–December 1928* (Shang-hai t'e-pieh-shih kung-tzu chih-shu chih shih-pien) (English and Chinese).

80. For example: H. D. Lamson, "The Standard of Living of Factory Workers," *Chinese Economic Journal* 7 (1930); Bureau of Social Affairs, City Government of Greater Shanghai, *The Cost of Living Index Numbers of Labourers, Greater Shanghai, January 1926–December 1931* (Shang-hai-shih kung-jen sheng-huo fei chih-shu) (1932) (English and Chinese); "The Living Standard of Shanghai Labourers," *China Critic* 7 (December 27, 1934); Shanghai Municipal Council, "Report of the Housing Committee, 1936–37," cited in *Shanghai Municipal Gazette*, March 30, 1937. See section on the expenditures of working-class families, reproduced in Wagner, *Labour Legislation in China*, p. 47.

81. T. Y. Tsha, "A Study of Wage Rates in Shanghai," p. 501, cited in Wales, *The Chinese Labour Movement*, p. 156.

82. See Lowe Ch'uan-hua, "Labour Conditions," in *Chinese Year Book*, 1937, p. 768.

83. See, for example, "Visite d'une filature de coton, Pékin," and "Visite de petites manufactures de tapis, Pékin" in "Visites d'Usines," manuscript, 1924, in dossier G/900/28/1 Voyage de M. Pierre Henry en Chine, in archives of International Labour Organization, Geneva (hereafter referred to as ILO, Geneva).

84. Honig, *Sisters and Strangers*, p. 155, and Hershatter, *The Workers of Tianjin*, p. 152.

85. Hershatter, *The Workers of Tianjin*, p. 164.

86. Eastman, *Family, Fields and Ancestors*, p. 207.

87. Orchard, "Man Power in China."

88. After 1932 wages tend to drop because of the depression.

89. T. Y. Tsha, "The Living Standard of Shanghai Labourers."

90. "Report of the Housing Committee, 1936–37," cited in the *Shanghai Municipal Gazette*, March 30, 1937, pp. 119–20. The survey covered a sample of families of 101 unskilled workers paid from $15 to $24 per month, 85 semiskilled workers paid from $25 to $34 per month, and 94 skilled workers paid from $35 to $60 per month; also 390 families of workers whose skill level and income was not specified.

91. "Regulation of Industrial Conditions," in *Annual Report of the Shanghai Municipal Council*, 1938, p. 43. Except where noted otherwise, these reports were consulted at the Foreign Office Library, London.

92. Ibid. It is not clear that this would have been the case. In cotton mills, for example, where much foreign capital was invested, the use of female labor was widespread, and in most mills women workers would probably have constituted a majority.

93. See appendix 1C. The greatest increase over the years 1937–39 was in the cost of accommodation, fuel and light, food, and clothing. See "Regulation of Industrial Conditions," 1939, pp. 46–47. A Chinese study, completed after Liberation, suggests that despite postwar fiscal reform the cost-of-living index in Shanghai had risen from a base of 100 in 1936 to over 3 million by 1947. See Chung-kuo k'o-hsueh-yuan Shanghai ching-chi yen-chiu-so, *Shang-hai chieh-fang ch'ien-hou wu-chia tzu-liao hui-pien, 1921–1957* (Commodity prices before and after the liberation of Shanghai, 1921–1957) (Shanghai, 1959), p. 330.

94. "Regulation of Industrial Conditions," 1935, p. 37.

95. Rawski, *Economic Growth in Prewar China*, p. 82. See appendix 1D below.

96. Cochran, *Big Business in China*, pp. 137, 155, 203.

97. Strand, *Rickshaw Beijing*, p. 29.

98. Hershatter, *The Workers of Tianjin*, pp. 58, 68.

99. Honig, *Sisters and Strangers*, p. 55.

100. Eastman, *Family, Fields and Ancestors*, p. 207. On this point see the discussion in chapter 5 below. This problem persisted in Hong Kong into the 1970s. See R. Porter, "Child Labour in Hong Kong and Related Problems: A Brief Review," *International Labour Review*, Geneva (May 1975).

101. Lowe, *Facing Labour Issues in China*, p. 118. Lowe notes that the Bureau of Social Affairs had not kept up-to-date data on unemployment in Shanghai.

102. Cited in ibid. Yet another source put the total number of unemployed in handicraft and modern industry for the peak (Chinese) depression year of 1934 at 12 million. See *Chung-kuo lao-tung nien-chien* (Chinese labour yearbook) (1934), p. 252.

103. "Regulation of Industrial Conditions," reprinted from the *Annual Report of the Shanghai Municipal Council*, 1937, pp. 2, 37, in dossier N/200/1/13/5, ILO Geneva.

104. "Regulation of Industrial Conditions," 1938, p. 31. These totals include workers in the so-called extra-settlement roads areas, which were under Municipal Council jurisdiction.

105. The level of economic activity began to decline after mid-1939, as the outbreak of the war in Europe made the commercial position of Shanghai progressively less secure. It is also likely that many workers were displaced by the previous Sino-Japanese conflict in Shanghai in the spring of 1932. See "Regulation of Industrial Conditions," 1939, p. 33.

106. Rawski, *Economic Growth in Prewar China*, p. xxviii.

107. See Strand, *Rickshaw Beijing*, chap. 9.

108. See Hershatter, *The Workers of Tianjin*, p. 35.

109. Honig, *Sisters and Strangers*, pp. 79–87, 101, 104.

110. Eastman, *Family, Fields and Ancestors*, p. 207.

111. "Report of the Child Labour Commission," part 1 (unpublished manuscript located among the Agatha Harrison Papers).

112. A detailed description of the process of decay caused by phosphorous poisoning in the case of one worker who subsequently died is given in a memorandum entitled "Phossy-Jaw," text indicates ca. 1925, in the archives of the World's YWCA, Geneva (hereafter referred to as YWCA, Geneva), (C). The worker maintained that if he had known more about the dangers of working with phosphorous, he would have sought other employment.

113. See "Visite de petites manufactures de tapis, Pékin," and "Visite d'une fabrique de cloisonnés, Pékin," in "Visites d'Usines."

114. Letter Eleanor Hinder to "My Dears," Feb. 25, 1933, YWCA, Geneva, (L).

115. "Kwong Song Glass Factory, Hong Kong," in "Visites d'Usines."

116. Honig, *Sisters and Strangers*, p. 108.

117. Hershatter, *The Workers of Tianjin*, p. 74.

118. Honig, *Sisters and Strangers*, pp. 113, 144, 150.

119. "Regulation of Industrial Conditions," 1937, pp. 13, 14. The studies were undertaken jointly by the Industrial Section of the Shanghai Municipal Council and the Henry Lester Institute of Medical Research. They appear to have been published by the Chinese Medical Association.

120. See, for example, the testimony of Dr. Fullerton and Dr. New, in "Minutes of the Child Labour Commission of Shanghai" (unpublished manuscript among the Agatha Harrison Papers).

121. For the risk of fire, see, for example, "Regulation of Industrial Conditions," 1939, p. 38.

122. "Regulation of Industrial Conditions," 1937, pp. 12–13, and 1938, pp. 34–37.

123. The annual totals were 1934: 1,788 accidents (112 fatal); 1935: 2,301 accidents (104 fatal); 1936: 2,200 accidents (95 fatal); 1937: 1,976 accidents (58 fatal); 1938: 1,513 accidents (88 fatal); 1939: 1,942 accidents (110 fatal); 1940: 1,487 accidents (79 fatal). See "Regulation of Industrial Conditions," accident report tables for each year.

124. For example, in 1938 the most accidents occurred in transport and the most fatalities in construction; in 1939 the most accidents and the most fatalities occurred in the textile industry; while in 1940 the most accidents occurred in the machine tool and metal products industry, and the most fatalities again in textiles. See ibid., 1938, pp. 33–35; 1939, p. 37; and 1940, p. 66.

125. M. T. Tchou, *Housing and Social Conditions among Industrial Workers in Shanghai*, Industrial Department, National Committee of the YMCA of China, Shanghai, May 1926, in archives of the library at the World's YMCA, Geneva, Box X358.3. The YMCA's own "model village" project is considered below.

126. A good description of a typical Chinese house is contained in Eleanor Hinder, *Life and Labour in Shanghai* (New York, 1944), pp. 83–84.

127. Hershatter, *The Workers of Tianjin*, p. 69.

128. Ibid., p. 79; Honig, *Sisters and Strangers*, pp. 23, 61.

129. Cochran, *Big Business in China*, pp. 137, 157.

130. "Regulation of Industrial Conditions," 1938, p. 42.

131. *Regulations for Welfare Work for the Commercial Press Employees*, n.d., text indicates ca. 1924, in dossier G/900/28/1, ILO Geneva.

132. These apparent concessions to workers may not have been honored in their entirety. Pierre Henry reported dissatisfaction over the failure to provide an eight-hour working day on his visit to the Commercial Press in 1924. See "Commercial Press, Shanghai," in "Visites d'Usines." In June 1925 workers at the company struck and formed a union demanding, among other things, an eight-hour day, abolition of contract labor, improved wages, and better treatment for apprentices. See Lowe, *Facing Labour Issues in China*, pp. 63–64.

133. Cochran, *Big Business in China*, pp. 137, 157. See also Richard W. Rigby, *The May Thirtieth Movement*, p. 10, and "Minutes of the Child Labour Commission of Shanghai" (unpublished manuscript located among the Agatha Harrison Papers), testimony of Su, and "Statement by the Naigai Wata Kaisha Ltd" cited in Lowe, *Facing Labour Issues*, p. 133. BAT offered a savings scheme, though conditions for withdrawal of money deposited were stringent.

134. See Lowe, *Facing Labour Issues in China*, p. 133. A discussion of private welfare schemes as they had evolved by the 1930s is contained in Ch'en Ta, *Chung-kuo lao-kung wen t'i* (Labor problems in China) (Shanghai, 1933), pp. 491–502. Ch'en was a firm advo-

cate of private welfare, but he conceded that many employers had yet to see the need for it.

135. Hershatter, *The Workers of Tianjin*, p. 165.

136. Strand, *Rickshaw Beijing*, pp. 128–29, 242.

137. *Provisional Factory Law, General Regulations*, promulgated by Ministerial Order no. 223 of the Ministry of Agriculture and Commerce, March 29, 1923. The text of the regulations is given in appendix 2A.

138. See *Labour Conditions in China*, cmd. 2442.

139. Wagner, *Labour Legislation in China*, p. 101.

140. Chesneaux, *The Chinese Labour Movement*, p. 308.

141. Wagner, *Labour Legislation in China*, p. 100.

142. In October 1923 the Peking government also promulgated a new set of factory regulations, with provision for inspection and enforcement, but as the government was shortly overthrown, these regulations were not put to the test.

143. The principal items of legislation were *Regulations Governing the Enforcement of Workers' Education*, promulgated in two stages in 1932 and 1934; *Provisional Regulations Governing Minimum Wages for Workers in Government Enterprises* and *Minimum Wage Law*, promulgated in 1934 and 1936, respectively; and *Factory Safety and Health Inspection Regulations*, issued in 1935. See ibid., pp. 104–5.

144. For example, while a regular weekly rest day was stipulated, no provision was made to cover the loss of earnings that this would cause. While the duties of employers to apprentices were set forth, apprentices were prohibited from quitting their employment during this term. The factory councils, in their pursuit of greater efficiency in the factory, were to explore the possibility of extending the working day in particular cases.

145. Ibid., pp. 140–42. Payment of medical expenses for sickness or injury contracted on the job was also supposed to be achieved during stage one. In stage two, the emphasis was to be on accident prevention and sanitation; in stage three, on hours of work and supplementary education; in stage four, on protection for child workers, apprentices, and women; and in stage five, on further regulation of hours of work and annual leave. Ch'en, *Chung-kuo lao-kung wen t'i*, pp. 557–58, in 1933 had advocated legislation at a level appropriate to Chinese conditions, seeming not to recognize that this argument could be turned about to justify no legislation at all.

It is beyond the scope of the present work to consider the progress of the trade union movement in China during the period under review. By and large, industrial welfare work and the trade unions proceeded in parallel, and there were few points of contact. For an account of trade union activity, see the two classic works on this subject: Wales, *The Chinese Labour Movement*, and Chesneaux, *The Chinese Labour Movement*.

Chapter 2

1. The most comprehensive account of the early work of the YMCA in China is Shirley Garrett's *Social Reformers in Urban China: The Chinese YMCA, 1895–1926*. See also K. S. Latourette, *World Service: A History of the Foreign Work and World Service of the YMCA's of the US and Canada*.

2. On James Yen, see Charles Hayford, *To the People: James Yen and Village China*.

3. C. C. Shedd, "Statement of Returned Labourer Work," May 26, 1920, manuscript, Industrial Department, Wu-Han YMCA, YMCA Historical Library, New York (R1).

4. G. A. Fitch, "Annual Report for the Year Ending 31 October 1921," Shanghai YMCA, manuscript, YMCA Historical Library, New York (R1).

5. The seven factories were the Yah Zung Safe Factory, San Yiu Towel Factory, China Industrial Corporation, Chi Ming Dye Works, Commercial Press, Chung Hwa Book Company, and Amos Bird Company, which dealt in egg products. No foreign firms were involved in the program.

6. Fitch, "Annual Report."

7. Ibid.

8. See "Industrial Department, Secretaries G. A. Fitch and W. S. Chen," manuscript, Jan. 1, 1921, YMCA Historical Library, New York (R5).

9. Fitch, "Annual Report." This report gives the date of destruction of the hut as June 1921, while a published report records that the hut was burned in the winter of 1920. See *A Community Enterprise: Review of the Work of the YMCA of Shanghai for the Year 1921*, Shanghai YMCA, 1921, World's YMCA, Geneva, Box X392.21 (51).

10. Fitch, "Annual Report."

11. Ibid.

12. It would appear that this seminar was repeated in the autumn of 1922. See Fitch, "Annual Report for 1922," manuscript, YMCA Historical Library, New York (A).

13. "Statement of Returned Labourer Work" and "A Few Hopes and Suggestions for the Development of the Industrial Department Work in Wu Han," manuscript, January 1921, YMCA Historical Library, New York (R1).

14. "Memorandum Regarding the Industrial Work of Shanghai Young Men's Christian Association," manuscript, n.d., attached to letter W. W. Lockwood to C. A. Herschleb, March 8, 1922, YMCA Historical Library, New York (R9).

15. "Mr Brockman's Address," manuscript, n.d., in file "Jan.-March 1920," YMCA Historical Library, New York (R2).

16. "Memorandum Regarding the Industrial Work."

17. Letter W. W. Lockwood to E. C. Jenkins, April 3, 1921, in YMCA Historical Library, New York (R1).

18. Letter E. C. Jenkins to Fletcher Brockman, Sept. 29, 1921, YMCA Historical Library, New York (R4).

19. Letter W. W. Lockwood to E. C. Jenkins, April 3, 1921.

20. M. T. Tchou, "Report on Industrial and Social Survey," manuscript, December 1922, World's YMCA, Geneva, Box X358.3.

21. A sample questionnaire is attached to the report sent in by C. C. Shedd of Wuhan, along with a covering letter, C. C. Shedd to Frank Lenz, July 6, 1922, YMCA Historical Library, New York (R6).

22. Ibid.

23. J. W. Nipps, "Report for the Eddy Campaign," manuscript, YMCA Historical Library, New York (R6).

24. Tchou, "Report on Industrial and Social Survey."

25. Ibid., p. 12.

26. "Conference on Industrial Work of Local and National Staff," November 28, 1922, manuscript, YMCA Historical Library, New York (R9).

27. Sherwood Eddy, "The Social Gospel in China," *Chinese Recorder* (February 1923), p. 77.

28. "Report on the Industrial Work of the YMCA's of China: 1923," manuscript, World's YMCA, Geneva, Box X358.3. Others Tchou met included Governor William Sweet, A. H. Lichty, J. B. Matteson, A. B. Minear, Samuel Gompers, A. A. Hyde, W. C. Coleman, Ben Charrington, A. G. Studer, Augustus Nash, Harry F. Ward, F. E. Johnson, Kirby Page, Robert W. Bruere, E. B. Chaffee, Cedric Long, Spencer Miller, J. N. Sayre, Brewer Eddy, Raymond Robbins, and Mary McDowell in the United States, and Ramsay MacDonald, Arthur Henderson, Lord Haldane, Lady Astor, J. J. Mallon, and Margaret Bondfield in Britain. Tchou also attended Sherwood Eddy's "American Seminar" in London in the summer of 1923.

29. M. T. Tchou, "Report of Fall Trip: Aspcts of Co-operation with Various Agencies," manuscript, received April 1924, World's YMCA, Geneva Box 315 (51). The cities visited were Hangchow, Tsinan, Tientsin, Peking, Chefoo, Chengchow, and Wuhan, along with the Chi Ming Shan coal mine.

30. M. T. Tchou, letter beginning "Dear Friends," April 13, 1924, YMCA Historical Library, New York (R9).

31. M. T. Tchou, "Statement on YMCA Industrial Work,' manuscript, July 1925, YMCA Historical Library, New York (R12). The cities, approximately in the order in which work was commenced in them, were Wuhan, Shanghai, Tientsin, Nanking, Tsinan, Chowtsun, Tsingchow, Chengchow, Changsha, Canton, Hangchow, Chefoo, Peking, Mukden, Antung, and Foochow. Industrial work ceased in Nanking after 1922, and Antung had only a summer program in 1924.

32. "Annual Report for 1925 of T. C. McConnell," manuscript, YMCA Historical Library, New York (R11).

33. Tchou, "Statement on YMCA Industrial Work."

34. Ibid. In this he anticipated James Yen, who later became concerned to embrace all aspects of the people's livelihood in his work at Tinghsien.

35. M. T. Tchou, "Outlines of Report on Housing and Social Conditions Among Industrial Workers in Shanghai," Industrial Department, National Committee of the YMCA of China, Shanghai, May 1926, World's YMCA, Geneva, Box X358.3, pp. 5–9, 14.

36. M. T. Tchou, "Outlines of Plan for Model Villages for Working People," Industrial Department, National Committee of the YMCA of China, Shanghai, n.d., World's YMCA, Geneva, Box X358.3. As the text indicates that this pamphlet was published after the housing survey above but before construction of the YMCA Model Village, the date of publication must be 1926. The quotations are from pages 1 and 10.

37. Letter W. W. Lockwood to Fletcher Brockman, Oct. 13, 1926, YMCA Historical Library, New York (R15); Letter J. C. Clark to C. A. Herschleb, Oct. 19, 1926, YMCA Historical Library, New York (R14); "Shanghai's Model Village: The Pootung Branch of the Shanghai YMCA," publicity handout, n.d., World's YMCA, Geneva, Box X358.3. Text indicates that the date of publication must be 1928. The cornerstone of the first house was laid by Dr. Rufus Jones, the noted American Quaker.

38. Letter W. W. Lockwood to Fletcher Brockman, Oct. 13, 1926.

39. "The Model Village Regulations," manuscript, received Feb. 21, 1928, YMCA Historical Library, New York (R20). The composition of the village "board" is nowhere given, but it would appear that the board is the same body as the committee of the Shanghai YMCA in charge of the Pootung Village mentioned in correspondence. "The Committee is composed of strong men, leaders in Shanghai, the Chairman being Mr N. L. Han, General Manager of the China Express Company and Treasurer of our National Committee." See letter E. E. Barnett to C. A. Herschleb, April 29, 1929, YMCA Historical Library, New York (R25). This committee was in fact the regular Industrial Committee of the Shanghai YMCA.

40. "Shanghai's Model Village."

41. "The Model Village Activities," manuscript, received Feb. 21, 1928, YMCA Historical Library, New York (R20).

42. Industrial Work of the Shanghai YMCA: Anniversary Report, 1935, November 1935, p. 9, YMCA Historical Library, New York, Box "China: Industrial Work." Text indicates that the pamphlet was published by the Industrial Department of the Shanghai YMCA, X951.03.

43. "The Model Village Activities."

44. "Pootung Model Village Proves Boon to Workers," The China Press, May 5, 1933, YMCA Historical Library, New York (R30).

45. Figures cited from "Shanghai's Model Village"; "Pootung Model Village"; and Industrial Work of the Shanghai YMCA.

46. "The Model Village Activities"; "Pootung Model Village"; "Shanghai's Model Village"; and Industrial Work of the Shanghai YMCA.

47. Industrial Work of the Shanghai YMCA.

48. "The Model Village Activities" and "Shanghai's Model Village."

49. The population of the Model Village in 1935, with the same number of houses, is given as eighty-eight. See Industrial Work of the Shanghai YMCA, p. 2.

50. "Social Centre More Popular than Jessfield," The China Press, May 12, 1933, YMCA Historical Library, New York (R30).

51. "Shanghai's Model Village."

52. See *Industrial Work of the Shanghai YWCA*. Thomas Tchou occupied a variety of posts concerned with industry within the Nationalist government after his departure from the YMCA in 1929 (see below), including that of chief representative for China to the ILO in Geneva in the early 1930s. For its part, the KMT was undoubtedly interested in eliminating causes of urban social unrest and was persuaded that the model villages would contribute to this end.

53. "Formal Opening of Model Villages Scheduled Today," *The China Press*, Feb. 29, 1936, YMCA Historical Library, New York (R32).

54. From a letter to Sidney Gamble, author unknown, enclosed with a letter from C. A. Herschleb to E. E. Barnett, March 28, 1929, YMCA Historical Library, New York (R25).

55. Letter E. E. Barnett to C. A. Herschleb, April 29, 1929, YMCA Historical Library, New York (R25). Barnett was anxious to establish that the YMCA itself made no money out of the undertaking.

56. Letter Eleanor Hinder to Mack Eastman, Dec. 7, 1937, International Labour Office, Geneva, Dossier N/200/1/13/5.

57. Letter Sherwood Eddy to Fletcher Brockman, May 8, 1925, YMCA Historical Library, New York (R14).

58. Letter G. T. Schwenning to Sherwood Eddy, Dec. 26, 1925, YMCA Historical Library, New York (R14).

59. Letter Eugene Barnett to Sherwood Eddy, April 12, 1926, YMCA Historical Library, New York (R14).

60. Tchou had compiled the "Report on Industrial and Social Survey" in 1922, *Outlines of Report on Housing* and *Social Conditions Among Industrial Workers in Shanghai* in 1926, and *The Present-Day Industrial Situation and the Labour Movement in China*, also in 1926, as well as writing articles for several journals and drawing up many unpublished internal reports and memoranda on the conditions of working people.

61. Letter H. A. Wilbur to D. W. Lyon, Nov. 29, 1922, YMCA Historical Library, New York (R9).

62. Letter Eugene Barnett to Sherwood Eddy, April 12, 1926, YMCA Historical Library, New York (R14).

63. Letter Pierre Henry to G. T. Schwenning, June 14, 1926, International Labour Office, Geneva, Dossier G/900/28/2.

64. Pierre Henry, in "Oeuvres sociales," section 4 of his "Rapport Général sur mon Sejour en Chine," International Labour Office, Geneva, Dossier G/900/28/1, jacket 2.

65. Letter Lily Haass to Mary Dingman, Dec. 22, 1926, World's YWCA, Geneva (C).

66. "Shanghai's Model Village."

67. Letter Mary Dingman to Lelia Hinkley, Aug. 3, 1929, World's YWCA, Geneva (C).

68. "A Statement of the Industrial Work of the YMCA Movement in China with Special Reference to the Rockefeller Fund," manuscript, with covering letter J. W. Nipps to C. A. Herschleb, April 26, 1930, YMCA Historical Library, New York (R25).

69. On the cover of the report of the fall 1928 tour a senior association official had written: "I hope they get down to some experimental work and do not over-itinerate. Don't think JDR (Rockefeller) will recognise value in much of this."

70. Letter from J. W. Nipps to Eugene Barnett, Nov. 15, 1929, YMCA Historical Library, New York (R22).

71. "Report of the 1930 Special Study of YMCA's of China, summarised edition," manuscript, (III–24), YMCA Historical Library, New York (R24).

72. *Building Up the Shanghai YMCA Social Centre*, July 1931, p. 3, YMCA Historical Library, New York (R28). Text indicates that the pamphlet was published by the Industrial Department of the Shanghai YMCA.

73. This is according to Nipps, in his letter to Eugene Barnett of November 15, 1929. In time Lowe became an acknowledged authority on labour matters, writing, among other things, the book entitled *Facing Labour Issues in China*, which was published in 1933.

74. "A Statement of the Industrial Work of the YMCA Movement."

75. Extract from a report on John Nipps by Sherwood Eddy during his visit to China in the spring of 1930, reproduced in a letter from Gerald Birks to Eugene Barnett, June 19, 1930, YMCA Historical Library, New York (R26).

76. Extract from a conversation between David Yui and Gerald Birks, recorded in Birks's letter to Eugene Barnett of June 19, 1930.

77. Letter C. A. Herschleb to Gerald Birks, Sept. 29, 1930, YMCA Historical Library, New York (R26).

78. The letter expressed appreciation of Nipps's "faithful and helpful service" and of the "poise, caution, and judgement" with which he approached industrial problems. It was signed by, among others, J. B. Tayler of Yenching University, Cora Deng and Eleanor Hinder of the National Industrial Committee of the YWCA, and H. D. Lamson of Shanghai Baptist College. The letter was forwarded to the YMCA with a covering note of support by Frank Rawlinson, editor of the *Chinese Recorder*. The letter, along with the covering note to C. A. Herschleb dated March 4, 1931, is in the archives of the YMCA Historical Library, New York (R27).

79. Letter Sherwood Eddy to David Yui, May 8, 1929, YMCA Historical Library, New York (R22).

80. Letter Arthur Packard to Sherwood Eddy, Feb. 10, 1931, YMCA Historical Library, New York (R27).

81. Letter Sherwood Eddy to David Yui, May 8, 1929.

82. "A Statement of the Industrial Work of the YMCA Movement." From mid-1926 to mid-1930 only Mex. $8,200, or approximately U.S. $3,200, was dispensed to local associations, all of this going to Canton, Shanghai, and Foochow, the only branches able to find the money to share costs of industrial work with the National Committee. Most of this went to pay the salaries of local industrial secretaries engaged in particular experiments or pieces of research. This money came from the "Chinese secretaries half" of the total Rockefeller grant to the YMCA of U.S. $30,000 over three years. Of this $15,000, it is reasonable to assume that the national secretary's salary for three years would not have exceeded $7,500 even if it had all been drawn, which left $7,500 for local projects. It is of this $7,500 that the local associations claimed only $3,200.

83. Letter from W. W. Lockwood to C. A. Herschleb, May 26, 1933, for example, YMCA Historical Library, New York (R29).

84. *Industrial Work of the Shanghai YMCA*, p. 17.

85. Bush, p. 169.

86. Ibid., p. 173.

Chapter 3

1. Hershatter, *The Workers of Tianjin*, p. 56.

2. Honig, *Sisters and Strangers*, pp. 24–25, taken from a study by the Bureau of Social Affairs of Greater Shanghai.

3. Hershatter, *The Workers of Tianjin*, p. 55.

4. Honig, *Sisters and Strangers*, pp. 57–58, 70, 72–73. Honig's assertion that reeling workers were paid least is not fully borne out by her table 6, p. 179.

5. See, for example, Hershatter, *The Workers of Tianjin*, pp. 148–49, and Honig, *Sisters and Strangers*, p. 55.

6. See the discussion of the transition from *bao fan* to *dai fan* in Honig, *Sisters and Strangers*, p. 109.

7. Honig, *Sisters and Strangers*, pp. 103, 108, 150–51, and Hershatter, *The Workers of Tianjin*, p. 63.

8. Honig, *Sisters and Strangers*, pp. 150–51.

9. Ibid., p. 157; Hershatter, *The Workers of Tianjin*, p. 59; and Zhong Shaoqin, "Wosuo kanjiande nugong shenghuo," in *Nu qingnian yuekan* 12, 5 (1933): 42–50, cited in Honig, p. 193.

10. There is no comprehensive account of the work of the YWCA in China, though the association's own publications *History of the YWCA in China, 1896–1930* (Shanghai: YWCA, ca. 1931) and *The YWCA of China, 1933–47* (Shanghai: Mercury Press, 1947) give a good idea of the kind of activity undertaken. Very few copies of either survive. The former was located in the archives of the World's YWCA, Geneva (K), and the latter in the library of the World's YMCA, Geneva.

11. "Annual Report, Agatha Harrison, Feb. 23, 1921–March 23, 1922," World's YWCA, Geneva, (A).

12. Irene Harrison, *Agatha Harrison* (London, 1956).

13. Letter W. W. Lockwood to E. C. Jenkins, June 23, 1921, in the archives of the YMCA Historical Library, New York (R5/3).

14. Agatha Harrison maintained no particular religious affiliation while working for the YWCA, and when approached to serve on the Bureau of Social and Industrial Research of the International Missionary Council in New York some years later she protested that she would feel ill at ease working for such a body as "in spite of the fact that she has worked with the YWCA and the NCC, she persists in regarding herself as too unorthodox to be called a Christian." A. L. Warnshuis, writing of her to John Mott, goes on to say, "This is slightly a pose, or perhaps I should rather say, she has so long become accustomed to regarding herself in this light that she does not realise how identical her outlook is with that which we call Christian." See letter A. L. Warnshuis to John Mott, April 9, 1930, in the archives of library of World Council of Churches, Geneva (RD23). Only in 1941 did Agatha Harrison manifest a firm commitment to Christianity when she joined the Society of Friends in London.

15. "Miss Agatha Harrison's Itinerary While in America," March 1, 1921, manuscript in the archives of the library at the Friends Meeting House, London, Agatha Harrison Papers, Temporary Box 50-B. Among the people Harrison met were Herbert Hoover, secretary of commerce; Mary Anderson, director of the Women's Bureau of the U.S. Department of Labor; and Mrs. Raymond Robbins of the Women's Trade Union League.

16. Letter Agatha Harrison to Mary Dingman, Nov. 26, 1921, World's YWCA, Geneva, (F).

17. Ibid.

18. "Minutes, National Committee, YWCA of China, June 16, 1921," World's YWCA, Geneva (A).

19. Helen Thoburn, "The Church and Modern Industry," n.d., text suggests 1923, manuscript, World's YWCA, Geneva (B). After Coppock's death, the chairmanship was shared by Zung Wei-tsung and C. F. Remer of St. John's University.

20. Letter Agatha Harrison to Mary Dingman, Nov. 26, 1921. A similar correspondence in the columns of the *South China Morning Post* had preceded the appointment of the child labor commission in Hong Kong.

21. Letter Agatha Harrison to Mary Dingman, Nov. 26, 1921.

22. Among the enterprises Zung inspected in Britain were Lewis's department store and the Port Sunlight factory in Liverpool, a weaving mill of the Tootal Broadhurst Lee group in Manchester, and Debenham's department store and the factories of Peek Frean and Co. and MacFarlane Lang and Co. in London. Apart from individual welfare workers, YWCA staff, and faculty at the London School of Economics, Zung met officials of the Home Office, the Co-operative Society, the Bermondsey Settlement, the International Women's Suffrage Alliance, the Welfare Workers' Institute, and the "Residential College for Working Women"—an experiment begun by the British YWCA with the object of "training leaders among the rank and file." Of this latter Zung remarked, "These students are genuine factory workers, but they are picked ones." "Report on My Visit to Europe," Nov. 18, 1921, manuscript, World's YWCA, Geneva (A).

23. "Review of the Industrial Situation, Shanghai, China," Sept. 11, 1922, manuscript, World's YWCA, Geneva (A).

24. "Second Interview with Mr X," Agatha Harrison, manuscript, text indicates Nov. 25,

1921, recorded together with the summary of a "Third Interview with Mr X," which evidently took place early in January 1922. World's YWCA, Geneva (A).

25. "Further Stage," typed note recording details of another meeting between Harrison and "Mr. X," shortly before the Rotary Club was to discuss industrial reform on Feb. 9, 1922. World's YWCA, Geneva (A).

26. "Second Interview with Mr X," giving details of the third meeting as well.

27. "Copy of letter sent to the Chairman of the Foreign Mill Owners' Association," Jan. 13, 1922, World's YWCA, Geneva (A).

28. "Meeting with the Committee of the Foreign Mill Owners' Association," Agatha Harrison, date given as Feb. 20, 1922, but text suggests that it should be Jan. 20, World's YWCA, Geneva (A).

29. C. F. Remer of St. John's University and Dr. Henry Hodgkin of the China Continuation Committee also spoke at this meeting. Both were members of the special Committee on the Church's Relation to Economic and Industrial Problems, which was preparing a report for the National Christian Conference to be held in May. See "Annual Report, Agatha Harrison."

30. "Review of the Industrial Situation, Shanghai."

31. "Minutes, National Committee of China," Oct. 19, 1922, World's YWCA, Geneva (A).

32. Letter Agatha Harrison to Mary Dingman, Nov. 26, 1921.

33. Letter Agatha Harrison to Mary Dingman, March 24, 1922, World's YWCA, Geneva (F).

34. Manuscript entitled "Suggestions," attached to letter Agatha Harrison to Mary Dingman, July 22, 1922, World's YWCA, Geneva (F). The person at the home office to be approached was Constance Smith, deputy chief inspector of factories.

35. "Review of the Industrial Situation, Shanghai."

36. The first woman to take up this scholarship was Shin Tak-hing of the Hong Kong YWCA, who left for London in November 1922.

37. Ibid.

38. The conference was an assembly of YWCA officials, student members of the association, and their faculty advisers. "Findings: Student Workers' Conference, Shanghai and Hangchow, Nov. 1–10, 1922," manuscript, World's YWCA, Geneva (A). In 1922 there were twelve city branches of the YWCA and ninety-two branches in schools and colleges. See *The YWCA in China, 1922*, World Council of Churches, Geneva, Box (W).

39. Dingman's presence is first recorded at a meeting of the National Committee of the Chinese YWCA on Jan. 18, 1923, and her anticipated date of departure is later given as July 13. See "Minutes, National Committee of the YWCA of China, 18 Jan 1923," manuscript in archives of World's YWCA, Geneva (B), and "Summary of Recent Events, 20 June 1923," manuscript, World's YWCA, Geneva (F). See also *Chinese Triangles: The YWCA in a Changing China* (Shanghai: YWCA, 1924), p. 59, World's YWCA, Geneva (B).

40. *Chinese Triangles*, pp. 60, 61. Harrison had also been the mainstay of the YMCA's industrial seminars of 1921–22 and 1922–23, as the YMCA had no qualified staff of its own to take the initiative in such work. See Fitch, "Annual Report for 1922."

41. For staff movements see "Summary of Recent Events, October 11, 1923," manuscript, World's YWCA, Geneva (G); "Harriet Rietveld, (America)," text indicates end of 1922, World's YWCA, Geneva (B); and *Chinese Triangles*, p. 62.

42. "Summary of Recent Events, 20 June 1923," along with "Suggested Outline of Speech to Be Given by Miss Shin at International Working Women's Conference, Cologne, August 1923," World's YWCA, Geneva (F).

43. "How the Industrial Question Was Presented to the National Convention, Hangchow, October 1923," manuscript, World's YWCA, Geneva (G).

44. *Chinese Triangles*, p. 61.

45. "Review of the Industrial Situation, Shanghai."

46. Letter John D. Rockefeller to Sherwood Eddy, Jan. 22, 1924, YMCA Historical Library, New York, (R10/1).

47. The International Committee of the YMCA in New York represented the American and Canadian YMCAs in their mission work overseas. This was a different entity from the World's YMCA, later to have its headquarters in Geneva. It would appear that at this time, as far as foreign mission work was concerned, within the YMCA much of the initiative and direction came from the International Committee in New York, reflecting American predominance in the YMCA movement, while within the YWCA initiative and direction tended to come from the World's YWCA in London, and later Geneva, reflecting more genuinely international participation. This difference in inspiration may have been responsible in part for the different degrees of success attained by the two organizations in their industrial programs. See chapter 8.

48. Letter Mary Dingman to Ella MacLaurin, April 11, 1924, also letter "My dear . . . ," unsigned, Sept. 12, 1924, probably by Mary Dingman, World's YWCA, Geneva (G).

49. Letter Mary Dingman to Ella MacLaurin, April 11, 1924.

50. Letter Henry Hodgkin to B. R. Barber, June 25, 1924, and letter E. C. Jenkins to C. W. Harvey, June 26, 1924, YMCA Historical Library, New York (R10/1).

51. No records appear to have survived of this meeting, but reference to it is made in the letter beginning "My dear . . . ," probably by Mary Dingman, Sept. 12, 1924, and three days later Dingman submitted a budget to C. W. Harvey for the YWCA part of the Rockefeller money based on what the YWCA itself considered to be priorities. See letter Mary Dingman to C. W. Harvey, Sept. 15, 1924, World's YWCA, Geneva (G).

52. Letter "My dear . . . ," probably by Mary Dingman, Sept. 12, 1924.

53. Ibid.

54. Letter to Agatha Harrison, Feb. 23, 1925, text indicates author was Mary Dingman, World's YWCA, Geneva (G).

55. Letter Sherwood Eddy to Fletcher Brockman, May 8, 1925, YMCA Historical Library, New York (R14).

56. "A Statement of the Industrial Work of the YMCA Movement in China, with Special Reference to the Rockefeller Fund," manuscript, with covering letter J. W. Nipps to C. A. Herschleb, dated April 26, 1930, YMCA Historical Library, New York (R25).

57. Letter to Charlotte Niven, unsigned, text indicates author was Mary Dingman, Feb. 24, 1925; also letter Mary Dingman to Agatha Harrison, April 30, 1925, World's YWCA, Geneva (G).

58. Letter Mary Dingman to "My dear family and friends," May 24, 1925, World's YWCA, Geneva (G).

59. Letter Mary Dingman to "My dear friends," Oct. 9, 1924, World's YWCA, Geneva (G).

60. Letter Mary Dingman to Charlotte Niven, Feb. 24, 1925, World's YWCA, Geneva (G).

61. Letter "F.G.S." (probably Florence Sutton) to Mary Dingman, May 11, 1925, World's YWCA, Geneva (G).

62. "The Industrial Work of the China YWCA—1924–1925 as noted by the Office Secretary, Hilda S. Murray," manuscript, World's YWCA, Geneva (G).

63. Soong Mei-ling and Chiang Kai-shek were married in 1927. It would appear that Soong Mei-ling took no further part in the YWCA's industrial work after the collapse of the campaign against child labor in 1925.

64. Letter Mary Dingman to Agatha Harrison, April 30, 1925, World's YWCA, Geneva (G).

65. Letter Lily Haass to Mary Dingman and Agatha Harrison, Sept. 28, 1926, World's YWCA, Geneva (C). Zung's married name was Chiu.

66. Letter to Mary Dingman and Agatha Harrison, text indicates the most likely author to be Lily Haass, Oct. 7, 1925, World's YWCA, Geneva (V).

67. Letter Lily Haass to Mary Dingman, no date, attached to letter apparently from Mary Dingman to Lily Haass and Eleanor Hinder, Nov. 25, 1926, World's YWCA, Geneva (C).

68. Letter Lily Haass to Mary Dingman, Dec. 29, 1926, World's YWCA, Geneva (C).

69. Having returned from a period of industrial training, apparently while on furlough in

England and the United States, Rietveld spent several months at the North China Language School before beginning welfare work in Chefoo in the autumn of 1925. "The Industrial Work of the China YWCA—1924–1925."

70. Minutes, National Committee, YWCA of China, March 19, 1925, World's YWCA, Geneva (B).

71. Letter to Mary Dingman and Agatha Harrison, Oct. 7, 1925.

72. Letter Lily Haass to Mary Dingman, Dec. 22, text indicates 1926, World's YWCA, Geneva (C).

73. Letter Lily Haass to Mary Dingman and Agatha Harrison, Sept. 28, 1926.

74. "The Beginning of the Chapei Centre—Report to the Board, 21 December 1926," manuscript, World's YWCA, Geneva (C).

75. Ibid.

76. Concern is repeatedly expressed that the YWCA's purpose not be "misunderstood." See, for example, the report cited immediately above. The association's attitude to labor and management will be explored more fully in chapter 8.

77. Letter Eleanor Hinder to Mary Dingman, Sept. 15, 1927, World's YWCA, Geneva (C).

78. "Industrial Developments in YWCA Work," in *Green Year Supplement*, Oct. 20, 1927, no. 13, pp. 12–15. This periodical, "issued irregularly, several times between October and June," was "the English supplement to 'The Green Year,' the magazine of the National YWCA of China [name based on literal translation of Young Women's Christian Association]." An incomplete set of the *Green Year Supplement* is to be found in archives of library at National Headquarters, YWCA of the United States, New York (E). The English-language "Supplement" in general reproduced in somewhat reduced form those items in the Chinese publications that it was felt would be of most interest to foreign subscribers, to association personnel in other countries, and, it may be supposed, to potential benefactors.

79. *Green Year Supplement*, July–August 1926, p. 5.

80. "Industrial Developments in YWCA Work," p. 12.

81. "YWCA Industrial Secretaries Conference, 29–30 Aug. 1927: Tentative Program," manuscript, YWCA of the United States, New York (D).

82. Letter Lily Haass to Mary Dingman, Oct. 19, 1927, World's YWCA, Geneva (C).

83. *Green Year Supplement*, Oct. 20, 1927, p. 14.

84. For example, toward the end of the year it was reported that through literacy classes and discussion groups YWCA personnel were in contact with women workers at the social center of the YMCA Model Village in Pootung, in Chapei near the former YWCA house there, and in the Nanyang and China Merchants tobacco factories. The numbers reached in this way were still small, however—23 tobacco and cotton workers in Pootung, a "small group" of silk workers in Chapei, and "between twenty and thirty" women workers at the other tobacco factories, together with some forewomen at the Nanyang Brothers factory. YWCA Secretary Kyong Bae-tsung was asked in late autumn of 1927 to work part-time for the Department of Labor of the new Kuomintang government of the Municipality of Greater Shanghai, "to supervise the study of the working conditions of women and children, preparatory to the making of regulations." See letter Eleanor Hinder to Mary Dingman, Nov. 8, 1927, World's YWCA, Geneva (C).

85. There was a much greater recognition of the strength of the labor movement as a result of the events of 1925–27. It is ironic that just as the Nationalist government was consolidating its control and the power of the unions had begun to decline, the YWCA redoubled its efforts to reach the unions. See, for example, letter Eleanor Hinder to Mary Dingman, Sept. 15, 1927; "Industrial Developments in YWCA Work"; and letter Eleanor Hinder to Mary Dingman, Nov. 8, 1927. For a consideration of the evolving YWCA attitude to the labor movement, see chapter 8.

86. A Scottish secretary, Margaret Chisholm, whom Hinder had intended should suc-

ceed her as national industrial secretary, did not do so. The promising Chinese trainee Kyong Bae-tsung left the YWCA in 1929 to get married. See letter Eleanor Hinder to Mary Dingman, Jan. 3, 1927, in the archives of the World's YWCA, Geneva (C), and "An Account of the Industrial Work of the Shanghai YWCA, 1904–1929," by May Bagwell, n.d., manuscript in a folder entitled "YWCA China: History," in the archives of the World's YWCA, Geneva. In 1929 also, both Gideon Chen and Lily Haass resigned from the Industrial Commission of the National Christian Council. See chapter 4.

87. Eleanor Hinder, "Toward the End of a Two Year Term: Phases in an Evolution," Jan. 1, 1928, manuscript, in archives of World's YWCA, Geneva (C).

88. Letter Lily Haass to Mary Dingman, Sept. 9, 1929.

89. Ibid.

90. *Green Year Supplement*, no. 17, Nov. 1928. This issue contained descriptions of industrial conditions in factories in various parts of the country, and of YWCA work with "industrial girls."

91. *Green Year Supplement*, no. 14, Jan. 4, 1928, p. 14.

92. Lydia Johnson, "Workers' Education in Tientsin, China," 1929, manuscript, YWCA of the United States, New York (C).

93. Ibid., and *History of the YWCA in China, 1896–1930*, YWCA Shanghai, n.d., text suggests 1931, p. 195, World's YWCA, Geneva (K).

94. Johnson, "Workers' Education in Tientsin, China."

95. *History of the YWCA in China*, p. 195. This was the wage of one of the instructors, probably at Ta Wang, in 1929.

96. Johnson, "Workers' Education in Tientsin, China."

97. *History of the YWCA in China*, pp. 196–97.

98. "China," typed memorandum noting recent developments in YWCA industrial work, n.d., marked "arrived 12.6.28," World's YWCA, Geneva (C).

99. Letter Cora Deng to Mary Dingman, Oct. 16, 1930, World's YWCA, Geneva (J).

100. Lily Haass, "YWCA Industrial Work in China," 1929, typescript, YWCA of the United States, New York (C).

101. "A Few Facts about the Industrial Department and its Work," YWCA, Shanghai, Nov. 1930, printed fact sheet, YWCA of the United States, New York (B).

102. Haass, "YWCA Industrial Work in China."

103. "A Few Facts about the Industrial Department." The distinction made in this report between "popular education" and "mass education" is not made clear.

104. See, for example, the list of publications made available by the National Christian Council (chapter 4), on which the YWCA relied heavily for its Chinese-language reading material.

105. "A Few Facts about the Industrial Department."

106. Letter Cora Deng to Mary Dingman, Oct. 16, 1930.

107. "A Few Facts about the Industrial Department." It is evident that these figures may have overlapped to some extent.

108. Haass, "YWCA Industrial Work in China." The house, ominously, was situated between a workers' village and a graveyard. The absence of local support is given as a cause of the subsequent closure of the center in 1934. See YWCA, *The YWCA of China, 1933–47* (Shanghai: Mercury Press, 1947), p. 71, World's YWCA, Geneva.

109. Letter Cora Deng to Mary Dingman, Oct. 16, 1930. The problem of lack of staff also prevented the association from starting industrial work in Wuchang, as it had hoped.

110. Letter Lily Haass to Mary Dingman, Sept. 9, 1929.

111. Letter Cora Deng to Mary Dingman, Oct. 16, 1930.

112. *The YWCA of China, 1933–47*, p. 71.

113. The suggestion that the municipal government would employ Kyong Bae-tsung to organize such a study is made in January 1928 by Eleanor Hinder, in "Toward the End of a Two Year Term." However, it would appear from later correspondence that Kyong did not in

fact undertake this task, but remained a little longer with the YWCA. See letter Eleanor Hinder to Mary Dingman, April 26, 1928, World's YWCA, Geneva (C).

114. Lydia Johnson, "Progressive Movements in Tientsin, China," 1929, manuscript, YWCA of the United States, New York (C).

115. Letter Lily Haass to Mary Dingman, Sept. 9, 1929.

116. May Bagwell, "Why an Industrial Department?" in *Green Year Supplement*, no. 21, July 1930, pp. 10–14, YWCA of the United States, New York (E).

117. Hinder, "Toward the End of a Two Year Term."

118. Letter Lily Haass to Mary Dingman and Agatha Harrison, Sept. 24, 1927, World's YWCA, Geneva (C).

119. It would appear that at one stage early in 1929 Cora Deng had decided not to go ahead with her training for industrial work. See letter Mary Dingman to Lily Haass, Jan. 25, 1929, World's YWCA, Geneva (C). Later, however, Lily Haass wrote of Cora Deng in the spring of 1929, "After two months travel with her I am more enthusiastic than ever about her personal qualities and her future contribution to industrial work." See letter Lily Haass to Mary Dingman and Agatha Harrison, May 16, 1929, World's YWCA, Geneva (C).

120. Letter Sherwood Eddy to David Yui, May 8, 1929, YMCA Historical Library, New York (R22).

121. Letter Lily Haass to Mary Dingman, Sept. 9, 1929.

122. Letter Arthur Packard to Sherwood Eddy, Feb. 10, 1931, YMCA Historical Library, New York (R27).

123. Letter Cora Deng to Mary Dingman, Oct. 16, 1930. With respect to this project, Cora Deng observed, "We have heard unofficially that the YMCA does not want to make the appeal." The YMCA's lack of initiative in industrial matters, here and elsewhere, must be in part responsible for its failure to obtain a renewal of its grant from the Rockefeller Foundation at a time when the other two agencies were successful in this quest.

124. Ibid. Regrettably, neither "Women and Money" nor any of the other items on economic and labor problems appear to have survived in YWCA archives.

125. Ibid.

126. Deng Yu-dji and May Bagwell, "A Developing Industrial Program," in *Green Year Supplement*, no. 24, May 1931, p. 12.

127. Circular letter beginning "Dear Fellow Workers . . . ," from Cora Deng, Industrial Department of the National Committee, YWCA, Shanghai, May 8, 1931, YWCA of the United States, New York (D).

128. Deng and Bagwell, "A Developing Industrial Program."

129. Circular letter beginning "Dear Fellow Workers . . . ," from Cora Deng, May 8, 1931.

130. Ibid.

131. "Report of the Third Conference of Industrial Secretaries, YWCA of China," YWCA, Shanghai, manuscript, YWCA of the United States, New York (D). The conference was held from January 19 to 25, 1933. Among the guest lecturers was C. H. Lowe, who spoke on "Industrial Legislation." From the YWCA itself Maud Russell spoke about "Workers in Russia."

132. Ibid., pp. 2–5. Obstacles in the way of improved attendance were said to be "night work, tiredness, distance, sickness, hours of work too long, busy with home duties, political situation not favourable, weather, poor teaching, marriage, child birth, education not considered important, family attitude unfavourable, family quarrels, period of study too long, and fear for safety in the dark."

133. Ibid., p. 6.

134. Ibid., pp. 9–10. It is not clear whether these meetings were to be open to the public, or whether they were to be for the benefit of a more limited constituency within the association.

135. "Report of the Third Conference of Industrial Secretaries, YWCA of China," p. 11.

136. *Green Year Supplement*, no. 28, Dec. 1933, pp. 17–18. The high points of the

assembly appear to have been formal lectures given by Gideon Chen (formerly of the National Christian Council's Industrial Commission, now of Yenching University) on "Trade Unionism," and by a Dr. W. T. Rao on "Workers' Education."

137. See *The YWCA of China, 1933–47*, p. 17, and the file "Classeur: Sections, 1/132," "Social, Industrial, and Public Affairs News Items, 1 Sept 1937," in the archives of World's YWCA, Geneva. The specific resolutions with respect to industrial work adopted at the Third National Convention were (1) that the convention address the national government to enforce immediately the articles regarding working hours, health and safety devices, night work, child labor, and other protective measures for women workers; (2) that the YWCA should within the next five years have a systematic and organised program for creating public opinion to support the enforcement of the factory law; (3) realizing that the way for solving the problems of workers is through their own organized effort, the YWCA should be encouraged to create public opinion for supporting the workers in organizing themselves; (4) that the YWCA intensify its program of workers' education as a foundation, but also emphasizing group education to help workers to realize and cultivate their own ability to organize to the solution of their own problems. It had been proposed that the World's Committee of the YWCA would meet in China later in 1933, at which time industrial work would have been discussed as a matter of course. Political developments in Europe and in North China prevented the meeting from taking place, however.

138. Deng attributes the full range of social problems in industry to the "profiteering" system of production. See *China Christian Yearbook, 1934–35*, reprint, p. 19, in the library of the YWCA, New York. See also below, chapter 8.

139. See Honig, *Sisters and Strangers*, especially pp. 233–43.

140. "Classeur: Sections 1/132," and *The YWCA of China, 1933–47*, pp. 70–71. Shanghai, Tientsin, and Chefoo had already begun industrial work before 1930. Tsinan and Taiyuan appear to have begun in 1934 and 1935 respectively. With respect to industrial work in "Hankow," different sources seem to refer to Hankow and Wuchang interchangeably, the commonly used name among foreigners for what are now the Wuhan cities then being Hankow. In either Wuchang or Hankow, therefore, industrial work was begun in 1935.

141. "Classeur: Sections, 1/132."

142. Letter Cora Deng to Mary Dingman, Oct. 16, 1930.

143. For example, in Tientsin in 1931 work is reported to have expanded so as to have embraced a new center, with a clinic, among cotton mill workers in Hsiao Liu Chuang, another one among tobacco workers, and classes for a limited number of women who worked at home finishing stockings and making match boxes. In Wusih, a clinic and a bath house were among new facilities offered. It is to be regretted that Cora Deng's most comprehensive report on developments during her tenure as national industrial secretary, covering the years 1929 to 1934, has been lost with the passage of time. In a covering letter to the World's YWCA in Geneva, she says of it, "I wrote about our work since 1929, because since then there has been a great change in the emphasis on the industrial work in the movement here, and I think it is worthwhile to show how these new emphasis [*sic*] developed in the last few years. It is rather a lengthy report, but there is so much to say and one cannot make things clear without going into some of the details." See letter Cora Deng to C. B. Fox, July 20, 1934, World's YWCA, Geneva (L).

144. *The YWCA of China, 1933–47*, p. 71.

145. It may be supposed that financial support for industrial work was always more difficult to obtain outside Shanghai. In Tientsin, Lydia Johnson observed in 1931, "Our work here is developing rather slowly, and is being financed entirely locally by our own Board—which means that no large amounts have been available for demonstration work on a large scale such as in Shanghai where they have had the benefit of the Rockefeller Fund." She noted that priority was being given to a campaign to raise money for a new headquarters building in Tientsin, "which accounts largely for the slower development of our industrial program here." See letter Lydia Johnson to Mary Dingman, May 20, 1931, World's YWCA, Geneva (J). Apparently the lack of adequate financial support forced suspension of part of the

work in Tientsin about 1935. The following account describes the circumstances of one center's closure, and of its subsequent resurrection: "Upon learning the unexpected news of the Board's decision to close down one of the industrial centers . . . the girls gathered together and decided that they would petition the Board not to do so. Three or four representatives were chosen to go to speak to the Board about it. A letter signed by all of them was sent to their national industrial secretary to help in pushing along their views. But it was too late, and the centre had to be closed because there were no funds to run it. But the industrial girls persisted and thought and worked. Through these group meetings the girls came to realize that they really can carry part of the work themselves. Finally it was agreed by the Board that they could go ahead and reopen the night school in a different form. So the girls worked many a night in group meetings to plan how they could carry the school themselves. A committee of four was chosen and they were delegated the task of running the school as well as teaching the beginners' classes. A voluntary teacher was secured to help with the advanced classes. So in the beginning of May the night school was reopened with the industrial girls themselves heading it up instead of the paid teachers." "Classeur: Sections, 1/132."

Chefoo, where industrial work was begun in the 1920s, is not mentioned as a city where such work was currently being pursued either in Cora Deng's memorandum from the National Committee of May 8, 1931, or in the review of the industrial program in *Green Year Supplement*, no. 24, published in the same month. By 1933, however, the industrial program in Chefoo appears to have been revived, as the city sent delegates both to the Industrial Secretaries Conference in January and to the Industrial Assembly later in the year. See Circular letter beginning "Dear Fellow Workers . . . ," from Cora Deng, May 8, 1931; *Green Year Supplement*, no. 24, May 1931; Deng and Bagwell, "A Developing Industrial Program," pp. 1–13; "Report of the Third Conference of Industrial Secretaries"; and *Green Year Supplement*, no. 28, Dec. 1933, p. 17.

Chapter 4

1. Helen Thoburn, "The Church and Modern Industry," n.d., text indicates 1923, YWCA, Geneva (B).

2. These were the "COPEC" conference on "Christian Politics, Economics and Citizenship" in Britain and the conference on the "Christian Way of Life" in the United States. *Christian Industry*, March 1, 1924, no. 1, Friends' Meeting House, London, Agatha Harrison papers, Temporary Box 50-B. This short news sheet is described as having been "issued occasionally by the Industrial Commission of the NCC."

3. Henry Hodgkin, "First Impressions of the Situation in China, November 1920," attached to letter dated November 24, 1920, Henry Hodgkin Papers, Box W, file "Letters Concerning His Work in China," 22.xi.1920–1.vi.1922, Friends' Meeting House, London.

4. Thoburn, "The Church and Modern Industry."

5. Ibid. It was apparently only at Coppock's insistence that the industrial question was retained for consideration at the conference. The conference was attended by students from thirty-seven countries and included six hundred delegates from China. The resolutions passed were the following: (1) Cooperation should be the principle of economic development; (2) Economic efficiency should seek the good of society and not the selfish interests of individuals; (3) Neither private nor group ownership of capital is absolute. All possessions are a trust from the community; (4) Ownership of capital and the receipt of income entails a duty to render some corresponding service to the community; (5) In accordance with these principles there should be the utmost development of natural resources with as little waste as possible and with the fullest measure of productivity from the labor of each worker; (6) There should be the largest measure of industrial self-government with real freedom for the worker and a guarantee of continued service in the industry and maintenance from it; (7) Society should take responsibility for seeing that every member has a suitable occupation which will provide

for life and health. Special provision should be made for the crippled in mind or body who are unable to work; (8) The community should be responsible for the regulation of conditions of labor especially in the case of women and children, and in dangerous trades and also for the steady improvement of standards in these matters; (9) There should be strict limitation of the amount of wealth that can be bequeathed; (10) Women should have economic opportunity equal to that of men. Among the members were almost certainly Agatha Harrison, Frank Rawlinson of the missionary journal, the *Chinese Recorder*, Henry Hodgkin, Gideon Chen, and "several employers."

6. *National Christian Conference, Shanghai 1922, Proceedings* (Shanghai: NCC, 1922), World Council of Churches, Geneva, pp. 326–29. This leads to the now familiar argument that better seeds and tools can in themselves be the key to a dramatic increase in productivity, and that major social reorganization is not necessary. The only reference to social relations in the countryside is the statement "We believe that it is the duty of the Christian Church to bring home to the landowners of China their duty toward their tenants and their responsibility for the introduction of better methods of agriculture, for the promotion of education, and for the improvement of village life." The report and recommendations on conditions in agriculture and in handicraft industry, however, may be supposed to have been largely the work of missionary correspondents in the hinterland, rather than of the committee in Shanghai.

7. Ibid., p. 330. Failure of handicraft industry "to develop" in the face of machine competition was attributed to the following causes: "lack of adequate training of the workers, lack of initiative and ambition on their part, ignorance of new demands and failure to produce new designs, lack of capital for experiment and improvement, inadequate advertisement, crude tools, production on too small a scale, and ignorance of the principles and methods of co-operation which might, to a considerable extent, be carried out through the guilds" (p. 331).

8. Ibid., pp. 331–32. The worst evils of domestic industry were found to be: "the neglect of children, child labor of such a nature as to be beyond control, injuries to health especially during pregnancy, the increase of unsanitary conditions in the home, and the indirect effect upon the wages of the men in the family."

9. Ibid., pp. 335–36.

10. Ibid.

11. Ibid., pp. 337–38. The committee understood the essential points of the Draft Conventions adopted by the League of Nations (and later expanded on by its agency the International Labour Office) to be as follows:

(1) On Limiting Hours of Work: The adoption of an eight-hour day or forty-eight hour week was set as the standard to be aimed at where it has not already been attained; (2) On Unemployment: Measures for dealing with and combating unemployment were recommended, and suggestions made for setting up free public employment agencies under the control of a central authority, for insurance schemes, etc.; (3) Employment of Women Before and After Childbirth: It was recommended that women should not be permitted to work for six weeks before or after childbirth. The subject of maternity benefits was also discussed; (4) Night Work for Women and Young Persons Under 18: With the exception of certain trades, women and young persons are not to work between the hours of 11 P.M. and 5 A.M.; (5) Safeguarding the Health of Workers: Protection was planned for workers in dangerous trades, and the establishment of health services and of systems of efficient factory inspection were recommended; (6) Child Labor: Fourteen years was set as a minimum age for entering industry. In the cases of India and Japan this was modified to twelve years for the present.

12. Ibid., pp. 338–39. The Christian principles referred to were: "The inestimable value of every individual life; involving the duty of safeguarding the individual from conditions and hours of labor directly injurious to life, and the recognition of the right of the individual to a certain amount of leisure and to opportunities for development and self-expression.

The dignity of all labour, whether skilled or unskilled, that ministers to the common good; involving the right of every worker to a fair reward for labour performed.

The brotherhood of man; involving the conception of cooperation in service, and such mutual relationships in industry as exclude the selfish exploitation of labor by employers and capitalists."

13. Ibid., p. 462. C. C. Nieh was the owner of the Heng Foong Cotton Mill in Shanghai and a leading figure in the cotton industry. He was also vice-chairman of the Executive Committee of the Chinese YMCA. See *Annual Report, National Committee of the YMCA of China, 1921* (Shanghai: YMCA, 1921), Geneva, Box 392.21(51). Harrison also claimed in her address to the conference to have support for the NCC industrial standard from a Mr. Brooke-Smith of Jardine Mathieson, Mr. C. Arnhold of Arnhold and Co., Mr. G. Okada of Naigai Wata Kaisha, and a Sir Edward Pearce. See pp. 464–65.

14. Ibid., p. 469. The resolution was passed with a majority of 1,189 to 1. See Thoburn, "The Church and Modern Industry."

15. "Report of the Committee on the Church and Industrial and Economic Problems," n.d., text indicates May 10, 1923, manuscript, YWCA, Geneva (F).

16. Thoburn, "The Church and Modern Industry."

17. "Report of the Committee on the Church and Industrial and Economic Problems." The conference was said to have been attended by forty-three delegates from eight cities. Among the "visitors" were Zung, Tchou, Rawlinson, Agatha Harrison, and Mary Dingman of the YWCA, and Rev. C. E. Patton of the NCC.

18. By May 1923 the committee had published the *Report of Commission II*, including the recommendations made on industry at the 1922 conference, in English and Chinese; *The Church and Modern Industry* by Helen Thoburn, in English and Chinese; and *Commercial, Financial, and Economic Development* by Thomas Tchou, in English and Chinese, and had reprinted the article "Church and Industry" by Sherwood Eddy, in English and an "article prepared for Association Progress" by Zung Weitsung, in Chinese.

19. Ibid.

20. "Summary," attached to letter Agatha Harrison to Charlotte Niven, June 20, 1923, YWCA, Geneva, (F).

21. "Summary of Recent Events, October 11, 1923," in archives of World's YWCA, Geneva (G). Harrison dropped out in order to return to England in January 1924. Dingman began sitting on the commission upon her return to Shanghai in December 1923. The other members of the Industrial Commission were: Rev. C. E. Patton (chairman); L. T. Chen; Mrs. S. F. Chao; C. L. Bau; Dr. Josephine Lawney; Dr. J. Y. Lee; Rev. E. W. Wallace; Dr. S. M. Woo; Rev. J. M. Yard; and Rev. T. S. Sing. See *Report of the Commission on the Church and Industry* (Shanghai: National Christian Council, 1924), ILO, Geneva, Dossier G/900/28/1, jacket 2. Lord Addington was added to the commission in the spring of 1924. See letter Mary Dingman to Agatha Harrison, March 12, 1924, YWCA, Geneva (G).

22. *Report of the Commission on the Church and Industry.*

23. "Recommendations from the Cabinet to the Commission on Church and Industry as Adopted at the Meeting on 7 January 1924," YMCA, Geneva, Box X315(51). The bulletin was to be "issued occasionally by the Industrial Commission of the National Christian Council." See *Christian Industry*, no. 1, March 1, 1924, Friends' Meeting House, London, Agatha Harrison Papers, Temporary Box 50-B. In fact it appeared spasmodically until about 1927.

24. The questions proposed in the report for consideration at the local conferences show that the focus of the NCC had yet to shift decisively from the abstract and general to the particular. These were Social and Personal Religion; The Task of the Church in Industrial Progress; New Motives for Old; The Family Spirit and Co-operation in Industry; Apprenticeships in China; Application of the Three Standards; The Old Civilization and the New Order. See *Report of the Commission on the Church and Industry.*

25. By May 1924 the commission had published the following items:

Report of Commission II (of 1922)
The Social Gospel in China, by Sherwood Eddy

The Way of Jesus, by Henry Hodgkin
Some Vital Life Problems, by Frank Rawlinson
The Commercial, Industrial, and Economic Development of China, by Thomas Tchou
Report on Industrial and Social Survey, by Thomas Tchou
Changing Industrial Conditions, no author given
Peking Rugs and Peking Boys, by H. C. Blaisdell and C. C. Chu

"Industrial Reconstruction Series":

An Industrial Program for a Chinese City, no author given
The Church in China and Industrial Problems, no author given
The Church's Labor Standard, no author given
History of the Industrial Revolution and its Consequences, by Thomas Tchou
Modern Industry in China, by Zung Wei-tsung
An Interpretation of Modern Industrial Development, by Gideon Chen
Methods of Industrial and Social Research and Survey, by H. C. Blaisdell
Co-operative Movements, by Thomas Tchou
See *Report of the Commission on the Church and Industry.*

26. See *An Industrial Program for a Chinese City*, Industrial Reconstruction Series no. 1 (Shanghai: National Christian Council, n.d., but probably 1924), ILO, Geneva, Dossier G/900/28/1.

27. For example, the NCC published *Peking Rugs and Peking Boys*, a study undertaken by H. C. Blaisdell and C. C. Chu in 1923, while another study was apparently in process of being conducted by "Mr. G. A. Parker and his sociological classes" with respect to thirty factories in Tsinan. See *Report of the Commission on the Church and Industry.*

28. Ibid.

29. "Summer School Letter," n.d., text indicates 1924, in archives of World's YWCA, Geneva (G). Mary Dingman and Gideon Chen took part in the teaching of the courses. The program lasted four weeks and cost $30 Chinese per student.

30. *Report of the Commission on the Church and Industry.* Of the new budget, however, $2,500 was allocated to pay Gideon Chen's salary, while other amounts were provided for literature, traveling expenses, and other purposes.

31. Letter Mary Dingman to Agatha Harrison, May 6, 1924, YWCA, Geneva (G).

32. Letter "My Dear . . . ," Sept. 12, 1924, text indicates was written by Mary Dingman, YWCA, Geneva (G).

33. "The Industrial Work of the China YWCA."

34. Letter to Dame Adelaide Anderson, Dec. 16, 1924, text indicates was written by Mary Dingman, YWCA, Geneva (G).

35. "The Industrial Work of the China YWCA."

36. Ibid.

37. Letter to Dame Adelaide Anderson, Dec. 16, 1924.

38. Of the original chairmen of various subcommittees of the Shanghai Industrial Committee, Zung Wei-tsung was from the YWCA and Dr. Josephine Lawney from the NCC Industrial Commission, while a Dr. R. Y. Lo, Miss Morrison, Mr. Keys, and Mrs. Anderson do not appear to have any connection with other groups. *Christian Industry*, no. 1, March 1924. In 1924–25 Edith Johnston of the YWCA seemed to bear the main burden of responsibility for the committee. See "The Industrial Work of The China YWCA."

39. Edith Johnston, "Annual Report: September 1923–September 1924," manuscript, YWCA, Geneva (B).

40. "The Industrial Work of the China YWCA." On the opening night there were reported to have been 120 people in attendance, and in the discussion groups an average of 40 to 50.

41. Letter Mary Dingman to Dame Adelaide Anderson, Feb. 26, 1925, YWCA, Geneva (G).

42. Eleanor Hinder, "Toward the End of a Two Year Term: Phases in an Evolution," Jan. 1, 1928, manuscript, YWCA, Geneva (C). The preliminary survey was undertaken under the direction of the Department of Social Research of the China Foundation, successor to J. B. Tayler's "Reconnaissance Committee."

43. Letter Eleanor Hinder to Mary Dingman, Jan. 3, 1927, YWCA, Geneva (C).

44. Hinder, "Toward the End of a Two Year Term." This group was started by Eleanor Hinder early in 1927 with the expectation that "if there comes the rule of the South to the regions of Shanghai outside the Settlement, there will be a need of a liberal thinking group in the Settlement to stir up action." See letter Eleanor Hinder to Mary Dingman, Jan. 3, 1927. As the Kuomintang became increasingly conservative, it would appear that public interest in industrial reform went into decline.

45. "Report of the Committee on the Church and Industrial and Economic Problems."

46. "Memorandum Regarding the Proposed Institute of Social Research in China, Addressed by the Institute of Social and Religious Research to the Industrial Commission of the China National Christian Council," June 10, 1924, YWCA, Geneva (G).

47. "The Industrial Work of the China YWCA."

48. Letter John D. Rockefeller to Sherwood Eddy, Jan. 22, 1924, YMCA Historical Library, New York (R10).

49. "Memorandum Regarding the Proposed Institute of Social Research in China."

50. Letter Mary Dingman to Charlotte Niven, Dec. 30, 1924, YWCA, Geneva (G). Royal Meeker was formerly head of the Legislative Department of the International Labour Office in Geneva. See letter to Dame Adelaide Anderson, Dec. 16, 1924. It is not clear who else served on the committee, but among those considered were Thomas Tchou, Zung Wei-tsung, Agatha Harrison (by now in England), C. F. Remer of St. John's University, a "Mr. Sarvis in Nanking," and a Mr. Cressy, none of whom was apparently available, for one reason or another. See letter to Lily Haass and Agatha Harrison, Oct. 9, 1924, text indicates was written by Mary Dingman, YWCA, Geneva (G).

51. This may be inferred from the skills of those people considered for membership in the group. That the committee proposed to visit a number of cities is evident, though it may be supposed that its travels were curtailed somewhat after the May Thirtieth incident. See letter to Dame Adelaide Anderson, Dec. 16, 1924.

52. Letter Lily Haass to Mary Dingman, Aug. 3, 1926, YWCA, Geneva (C).

53. Letter Lily Haass to Mary Dingman and Agatha Harrison, Sept. 28, 1926, YWCA, Geneva (C).

54. "Memorandum to the British Boxer Indemnity Commission from the Industrial Committee of the National Christian Council Re Institute of Social and Economic Research," n.d., text indicates 1926, YWCA, Geneva (C). Under the terms of the original Rockefeller grant, it was understood that the institute, once established, would be financed locally or by other international organizations. See letter John D. Rockefeller to Sherwood Eddy, Jan. 22, 1924. The "Tayler-Meeker committee" and its successor institute were permitted to draw up to $5,000 gold per year for three years; in fact they drew $11,000 and returned $4,000, rather inexplicably in the circumstances. Letter Sherwood Eddy to David Yui, May 8, 1929, YMCA Historical Library, New York (R22).

55. "Memorandum to the British Boxer Indemnity Commission." The appeals were made by J. B. Tayler and by the NCC. An appeal to the British Boxer Indemnity Commission for money to support such an institute had first been suggested at the Annual Meeting of the National Christian Council in May 1923. See "Report of the Committee on the Church and Industrial Economic Problems," and *Christian Industry*, no. 9, Aug. 1, 1927, World Council of Churches, Geneva (21).

56. Letter "My Dear family and friends," from Mary Dingman, May 24, 1925, YWCA, Geneva (G).

57. Letter Lily Haass to Agatha Harrison and Mary Dingman, Nov. 4, 1925, YWCA, Geneva (C).

58. "Minutes, National Committee, YWCA of China," March 19, 1925, YWCA, Geneva (B).

59. Letter to Mary Dingman and Agatha Harrison, Sept. 19, 1925, text indicates written by Lily Haass, YWCA, Geneva (C); letter Lily Haass to Agatha Harrison and Mary Dingman, Nov. 4, 1925.

60. Letter John D. Rockefeller to Sherwood Eddy, Jan. 22, 1924, YMCA Historical Library, New York (R10).

61. Letter to Mary Dingman and Agatha Harrison, Sept. 19, 1925.

62. Ibid.

63. Letter Lily Haass to Agatha Harrison and Mary Dingman, Nov. 4, 1925.

64. Ibid. It would appear that in the turbulent political circumstances of 1926 the conferences were not in fact held.

65. Letter Lily Haass to Mary Dingman and Agatha Harrison, Oct. 30, 1926, YWCA, Geneva (C).

66. Letter Lily Haass to Mary Dingman, Dec. 22, 1926, YWCA, Geneva (C).

67. Letter Eleanor Hinder to Mary Dingman, Sept. 15, 1927, YWCA, Geneva (C).

68. From the foreword by Lily Haass to the *Report of the Conference on Christianising Economic Relations, held under the auspices of the National Christian Council of China, Shanghai, 18–28 August 1927* (Shanghai: NCC, 1927), p. 2, World Council of Churches, Geneva (X).

69. Among the delegates were Henry Hodgkin and Frank Rawlinson of the NCC, Cora Deng, Dju-yu Bao, Eleanor Hinder, Lily Haass, Ruth Hoople, Harriet Rietveld, Tao Ling, and Lydia Johnson of the YWCA, and E. E. Barnett and other representatives from the YMCA, along with M. T. Tchou, Gideon Chen, J. L. Buck, Lord Addington, and others concerned with problems of economic welfare. *Report of the Conference on Christianising Economic Relations*, pp. 3–4.

70. Ibid.

71. Eleanor Hinder, "Some Facts About the Present Industrial Situation in Shanghai," in ibid., pp. 75–83, 89–91.

72. Ibid., p. 106.

73. Ibid., pp. 106–7.

74. Ibid., pp. 109, 111.

75. Ibid., p. 116. Protection for women involved prohibition of night work and/or work in dangerous trades, and provision for absence from work with pay for a month at the time of childbirth.

76. Ibid., p. 117.

77. Ibid., pp. 118–21.

78. Ibid., pp. 122–23. The following passage from the *Li chi*, ch. 9 (*Li-yun p'ien*), was offered in support of the principle "to each according to his need": "When universal virtue is practiced, the aim is the good of all. The wise and capable are elected, sincerity and friendship are created. Thus man is not only filial to his own parents and not only kind to his own children; the aged are comforted, men are properly employed, the youth is rightly cared for; widowers, widows, orphans and the infirm are all well supported; men and women are tranquilly settled. Resources will not be wasted on earth, but shared by all, not enjoyed by oneself; energy will not be used selfishly, but used for all, not for oneself only. Therefore selfish devices cease, robbery, stealing and all other illegal disturbances disappear, the doors are left wide open and never closed. This is the meaning of the 'great harmony.'"

79. Letter Lily Haass to Mary Dingman and Agatha Harrison, Sept. 24, 1927, YWCA, Geneva (C); letter Henry Hodgkin to Charlotte Niven, Nov. 4, 1927, YWCA, Geneva (C).

80. By 1927 the NCC had added the following items on industrial problems to those listed for sale in 1924:

"Factory System and Regulation of Labor Conditions by National and International Laws"
"Brief History of Factory Legislation in the United Kingdom"
"An Industrial Miracle and How It Happened"
"Christianity and Industry in China"
"Shanghai Committee on the Church and Industry"
"Report of Child Labor Commission of Shanghai Municipal Council"
"Phosphorous Poisoning in Match Factories in China"
"The Church and the Economic and Industrial Problems of China's Labor Today"

In addition to these pamphlets, usually ten to twenty pages in length, the following one-page broadsheets had been published:

"Prohibiting Use of White Phosphorous Movement"
"What Have I to Do with Labor Problems?"
"Church and Labor"

All of the above were published in Chinese, while some of the pamphlets were also published in English. See "Bibliography of Publications by the National Christian Council," in *The National Christian Council, 1922–27* (Shanghai: NCC, 1927), pp. 39–41, Friends' Meeting House, London. By late 1927, nine editions of the bulletin *Christian Industry* had also been published, both in English and (separately) in Chinese.

81. Letter Henry Hodgkin to Charlotte Niven, March 6, 1928, YWCA, Geneva (C); Gideon Chen, "The YWCA and the Chinese Labour Movement," in *History of the YWCA in China, 1896–1930* (Shanghai: YWCA, n.d., probably 1931), p. 113, YWCA, Geneva (K).

82. Letter Gideon Chen to Mary Dingman, Feb. 9, 1929, YWCA, Geneva (C).

83. Letter Mary Dingman to Gideon Chen, Nov. 19, 1929, YWCA, Geneva (C). Tayler had first approached Chen about the possibility of his working at Yenching in 1927. See letter Gideon Chen to Mary Dingman Feb. 17, 1927, YWCA, Geneva (C).

84. Letter Lily Haass to Mary Dingman and Agatha Harrison, May 16, 1929, YWCA, Geneva (C).

85. Letter Gideon Chen to Mary Dingman, Feb. 9, 1929.

86. Letter Mary Dingman to Cora Deng, Nov. 28, 1930, YWCA, Geneva (J).

87. Letter Lily Haass to Mary Dingman, Sept. 9, 1929, YWCA, Geneva (C).

88. Letter J. B. Tayler to William Paton, Feb. 12, 1930, World Council of Churches, Geneva (114).

89. Letter J. B. Tayler to William Paton, April 14, 1930, World Council of Churches, Geneva (114).

90. See chapter 2 above. Undoubtedly these visits were of considerable benefit to the visitors and did much to increase their awareness of the problems facing China, but the extent to which they had any lasting impact on China is very much open to question.

91. Letter J. B. Tayler to William Paton, April 14, 1930.

92. Letter to J. B. Tayler, May 22, 1930, text indicates written by William Paton, World Council of Churches, Geneva (114).

93. Letter J. B. Tayler to William Paton, April 14, 1930.

94. Letter J. B. Tayler to William Paton, July 10, 1930, World Council of Churches, Geneva (114). Tayler was heartened by the fact that Kung was a Christian.

95. Letter J. B. Tayler to William Paton, April 14, 1930.

96. Ibid.

97. Ibid. This department was set up in the autumn of 1930 to promote research work on

industrial and social problems as a result of a decision taken at the Jerusalem meeting of the International Missionary Council in 1928. It had its headquarters in Geneva, and was administered by the American Merle Davis and the German Otto Iserland. At one stage, Agatha Harrison had been considered for a position with the department. See letter to John Mott, April 9, 1930, probably from William Paton, World Council of Churches, Geneva (RD23).

98. It would appear that the department's directors, Davis and Iserland, decided to limit their assistance to Tayler to "finding the technical experts he needs," feeling that criticism of their new bureau by various continental mission bodies prescribed "caution in accepting as one of our first tasks a project that apparently opens itself so wide to criticism as this proposed enterprise in China." See letter J. Merle Davis to A. L. Warnshuis, Nov. 24, 1930, World Council of Churches, Geneva (RD16). The two may have been influenced by the observation of an ILO official that "certain concrete labour situations in Africa form a more immediate and important field for the attention of our department than China." See "Notes of an Interview with Deputy Director-General Alfred Butler and Mr. Phelan at the International Labour Office," Sept. 25, 1930, manuscript, World Council of Churches, Geneva (RD23).

99. Letter J. B. Tayler to William Paton, May 2, 1930, World Council of Churches, Geneva (114).

100. Letter J. B. Tayler to R. H. Tawney, May 2, 1930, World Council of Churches, Geneva (114).

101. Letter J. B. Tayler to William Paton, July 10, 1930.

102. *Papers, Abstracts, and Extracts from Papers Contributed as the Basis of a Discussion to the Conference on the People's Livelihood, Shanghai, 21–28 Feb 1931* (Shanghai: NCC, 1931), pp. 2–3, World Council of Churches, Geneva (X).

103. Ibid., pp. 4–5.

104. Ibid., p. 4.

105. Ibid., p. iv.

106. "Report of the Conference on the People's Livelihood, Shanghai, Feb. 21–28, 1931," World Council of Churches, Geneva (X). This version is longer and somewhat more complete in certain respects than the published version.

107. *Papers, Abstracts, and Extracts from Papers*, p. 14.

108. Ibid., p. 65.

109. Ibid., p. 76.

110. Ibid., pp. 78, 80. The councils' functions were to be as follows: "To promote working efficiency; to improve the relations between the employers and the employees and to settle disputes between them; to assist in the enforcement of contracts and factory regulations; to deliberate and decide upon overtime work; to improve safety and health conditions in the factory; to propose improvements in factories or workshops; [and] to make plans for the workers' welfare."

111. Ibid., p. 84.

112. Ibid., pp. 18–19.

113. "Report on the Conference on the People's Livelihood."

114. *Papers, Abstracts, and Extracts from Papers*, pp. 53–55.

115. Ibid.

116. Ibid., pp. 103–4.

117. Ibid., pp. 104–7.

118. Ibid., p. 109.

119. J. B. Tayler, "NCC Committee on Christianising Economic Relations: Report and Forecast," Dec. 31, 1930, manuscript, World Council of Churches, Geneva (114).

120. Ibid. Tayler hoped to bring H. J. May, secretary of the International Co-operative Alliance, to China in 1932. This hope was not realized.

121. "Present Position of CCER Projects, and Plans for the Immediate Future," n.d., text indicates written by J. B. Tayler, early spring 1931, World Council of Churches, Geneva (114).

122. Ibid.

123. Ibid. For example, for the Nankai studies, it was hoped that funds might be forthcoming from the Institute of Social and Religious Research in New York, for Dean's experiments money was hoped for from the International Famine Relief Fund or from the Penney Foundation, and for securing experts in cooperative organization an appeal was to be made for money to the Agricultural Missions Boards. Most sources were now likely to have been more difficult to tap because of the impact of the world depression.

124. Tayler, "NCC Committee on Christianising Economic Relations." In particular, Tayler refers to a Miss Senger, who was attempting to develop the knitting and weaving of wool as a village industry "in the Northwest."

125. *Papers, Abstracts, and Extracts from Papers*, p. iii.

126. "John Bernard Tayler, M.Sc." Hilda Brown and Gladys Yang (later of the Foreign Language Press in Beijing) are Tayler's daughters.

127. "Report of Informal Discussion on Rural and Industrial Problems in China," Sept. 21, 1931, World Council of Churches, Geneva (RD3).

128. "Report of J. B. Tayler's Trip to Shansi," n.d., text indicates 1932, World Council of Churches, Geneva (114).

129. "Social and Economic News," issued by the Department of Social and Industrial Research and Counsel, International Missionary Council, April 1933, World Council of Churches, Geneva (RD24).

130. "North China Industrial Service Union," n.d., text indicates Sept. 17, 1932, World Council of Churches, Geneva (RD3). Those present at the inaugural meeting were Chang Po-ling and Franklin Ho of Nankai University; Leighton Stuart, Gideon Chen, E. O. Wilson, and J. B. Tayler of Yenching University; Gene L. Chiao of Oberlin in Shansi; A. L. Carson of Cheloo University; S. M. Dean and Liu Chao of the North China School of Engineering Practice in Peking; J. A. Hunter of the North China Christian Rural Service Union; W. H. Wong of the National Geological Survey; and Y. T. Tsur, whose affiliation is not given. Apparently the North China Christian *Rural* Service Union "had planned to have an industrial section but desired to leave this field to the proposed Industrial Union, co-operating with it as much as possible."

131. Tayler, "Rural Reconstruction in China," p. 26. It was also proposed that Yenching and Nankai universities form a joint Industrial Service Institute, possibly with Tayler as its "foreign secretary." No record appears to have remained of such an institute, however.

132. Ibid.

133. "John Bernard Tayler, M.Sc."

134. J. Merle Davis, "Notes on an Interview with Dr. J. B. Tayler of Yenching University," Shanghai, June 13, 1937, World Council of Churches, Geneva (RD3).

135. J. B. Tayler, "Rural Reconstruction in China," in *The Home Messenger*, Feb. 1934, p. 26, in the private papers of J. B. Tayler in the possession of Mrs. Hilda Brown, London.

136. "John Bernard Tayler, M.Sc."

137. *Bibliography of Publications of the National Christian Council of China, March 1, 1934*, NCC Shanghai, YMCA, Geneva, Box X315.51.

138. Letter Arthur Packard to Sherwood Eddy, Feb. 10, 1931, YMCA Historical Library, New York (R27). There was also a further final $4,000 for the NCC to use to bring "experts" to China; it does not appear that this sum was drawn.

139. Letter J. B. Tayler to William Paton, April 14, 1930. Tayler's "extensive plan . . . for establishing subsidiary industries" met with a cool reception.

140. Letter J. B. Tayler to Henry Hodgkin, June 3, 1931, World Council of Churches, Geneva (114).

141. Letter F. Hawkins to Lena Tayler, April 24, 1934, in the private papers of J. B. Tayler in the possession of Mrs. Hilda Brown, London, and Tayler, "Rural Reconstruction in China," p. 26.

142. See letter Howard Galt to Manchester University Senate, March 7, 1933, in the

private papers of J. B. Tayler, in the possession of Mrs. Hilda Brown, London. See also letter Selina Tayler to the Registrar, University College Bangor, June 1, 1934, in the private papers of J. B. Tayler in the possession of Mrs. Hilda Brown, London.

143. "John Bernard Tayler, M.Sc."

144. Letter J. Merle Davis to John Mott, Dec. 8, 1936, World Council of Churches, Geneva (42) Davis conceded that some research had been carried out on economic and social matters but complained that the material had been "secured in the first instance without reference to the problems of the Church."

145. Ibid. In connection with the Hangchow conference, Davis sent out a questionnaire, in response to which some of the most pointed comments came from Augusta Wagner of the Economics Department of Yenching University, later to write *Labor Legislation in China*. "Studies in the use of leisure, opium, narcotics, financing the Church, economic organisation of Chinese religious foundations, the pastor's budget, the Church and the co-operative movement, the economic life and organisations of rural and urban families are of academic and administrative interest to the organised Christian movement in China but offer very little light on what seems to me to be the topic of most vital concern—why Christianity does not take root in China; why it is not accepted; why it is definitely rejected. . . . There do not seem to be any questions raised as to what the Chinese think of Christianity . . . you raise the question of the influence of Communism upon Christian thought . . . but you raise no question as to its influences on *Chinese* thought—Christian or non-Christian. I think you would get a good deal more if you did not limit your question to Christian thought." See letter Augusta Wagner to J. Merle Davis, Jan. 4, 1937, World Council of Churches, Geneva (RD2). Because of the war between China and Japan, the conference was held at Tambaram, near Madras in India.

146. Letter J. Merle Davis to John Mott, Dec. 8, 1936.

147. "Notes on a Conference with Members of the Sociological Faculty at Yenching," June 8, 1937, text indicates written by J. Merle Davis, World Council of Churches, Geneva (RD3). The faculty members agreed that they would "help a joint study group, as counsellors and advisers, in the setting up of studies and in suggestions for procedure; assign to one of their best students a study of the Presbyterian Church and its members in the village of Ching Ho near the university—a centre which has already been the object of intensive studies by the Sociology Department; . . . endeavour to assign two of their students, preferably a man and a woman, to studies of Peiping churches in relation to their environment; . . . select a village in which a Christian church is located, and would include studies of the church and its environment in their program." One of those present suggested that the Sociology Department might accept research by students into Christian churches and their communities for credit.

148. Davis, "Notes on an Interview with Dr. J. B. Tayler." Tayler estimated that about $350 to $500 in new Chinese currency (or about U.S. $35 to $50) would be necessary to set up each of the cooperatives initially. Davis had earlier promised up to U.S. $750 for the study to be conducted by Frank Price of Nanking Theological Seminary into the "Church and its Rural Environment." Letter J. Merle Davis to John Mott, Dec. 8, 1936.

Chapter 5

1. *Labour Conditions in China*, cmd. 2442, 1925, p. 83.

2. A. Kotenev, *Shanghai: Its Municipality and the Chinese*, pp. 306–10, cited in Chesneaux, *The Chinese Labour Movement*, p. 74. It was so common for children to work from an early age that workers describing their early years often refer to it only in passing, as an unavoidable fact of life. See *Lao gongren hua dangnian* (Narratives of the lives of old workers (Beijing, 1958).

3. Chesneaux, *The Chinese Labour Movement*, p. 74. The role of women in the cotton

industry in particular has been dealt with very comprehensively by Emily Honig in her *Sisters and Strangers*. For a view in the broader historical perspective see Yen Chung-p'ing, *Chung-kuo mien-fong-chih shih-kao* (Draft history of the Chinese cotton-spinning industry, 1289–1937) (Peking, 1955).

4. Cited in Honig, *Sisters and Strangers*, p. 24.

5. Hershatter, *The Workers of Tianjin*, pp. 53–54.

6. *China Year Book*, 1925, pp. 908–9.

7. George Sokolsky, "The Strikes of Shanghai," in the *North China Herald*, Sept. 24, 1926.

8. *North China Herald*, April 18, 1925.

9. *International Labour Review* 20 (1929): 252; Chesneaux, *The Chinese Labour Movement*, p. 215. Only in relatively few industries, where workers were better organized, was any serious attempt made to monitor wages, as with respect to the railway workers, for example, noted in Ch'en Ta, *Chung-kuo lao-kung wen-t'i* (China's labour problems) (Shanghai, 1933). It is hard to see how the International Labour Organization, which in 1929 was still unrepresented in China, would have known enough to make this assertion.

10. See, for example, the testimony of Heygate, Armstrong, Han, Mrs. Noh, and Miss Wang in the "Minutes of the Child Labour Commission of Shanghai," 1923–24, in archives of library at Friends' Meeting House, London, Agatha Harrison Papers, Temporary Box 50-B. Testimony shows that the wages paid to children were pitiful enough, ranging from 7 cents per day for a "small girl" at a Chinese cotton mill (McNicol), to 30 cents and more per day for child workers at the British-American Tobacco plants (Heygate). Apprentice boys were often not paid at all (Chen). H. D. Lamson, in a survey published in 1930, concludes that even then the contribution by girls under fifteen to the family budget was critical, constituting an average 19.7 percent of the entire family income. Without the contribution of these working children the families would have an annual deficit of $75.95; with it this would become an annual surplus of $36.07. See H. D. Lamson, "The Standard of Living of Factory Workers: A Study of Incomes and Expenditures of 21 Working Families in Shanghai," *Chinese Economic Journal* 7 (1930), cited in Honig, *Sisters and Strangers*, p. 169.

11. Letter Agatha Harrison to Lily Haass and Eleanor Hinder, Nov. 26, 1926, World's YWCA, Geneva (C).

12. *Report of the Joint Committee of Women's Organisations* (Shanghai, 1927), p. 6.

13. In statements to the Child Labor Commission the Foreign Cotton Mill Owners Association of China subsequently affirmed that it would accept legislation that would be applied at least both in the settlement and in the neighboring province of Kiangsu, while the Chinese Cotton Mill Owners Association insisted that it be applied also both in Kiangsu and Chekiang. See "Report of the Child Labour Commission," in *Shanghai Municipal Gazette*, July 19, 1924. Copy at Friends' Meeting House, London, Agatha Harrison Papers, Temporary Box 50-B.

14. *Report of the Joint Committee of Women's Organisations*, p. 9.

15. Ibid., pp. 7–8. The Joint Committee nominated five employers, five persons locally concerned with industrial welfare, and seven "others," one of whom was J. B. Powell, editor of the *China Weekly Review*. Six of these total actually served on the commission.

16. "Report of the Child Labour Commission." The manufacturers were: R. J. McNicol, manager of the Cotton Mills Department of Jardine Mathieson and chairman of the Foreign Cotton Mill Owners Association of China; G. Okada, manager, Naigai Wata Kaisha; J. S. S. Cooper, vice-chairman and director, Arnhold and Co.; Edwin J. Cornfoot, silk merchant, Dyce and Co.; and a Mr. H.Y. Noh, apparently an industrialist, but whose affiliation is not given. The chairman was H. Lipson Ward. The women from the YWCA were Agatha Harrison, and Soong Mei-ling, soon to marry Chiang Kai-shek. The missionary wife was Mrs. L. MacGillivray, while the doctor was Mary Stone. Agatha Harrison left for England in January 1924 and was replaced by Mary Dingman of the YWCA World's Committee. Mrs. MacGillivray left for Canada and England in May, while Mrs. Moh and Dr. Stone were able to attend only a few of the meetings.

17. Ibid. These thirty witnesses were as follows:

Employers:
James Harrof, manager, Ewo Cotton Mills, Jardine Mathieson
Mr. Nishikawa, managing director, Toyoda Cotton Mill
Mr. Nieh, manager, Gen Foong Cotton Mill
Woo Tao-yin, manager, Say Lun Silk Filature
Mr. Heygate, manager, British-American Tobacco, Pootung
George Su, general secretary, Nanyang Brothers Tobacco Co.
Mr. Bau, assistant works superintendent, Commercial Press
C. A. Skinner, manager, New Engineering and Shipbuilding Works
R. J. McNicol, manager, Ewo Cotton Mills Department, Jardine Mathieson
E. J. Cornfoot, silk merchant, Dyce and Co.
Chen Chin-kee, building contractor, Shanghai Land Investment Co.

Police:
Inspector Johnston (Yangtzepoo)
Detective Inspector Price (West Hongkew)
Major Hilton Johnson, deputy commissioner of police
W. Armstrong, director of criminal intelligence

Medical:
Dr. Fullerton, St. Elizabeth's Hospital
Dr. Decker, Yangtzepoo Social Center
Dr. New, Red Cross Hospital
Miss Hille, Nantao Institute
Dr. Lawney, Margaret Williamson Hospital

Social Agencies:
Miss Zung Wei-tsung, YWCA
Mr. Tsien, Yangtzepoo Social Center
Miss Wang, YMCA
Mr. T. L. Chang, YMCA

Labor Contractors:
Mr. Chang, contractor to Ewo Mills
Han Sung-wen, contractor to a Jessfield waste silk filature

Compradore: Mr. Liu, compradore, Ewo Silk Filature

Architect: G. W. Shipway, architect and civil engineer

Editor: Cao Hwei, editor, *Min Kuo Shih Bao*

Worker: Mrs. Moh, ex-silk filature worker, attempting to form a union

18. Supplementary material attached to "Minutes of the Child Labour Commission of Shanghai." Figures given by the police for the number of children in mills and factories in the International Settlement and Chapei and Pootung, though undoubtedly partial and inaccurate, show a total of 4,485 boys under twelve, foreign count, and 17,958 girls. See appendix 1, "Report of the Child Labour Commission."

19. Tours of inspection were arranged on October 16 and November 24, for example, though there were almost certainly others. See "Minutes of the Child Labour Commission." The form of inquiry, and the comments registered in response to it on the occasion of one particular visit, are reproduced in Appendix 3.

20. Testimony of Heygate, Johnston, Armstrong, Liu, Moh, Tsien, and Zung, "Minutes of the Child Labour Commission of Shanghai."

21. Testimony of Harrof, Heygate, Nieh, Tsien, and Chang.

22. Testimony of New and Cao Hwei. The latter qualified his position by saying that while children might be allowed to work in the more traditional Chinese workshops at the age of twelve, Chinese count, they ought to be debarred from modern factories until they were fifteen.

23. Testimony of Prince.

24. Testimony of Liu.

25. Testimony of Heygate, Johnston, Armstrong, Prince, Su, New, and Liu.

26. Testimony of Armstrong.

27. Testimony of Moh.

28. Testimony of Prince, Han and Harrof.

29. James Harrof, manager of the Ewo Cotton Mills, owned by Jardine Mathieson.

30. Testimony of McNicol.

31. Testimony of Han, and McNicol.

32. R. J. McNicol, based on the calculation that in his own mills one-third of the labor employed was under fifteen, Chinese count, and that for every six children dismissed one adult might also leave.

33. Testimony of Harrof and Liu.

34. Testimony of Woo. Apart from this process in the filatures, there were undoubtedly other stages of manufacture or tasks in various industries which were felt to be particularly suited to small children, such as the cleaning of the inside of boilers on steam launches (testimony of Skinner), and the boxing of matches (testimony of Zung). There were rumors, neither confirmed nor denied, that small machines were in process of manufacture in the United States for shipment to China and use in factories where child labor was commonplace. See letter Charlotte Niven to Florence Simms, Nov. 21, 1922, YWCA, Geneva (F).

35. Testimony of R. J. McNicol.

36. Testimony of McNicol, Heygate, and Johnston.

37. Testimony of Harrof, McNicol, Prince, Bau, Woo, and Nieh. See especially the testimony of McNicol.

38. Testimony of Liu, Nieh, Harrof, Nishikawa, and Prince.

39. Testimony of Prince; J. S. S. Cooper, vice-chairman, Arnhold and Co.

40. Testimony of Zung.

41. Testimony of Cao Hwei.

42. In the latter category notably were Bau, Moh, Shipway, the representatives of the YM and YWCA, certain of the doctors, and one police witness, Inspector Johnston.

43. For example, Heygate, McNicol, Nieh, Liu, Nishikawa, Skinner, and the Naigai Wata Kaisha.

44. Testimony of Armstrong. These were Armstrong and Hilton Johnson.

45. Testimony of Hilton Johnson.

46. See testimony of both Armstrong and Hilton Johnson.

47. Dame Adelaide Anderson on the occasion of the fifteenth meeting. Even Ch'en Ta, probably the most prominent Chinese writer on labor matters of the time, does not take up this point, and indeed gives little attention to child labor at all in his work of 1929–33. See Ch'en Ta, *Chung-kuo lao-kung wen-t'i* (China's labour problems).

48. "Report of the Child Labour Commission."

49. Ibid.

50. *Report of the Joint Committee of Women's Organisations*, pp. 12–14.

51. Adelaide Anderson, *Humanity and Labour in China* (London, 1928), pp. 163–203.

52. *North China Herald*, June 21, 1924.

53. "Child Labour in Shanghai," n.d., memorandum of the Joint Committee of Women's Organizations, archives of World's YWCA, Geneva (G).

54. *Report of the Joint Committee of Women's Organisations*, pp. 60–62.

55. "The Industrial Work of the China YWCA."

56. See the *Times*, Oct. 15, 1924; the *Manchester Guardian*, Feb. 13, 1925; and the *New Statesman*, Feb. 21, 1925.

57. Letter to Lady Portsmouth, chairman, Industrial Law Bureau, text indicates from Agatha Harrison, Feb. 17, 1925, World's YWCA, Geneva (G).

58. See "People to be invited to the 'At Home' to Dame Adelaide Anderson and Miss Agatha Harrison, February 3, 1925"; and letter Charlotte Niven to Mary Dingman, Feb. 4, 1925, both in World's YWCA, Geneva (G).

59. See "Meeting of Feb. 5th, 1925," in "Minute Book 1925–26, China and Far East Section," p. 170, in archives of Manchester Chamber of Commerce, Manchester. There was some controversy over whether or not pressure should be brought to bear outside China to further the campaign. George Sokolsky of the *North China Herald,* for example, felt that "the utilisation of publicity in England, the United States and Japan to affect opinion in China is ill-conceived." See letter George Sokolsky to Mary Dingman, March 24, 1925, World's YWCA, Geneva (G). On the other hand, it became clear that "the British Chamber [of Commerce in Shanghai] would be compelled to take some notice of the Child Labour Report because they had had word from the Manchester Chamber of Commerce," a fact conceded by the secretary of the British Chamber himself. See letter Mary Dingman to Dame Adelaide Anderson, Feb. 26, 1925, World's YWCA, Geneva (G).

60. Murray, "The Industrial Work of the China YWCA."

61. *Report of the Joint Committee of Women's Organisations*, pp. 15–16.

62. Ibid. The firms were: **British**: Jardine Mathieson, Butterfield and Swire, Mackenzie and Co., the China Soap Co., Liddel Bros., Arnhold and Co., and the British-American Tobacco Co.; **Chinese**: Sincere Co., Commercial Press, Wing On Co., K. Willey Commercial Co., C. C. Nieh Cotton Mills, and Sung Sing Cotton and Weaving; **Japanese**: Mitsui Bussan Kaisha, Nippon Yusen Kaisha, Osaka Shosen Kaisha, South Manchuria Railway, Mitsubishi Kaisha, and Dah Dong Spinning Co.; **American**: Robert Dollar Co., American Trading Co., Shanghai Building Co., Standard Oil, and China General Edison.

63. Ibid., Appendix 5, "Extracts from Manifesto, Chinese General Chamber of Commerce, Shanghai," pp. 63–64.

64. Dame Adelaide Anderson, in International Industrial Welfare Congress, *Report of the Proceedings Held in Flushing, Holland* (Zurich, 1925), p. 233.

65. *North China Herald,* April 18, 1925.

66. Ibid., May 9, 1925.

67. Letter Mary Dingman to Agatha Harrison, April 30, 1925, World's YWCA, Geneva (G). Thirty-four of the signatories were to be found in the current *China Who's Who.*

68. This point, made in a letter to the *North China Herald,* was not disputed.

69. Memorandum of the Joint Committee of Women's Organisations, untitled, text indicates May 28, 1925, World's YWCA, Geneva (G).

70. Letter Mary Dingman to Agatha Harrison, April 30, 1925.

71. *China Year Book*, 1926, p. 908.

72. *Report of the Joint Committee of Women's Organisations*, p. 23.

73. Ibid., p. 15.

74. Letter "Dear Family and Friends . . . ," by Mary Dingman, May 24, 1925, YWCA, Geneva (G).

75. John Pratt, in *Labour Conditions in China*.

76. Letter Mary Dingman to "World Colleagues," May 26, 1926, World's YWCA, Geneva (G).

77. "The Industrial Work of the China YWCA."

78. Peter Finch of the *Shanghai Sunday Times* writing in *Current History,* vol. 22 (August 1925): 759. A recent thoughtful account of the political factors surrounding this second meeting is contained in Richard Rigby, *The May Thirtieth Movement,* appendix 2. Rigby emphasizes British Foreign Office support for the proposed bylaw, and Chinese opposition to it. He notes the significant failure of mainland Chinese historians since 1949 to refer to it.

79. In 1925 the Municipal Council was made up of nine members, of whom six were British, two were American, and one was Japanese. Council was elected by the ratepayers, who were the foreign owners of land and buildings; Chinese were not given the vote. The most recent census figures available for the settlement showed a population of approximately 6,300 Britons, 2,300 Americans, 10,200 Japanese, 3,700 other foreign nationalities, and 760,000 Chinese living in its bounds. See *Parliamentary Debates,* 1924–25, vol. 185, p. 531.

80. *Report of the Joint Committee of Women's Organisations,* pp. 63–64.

81. Wagner, *Labour Legislation in China,* p. 92.

82. See, for example, the *North China Herald,* July 12, 1924, Aug. 6 and 7, 1924, Feb. 7, 1925, and April 11, 1925. Quote is from April 11.

83. Ibid., June 6, 1925.

84. Ibid., July 2, 1927. The *Herald* went on to reason: "If the complete industrialisation of China is the only possible solution of China's economic unrest, surely a partial industrialisation is at least a palliative of her trouble. Some praise must be due to the pioneers who, in the early days, ventured to invest their capital in industrial undertakings, took the sweepings of the labour market, and trained the incompetents into efficient technical workers —cotton spinners, engineers, and constructors of the skyscrapers that astonish the tourist as he sails up the Huangpu. The men who did these things benefitted China in two ways. They provided a livelihood for a large number who would otherwise have been hard put to it to find daily bread, and in the process conducted an educational work of great value."

85. See the letter of "Welfare," for example, in the *North China Herald* of Jan. 10, 1925, and that of "Inquirer," in ibid., April 25, 1925.

86. Letter of Mrs. L. MacGillivray in the *North China Herald,* March 28, 1925. See also, for example, the letters of Dame Adelaide Anderson and of Fong Sec in ibid., March 28, 1925, and April 4, 1925, respectively.

87. The Theosophical Society, in ibid. April 11, 1925.

88. John Pratt in *Labour Conditions in China,* p. 107.

89. "Shanghailander," in the *North China Herald,* March 28, 1925.

90. "Old Resident," in ibid., April 4, 1925.

91. Ibid. Also Wang Mau in ibid.

92. See especially the letter of "Shanghailander" in ibid., March 28, 1925.

93. *New Statesman,* Feb. 21, 1925, and June 13, 1925.

94. *Report of the Annual Labour Party Conference,* 1925, p. 63.

95. *Parliamentary Debates,* vol. 185, 1924–25, p. 932.

96. For example, according to the British White Paper *Memorandum on Labour Conditions in China,* cmd. 2846, published in 1927, Jardine Mathieson's Ewo Cotton Mills no longer hired boys under ten or girls under twelve—a reform dating back to September 1923. BAT claimed not to admit children under fourteen, Naigai Wata Kaisha did not employ children under four feet tall, while Arnhold and Co. was reported as having taken steps to end child labor in their Oriental Cotton Mills. The Chinese-owned Commercial Press had sought from the beginning to ban child labor. A memorandum submitted to the Child Labor Commission in 1924 suggested that the Silk Reeling Guild would enforce a ban on child labor in Chinese filatures, "as the children often spoil the raw material," but there is no evidence that the ban was put into practice. See "Shanghai Silk Filatures and Labour Regulations," Jan. 5, 1924, at Friends' Meeting House, London, Agatha Harrison Papers, Temporary Box 50-B.

97. *China Weekly Review,* Oct. 10, 1928, p. 94.

98. *International Labour Review* 25 (1932): 539; Wagner, *Labour Legislation in China,*

pp. 92–94. For this particular improvement see also *Report of Mr. Justice Feetham to the Shanghai Municipal Council, 1931*, vol. 2, p. 28. With the range of new information available by the late 1930s it was at least possible for critics to make a stronger case for reform. See, for example, Ho Te-ming, *Chung-kuo lao-tung wen-t'i* (Chinese labor problems) (Shanghai, 1935).

99. *Report of Mr. Justice Feetham*, p. 28.

100. Honig, *Sisters and Strangers*, pp. 24–25, and Hershatter, *The Workers of Tianjin*, p. 53.

101. "Regulation of Industrial Conditions," p. 39, in *Annual Report of the Shanghai Municipal Council*, 1935.

102. Hinder, *Life and Labour in Shanghai*, p. 24.

103. See, for example, the *Proceedings of the International Labour Conference 1919*, and subsequent years, the speeches by Chinese delegates.

104. See letter from the British minister in Peking to Ramsay MacDonald in *Labour Conditions in China*, cmd. 2442, 1925, p. 5.

105. Anderson was co-opted for this task because of her experience on the Shanghai Child Labor Commission, noted above. Pone had no previous experience of China.

106. Participating in the discussions were the vice-minister and other officials of the Ministry of Industries, the director of the Bureau of Social Affairs of the Chinese municipality, the chairman and the secretary-general of the Municipal Council of the International Settlement, and the French consul-general and the director of municipal services of the French Concession, as well as Pone and Anderson. See Wagner, *Labour Legislation in China*, p. 159.

107. See letter Eleanor Hinder to "My Dears," March 18, 1933, and letter Eleanor Hinder to Mary Dingman, March 20, 1933, both World's YWCA, Geneva (L). Even the YWCA joined in the protest against this proposed extension of the council's power.

108. Hinder, *Life and Labour in Shanghai*, p. 10.

109. Letter Eleanor Hinder to Mary Dingman, April 5, 1935, World's YWCA, Geneva (L).

110. "Survey of 1936," pp. 1–2, in *Annual Report of the Shanghai Municipal Council, 1936*.

111. Ibid.

112. Letter Eleanor Hinder to Camille Pone, June 20, 1934, in dossier N/200/1/13/3, ILO, Geneva.

113. Letter Eleanor Hinder to "My Dears," Feb. 25, 1933, World's YWCA, Geneva (L).

114. Letter Eleanor Hinder to "My Dears," March 18, 1933.

115. "Regulation of Industrial Conditions," pp. 2–3, reprint from *Annual Report of the Shanghai Municipal Council, 1934*, in N/200/13/3, ILO, Geneva.

116. Letter Eleanor Hinder to "My Dears," Feb. 25, 1933.

117. "Regulation of Industrial Conditions," 1935, pp. 42–43.

118. Ibid., 1936, p. 36.

119. Ibid., 1937, p. 13.

120. Ibid., 1934, p. 6.

121. Letter Eleanor Hinder to Mary Dingman and Evelyn Fox, Nov. 2, 1933, World's YWCA, Geneva (L).

122. "Regulation of Industrial Conditions," 1935, p. 45.

123. "Regulation of Industrial Conditions," 1935, p. 38.

124. This was the view of a section official expressed in a paper given before the China branch of the Institution of Electrical Engineers on December 6, 1937. See ibid., 1937, p. 8.

125. Ibid., 1935, p. 44.

126. Ibid., 1937, p. 14.

127. Ibid., p. 15.

128. Ibid., 1934, p. 1.

129. Letter Eleanor Hinder to "My Dears," Nov. 1, 1933, World's YWCA, Geneva (L).

130. Hinder, *Labour Legislation in China*, p. 131.

131. "Regulation of Industrial Conditions," 1936, pp. 40–41. The Social Affairs Bureau of the Municipality of Greater Shanghai was by the mid-1930s also producing statistics with regard to wage rates in Shanghai; though by no means comprehensive, they give an approximate idea of wages in various trades. See Shang-hai shih cheng fu, she-hui-chu, *Shang-hai shih kung-tzu-li* (Wage rates in Shanghai) (Shanghai, 1935). The situation with respect to information on prices began also to clarify somewhat by the mid-1930s. See this progression in Chung-kuo k'o-hsueh-yuan Shanghai ching-chi yen-chiu-so, *Shang-hai chieh-fang ch'ien-hou wu-chia tzu-liao hui-pien, 1921–1957* (Commodity prices before and after the liberation of Shanghai, 1921–1957) (Shanghai, 1959).

132. Ibid., 1936, p. 32.

133. Letter Eleanor Hinder to Mary Dingman and Evelyn Fox, Nov. 2, 1933.

134. "Regulation of Industrial Conditions," 1936, p. 31, and 1937, p. 4.

Chapter 6

1. See Robert Barnett, *Economic Shanghai: Hostage to Politics, 1937–1941*, pp. 44–45.

2. Honig, *Sisters and Strangers*, p. 198.

3. Barnett, *Economic Shanghai*, p. 46.

4. See, for example, Lewis S. C. Smythe, *War Damage in the Nanking Area, Dec. 1937 to March 1938* (Nanking International Relief Committee, June 1938).

5. Barnett, *Economic Shanghai*, pp. 44–45. By 1939 the numbers had been reduced to 31,000, and by December 1941 to 16,000. The camps were then closed, and the inmates dispersed. See Honig, *Sisters and Strangers*, p. 199.

6. A critique of the bureau's data is given in D. K. Lieu's *The Growth and Industrialisation of Shanghai*, chap. 3.

7. "Regulation of Industrial Conditions," 1938, p. 43.

8. Ibid. Consideration was given in 1940 to the possibility of soliciting information from foreign factories (see ibid., p. 53), but it would appear that no practical steps had been taken in this direction by the time of the Japanese invasion in December 1941.

9. In 1939 a study was undertaken of the "foreign" cost of living in Shanghai for similar purposes. See "Regulation of Industrial Conditions," 1939, p. 42, and 1940, p. 44. One enterprising firm in 1940 apparently conducted its own study in order to discover "the extent to which its women workers are the breadwinners in their families, to see whether their earnings are sufficient."

10. Ibid., 1938, p. 60.

11. Ibid., 1939, p. 41; 1940, pp. 57–58.

12. Ibid., 1939, p. 41.

13. Ibid., 1940, p. 57.

14. Hinder, *Life and Labour in Shanghai*, p. 76.

15. Ibid., pp. 75–76.

16. "Regulation of Industrial Conditions," 1940, p. 58.

17. Ibid., pp. 75–76.

18. See ibid., 1937, p. 5; 1940, p. 44. Initially, thirty foreign-owned engineering establishments were approached. In one, the existing standard of apprentice training conformed to that required, while eight others expressed interest in the scheme. Some claimed not to employ apprentices on a regular basis. Only preliminary approaches were made to Chinese concerns in 1940.

19. Ibid., 1938, pp. 40–42; 1937, p. 4.

20. Ibid., 1939, pp. 54–55.

21. Ibid., p. 58.

22. Ibid., 1940, p. 62.

23. Ibid., p. 63.

24. Ibid., 1939, pp 57, 59; 1940, p. 61.

25. Hinder, *Life and Labour in Shanghai*, p. 85.

26. Ibid.

27. "Regulation of Industrial Conditions," 1938, p. 4; 1940, p. 59.

28. Hinder, *Life and Labour in Shanghai*, pp. 89–90.

29. "Regulation of Industrial Conditions," 1940, pp. 59–60.

30. Hinder, *Life and Labour in Shanghai*, p. 106.

31. "Regulation of Industrial Conditions," 1939, pp. 40–41; 1940, pp. 43–44.

32. Facilities for regular technical education were provided by the China Institute of Industrial Training, organized in 1940. See ibid., 1940, pp. 43–44.

33. Hinder, *Life and Labour in Shanghai*, pp. 111–12.

34. "Regulation of Industrial Conditions," 1939, p. 37.

35. "A Letter from Shanghai YWCA Industrial Club Girls to YWCA Industrial Girls in America," Oct. 2, 1937, World's YWCA, Geneva (N).

36. *The YWCA of China, 1933–47*, p. 72; and "Annual Report, YWCA of China, 1 Sept. 1939–31 Aug. 1940, Section A, Education: Industrial Statistics 1939–40 by Cities," World's YWCA, Geneva (S). Industrial work is mentioned as having continued in Tientsin "for a time," but the last report showing any activity there was submitted in 1940.

37. Lily Haass, "The Social and Industrial Programme of the YWCA in China," May 9, 1939, World's YWCA, Geneva (Q).

38. "Annual Report, YWCA of China."

39. "World's YWCA: Report on a Visit to China, by Miss Woodsmall, prepared for the Executive Committee Meeting, June 1941," World's YWCA.

40. *The YWCA of China, 1933–47*.

41. "A Letter from Shanghai YWCA Industrial Club Girls."

42. Eleanor Hinder, "YWCA Faces Effects of War in Shanghai," in *Green Year Supplement*, 1937, pp. 15, 17. The camp later moved to a site in Brenan Road.

43. Ibid.

44. Ibid., p. 18.

45. Ibid., p. 17.

46. "Classeur: Sections 1/132, 'The Refugee Problem—Further Reports from Associations, 23 June 1939,'" World's YWCA, Geneva.

47. "A Brief Summary of the YWCA Industrial Camp for Refugee Women and Children," n.d., text indicates 1938, World's YWCA, Geneva (Q).

48. "Classeur: Sections 1/132." This was the camp in Yu Yuen Road. Of the other two camps, one was that at YWCA Headquarters, and the other is unidentifiable. The refugee center at the Continental Bank Building, later in Brenan Road, was administered jointly with several Christian agencies.

49. "A Letter from Shanghai YWCA Industrial Club Girls." Some sixty YWCA Industrial Club girls entered the Women Labourers' War Area Service Corps and accompanied the army to the front to do "liaison work" between the peasants and soldiers, along with similar groups from Canton and Hankow. In a similar vein, the YWCA later in the war started a program to assist soldiers' families in various parts of the country. This program consisted of mass education, health work, the holding of meetings to boost morale, and extensive case work among young widows and other women. See *The YWCA of China, 1933–47*, pp. 72, 75.

50. "Hardly Human Habitation," National YWCA, Chengtu, China, Feb. 2, 1943, World's YWCA, Geneva (T).

51. *The YWCA of China. Industrial Co-operative Work* (Shanghai: YWCA National Committee, n.d., text indicates 1940), World's YWCA, Geneva (S).

52. *The YWCA of China, 1933–47*, p. 75.

53. "Recent News from the National Committee of the YWCA of China: Industrial Co-operative Work," n.d., text indicates early 1940, World's YWCA, Geneva (S).

54. *The YWCA of China: Industrial Co-operative Work.*

55. *The YWCA of China, 1933–47.*

56. Proposed cooperatives for Kunming and "four other" interior cities are mentioned in "Recent News from the National Committee of the YWCA of China," but are not mentioned in any subsequent reports.

57. "Annual Report, National Committee YWCA of China, 1 Aug 1942—1 Aug 1943: 'Mass Education and Industrial Co-operatives,'" in archives of World's YWCA, Geneva (T). It is not made clear in this or other documents to which pattern the remaining co-ops conformed.

58. Ibid. At the time this report was written, the wool spinning co-op had only two outworkers as members of the co-op.

59. Training for the Chengtu sewing co-op is said to have lasted only a few weeks, while a period of three months is given as normal in the annual report for 1942–43, and four months seems to have been required at the Penghsien wool-spinning co-op. See, respectively, *The YWCA of China: Industrial Co-operative Work*; "Annual Report, National Committee YWCA of China"; and "A Co-operative Venture in Lung Feng Ch'ang [Glorious Abundance Market]," May 27, 1943, World's YWCA, Geneva (T).

60. "Annual Report, National Committee YWCA of China."

61. *The YWCA of China: Industrial Co-operative Work.*

62. For example, in Kweiyang, where the YWCA organizer was faced with the task of setting up a cooperative to create work, there was regularly a heavy rainfall. Although umbrellas had always been imported from the neighboring province, all the raw materials necessary for their manufacture—bamboo to make the poles and paper sections, nuts for the oil and shellac, and glue from the hoofs and horns of water buffalo—were available locally. "Everything seemed possible. It did not require heavy physical labor, women's hands were suited to the delicate spokemaking and fitting of the framework and to the painting of designs—raw materials were at hand." See Josephine Brown, "The Umbrella Making Co-operative of the YWCA of Kweiyang," n.d., text indicates early 1942, YWCA of the United States, New York (D).

63. In a publicity release in 1940, YWCA officials maintained that the overall purposes of the cooperative movement were (1) to give basic constructive relief to refugees; (2) to help in the patriotic work of production, meeting China's immense need of goods; and (3) to educate toward good citizenship in a cooperative society. They further observed that the YWCA "recognises the co-operative as a basic form of mass education educating the members of co-operatives for understanding, participating, and responsible citizenship. " Under Chiang Kai-shek, however, it may be supposed that the opportunity to practice responsible citizenship was still a long way off. See "Recent News from the National Committee of the YWCA of China: Industrial Cooperative Work."

64. "Annual Report, National Committee YWCA of China." The theme of the emancipation of working women through participation in the cooperatives is an important one, and is elaborated upon in this document. Two examples are given: "The Chairman of a certain co-op is a girl who once lost her mind because her husband went to the front and never returned, thus losing her source of support. When she first entered the co-op training class she wasn't sure that she could support herself. She was illiterate and inarticulate. But being in the co-op she gradually changed her ideas, and her mind came back, and last year she was elected to be the chairman of this co-op. Now she goes out to buy raw materials, and contracts for business, and has the roughest deals with men in the business world, and yet she manages to do it as efficiently and as calmly as an able person. The writer personally witnessed her presiding at their membership meeting at which they divided up their dividends for the year which amounted to forty thousand dollars for the co-op, and also heard her make a very good report of the work and kind of organisation to a group of highly-educated people including newspaper men who visited the co-op." Also, "Take for instance another girl who had been badly treated by her ignorant mother. After she freed herself from her opium-smoking hus-

band, and defied the will of her mother [for her] to marry a useless rich man after the word came that her husband had died at the front, and seeing the YWCA advertisement for enrolment of girls to the co-op training class, she joined. She remains to this day the best and quickest worker on the sewing machine, and is elected to be a member of the management committee of the co-op. She says, 'What a joy it is to be a free person.' She also says that since she is so benefitted by the co-op, she is going to devote her whole life to help others to get the same kind of freedom." Ibid.

65. Requests for assistance to set up co-ops (see "Recent News from the National Committee of the YWCA of China") appear not always to have met with a response for this reason. Only two YWCA secretaries seem to have been trained specifically for cooperative work. In general, the city cooperatives—two in Chengtu, one in Chungking, and one in Wusu—were under the supervision of the local YWCA, while those in rural districts—Weiyang and Penghsien—were run with the advice of the National Committee. See *The YWCA of China, 1933–47.*

66. For example, the limited experience of the Penghsien cooperative with outworker members was not put to use to encourage the incorporation of outworkers into cooperatives elsewhere.

67. "Annual Report, National Committee YWCA of China." This was especially true among outworkers.

68. "A Co-operative Venture in Lung Feng Ch'ang."

69. *The YWCA of China: Industrial Co-operative Work.*

70. Brown, "The Umbrella-Making Co-operative of the YWCA of Kweiyang."

71. "Annual Report, National Committee YWCA of China."

72. "A Co-operative Venture in Lung Feng Ch'ang." It is not made clear who purchased the shares.

73. "Annual Report, National Committee YWCA of China."

74. Ibid.

75. *The YWCA of China, 1933–47*, p. 76.

76. The visit had evidently been planned for some time. See letter, "Social and Industrial Secretary, World's YWCA" to Cora Deng, Sept. 28, 1938, World's YWCA, Geneva (P).

77. Lily Haass may have remained in Shanghai to be interned, along with Eleanor Hinder early in 1942, and later released, or she may have left Shanghai much earlier. The last correspondence in the YWCA's Geneva archives authored by Lily Haass in Shanghai is dated May 9, 1939 (Letter Lily Haass to Evelyn Fox, May 9, 1939).

78. Letter C. B. Fox to Tsai Kwei, June 12, 1939, in archives of World's YWCA, Geneva (P). Deng had visited the ILO on her previous trip to Europe in 1930 and, since 1936 at least, had been a member of the ILO's Committee of Experts on Women's Work. See letter C. B. Fox to Maud Russell, Nov. 19, 1936, World's YWCA, Geneva (N).

79. Letter, "Social and Industrial Secretary, World's YWCA," to Cora Deng, Sept. 28, 1938.

80. Letter C. B. Fox to Tsai Kwei, June 12, 1939.

81. Conversation with Mrs. Katharine Strong, niece of Anna Louise Strong, at the headquarters of the World's YWCA, Geneva, 1974; and letter from Rewi Alley to the author, Sept. 26, 1975. See also the numerous references to Cora Deng in Honig, *Sisters and Strangers.*

82. *The YWCA of China, 1933–47*, p. 80. Industrial work was also revived in Hong Kong, where a program had been initiated just before the outbreak of World War II. As Hong Kong was under British jurisdiction, however, the history of industrial welfare work there has not been considered here.

83. Ibid., p. 78.

84. In 1946 district conferences of "Mass Education Club Girls" were held in Chengtu, Shanghai, and Hong Kong; they were said, however, to be "primarily for the training of club leaders." Ibid., pp. 79–80.

85. See, for example, Nym Wales, *China Fights for Democracy*, for a contemporary account.

86. J. B. Tayler, "The Co-operative Movement in China During the War," n.d., text indicates 1941, p. 17, in the private papers of J. B. Tayler in the possession of Mrs. Hilda Brown, London.

87. J. B. Tayler, "Indusco: The Chinese Industrial Co-operatives," n.d., text indicates 1945, p. 1, in the private papers of J. B. Tayler in the possession of Mrs. Hilda Brown, London.

88. J. B. Tayler may have been instrumental in convincing the government to go ahead with Indusco. He records in a letter written after the war, "it was not until Dr. Kung had flown me down to Hankow from the N W and had got my OK that he was willing to become Chairman of the Committee and to cough up the millions." See letter J. B. Tayler to Arthur Hemstock and Laurie Pavitt, Nov. 1, 1948, in the private papers of J. B. Tayler in the possession of Mrs. Hilda Brown, London. Tayler was educational adviser to Indusco from 1939 until February 1945. See also Tayler, "Co-operative Movement in China During the War," p. 18.

89. "China: The Industrial Co-operative Movement," inscribed "ILO Co-operative Information," n.d., text indicates 1939, in archives of World Council of Churches, Geneva (RD3).

90. "Chinese Industrial Co-operatives: Statement by Mr. John H. Reisner, Committee on East Asia," probably YMCA New York, Sept. 24, 1940, World Council of Churches, Geneva (RD3).

91. Tayler, "The Co-operative Movement in China During the War," p. 18.

92. "China: The Industrial Co-operative Movement."

93. "Chinese Industrial Co-operatives."

94. Tayler, "The Co-operative Movement in China During the War," p. 30.

95. Tayler, "Indusco: The Chinese Industrial Co-operatives," pp. 5–6.

96. "Chinese Industrial Co-operatives," memorandum by Rewi Alley, Lanchow, Kansu, Nov. 27, 1943, in the private papers of J. B. Tayler in the possession of Mrs. Hilda Brown, London.

97. Tayler, "Indusco: The Chinese Industrial Co-operatives," p. 4.

98. Manuscript about Indusco, missing pp. 1–3, and title, text indicates by J. B. Tayler, 1945, pp. 7–8, in the private papers of J. B. Tayler in the possession of Mrs. Hilda Brown, London.

99. Tayler, "The Co-operative Movement in China During the War," p. 25.

100. Ibid., pp. 27–28.

101. Ibid., pp. 27–30. Nonmembers were expected to show their "willingness to assume the responsibility of the society by applying for membership within three months after the profit is declared."

102. Tayler, "Indusco: The Chinese Industrial Co-operatives," p. 5.

103. Tayler, "The Co-operative Movement in China During the War," p. 25.

104. Tayler, "Indusco: The Chinese Industrial Co-operatives," p. 6.

105. Manuscript about Indusco, p. 7.

106. Tayler, "The Co-operative Movement in China During the War," p. 23. For example, the "H F Small-Scale Carding and Spinning Set" for wool, imported from England, and the Ghosh small-scale cotton carding and spinning outfit, imported from India, were both adapted for use by Indusco co-ops. Charles Riggs of the University of Nanking in Chengtu adapted the weave of the Tibetan headdress to the manufacture of rugs, while William Sewell of West China Union University at Chengtu developed new natural dyes, extensively used in the manufacture of army blankets.

107. Manuscript about Indusco, p. 6.

108. Ibid., p. 7.

109. Tayler, "The Co-operative Movement in China During the War," p. 41; manuscript about Indusco, p. 7.

110. Tayler, "The Co-operative Movement in China During the War," p. 24.

111. Manuscript about Indusco, p. 7.

112. Ibid., pp. 8, 10.

113. Ibid., p. 10.

114. Ibid., p. 8.

115. An account of some of the conflicts that developed between association organizers and the government is given in the manuscript about Indusco. Rewi Alley, writing in 1943, saw the main obstacles to Indusco's progress as "opposition to the movement as conceived . . . from the following: (a.) Ambitious groups who wish to control and who do not understand the movement. The activities of such lead to the arrest of persons for dangerous thoughts, which scares away many able cooperative and technical men, thus limiting the amount of work that can be accomplished. (b.) Landlord and money lender class, who are jealous of economic power in any other hands but their own. (c.) Coastal industrialists, who fear the spread of the movement in the interior will interfere with their investments. (d.) Ignorant and reactionary elements in the bureaucracy." See "Chinese Industrial Co-operatives."

116. Tayler, "The Co-operative Movement in China During the War," pp. 31, 35. Later, Tayler listed the following conditions for the success of industrial cooperatives: "government assistance, without control; collaboration with educational and especially technical institutions capable of supplying needed services locally, a strong, competent promotional agency . . . ; in the early stage, much concentrated energy." See manuscript about Indusco, p. 11.

117. "Chinese Industrial Co-operatives." The minerals that Alley suggested could be mined by cooperatives were tin, wolfram, iron, gold, silver, lead, and antimony. His assessment and recommendations form part of a report drawn up for an American army officer.

118. "Christians and Co-operatives," n.d., text indicates by J. B. Tayler, 1941, pp. 4–6, in the private papers of J. B. Tayler in the possession of Mrs. Hilda Brown, London. Tayler illustrates his argument by quoting W. K. H. Campbell's description of peasant reactions to agricultural credit cooperatives: "At first, they survey the results of their own action with half-incredulous amazement, but gradually the conviction is borne in upon them that they are not nearly such helpless creatures as they had always been accustomed to suppose." Campbell was at one time League of Nations adviser to the Chinese government on cooperatives.

Chapter 7

1. See Article 405 of the Treaty of Versailles.

2. Wagner, *Labour Legislation in China*, p.176.

3. In 1925 an official of the Shanghai Municipal Council offered in confidence to provide the ILO with information about labor conditions in that city, but ILO staff, thinking he might wish to be paid for it, sought to discourage him. See letter J. A. Jackson to R. K. Burge, May 2, 1925, and other correspondence in dossier RL/13/5/1 in archives of International Labour Organization, Geneva (hereafter referred to as ILO Geneva).

4. Pierre Henry, "Rapport Général sur mon Séjour en Chine," Pierre Henry, 1924, in G/900/28/1, ILO Geneva.

5. Ibid., and letter Pierre Henry to G. A. Johnston, Dec. 3, 1924, in G/900/28/1, ILO Geneva.

6. Henry, "Rapport Général," preamble. Elsewhere in this report Henry remarks of the industrial effort of the YM and YWCA: "le groupe protestante . . . se déclare prêt à mener la lutte pour l'amélioration des conditions de travail des ouvriers chinois, soit par sentiments d'humanité, soit sur l'instigation de capitalistes des pays anglo-saxons qui s'inquiète (je crois à tort) le bon marché de la maind' oeuvre chinoise.' " See section 3, "Oeuvres sociales en général." Henry appears not to distinguish between the YM and YWCA.

7. Pierre Henry, "Visites d'Usines," 1924, in dossier G/900/28/1, ILO Geneva.

8. Henry, "Rapport Général," sec. 1, "conditions du travail."

9. Letter Pierre Henry to Sherwood Eddy, Dec. 21, 1925, in dossier G/900/28/2, ILO Geneva.

10. See letter Lily Haass to Mary Dingman and Agatha Harrison, March 11, 1926, and postscript, and letter Mary Dingman to Lily Haass, Dec. 11, 1926.

11. "William Caldwell's Mission," 1927, in G/900/29/2, ILO Geneva.

12. Albert Thomas, "A la Rencontre de l'Orient," 1929, no dossier number, ILO Geneva, pp. 178, 385, 392.

13. Letter H. H. Kung to Albert Thomas, Feb. 26, 1931, in F/1/13/1/0, ILO Geneva. The Factory Act of 1929 applied to all factories employing thirty workers or more. It contained provisions dealing with women and child workers, apprenticeship, working hours, rest days and holidays, dismissal procedures, welfare facilities, safety precautions, compensation for injury, sickness and death, and the creation of "factory councils" to mediate between management and labor and encourage production.

14. "Rapport de M. Pone," 1931, in F/1/13/1/1, ILO Geneva. The curriculum for the course comprised the following subjects: general labor questions, Chinese labor legislation, organization of factory inspection, industrial hygiene, prevention of accidents, scientific organization of work, industrial statistics, the study of Chinese industry, industrial accountability, industrial ethic, the printing of administrative documents in Chinese, and the principles of Sun Yat-sen.

15. Ibid.

16. C. Pone and Dame A. Anderson, "Towards the Establishment of a Factory Inspectorate in China," *International Labor Review* 25 (May 1932): 591–604.

17. "Rapport de M. Pone."

18. Letter C. S. Chan to Alfred Butler, Oct. 23, 1933, in F/1/13, ILO Geneva.

19. Wagner, *Labour Legislation in China*, pp. 165–66, 196.

20. Letter F. Maurette to Alfred Butler, March 19, 1934, in XT/3/1/1, ILO Geneva.

21. Memorandum by Mack Eastman, May 6, 1936, in XT/13/2/1, ILO Geneva. Almost all material pertaining to Eastman's stay in China appears to have been transferred at some stage to the personal files of the director of the ILO, which remain confidential.

22. See memoranda in XT/13/3/1, and letter Eleanor Hinder to Alfred Butler, June 2, 1937, in G/900/3/50, ILO Geneva.

23. See memorandum dated Sept. 16, 1937, in G/900/3/50, ILO Geneva.

24. See especially the letters Mary Dingman to Lily Haass, Dec. 11, 1926, and Lily Haass to Mary Dingman, Jan. 13, 1927, in archives of World's YWCA, Geneva (C), "China 1926–29, correspondence, Minutes Reports, etc." Inter alia, Dingman pointed out that it would be difficult in the uncertainty of the prevailing political situation to know with which Chinese government a Chinese office of the ILO should have official ties.

25. C. S. Chan, "La Question de l'Utilité du Bureau de Chine," November 1934, in XC/13/1/1, ILO Geneva. The university that invited Chan to become dean was Shanghai Labor University (l'Université du Travail de Shanghai), which was later closed down.

26. See comments contained in dossier N/200/1/13, ILO Geneva, in the margins of Chan's reports. Subsequent reports submitted by Chan's stand-in, Jennings Wong, suffered from similar deficiencies.

27. Chan, "La Question de l'Utilité du Bureau de Chine."

28. See memorandum dated Oct. 25, 1930, in N/200/1/13/2, ILO Geneva. At this time it had been suggested that "milieux syndicaux" in Europe were proposing to send a study delegation to China to meet their Chinese counterparts and it had been requested that Chan provide a list of names of "bona fide" unions. This he did.

29. See memorandum dated Oct. 14, 1932, in C/1802/1, ILO Geneva.

30. Letter M. T. Tchou to Albert Thomas, April 3, 1932, in RL/13/5/2, ILO Geneva. Tchou was a former official of the YMCA and was at one stage responsible for implementing factory inspection on behalf of the Nationalist government.

31. An anonymous memorandum to the director dated March 25, 1936, notes: "M. Cheng

. . . a été recommandé au Directeur par le Gouvernement chinois . . . et a garde toute la confiance de ce Gouvernement." See dossier XC/13/1/1. François Maurette had earlier observed that it would be necessary to preserve the goodwill of the Chinese government in choosing a successor to C. S. Chan. See letter F. Maurette to Alfred Butler, March 19, 1934, in XT/13/1/1. This is quite contrary to the impression given in unrestricted correspondence in which a letter is to be found from the minister of industries, K. P. Chen, to Alfred Butler, commending the ILO on its choice of candidate for the job. See letter K. P. Chen to Alfred Butler, Nov. 17, 1934, in N/200/1/3, ILO Geneva.

32. See "Traduction d'une lettre en chinois de M. Li ping-heng, premier délégué de la Chine à la conférence à Genève," July 14, 1934, in XC/13/1/1, ILO Geneva. It would appear that Cheng must for a time have occupied this post formerly held by M. T. Tchou.

33. Letter H. F. Cheng to "Chief of Extra-European Section," Dec. 10, 1934, in C/1802/1, ILO Geneva.

34. Letter H. F. Cheng to Director, Oct. 6, 1934, in C/1802/1, ILO Geneva.

35. Letter H. F. Cheng to Director, Sept. 21, 1934, in C/1802/1, ILO Geneva.

36. See letters H. F. Cheng to Director, Sept. 21, 1934, Oct. 6, 1934, and Nov. 17, 1934, in C/1802/1, ILO Geneva.

37. H. F. Cheng, "Report of Trip to Hankow and Changsha, October 16 to November 2, 1935," in C/1802/1, and "Report on Trip to Chingkiang and Wusih, Dec. 17 to Dec. 28, 1935," in C/1802/2 ILO Geneva.

38. H. F. Cheng, "Report on Trip to Hui Nan Coal Mine, and Anking, June 25th to July 4th, 1936," and "Report on Trip to Nantung, 26th to 30th November, 1930," in C/1802/2, ILO Geneva.

39. See letter H. F. Cheng to Mack Eastman, Feb. 2, 1938, in C/1802/2, ILO Geneva.

40. See, for example, Cheng, "Report on Trip to Hankow and Changsha," and "Report on Trip to Chingkiang and Wusih."

41. See Wagner, *Labour Legislation in China*, pp. 4–11, and D. K. Lieu, *The Growth and Industrialization of Shanghai*, pp. 61–64. Mack Eastman of the Geneva office, however, found the reports "interesting and useful." See Mack Eastman to H. F. Cheng, Jan. 22, 1936, in C/1802/2, ILO Geneva.

42. Cheng, "Report of Trip to Hankow and Changsha."

43. Letter H. F. Cheng to Director, Dec. 30, 1935, in C/1802/1, ILO Geneva.

44. See Cheng, "Report of Trip to Hankow and Changsha" and "Report on Trip to Hui Nan Coal Mine and Anking."

45. Cheng, "Report on Trip to Hankow and Changsha."

46. Ibid., and letter H. F. Cheng to Director, Oct. 7, 1936, in C/1802/2, ILO Geneva. In Hankow, the dockers' union is reported as having money collected on its behalf by the Dock Affairs Bureau of the municipal government, of which the bureau would keep 35 percent, a workers' school would take 25 percent, the provident fund 15 percent, and the union itself would receive only 25 percent. In the provinces named, many unions existed on money collected ostensibly to maintain schools for the children of workers, or union libraries.

47. See Chang, "Report on Trip to Chingkiang and Wusih."

48. Cheng, "Report of Trip to Hankow and Changsha." The official was the chief of the First Section of the Hankow municipal government. The secretary-general of the Hankow municipal government similarly observed: "Formerly, the Kuomintang was always on the side of the worker. Realising the political and economic conditions, they change their attitude."

49. Ibid. See also letter H. F. Cheng to Alfred Butler, Dec. 4, 1935, referring to the same incident, in C/1802/1, ILO Geneva. Mack Eastman of the Geneva staff noted that "misconceptions" about the nature of the ILO were widespread. "The tendency is, or at least used to be, in my country [Canada] for example, to think that the ILO is something like the Second International, or like the International Federation of Trade Unions." See letter Mack Eastman to H. F. Cheng, Jan. 22, 1936.

50. Letter H. F. Cheng to M. Staal, Jan. 18, 1938, in C/1802/2, ILO Geneva. See also letter H. F. Cheng to Director, Feb. 23, 1937, in ibid.

51. This letter was that of March 16, 1939. See C/1802/2, ILO Geneva.

52. Wagner, *Labour Legislation in China*, p. 180.

53. See untitled memorandum, n.d., in XC/13/1/1, ILO Geneva. Probably ca. 1934.

54. For example, in 1938 the worker delegate Chu Hsueh-fan wrote to Geneva for details of the "social legislation programme" of the IFTU, material on freedom of association, on social services in various countries, and on collective agreements. He sought this information to "help the Chinese trade unionists as well as the workers in their struggle for organising and developing the Chinese working class." See letter Chu Hsueh-fan to M. Staal, Nov. 18, 1938, in RL/13/3/1, ILO Geneva.

55. Wagner, *Labour Legislation in China*, p. 184.

56. Even if the Peking government had been committed to implementing factory legislation, and there is scant evidence that this was so, it in fact controlled little territory and was soon to be brought down to be replaced by the Nationalist government at Nanking. For details of these factory regulations, see *Papers Respecting Labor Conditions in China*, cmd. 2442, Foreign Office, London, 1925.

57. For details of this legislation see Wagner, *Labour Legislation in China*, appendix.

58. Ibid., pp. 187–91.

59. Lowe Chuan-hua, "China's Relations with the ILO," *China Critic* 3 (Nov. 13, 1930): 1090–92, cited in ibid., p. 199.

60. All that had been achieved with respect to the inquiry on China was the preparation of some 1,500 file cards. See memorandum dated Aug. 24, 1938, on cancellation of the project, in N/200/1/13/5. It would seem that the China bureau was only officially informed that the inquiry had been abandoned early in 1939. See letter Mack Eastman to H. F. Cheng, March 27, 1939, in N/200/1/13/5, ILO Geneva.

Chapter 8

1. "Annual Report, YMCA of China, 1921," World's YMCA, Geneva, Box X392.21 (51).

2. "Discussion," n.d., but in folder "Jan–March 1920" YMCA Historical Library, New York (R2).

3. For example, William Lockwood notes in a letter in May 1921 that the association's industrial work was "being liberally supported by the employers of labour," while as late as 1936, by which time the work was quite limited, the British-American Tobacco Company gave $1,500 Chinese toward a total budget of $3,600 for classes at the centers in Pootung and in Robison Road. In Chengchow in 1920 a "building was erected by Mr. H. Y. Moh in connection with a large new cotton mill and steps to organise an association," while in 1921 in Tienstin, Hankow, and Shanghai "work had begun." For Lockwood, see William Lockwood, "Occasional Letter, May 2nd, 1921" (series IV, no. 2), World's YMCA, Geneva, Box X392.22 (51). For the BAT, see S. Y. Chao, "Comment on the Proposed 1936 Budget, Jan. 21, 1936, YMCA Historical Library, New York (R32). For Chengchow, 1920, see "Annual Report, YMCA of China, 1920," World's YMCA, Geneva, Box X392.21(51). For Tientsin, Hankow, and Shanghai, 1921, see ibid., 1921.

4. For example, among members of the National Executive Committee of the Chinese YMCA in 1921 were Fong Sec, chairman, editor in chief of the Commercial Press in Shanghai; C. C. Nieh, vice-chairman, proprietor of the Heng Foong Cotton Mill, Shanghai; Y. H. Bau, manager of the Commercial Press; and A. O. Ben, manager of the Sincere Co. See "Annual Report, YMCA of China, 1921." Probably typical of local centers was Foochow, where T. C. McConnell noted in 1925, "[T]he Industrial Committee is composed almost entirely of managers and workers in whose shops work is being done." See "Annual Report

for 1925 of T. C. McConnell to the Foreign Committee of the National Councils of the YMCA's of the United States and Canada," at the YMCA Historical Library, New York (R11).

5. It is difficult to assess exactly what part of the Chinese YMCA's budget was found in the United States, and what part was found in China, but it is significant that when contributions to the American YMCA dried up because of the depression, the Chinese YMCA was also very hard hit, being obliged to sacrifice staff and cut back on its programs. See, for example, letter W. W. Lockwood to Charles Herschleb, May 26, 1933, YMCA Historical Library, New York (R29).

6. "Annual Report, Agatha Harrison, February 23, 1921–March 23, 1922," at the World's YWCA, Geneva (A).

7. Letter Mary Dingman to Agatha Harrison, March 30, 1922, World's YWCA, Geneva (F).

8. Agatha Harrison, "Meeting with the Committee of the Foreign Mill Owners' Association, Feb. 20, 1922," attached to "Second Interview with Mr. X," World's YWCA, Geneva (A).

9. Harrison observed: "[A]ny sane person will admit that honest and just dealing always does pay. But is there any hope for a future if the stress is laid 'Do this, it will pay'? Are we any further forward?" See "Review of the Industrial Situation, Shanghai, China," Sept. 11, 1922, text indicates by Agatha Harrison, World's YWCA, Geneva (A).

10. An aversion to welfare work carried on in the factories expressed here by Mary Dingman was shared by all the industrial secretaries. See letter Mary Dingman to Lily Haass, Nov. 24, 1927, World's YWCA, Geneva (C).

11. Letter Lily Haass to May Dingman, April 9, 1927, World's YWCA, Geneva (C).

12. "Report of the Third Conference of Industrial Secretaries, YWCA of China, Held at Shanghai, January 19–25, 1933," National Headquarters, YWCA of the United States, New York (D).

13. *National Christian Conference, Shanghai 1922.*

14. In the one case in which foreign employers actively participated in a movement for reform—during the child labor campaign—it may be argued that they were as much driven by the bad publicity they had been getting in their home countries as by any sense of shame (see chapter 5).

15. *Report of the Conference in Christianising Economic Relations*, pp. 122–23.

16. Ibid., p. 95.

17. Charles Shedd, "Industrial Work, Wu-Han Cities, China, 1922—Administration Report," YMCA New York (B).

18. M. T. Tchou, "Report of Fall Trip: Aspect of Co-operation with Various Agencies," received April 1924, World's YMCA, Geneva Box X315(51); and letter "Dear Friends," by M. T. Tchou, April 13, 1924, YMCA New York (R9).

19. "A Chinese 'Y' Secretary's Answer to Labour on 'What is the Attitude of the 'Y' Towards the Labour Unions'" text indicates 1925, YMCA New York (R12).

20. *Changing Industrial Life*, apparently part of a larger published report, printed separately as a pamphlet, by Kenneth Duncan, Charles Shedd, and John Nipps, attached to a report entitled "YMCA Chungking, April 15th, 1924," YMCA New York (R10).

21. Thomas Tchou, *The Present Day Industrial Situation and the Labour Movement in China*, YMCA Shanghai, text indicates 1926, p. 29, World's YMCA, Geneva, Box 392.21 (51); and Y. L. Lee, *Some Aspects of the Labour Situation in Canton*, Canton: YMCA, 1928, p. 13, YMCA New York (B).

22. E. H. Lockwood, "Mid-May Reflections on China, 1927," YMCA New York (A). Lockwood went on to observe: "Labour put restrictions on employers and enforced them with the weapons of terrorism. Their leaders tried to bring to labour the advantages enjoyed by labour in industrialised countries with their economic surplus and increased production through the use of machines, and led labour unions to apply these advantages in the economic order of China without economic surplus and with out the speeding up process of production

[*sic*] which exists in Western countries. Employers were caught between two millstones. They were ground by a government in need of funds which had to come largely from taxes on industry and commerce, and by a labouring class flushed with the pleasurable and novel experience of cracking the whip to which the employers danced."

23. In a letter to Mary Dingman, George Sokolsky, journalist with the *North China Daily News*, suggested that instead of publicly criticizing employers, "the best piece of work you could do would be to get the Chinese labour unions to adopt resolutions opposing the employment of children. . . . Unless the Chinese themselves are opposed to child labour, all efforts in this direction are bound to fail." Letter George Sokolsky to Mary Dingman, March 24, 1925, World's YWCA, Geneva (G).

24. Letter Lily Haass to Mary Dingman and Agatha Harrison, Sept. 19, 1925, World's YWCA, Geneva (C).

25. Letter Eleanor Hinder to Mary Dingman, March 23, 1926, World's YWCA, Geneva (C).

26. Ibid.

27. Letter Eleanor Hinder to "My Dears," May 16, 1926, World's YWCA, Geneva (C).

28. In a mid-1926 edition of the YWCA's official English-language bulletin, *Green Year Supplement*, it was noted that "[w]ith the astonishing development of Labour Unions in the last few years an entirely new element has entered. Our policy may need to be re-thought with a view to ascertaining in what ways we may co-operate with these groups." See *Green Year Supplement*, July–August 1926, YWCA, New York (E).

29. Eleanor Hinder, "The Industrial Situation in Shanghai," October 1926, World's YWCA, Geneva (C).

30. Ibid.

31. Letter Lily Haass to Mary Dingman, Aug. 3, 1926, World's YWCA, Geneva (C).

32. Eleanor Hinder, "The Beginning of the Chapei Centre—Report to the Board," Dec. 21, 1926, World's YWCA, Geneva (C).

33. See *Green Year Supplement*, Jan. 15, 1927, no. 10, p. 5.

34. Letter Eleanor Hinder to Mary Dingman, April 10, 1927, World's YWCA, Geneva (C).

35. Hinder, "The Industrial Situation in Shanghai." This attitude is further elaborated in a YWCA publication of 1927: "World history displays that it has been in the main the efforts of labour itself which have attained for it a measure of legal protection in the conditions of its employment. There have been, of course, sympathetic men who have advanced the cause of labour, though themselves not of the ranks of labour, and especially in the early days of struggle for emancipation, these friends have had a place. But in the main it is labour which accomplishes for itself, presupposing a growing intelligence toward its own problems." *The YWCA of China*, p. 26, in archives of World Council of Churches, Geneva (W). Hinder places the emphasis here on legal protection.

36. Hinder, "The Beginning of the Chapei Centre." Interestingly, YWCA staff in Chapei at this time called upon a Mrs. Moh, "formerly a silk worker, and now employed in an organising position by owners of the filature," whom they had known previously. Discovering that her status had changed, and that "her group is not now regarded as loyal by the General Federation of Labour . . . we are not therefore anxious to have much to do with her, so that we shall not be misunderstood by Labour."

37. See letter Eleanor Hinder to Mary Dingman, Sept. 15, 1927, and letter Eleanor Hinder to Mary Dingman, Nov. 8, 1927, both World's YWCA, Geneva (C).

38. Eleanor Hinder, "Some Facts and Factors in the Labour Movement in China," *Chinese Recorder* (January 1928): 33.

39. See Eleanor Hinder, "Some Facts about the Labour Movement in China," n.d., text indicates 1927, in archives of World Council of Churches, Geneva (Box 21).

40. Lily Haass, "YWCA Industrial Work in China," 1929, YWCA New York (C).

41. "Report of the Third Conference of Industrial Secretaries."

42. Ibid. In a letter to Mary Dingman in 1933, Cora Deng reports the result of "a census of opinion among union people as to what YWCA work is . . . or should be." Deng found that unionists felt the association could be most helpful in pressing for enforcement of legislation on the protection of women workers, to which end Deng had begun collecting information on the effect of night work, long hours, and other occupational hazards on women workers. This emphasis on legislation on the part of the unions reflected both the conservative nature of the unions in existence at this time, and probably also a reluctance still to trust the YWCA with more than conventional "public opinion" work. Deng further noted that she had been unable to obtain accurate information on the extent of unionization among women workers, but that in general "(1) In trades where women and men are employed, they are in the same union, but women take very little active part—such as tobacco, match, silk weaving, food canning, textile, etc. industries. (2) In trades where women are in the dominant group they have a union by themselves, but the head of the union is usually a man and also the majority of the committee members are men in some unions. This is true of silk filatures in both Wusih and Shanghai. This is due to three reasons: (a) Lack of literate women and (b) Men are more experienced in public organisational matters; (c) Employers put their feelers in the unions." Deng also attributed the slow progress of the union movement generally to Kuomintang control, employers' frequent dismissal of unionists, and repression by the authorities of the foreign concessions. See letter Cora Deng to Mary Dingman, March 13, 1933, World's YWCA, Geneva (L).

43. Cora Deng, *Labour Problems*, p. 18. Article from the *China Christian Yearbook* reproduced as a pamphlet, YWCA New York (B). The growth in the radical commitment of the YWCA to labor coincided with the increasing impact of the depression on China. See especially *Chung-kuo lao-tung nien-chien* (Chinese labor yearbook), 1932–33, for the impact on employment.

44. "Report of the Third Conference of Industrial Secretaries."

45. See, for example, the list of executive officers in 1930, in letter Cora Deng to Mary Dingman, Oct. 16, 1930, World's YWCA, Geneva (J).

46. The precise sources of funds for YWCA work are difficult to pinpoint. It would seem, however, that each local YWCA raised funds by means of financial campaigns, membership and activity fees, hostels and room rentals, bazaars, and similar activities. The National Committee relied for support on contributions from the branches, and sometimes also from overseas, and in addition held its own fund drives.

47. *The YWCA of China*, p. 28. This resolution was passed at the 1926 annual meeting of the NCC.

48. Letter Lily Haass to Mary Dingman, Dec. 29, 1926, World's YWCA, Geneva (C). Lily Haass's frustration with the NCC Executive on this question is expressed in another letter to Mary Dingman: "There is no dodging that I am up against something here about Labour Unions. E. C. L. [E. C. Lobenstine] is so afraid that he got the executive to re-iterate that no committee get out anything in statement or policy without referring back to the NCC Exec. It's not of course that he's against Labour Unions but he's so afraid of the conserva-tives who feel we're 'butting in' to secular fields—and ignorantly at that—I think we have the best answer in the world to the anti-Christian movement attack on our 'Capitalism' etc. if we state where we stand with reference to Labour Unions, but it can't be done, at present at least." See letter Lily Haass to Mary Dingman, "Dear Mary," n.d., but attached to letter to Lily Haass and Eleanor Hinder, apparently from Mary Dingman, Nov. 25, 1926, World's YWCA, Geneva (C).

49. *Report of the Conference on Christianising Economic Relations, held under the aus-pices of the National Christian Council of China Shanghai, August 18–28, 1927* (Shanghai: NCC, 1927), pp. 95–96, 116. On the Kuomintang and the unions, Gideon Chen, conveying the news of his decision to leave the NCC in 1929, wrote to Mary Dingman: "There has been a general setback to the labour movement in China, owing to the attitude of the Nanking government and most of the big commanders . . . a system of Government guides to labour

has been instituted, that is to control trade unions through local Kuomintangs. . . . The shooting and arrest of 'communists' still goes on every day! This kind of policy couldn't go on forever. A reaction may come sooner or later." Letter Gideon Chen to Mary Dingman, Feb. 9, 1929, World's YWCA, Geneva (C).

50. *Papers, Abstracts and Extracts from Papers Contributed as the Basis of a Discussion to the Conference on the People's Livelihood Shanghai, February 21–28, 1931* (Shanghai: NCC, 1931), p. 2, archives of the World Council of Churches, Geneva (X). Typically, at the annual meetings of the China Christian Association held in the late 1930s, social issues in the broad sense, and industrial issues in particular, were not considered. See Chung-hua chi-tu-chiao hui, *Chung-hua chi-tu-chiao hui ti-liu chih ch'ang-hui i-lu* (Proceedings of the sixth regular general meeting of the China Christian association, 1936), annual, especially 1936–40.

51. Zung Wei-tsung, "The Woman's Viewpoint: The Chinese Church and the New Industrial System," *Chinese Recorder* (March 1922): 190.

52. Mary Dingman noted two examples in particular of the strength of this feeling among the foreign community, both taken from letters to the *North China Daily News*, as follows: Feb. 14, 1927—"Opposite to me [in a bus] was a number of Chinese of the coolie class. Presently one of them indulged in that disgusting peculiarity of expectorating on the floor of the bus. Nothing was said. In a little while he did this again even more disgustingly, so I gave him a kick on the shin and called him a dirty devil."

"Jan. 15, 1927—'Fear not, what Britain was is Britain still.

Soon all the scum thrown up to prance and preen

At Moscow's bidding will receive their fill

Of punishment, and seek their styes obscene,

Unwept, unhonoured. Britain, like God's mill

Grinds slowly. Britain is what she has been.' "

Another contributor deplored the fact that in Hankow British marines had been "desecrated by the ape-like creatures of Borodin and Chen." See letter Mary Dingman to Dr. T. Tatlow, n.d., text indicates 1927, World's YWCA, Geneva (C).

53. Letter Eleanor Hinder to Mary Dingman, Jan. 25, 1927, World's YWCA, Geneva (C).

54. That YWCA secretaries were unanimous in their early support for the United Front led by the Kuomintang, and for the possibilities for radical change that it was thought to represent, is the more remarkable when their attitude is contrasted with that of senior YMCA officials at the time. From the point of this schism it is possible to date the cessation of any attempt at cooperation with the YMCA.

The following passages taken from the correspondence of YWCA and YMCA officials are quoted to illustrate this divergence of view:

"I hope that I may still have faith in this nationalist movement, even if I am the victim of some of the excesses. . . . My mind tries to take in the import of the so-called 'red' element of this thing, and not unsympathetically, for we have not yet demonstrated that Russia is not right in her method, nor have we demonstrated the complete rightness of the capitalist system." Eleanor Hinder to Mary Dingman, Jan. 25, 1927.

"The movement that is sweeping from the south—the movement that is the most hopeful thing on the horizon for checking militarism." Lily Haass to Mary Dingman, Dec. 22, 1926.

"I hope the havoc these warlords have played with China is about over, and the foreign influence which was part of the havoc in many ways is about over too. . . . I hope we don't have to leave until we see the Southern flags flying." Harriet Reitveld (Chefoo) to Mary Dingman, June 23, 1927.

For the above, see the World's YWCA, Geneva (C).

Helen Thoburn also wrote sympathetically of the "revolution," as it was termed, early in 1927, while Maud Russell noted that more and more she had come to "revel in the challenge of it." See Helen Thoburn (a eulogy), by Eleanor Hinder, in *Green Year Supplement*, March 1932, and "Wuchang," no author given, in *Green Year Supplement* 11, March 12, 1927, both YWCA, New York (E).

On the other hand, E. E. Barnett of the YMCA complained that "agitators, schooled in the ideals and methods of Moscow, have engendered class consciousness, have stirred class hatred against the possessing classes, and at least in Hunan have boldly preached the doctrines and practised the methods of Marx and Lenin."

E. H. Lockwood wrote, "The most encouraging event in the politics of Canton in 1927 was the elimination of the communists as a party after the Red uprising in December." See Barnett, "Mid-May Reflections on China, 1927," and Lockwood, "Administrative Report for 1927."

55. A contemporary review of labor matters contained no suggestion that the Industrial Cooperative Movement would have any future beyond the war emergency. See *Chung-kuo lao-tung yueh-kan* (China labour review) (Chungking, 1942).

Glossary of Chinese Names

Chan, C.S.	陈宗城
Ch'en Ta	陈达
Chen, Gideon	陈其田
Chen, K.S. (?)	陈庚孙
Cheng Haifong (H.F. Cheng)	程海峰
Chu Mu-ch'eng (M.T./Thomas Tchou)	朱懋澄
Chung Shou-ching (Helen Chung)	锺韶琴
Deng Yu-chi (Cora Deng)	邓予祉
Fong Hsien-ting (H.D. Fong)	方显庭
Ho, Franklin	何廉
Hsu Ch'ing-yun (C.Y. Hsu?)	徐庆誉
Hu Han-min	胡汉民
Kung Hsiang-hsi (H.H. Kung)	孔祥熙
Li Ta-chao	李大钊
Lin Tung-hai (J.D. H. Lamb)	林东海
Lowe Ch'uan-hua (C.H. Lowe)	骆传华
Liu Ta-chun (D.K. Lieu)	刘大钧
Meng T'ien-pei (T. P. Meng)	孟天培
Soong Mei-ling	宋美龄
T'ao Ling	陶苓
Tchou, M. T (See Chu above)	朱懋澄

Select Bibliography

Archives

The present work draws heavily on reports, correspondence, and ephemeral printed matter in archives in Geneva, New York, and London. Most useful were the following archives:

World's YWCA, Geneva
Library at the World's YMCA, Geneva
World Council of Churches, Geneva
International Labour Organization, Geneva
National Headquarters, YWCA of the United States, New York
YMCA Historical Library, New York
Friends' Meeting House, London
The private papers of J. B. Tayler, in the possession of Mrs. Hilda Brown, London

Also consulted were the archives of the Public Record Office, the Foreign Office Library, and the Conference of British Missionary Societies in London, and of the Manchester Chamber of Commerce.

In each case, archive material was principally sought that had a direct bearing on the Christian industrial welfare movement in China or the functioning of supporting agencies such as the International Labour Organization or the Shanghai Municipal Council's Industrial Section. The items that follow were found to be of particular value. The letters that precede the file or box titles for material from the archives of the YWCA Geneva, the YWCA New York, and the YMCA New York have been assigned arbitrarily and serve only to identify material to which reference has been made in the notes. The existing designations employed for items from these archives, I felt, were too cumbersome to bear extensive repetition. Material from other archives has been identified in the notes by the file or box number normally employed for it.

World's YWCA, Geneva

A. 1920–22 China, Reports, Box 3/68
B. 1923–26 China, Minutes and Reports, Box 3/160
C. China 1926–29, Correspondence, Minutes, Reports, etc., Box 3/162
D. China 1926–29, Correspondence, Minutes, Reports, etc., Box 3/163
E. China 1928–31, Minutes and Reports, Box 3/69
F. China Correspondence, 1922–23, Box 3/70
G. China 1923–26, Correspondence, Box 3/159
H. China 1923–26, Minutes, Reports, Box 3/161
J. 1930–32 Finance, Box 11/15

K. Reports and Minutes, China, 1930–32, Box 11/165

L. China, India, 1933–34–35, Box 11/214

M. 1933–34 Minutes and Reports, China Box 11/233

N. Asia: China, India 1936–37, Box N/177

O. Asia: China, India, Japan, Korea, Malaya, Palestine, Philippines, Syria, 1936–37, Box 11/196

P. Asia: China, India 1938–39, Box 11/148

Q. Asia: Reports 1938–39, Box 11/167

R. China, India 1940–41–42, Box 11/78

S. 1940–41–42 China, Minutes and Reports, Box 11/103

T. China Reports, India Reports and Minutes, Japan Reports 1943–44, Box 11/65

U. China, India, 1945–46, Box 11/22

V. 1925–26 Circulars, Conferences, Minutes, Miscellaneous, Training, Industry, Cases, Box 3/223

W. 1926–27 Bible Study, Training, Conferences, Preparation for World Committee, Extension, Publications, Industry, Box 3/226

World's YMCA, Geneva

Box X358.3 China; National Committee

Box X314.119 Industrial Work

Box X392.21(51) Annual Reports, China

World Council of Churches, Geneva

In particular, the archives of the International Missionary Council:

Box 21 Jerusalem Conference, 1928

Box 24 Jerusalem, 1928 —

Box 42 Committees, Tambaram

Box 114 Industrial And Social Questions, China; NCC

Box 368 China Continuation Committee, NCC Conference May 1922, NCC Memoranda, etc.

Box 370 China Correspondence, NCC; Lobenstine, Hodgkin, etc.

Box 371 China, NCC Minutes

Box 374 China, Christian Literature 1922–28; Information about China 1925–28, NCC Bulletin, 1922–30

Also archives of the International Missionary Council's Research Department, classified separately:

Box RD.1 China: Canton, Foochow and Fukien, Nanking, Peiping, Shanghai, YMCA Shanghai

Box RD.2 China General; China in War, NCC of China; Hangchow (eventually Tambaram)

Box RD.3 China: Conference on the People's Livelihood; Co-operatives and Small Industries; Report on Visit to South China by J. W. Decker

Box RD.15 Industrial Schools

Box RD.16 Labour and Industry

Box RD.24 Correspondence on Industrial Questions

Box W Pamphlets, China

Box X Pamphlets, China

Box Y Pamphlets, China

The International Labour Organization

The files of the ILO are variously designated in English or French, usually depending on their contents; some have no adequate designation other than their dossier number, and in these cases a brief indication of their contents has been supplied below.

G/900/28/1 Voyage de M Pierre Henry en Chine
G/900/28/2 2ieme Mission de M Henry
G/900/29/2 William Caldwell's Mission, 1927
RL/13/5/1 Relations with Mr. Jackson, 1925
RL/13/5/2 Relations with Col. M. T. Tchou; relations with United China Relief
RL/13/3/1 Relations with Hsueh Fan-tu, 1936–40
C/1802/1 China correspondent, general correspondence 1930–35
C/1802/2 (further correspondence with ILO's Chinese agent, 1935–39)
N/200/1/13 Conditions of Labour, General, China 1920–38
N/200/1/13/2 (correspondence with trade unionists)
N/200/1/13/5 Enquiry on industrial labour in China, 1937–39
XT/13/1/1 Mission de M. Maurette
XC/13/1/1 Bureau de Chine, correspondence
F/1/13/0 Factory Inspection
F/1/13 (draft hygiene and safety regulations drawn up by Camille Pone and Dame Adelaide Anderson)
F/1/13/1/1 Rapport de M. Pone

YWCA New York

A. YWCA of China: Publicity Releases and a Few Reports, 1938–41
B. Industrial Work of the YWCA in China, 1926–35
C. Foreign Mail, 1929–34
D. YWCA of China, Information Bulletins and Some Reports
E. YWCA of China, Green Year Supplement

YMCA New York

A. Box X951.01 China Reports; China Yearbooks
B. Box X951.03 China, Labourers in France

Extensive use was made of material filed under the designation X951.09 China, World Service (Restricted), among which the following boxes yielded much relevant information:

R1 1920–21
R2 Jan.–March 1920
R3 Oct. 1920–March 1921
R4 Sept. 1921–April 1922
R5 April–June 1921
R6 May–Dec. 1922
R7 Jan.–April 1923
R8 May–Dec. 1923
R9 1922–24
R10 Jan.–Sept. 1924
R11 Oct.–Dec. 1924
R12 April–July 1925
R13 Aug.–Dec. 1925
R14 1925–26
R15 May–Dec. 1926

R16 April–June 1927
R18 Aug. 1927–Feb. 1928
R19 March–Dec. 1928
R20 1927–1929
R21 Jan.–April 1929
R22 May–Dec. 1929
R23 May 1930
R24 1930 Study of the YMCAs of China
R25 Jan.–April 1930
R26 May–Sept. 1930
R27 Jan.–May 1931
R28 1930–32
R29 1932–33
R30 1933
R31 1934–35
R32 Jan.–June 1936

Other

The Agatha Harrison Papers, Friends' Meeting House, London, Temporary Box 50-B.
The private papers of J. B. Tayler, in the possession of Mrs Hilda Brown, London; unclassified.

Official Publications

Annual Report of the Director, International Labour Office, Geneva, various years, 1920–1940.
Annual Report of the Shanghai Municipal Council, North China Daily News and Herald, Shanghai, 1933–40.
The Cost of Living Index Numbers of Labourers, Greater Shanghai, January 1926–December 1931, Bureau of Social Affairs, City Government of Greater Shanghai, Shanghai, 1932 (English and Chinese).
The Index Numbers of Earnings of Factory Labourers in Greater Shanghai, July–December 1928, Bureau of Social Affairs, City Government of Greater Shanghai, Shanghai, 1929 (English and Chinese).
Industrial Work of the Shanghai YMCA: Anniversary Report, 1935. YMCA: Shanghai, 1935.
Legislative Series, International Labour Office, Geneva, various years, 1920–1940.
Memorandum on Labour Conditions in China (cmd. 2846), Foreign Office, London, 1927.
Papers Respecting Labour Conditions in China (cmd. 2442), Foreign Office, London, 1925.
Parliamentary Debates, HMSO, London, 1924–25.
Report of the Annual Conference, International Labour Office, Geneva, various years, 1920–1940.
Shang-hai shih cheng-fu, she-hui-chu, *Shang-hai shih kung-tzu-li* (City Government of Greater Shanghai, Social Affairs Bureau, *Wage Rates in Shanghai*). Shanghai, 1935.

Books and Articles

Anderson, A. *Humanity and Labour in China*. London: S.C.M. Press, 1928.
———. "Labour Legislation and Its Relation to the Labour Movement." *Chinese Social and Political Science Review* 8 (July 1924).
———. "The Recommendations of the Shanghai Child Labour Commission." *International Labour Review* 11 (May 1925).
Arnold, J. *China: A Commercial and Industrial Handbook*. Washington, D.C.: U.S. Department of Commerce, 1926.
Barnett, R. W. *Economic Shanghai: Hostage to Politics, 1937–1941*. New York: Institute of Pacific Relations, 1941.
Burgess, J. S. *The Guilds of Peking*. New York: Columbia University Press, 1928.

Bush, Richard C. *The Politics of Cotton Textiles in Kuomintang China, 1927–1937*. New York: Garland, 1982.

Chan, C. S. "Social Legislation in China Under the Nationalist Government." *International Labour Review* 19 (January 1929).

Ch'en Chen et al. *Chung-kuo chin-tai kung-yeh-shih tzu-liao* (Source material for the history of modern Chinese industry). 2 vols. Peking: Three United Book Stores, 1957–58.

Ch'en Ta. *Chinese Migrations, with Special Reference to Labour Conditions*. Washington, D.C.: U.S. Government Printing Office, 1923.

———. *Chung-kuo lao-kung wen t'i* (China's labour problems). Shanghai: Commercial Press, 1933.

———. *Study of the Applicability of the Factory Act*. Shanghai: China Institute of Scientific Management, 1931.

———. "The Labour Movement in China." *International Labour Review* 15 (March 1927).

Cheng Hai-feng. "Labour Conditions in China During 1934." *Chinese Economic Journal* 16 (February 1935).

Chesneaux, J. *The Chinese Labour Movement, 1919–1927*. Stanford: Stanford University Press, 1968.

Chu, C. C., and Blaisdell, T. C. *Peking Rugs and Peking Boys*. Peking: Chinese Social and Political Science Association, 1924.

Chung-hua chi-tu-chiao hui. *Chung-hua chi-tu-chiao hui ti-liu chih ch'ang-hui i-lu* (Proceedings of the sixth regular general meeting of the China Christian Association) 1936, annual, especially 1936–40.

———. *Lao gongren hua dangnian* (The lives of old workers). Beijing: Gongren Chubanshe, 1958.

Chung Jui-chi. "The Cigarette Industry in China." *Chinese Economic Journal* 16 (1935).

Chung-kuo k'o-hsueh-yuan Shanghai ching-chi yen-chiu-so. *Nan-yang hsiung-ti yen-ts'ao kung-ssu shih-liao* (Source material for the history of the Nanyang Brothers Tobacco Company). Shanghai: People's Publishers, 1958.

———. *Shanghai chieh-fang ch'ien-hou wu-chia tzu-liao hui-pien 1921–1957* (Commodity prices before and after the liberation of Shanghai 1921–1957), Shanghai: People's Publishers, 1959.

Chung-kuo lao-tung nien-chien (Chinese labour yearbook). Shanghai, various issues.

Chung Shou-ching and Bagwell, M. *Women in Industry in the Chapei Hongkew, and Pootung Districts of Shanghai*. Shanghai: YWCA, 1931.

Coble, Parks M., Jr. *The Shanghai Capitalists and the Nationalist Government, 1927–1937*. Cambridge: Harvard University Press, 1980.

Cochran, Sherman. *Big Business in China: Sino-Foreign Rivalry in the Cigarette Industry, 1890–1930*. Cambridge: Harvard University Press, 1980.

Cohen, P. *China and Christianity*. Cambridge: Harvard University Press, 1963.

Decker, H. W. "Industrial Hospital Shanghai: A Review of 880 Cases from the Cotton Mills." *China Medical Missionary Journal* (March 1924).

Deng Yu-dji. *Economic Status of Women in Industry in China, with Special Reference to a Group in Shanghai*. Master's thesis, New York University, 1941.

Eastman, Lloyd. *The Abortive Revolution: China under Nationalist Rule, 1927–1937*, Cambridge: Harvard University Press, 1974.

———. *Family, Fields and Ancestors: Constancy and Change in China's Social and Economic History, 1550–1949*, New York: Oxford University Press, 1988.

Fang Fu-an. *Chinese Labour*. Shanghai: Kelly and Walsh, 1931.

Feetham, R. *Report of Mr. Justice Feetham to the Shanghai Municipal Council, 1931*. 3 vols. Shanghai: North China Daily News Publishers, 1931.

Feuerwerker, Albert, "Economic Trends in the Late Ch'ing Empire, 1870–1911," in *The Cambridge History of China*, Volume 11: Late Ch'ing 1800–1911, Part 2, ed. J. K. Fairbank and Kwang-ching Liu. New York: Cambridge University Press, 1978.

Fewsmith, Joseph. *Party, State, and Local Elites in Republican China: Merchant Organizations and Politics in Shanghai, 1890–1930*. Honolulu: University of Hawaii Press, 1985.

Finch, P. "Battle Against Child Labour in China." *Current History* 22 (August 1925).

Fong, H. D. *China's Industrialisation, a Statistical Survey*. Shanghai: China Council of the Institute of Pacific Relations, 1931.

———. *Toward Economic Control in China*. Shanghai: China Council of the Institute of Pacific Relations, 1936.

Gamble, S. D. *Peking Wages*, Peiping: Yenching University, 1929.

———. "Peiping Family Budgets." *Annals of the American Academy of Political Science* (November 1930).

Gamble, S. D. and Burgess, J. S. *Peking: A Social Survey*, conducted under the auspices of the Princeton University Centre in China and the Peking YWCA, Doran, New York, 1921.

Garrett, S. *Social Reformers in Urban China: The Chinese YMCA, 1895–1926*, Cambridge: Harvard University Press, 1970.

Harrison, I. *Agatha Harrison*. London: George Allen and Unwin, 1956.

Hayford, Charles. *To the People: James Yen and Village China*. New York: Columbia University Press, 1990.

Hershatter, Gail. *The Workers of Tianjin 1900–1949*. Stanford: Stanford University Press, 1986.

Hinder, E. M. *Life and Labour in Shanghai*. New York: Institute of Pacific Relations, 1944.

———. "China's New Factory Law as Affecting Women and Children." *Chinese Recorder* (January 1928).

Ho, F. L., and Fong, H. D. *The Extent and Effects of Industrialisation in China*. Tientsin: Nankai University, 1929.

Ho Han-wen. *Chung-kuo kuo-min ching-chi kai-k'uang* (Outline of the Chinese national economy). Shanghai: Sen-chow kuo-kung Book Store, 1932.

Ho Te-ming. *Chung-kuo lao-tung wen-t-i* (China's labour problems). Shanghai: Commercial Press, 1935.

Hodgkin, H. T. *Living Issues in China*. London: George Allen and Unwin, 1932.

Honig, Emily. *Sisters and Strangers: Women in the Shanghai Cotton Mills, 1919–1949*. Stanford: Stanford University Press, 1986.

International Industrial Welfare Congress. *Report of Proceedings Held in Flushing, Holland, 1925*. Zurich: IIWC, 1925.

Joint Committee of Women's Organisations. *Report of the Joint Committee of Women's Organisations*, privately published, Shanghai, 1927.

Koo Ping-yuan, ed. *China's Labour Laws, 1929–1935*. Shanghai: Commercial Press, 1935.

———. *Factory Safety and Health Inspection Regulations*. Shanghai: Commercial Press, 1936.

Kotenev, A. M. *Shanghai: Its Municipality and the Chinese*. Shanghai: North China Daily News Publishers, 1927.

Kyong Bae-tsung. *Industrial Women in Wusih*. Shanghai: YWCA, 1929.

Labour Party. *Report of the Annual Labour Party Conference, 1925*. London, 1925.

Lamb, J. D. H. (Lin Tung-hai). *The Labour Movement and Labour Legislation in China*. Shanghai: China United Press, 1933.

———. *Origin and Development of Social Legislation in China*. Peiping: Yenching University, 1930.

Lamson, H. D. *Social Pathology in China*. Shanghai: Commercial Press, 1935.

———. "Effect of Industrialisation upon Village Livelihood." *Chinese Economic Journal* 9 (October 1931).

———. "The Problems of Housing for Workers in China," *Chinese Economic Journal* 11 (August 1931).

———. "The Standard of Living of Factory Workers." *Chinese Economic Journal* 7 (November 1930).

Lang, O. *Chinese Family and Society.* New Haven: Yale University Press, 1946.

Latourette, K. S. *A History of Christian Missions in China.* London: SPCK Press, 1929.

————. *World Service: A History of the Foreign Work and World Service of the YMCA's of the US and Canada.* New York: YMCA, 1957.

Li Ta-chao. *Li Ta-Chao hsuan-chi* (Collected works of Li Ta-chao). Peking: People's Publishers, 1962.

Lieu, D. K. *Foreign Investments in China.* Nanking: Bureau of Statistics, 1929.

————. *The Growth and Industrialisation of Shanghai.* Shanghai: China Institute of Economic and Statistical Research, 1936.

Liu, Ta-chung and Yeh, Kung-chia. *The Economy of the Chinese Mainland: National Income and Economic Development, 1933–1959.* Princeton, NJ: Princeton University Press, 1965.

Lowe Ch'uan-hua. *Chin-jih Chung-kuo lao-tung wen-ti* (China's labor problems today). Shanghai: YMCA, 1933.

————. *Facing Labour Issues in China.* London: George Allen and Unwin, 1934.

————. "China's Labour Movement." *Chinese Economic Journal* 6 (May 1930).

————. "Enforcing China's Factory Law." *China Critic* 5 (August 25, 1932).

————. "Factory Inspection as a Political Football." *China Critic* 6 (May 11, 1933).

Lutz, J., ed. *Christian Missions in China: Evangelists of What?* Boston: Heath and Co., 1965.

Malone, C. E. *New China: Report of an Investigation.* London: Independent Labour Party, 1926.

Meng T'ien-pei and Gamble, S. D. *Prices, Wages and the Standard of Living in Peking.* Peking: Peking Express, 1926.

Morse, H. B. *The Guilds of China.* London: Longmans, 1932.

Murphey, R. *Shanghai: Key to Modern China.* Cambridge: Harvard University Press, 1953.

National Christian Council of China. *National Christian Conference, Shanghai 1922, Proceedings.* Shanghai: NCC, 1922.

————. *The National Christian Council: A Five Years' Review, 1922–27.* Shanghai: NCC, 1927.

————. *Papers, Abstracts, and Extracts from Papers Contributed as the Basis of a Discussion to the Conference on the People's Livelihood, Shanghai, February 21–28 1931.* Shanghai: NCC, 1931.

————. *Report of the Conference on Christianizing Economic Relations.* Shanghai: NCC, 1927.

Orchard, D. "Man Power in China." *Political Science Quarterly* 50 and 51 (December 1935 and March 1936).

Pone, C. and Anderson, D. A. "Towards the Establishment of a Factory Inspectorate in China." *International Labour Review* 25 (May 1932).

Porter, R. "Child Labour in Hong Kong and Related Problems: A Brief Overview." *International Labour Review* (May 1975).

Rawski, Thomas G. *Economic Growth in Prewar China.* Berkeley: University of California Press, 1989.

Remer, C. F. *Foreign Investment in China.* New York: Macmillan, 1933.

Rigby, Richard W. *The May Thirtieth Movement: Events and Themes.* Canberra: Australian National University Press, 1980.

Smith, A. H. *The Uplift of China.* London: Christian Missionary Society, 1907.

Smythe, Lewis. *War Damage in the Nanking Area, Dec. 1937 to March 1938.* Nanking International Relief Committee, Urban and Rural Surveys, June 1938.

Strand, David. *Rickshaw Beijing: City People and Politics in the 1920's.* Berkeley: University of California Press, 1988.

Tao Li-kung. *The Standard of Living Among Chinese Workers.* Shanghai: China Council Institute of Pacific Relations, 1931.

T'ao Ling and Johnson, Lydia. *A Study of the Working Conditions of Women and Girls.* Peking: Leader Press, 1928.

Tawney, R. H. *Land and Labour in China.* London: George Allen and Unwin, 1932.

Tayler, J. B. *Farm and Factory in China*. London: SCM Press, 1928.

———. "Christian Industry for China." *International Review of Missions* (October 1931).

———. "Rural Reconstruction in China." *Home Messenger* (February 1934).

Tayler, J. B., and Zung, W. T. "Labour and Industry in China." *International Labour Review*, Geneva, 8 (July 1928).

Tchou, M. T. *Housing and Social Conditions among Industrial Workers in Shanghai*. Shanghai: YMCA, 1926.

———. *Report on Industrial and Social Survey*. Shanghai: YMCA, 1922.

Teng Chung-hsia. *Chung-kuo chih-kung yun-tung chien-shih* (Short history of the Chinese working class movement). Shanghai: Hsin Hua Book Store, 1949.

Tsha, T. Y. "Labour Legislation, Wages, and Hours in Shanghai." *China Critic* 4, 23 (July 1931).

———. "The Living Standard of Shanghai Labourers." *China Critic* 7, 27 (December 1934).

Tsing Chin-chun. *Le Mouvement Ouvrier en Chine*. Paris: Libraitie Geuthner, 1929.

Tso Sheldon, S. K. *The Labour Movement in China*. Shanghai: Commercial Press, 1928.

Unsigned article. "An Enquiry into the Condition of Workers in China." *International Labour Review* 23 (June 1931).

———. "Some Recent Family Budget Enquiries in Shanghai." *International Labour Review* 23 (April 1931).

———. "Trade Unionism in China Since 1929." *International Labour Review* 25 (1932).

"Tsung ying-mei yen kung-ssu kan ti-kuo-chu-i ti ching-chi chin-lae" (Imperialist penetration of China as seen in the case of the British-American Tobacco Company). *Li-shih Yen-chiu* (Lishi Yanjiu—Historical research) no. 4, 1976.

Varg, P. A. *Missionaries, Chinese, and Diplomats: the American Protestant Missionary Movement in China, 1890–1952*. Princeton: Princeton University Press, 1958.

Wagner, A. *Labour Legislation in China*. (Columbia University Ph.D. thesis), Yenching University, Peiping, 1938.

Wales, N. *China Fights for Democracy: A Story of Co-operative Industry*. New York: Modern Age, 1941.

———. *The Chinese Labour Movement*. New York: Day and Co., 1945.

Wang, Simine (Wang Hsi-min). *Le Travail Industriel des Femmes et des Enfants in Chine*. Paris: A. Pedone, 1933.

Wehrle, E. *Britain, China, and the Anti-Missionary Riots, 1891–1900*. Minneapolis: University of Minnesota Press, 1966.

Wong, Jennings. "The New Factory Law and China's Industries." *China Weekly Review* 57, 22 (August 1931).

Wou Monpeng. *L'Evolution des Corporations Ouvrieres en Chine*. Paris: Librairie Geuthner, 1931.

Yang, S., and Tao, L. K. *A Study of the Standard of Living of Working Families in Shanghai*. Peiping: Institute of Economic and Social Research, 1931.

Yao Hsun-yuan. "Industrial Health in the Peiping Special Health Area." *China Medical Missionary Journal* (April 1929).

Yen Chung-p'ing. *Chung-kuo mien-fong-chih shih-kao* (Draft history of the cotton-spinning industry in China, 1289–1937). Peking: Science Publishers, 1955.

YWCA. *Chinese Triangles: The YWCA in a Changing China*. Shanghai:YWCA, 1924.

———. *History of the YWCA in China, 1896–1930*. Shanghai: YWCA, ca. 1931.

———. *The YWCA of China, 1933–1947*. Shanghai: Mercury Press, 1947.

Zhongguo Kexueyuan. *Lishi Yanjiu* (Historical research). Beijing, 1954, etc., various issues.

Index

ACLF. *See* All China Labor Federation
Addington, Lord, 227*n.21*, 230*n.69*
Agricultural Missions Boards, 233*n.123*
Agricultural sector, 74, 84–85, 85–86, 88–89,
    91–92, 93, 94, 98, 226*n.6*, 247*n.11*
All China Labor Federation (ACLF), 19
Alley, Rewi, 17, 58, 115, 129, 133, 138, 140,
    142, 143, 144, 176, 246*nn.115, 117*
American Friends Service Committee, 38
Anderson, Adelaide, 54, 77, 88, 102, 105,
    108–09, 116, 149–50, 240*n. 105*
Anderson, Mary, 218*n.15*
Anderson, Mrs., 228*n.38*
Apprenticeships, 13–14, 92, 172, 209*n.67*
    child labor, 14, 74, 120, 125, 235*n.10*, 241*n.18*
    legislation, 24, 25, 213*nn.144, 145*
    women workers, 209*n.69*
Armstrong, W., 236*n.17*, 237*n.44*
Arnhold, C., 227*n.13*
Association for the Advancement of Chinese
    Industrial Cooperatives, 139
Australia, xiii, 167, 206*n.13*

Bagwell, May, 61, 64, 65–66, 90, 91
Bailie, Joseph, 141
Bailie schools, 141–42
Barnett, E.E., 164, 206*nn.15, 17*, 230*n.69*,
    253–54*n.54*
BAT. *See* British-American Tobacco Company
Bau, C.L., 227*n.21*
Bau, Y.H., 236*n.17*, 237*n.42*, 249–50*n.4*
Ben, A.O., 249–50*n.4*
Biennial Meeting (NCC; 1931), 93
Blaisdell, H.C., 227–28*nn.25, 27*
Bonus system, 84
Boxer Uprising (1899), 3
Britian. *See* Great Britain
British-American Tobacco Company (BAT), 6,
    9, 61, 208*n.33*
    child labor, 105, 238*n.62*, 239*n.96*
    contract labor system, 14

British-American Tobacco Company (BAT),
    (continued)
    employee welfare plan, 23, 175, 212*n.133*
    as foreign investor/owner, 6, 9, 11, 209*nn.52, 58*
    housing issues, 22, 38
    pay rates/work hours, 18, 235*n.10*
    relations with welfare workers, 249*n.3*
British Boxer Indemnity Commission, 81, 96,
    229*n.55*
British Consular Service, 24
Brockman, Fletcher, 206*n.15*
Brooke-Smith, Mr., 227*n.13*
Brown, Hilda, 233*n.126*
Bryn Mawr (Pa.), 53
Buck, J.L., 230*n.69*
Bureau of Markets, 80, 84
Bureau of Social Affairs (Shanghai), 4, 19, 99,
    120, 123, 124, 173, 211*n.101*, 241*n.131*
Bureau of Social Affairs (Tientsin), 14
Bush, Richard, 5, 7–8
Butler, Alfred, 151, 247–48*n.31*

Caldwell, William, 148
Campbell, W.K.H., 246*n.118*
Canada, 8, 29, 220*n.47*
Cao Hwei, 236*n.17*, 237*n.22*
Carson, A.L., 233*n.130*
CCC. *See* China Continuation Committee
CCER. *See* Committee on Christianizing
    Economic Relations
Central Factory Inspection Bureau, 25
Chambers of Commerce, 61, 76, 110, 112,
    238*n.59*
Chan, C.S., 150, 151–53, 155, 247*nn.25, 28*,
    247–48*n.31*
Chang, John, 9
Chang, Mr., 236*n.17*
Chang, T.L., 236*n.17*, 237*n.42*
Chang Po-ling, 233*n.130*
Chao, Mrs. S.F., 227*n.21*
Chapei, xvi, 37, 46, 58–59, 166, 251*n.36*

Chefoo Christian Women Workers' Society, 33
Chefoo industrial program (YWCA), 71, 72, 130, 224–25nn.140, 145
Chen, Chin-kee, 236n.17
Chen, Gideon, 77, 78, 82, 86–87, 90, 221–22n.86, 223–24n.136, 225–26n.5, 227–28nn.25, 29, 30, 230n.69, 231n.83, 233n.130, 252–53n.49
Chen, K.P., 150, 247–48n.31
Chen, K.S., 156
Chen, L.T., 227n.21
Chen, Mrs. C.C., 167
Cheng, H.F. (Cheng Hai-fong), 117, 153–56, 158, 247–48nn.31, 32
Cheng, Philip, 90
Chen Ta, 44, 90, 94, 168, 212n.134, 237n.47
Chesneaux, Jean, 13, 14, 99, 100
Chiang Kai-shek, 25, 46, 54, 57, 155, 168, 169, 220n.63, 235n.16, 243n.63
Chiao, Gene L., 233n.130
Child labor, 239–40n.98
 apprenticeships, 14, 74, 120, 125, 235n.10, 241n.18
 and Confucian values, 99–100
 contract labor system, 14–15, 210n.76
 cotton industry, 99, 101, 106, 235n.13, 237n.32, 239n.96
 and foreign employers, 250n.14
 health/safety issues, 20, 105, 174
 and ILO, 101, 107, 148, 149, 235n.10
 legislation, xvii, 24, 25, 35, 46, 161–62, 164, 169, 172
  See also Child Labor Commission
 match industry, 7, 107, 237n.34
 mui tsai, 125–26
 Municipal Council reform efforts. See Child Labor Commission
 National Christian Conference (1922), 226nn.8, 11
 National Christian Council reform efforts, 80, 84, 101
 pay rates/work hours, 16, 17, 18, 100, 105, 226n.11, 235n.10
 printing industry, 99, 107, 239n.96
 silk industry, 99, 103, 106, 237n.34, 239n.96, 239–40n.98
 study findings, 98–100, 114, 234n.2
 tobacco industry, 99, 106–07, 239–40n.96
 YMCA reform efforts, 35, 36
 Young Workers' Employment Contract, 126
 YWCA reform efforts, 50, 53–54, 57, 101, 161–62, 164, 218n.20
Child Labor Commission (Shanghai Municipal Council), 77, 98–114
 creation of, 50, 53–54, 79, 100–101
 findings/recommendations, 14–15, 105–08, 172, 174, 203–04

Child Labor Commission (Shanghai Municipal Council) (continued)
 legislative efforts/failure, 108–14, 169, 172, 238nn.59, 62, 67, 239nn.78, 84, 96
 membership/investigative approach, 102, 235n.16, 236–37nn.18, 19
 witness testimony, 102–05, 209n.67, 236n.17, 237nn.22, 32, 34, 42, 44, 47
Child Protection Section (Shanghai Municipal Council), 125–27
China Bureau (ILO), 151–56, 173, 247n.24, 249n.60
 under C.S. Chan, 151–53, 155, 247nn.25, 26, 28
 under H.F. Cheng, 153–56, 248–49nn.31, 41, 46, 48, 49
China Christian Association, 253n.50
China Christian Educational Commission, 81
China Continuation Committee (CCC), 73, 74
 National Christian Conference (1922), 32, 33, 73, 74–76, 81, 162, 168, 225–27nn.5, 6, 7, 8, 11, 12, 13, 14
China Foundation, 81, 229n.42
China Institute of Industrial Training, 242n.32
China Medical Missionary Association, 79
China Weekly Review, 113
China Year Book, 100, 111
Chinese Cotton Mill Owners Association, 6, 101, 235n.13
Chinese Industrial Cooperative Association, 139
Chinese Industrial Cooperative Movement (CIC), 123, 130, 133–34, 136, 138–44, 170–71, 176, 245nn.101, 106, 246nn.116, 117, 118, 254n.55
 See also Indusco
"Chinese Labour Since 1927" (report), 90
Chinese Mill Owners' Association, 51, 52
Chinese Statistical Society, 123
Ch'ing dynasty, xvi
Chisholm, Margaret, 221–22n.86
Christian Industry (newsletter), 77, 83, 227n.23, 231n.80
Christianity
 evangelism, 39, 73, 88
 impact on reform movement, xii–xiii, 205n.9
Chu, C.C., 227–28nn.25, 27
Chu Hsueh-fan, 249n.54
Chu Mu-ch'eng. See Tchou, M.T.
Chung, Helen (Chung Shou-ching), 61, 132
Chung Hwa Book Company, 33, 213n.5
Church of England, 73, 76
CIC. See Chinese Industrial Cooperative Movement
Cigarette industry. See Tobacco industry
Class struggle, 69, 70, 167
Coble, Parks M., Jr., 7–8
Cochran, Sherman, 11, 18

Commercial Press, 23, 33, 38, 61, 175, 212*n.132*, 213*n.5*, 238*n.62*, 239*n.96*
Commission on Labor Problems, xii
Committee on Christianizing Economic Relations (CCER), 59, 83, 85, 86–88, 92, 93–94, 95
  See also Industrial Commission
Committee on the Church's Relation to Economic and Industrial Problems. *See* Industrial Commission
Communism/communists, 8, 15, 85, 91, 122, 133, 138, 143, 148, 155, 164, 166, 169, 210*n.76*
Concession areas, xiv, xvi, 98, 115–16, 252*n.42*
  See also French Concession
Conference of Christian Colleges and Universities, 81
Conference of Missionary Societies, 94
Conference on the People's Livelihood (1931), 89–93, 168, 170
Confucian values, 23, 99–100
Contract labor system, 13, 14–15, 84, 92, 172
  child labor, 14–15, 210*n.76*
  dormitories, 22
  women workers, 14, 15, 48, 125
Contract work system, 15
Cooperatives, 74, 93
  Chinese Industrial Cooperative Movement, 123, 130, 133–34, 136, 138–44, 170–71, 176, 245*nn.101, 106*, 246*nn.116, 117, 118*, 254*n.55*
  and National Christian Council, 88–89, 91–92, 94, 96, 97, 130, 162, 170–71, 176, 232*n.120*, 233*nn.123, 124*, 234*n.148*
  YWCA-sponsored, 130, 133–37, 243–44*nn.56, 57, 58, 59, 62, 63, 64, 65, 66, 67, 72*
Cooper, J.S.S., 235*n.16*
Coppock, Grace, 49, 50, 74, 218*n.19*, 225–26*n.5*
Cornfoot, Edwin J., 235*n.16*, 236*n.17*
Cost-of-living rates
  research/study findings, 18, 80, 81, 100, 123–24, 170, 173, 211*n.93*, 229*n.42*, 235*n.10*, 241*n.9*
  summary table, 182
Cotton industry
  child labor, 99, 101, 106, 235*n.13*, 237*n.32*, 239*n.96*
  employee welfare plans, 23
  health/safety issues, 20, 21
  industry profile, 5–6, 7, 8, 9, 207*n.18*
  pay rates/work hours, 16, 18, 211*n.92*, 235*n.10*
  women workers, 6, 15, 21, 47, 168, 208*n.24*, 211*n.92*, 217*n.4*
Cressy, Mr., 229*n.50*

Davis, J. Merle, 96–97, 231–32*nn. 97, 98*, 234*nn.144, 145, 148*
Dean, Sam, 94, 95, 233*nn.123, 130*
Decker, Dr., 236*n.17*
Deng, Cora (Deng Yu-chih), xv, 63, 65, 66–69, 71, 90, 132, 136–38, 144, 166–67, 176, 217*n.78*, 223*nn.119, 123*, 224*nn.138, 143*, 230*n.69*, 244*nn.76, 78*, 252*n.42*
  as Industrial Department director, 175
  as YWCA industrial secretary, 169
  as YWCA trainee secretary, 170
Dennison (no first name), 88
Department of Labor (U.S.), 109
Diet. *See* Health/safety issues
Dingman, Mary, 52, 53, 54, 55, 56, 57, 77, 80, 82, 87, 161, 219*n.39*, 220*n.51*, 227*nn.17, 21*, 228*n.29*, 235*n.16*, 247*n.24*, 250*n.10*, 253*n.52*
Dispute mediation, 124–25
Dju Yu-bao, 57–58, 84, 120, 230*n.69*
Dockers' Union (Hankow), 155, 248*n.46*
Domestic service. *See* Mui tsai
Dormitories, 22, 36–37, 120, 128, 174

East China University Summer School (1924), 78
Eastman, Lloyd, 7, 11, 13, 18
Eastman, Mack, 150–51, 247*n.21*, 248*n.41, 49*
Eddy, Sherwood, 32, 33–34, 35, 42, 45, 55, 56, 67, 76, 79, 88, 227–28*nn.18, 25*
Education/training programs, 13, 59, 74, 78, 92, 93, 228*n.29*
  Chinese Industrial Cooperative Movement, 141–42, 245*n.106*
  Industrial Section, 127, 128–29, 242*n.32*
  women workers, 40, 61–63, 64, 69, 164–65, 174–75, 223*n.132*
  YMCA, 30–31, 39–40, 169, 174
  YWCA, 40, 134–35, 137, 138, 165–66, 174–75, 221*n.84*
Employee welfare plans, 23–24, 212*nn.132, 133*
Employers, and welfare workers' relations, 160–63, 175, 249–50*nn.3, 4*
Engineering Society of China, 125, 172
Episcopal Church. *See* Church of England
Escreet, Miss, 57
Evangelism, 39, 73, 88
Extraterritoriality, xiv, xv, xvi-xviii, 11–12, 93, 115–16, 129, 158, 240*n.106*

Factory, defined, 207*n.15*
Factory Act (1923). *See* Provisional Factory Regulations (1923)
Factory Act (China; 1929–31), xiv, xvii, xviii, 8, 23, 25, 68, 90, 91, 93, 94, 116, 117, 120, 149–50, 152, 157, 189–202, 207*n.15*, 213*nn.144, 145*, 247*n.13*

Factory Act (Great Britain; 1847), xv
Factory councils, 25, 91, 213n.144, 232n.110
Factory Inspection Act (1929), 25, 90, 91, 93, 149
Factory Safety Association, 121
Farming. See Agricultural sector
Feetham, Richard, 113
Feetham Commission (1931), xviii
Feng Yu-hsiang, 43
Filatures. See Silk industry
First Opium War, xvi
First Special District Court (Shanghai), xvii, 116, 119, 125, 129
Fong, H.D. (Fong Hsien-ting), 6, 90, 207n.11
Fong, Mrs. Sec, 167
Fong Sec, 23, 249–50n.4
Foreign Cotton Mill Owners Association, 7, 101, 235n.13
Foreign Mill Owners' Association, 51
Foreign residents/employers
   and child labor, 250n.14
   exploitation by, xiv
   and extraterritoriality, xiv, xv, xvi-xviii, 11–12, 93, 115–16, 129, 158
   industrial investment/ownership, 3, 8, 10–12, 50–51, 209n.52
   and industrial reform, xv, xvi-xviii, 88–89, 231n.90, 250n.14
   legal position, xvi-xviii
   See also Ratepayers
France, 29
Frankfurter, Felix, 51
Freely negotiated agreement, 13
French Concession, xi, xvi, 116, 122, 150, 206n.22
French Tramway Company, 14
French Women's Union, 109
Fullerton, Dr., 236n.17

Gear, H.S., 21
Germany, 8
Gold standard, 8
Goodrich, Carrington, 43
Great Britain, xiii, xv, xvi, 8, 94, 206n.13
   child labor, 109, 113, 145
   employee welfare plans, 23
   factory legislation, xv, 102
   industrial investment/ownership, 10–11, 207n.12
   YMCA, 29
   YWCA, 48, 167
Great Depression, 8–9, 45, 67, 166, 210n.88, 233n.123, 250n.5, 252n.43
Green Gang, 8, 15–16, 20
Greenwood, Arthur, 34
Green Year Supplement, 61, 221n.78, 222n.90, 251n.28
Gunpowder manufacture, 5

Haass, Lily, 54, 57–58, 59, 60, 65, 66, 68, 71, 82–84, 86, 87, 136, 162, 164, 165, 166, 168, 221–22n.86, 223n.119, 230n.69, 244n.77, 252n.48, 253–54n.54
Handicraft industry, 4, 19, 74, 82, 84, 98, 211n.102, 226nn.6, 7
Han Sung-wen, 236n.17
Hapgood (no first name), 88
Harrison, Agatha, 31, 49–54, 55, 73, 76, 77, 94, 102, 109, 161, 164, 170, 218nn.14, 15, 219n.40, 225–26n.5, 227nn.13, 17, 21, 229n.50, 231–32n.97, 235n.16, 250n.9
Harrof, James, 236n.17
Harvey, C.W., 55, 56, 220n.51
Hatem, S.C. (Ma Hai-teh), 21
Health/safety issues, 20–21, 92, 213n.145, 226nn.8, 11
   child labor, 20, 105, 174
   industrial accidents, 21, 117–20, 212nn.123, 124
   phosphorous poisoning, 20, 21, 79, 107, 174, 211n.112
   reform efforts, 117–21, 127, 128, 129, 173–74
   women workers, 20, 21, 174, 226nn.8, 11, 230n.75
Henry, Pierre, 16, 20, 43, 79, 146–48, 151, 212n.132, 246n.6
Henry Lester Institute of Medical Research, 119, 120, 128
Herschleb, Charles, 56
Hershatter, Gail, 12, 13, 18, 20, 23, 99, 114
Heygate, Mr., 236n.17
Hille, Miss, 236n.17
Hinder, Eleanor, 17, 58, 59, 60, 66, 71–72, 80, 84, 89, 90, 115, 116, 117–18, 120, 121, 127, 131, 144, 164–66, 169, 217n.78, 221–22n.86, 222–23n.113, 229n.44, 230n.69, 244n.77, 251n.35, 253–54n.54
Ho, Franklin, 6, 207n.11, 233n.130
Hodgkin, Henry, 54, 55, 56, 73, 77, 82, 86, 96, 219n.29, 225–26n.5, 227–28n.25, 230n.69
Hong Kong, 101, 103, 244n.82
Honig, Emily, 6, 12, 15, 18, 47, 48, 71, 114
Hoople, Ruth, 230n.69
Hoover, Herbert, 218n.15
Housing, 21–22, 36–42, 92, 127–28, 174
   See also Dormitories
Housing Committee (Shanghai Municipal Council), 127
Hsu, C.Y. (Hsu Ch'ing-yun), 85
Hu Han-min, 46
Hunter, J.A., 233n.130

ILO. See International Labor Organization
India, 48, 158, 226n.11
Indochina, 158

Indusco, 139, 140, 142, 143, 245nn.88, 106, 246n.115
    See also Chinese Industrial Cooperative Movement
Industrial accidents. See Health/safety issues
Industrial Advisory Committee (YWCA), xii
Industrial and Social Division (Industrial Section), 123
Industrial Commission (NCC), 227nn.18, 24, 228n.30, 230n.64
    creation of, 74–79
    employer relations, 162
    Industrial Cabinet, 77, 82, 227n.21
    Institute of Social and Economic Research, 80–81, 229nn.54, 55
        Reconnaissance Committee, 81, 170, 229nn.42, 50, 51
    and labor unions, 168
    leadership changes, 82
    name change, 83
    publications, 227–28n.25
        Industrial Reconstruction Series, 78, 227–28nn.25, 27
    reform efforts, 172, 173–74
    Shanghai Committee on the Church and Industry, 79–80, 228nn.38, 40
    See also Committee on Christianizing Economic Relations
Industrial Cooperative Movement. See Chinese Industrial Cooperative Movement
Industrial Department. See Young Women's Christian Association, reform efforts
Industrial development, 3–25
    Christian church evaluation of, 74–76
    during World War II, 123–44
    employer relations, 160–63, 175, 249–50nn.3, 4
    foreign investment/ownership, 3, 8, 10–12, 50–51, 209n.52
    human factors, 12–22
    See also Health/safety issues; Housing; Pay rates/work hours; Recruitment, employee; Rural-urban mobility; Unemployment
    labor relations. See Unions, labor
    manufacturing profile, 3–12
    National Conference on Christianizing Economic Relations (1927), 83–86, 162, 163, 168, 230nn.69, 75, 78
"Industrial Handbook for Social Workers," 87
Industrial Reconstruction Series (NCC publications), 78, 227–28nn.25, 27
Industrial reform
    child labor. See Child Labor Commission; Child Protection Section
    early history, xi–xviii
    employee welfare plans, 23–24, 212nn.132, 133

Industrial reform (continued)
    and foreign residents/employers, xv, xvi-xviii, 88–89, 231n.90
    health/safety issues, 117–21, 127, 128, 129, 173–74
    legislation. See Legislation
    Nationalist movement/government impact, xiv-xvi, 101, 114, 253–54n.54
    welfare workers' intermediary role, 160–71
        employer relations, 160–63, 175, 249–50nn.3, 4
        labor union relations, 163–68
        nonpaternalistic approach, 168–71, 176
    World War II activities, 123–44
        Chinese Industrial Cooperative Movement, 123, 130, 133–34, 136, 138–44, 170–71, 176, 245nn.101, 106, 246nn.116, 117, 118, 254n.55
        See also Indusco
        Industrial Section, 123–29, 173, 174, 241nn.8, 9, 242n.32
        YWCA, 123, 129–38, 242–44nn.42, 48, 49, 56, 57, 58, 59, 62, 63, 64, 65, 66, 67, 72, 84
    See also International Labor Organization; Municipal Council; National Christian Council of China; Young Men's Christian Association; Young Women's Christian Association
Industrial Secretaries' Conferences (YWCA), 59–60, 68, 69, 70, 162, 166, 167, 170, 223n.131
Industrial Section (Shanghai Municipal Council)
    Child Protection Section, 125–27
    creation of, 58
    Industrial and Social Division, 123
    reform efforts, 114–21, 172, 240n.106
    World War II activities, 123–29
        child protection, 125–27
        dispute mediation, 124–25
        economic data collection, 123–24, 173, 241nn.8, 9
        education/training programs, 127, 128–29, 242n.32
        health/safety issues, 127, 128, 129, 174
        housing standards, 127–28, 174
Industrial Service Union. See North China Industrial Service Union
Industrial welfare. See Industrial reform
Industrial Women in Wusih, 61
Institute of Pacific Relations, 120, 148
Institute of Social and Economic Research (NCC), 80–81, 229nn.50, 51, 54, 55
Institute of Social and Religious Research (N.Y.), 81, 96, 229nn.50, 51, 233n.123

International Committee (YMCA), xiii, xv-xvi, 44, 45, 55, 56, 161, 206nn.15, 17, 220n.47, 250n.5
International Congress of Working Women (1923), 54
International Famine Relief Fund, 233n.123
International Labor Conferences, xii, 24, 115, 156, 158, 205n.6
International Labor Organization (ILO), 137, 145–59, 232n.98, 244n.78
  child labor, 101, 107, 148, 149, 235n.10
  China Bureau, 151–56, 173, 247n.24, 249n.60
    under C.S. Chan, 151–53, 155, 247nn.25, 26, 28
    under H.F. Cheng, 153–56, 247–48nn.31, 41, 46, 48, 49
  Chinese representation in Geneva, 156–59, 249n.54
  conventions ratification, 157–58
  extraterritoriality issue, 116, 240n.106
  fact-finding missions, 146–51, 246n.3
    Caldwell/Thomas reports, 148
    Henry investigation, 146–48, 151, 246n.6
    Maurette/Eastman/Butler trips, 150–51, 247n.21
    Pone/Anderson investigation, 149–50
  factory legislation, 149–51, 152, 157, 247n.14
  and Kuomintang, 115, 156
  and labor unions, 145–46, 151, 153, 155, 249n.54
  and Nationalist movement/government, 153
  reform efforts, xi-xii, xiv, xviii, 172
  and Rockefeller Foundation, 148
  and YMCA/YWCA, 146, 246n.6
International Labor Review, 100, 113
"International Labour" (newsletter), 152
International Missionary Council, xiii, 89, 96, 231–32nn.97, 98, 233n.139
International Settlement (Shanghai), xvi-xvii, 169
  child labor, 53–54, 161–62
    See also Child Labor Commission
  factory legislation, xviii, 149–50, 151
  housing, 37
  industrial data, 5
  Industrial Section reform efforts, 114–17
  match industry legislation, 79
  Nationalist movement/government impact, xv
  Public Works Department, 14
  Sino-Japanese War (1937), xiv, 9, 19–20, 122, 123
  unemployment, 173
  World War II, 122–29, 130, 131
Iserland, Otto, 231–32nn.97, 98

Japan, 3, 8, 158, 226n.11
  industrial investment/ownership, 10, 11

Japan (continued)
  Sino-Japanese War (1937), xiv, 5, 9, 19–20, 42, 122, 123, 151
  World War II, 122, 123
  YWCA, 48
Jenkins, E.C., 55
Johnson, Hilton, 236n.17, 237n.44
Johnson, Lydia, 61, 63, 224–25n.145, 230n.69
Johnston, Edith, 50, 54, 58, 79, 228n.38
Johnston, Inspector, 236n.17, 237n.42
Jones, Rufus, 215n.37
Jordan, John, 52
Judicial system
  First Special District Court (Shanghai), xvii, 116, 119, 125, 129
  foreign residents/employers and extraterritorial privileges, xvii
  Mixed Court (Shanghai), xiv, xvii
  Provisional Court (Shanghai), xvii

Kerr, Archibald Clark, 138–39
Keys, Mr., 228n.38
Kropotkin's principles, 92
Kulp, D.H., 31
Kung, H.H. (Kung Hsiang-hsi), 46, 88, 89, 139, 149, 231n.94, 245n.88
Kuomintang
  and Chinese Industrial Cooperative Movement, 136, 171
  employee recruitment, 15
  and ILO, 115, 156
  industrial legislation program, 24–25, 114–15, 121, 149, 175
  and labor unions, 7–8, 87, 90–91, 148, 153, 166, 169, 208–09n.43, 248n.48, 252–53nn.42, 49
  and YMCA, 44
  and YWCA, 60, 221n.84, 253–54n.54
  See also Nationalist movement/government
Kyong Bae-tsung, 59, 61, 64, 65, 221–22nn.84, 86, 222–23n.113

Labor. See Men workers; Unions, labor; Women workers
Labor Conditions in China, 98–99, 115
Labor contract. See Contract labor system
Labor Union Law, 90, 91, 166, 168, 175
Lacquerware industry, 4
Laissez-faire, 176
Lamb, J.D.H. (Lin Tung-hai), 90
Lambeth Conference (1921), 73
Lamson, H.D., 90, 217n.78, 235n.10
Land Regulations (1845), xvii, xviii
Lao-pan, 14, 143
Law Governing Penalties for Police Offenses, 129
Lawney, Josephine, 227n.21, 228n.38, 236n.17

League of Nations, 75, 145, 226n.11
    See also International Labor Organization
Lee, J.Y., 227n.21
Lee, Y.L., 41, 163–64
Legislation, xvi, 46, 161, 170, 175
    child labor, xvii, 24, 25, 35, 46, 161–62, 164,
        169, 172
        See also Child Labor Commission
    Factory Act (1929–31), xiv, xvii, xviii, 8, 23,
        25, 68, 90, 91, 93, 94, 116, 117, 120,
        149–50, 152, 157, 189–202, 207n.15,
        213nn.144, 145, 247n.13
    Factory Inspection Act (1929), 25, 90, 91, 93,
        149
    general factory-related, 213n.143
    health/safety-related, 118–19, 174
    Kuomintang industrial program, 24–25,
        114–15, 121, 149, 175
    Labor Union Law, 90, 91, 166, 168, 175
    Land Regulations (1845), xvii, xviii
    Law Governing Penalties for Police
        Offenses, 129
    licensing regulations, 116–17
    match industry-related, 79
    Provisional Factory Regulations (1923), 53,
        101, 102, 110, 145, 157, 175, 184–88,
        213n.142, 249n.56
    Trade Union Law (1929), xiv, 25, 65
Li, Grace, 65
Lieu, D.K. (Liu Ta-chun), 4–5, 155
Lin Tung-hai. See Lamb, J.D.H.
Li Ta-chao, 210n.76
Literacy. See Education/training programs
Liu, Mr., 236n.17
Liu Chao, 233n.130
Liu Ta-chung, 5, 6, 7
Lo, R.Y., 228n.38
Lobenstine, E.C., 252n.48
Lockwood, E.H., 164, 250–51n.22, 253–54n.54
Lockwood, William, 206n.15, 249n.3
London School of Economics, 53, 57, 67, 219n.36
Lowe, C.H. (Lowe Ch'uan-hua), 43–44, 158,
    216nn.69, 73, 223n.131
Lyon, D.W., 29

MacGillivray, Mrs. L., 235n.16
Ma Hai-teh. See Hatem, S.C.
Maitland, C.T., 79
Maitland, G.T., 21
Malone, l'Estrange, 164
Manchuria, 8, 11
Masaryk, Alice, 109
Mass Education Movement, xii, xv, 29, 174,
    206n.12
Match industry
    child labor, 7, 107, 237n.34
    health/safety issues, 20, 21

Match industry (continued)
    industry profile, 5, 6–7, 9, 208n.34
    pay rates/work hours, 16, 18
    phosphorous poisoning, 20, 21, 79, 107, 174,
        211n.112
Maurette, Francois, 150, 247–48n.31
May, H.J., 232n.120
May Thirtieth Incident, 57, 58, 80, 81, 101,
    111, 169
McConnell, T.C., 249–50n.4
McKinley, William, xii
McMurray (no first name), 206n.17
McNicol, R.J., 235n.16, 236n.17, 237n.32
Mediation, dispute, 124–25
Meeker, Royal, 81, 229n.50
Meng, T.P. (Meng T'ien-pei), 82, 83
Men workers, 17, 18, 40, 179, 226nn.8, 11
Migration, rural-urban, 12–13, 172
Ministry of Finance, 42
Ministry of Industries, 25, 121, 152, 154, 155
Minsheng, 23
Mixed Court (Shanghai), xiv, xvii
Model Village (YMCA), 36–42, 43, 46, 60, 63,
    169, 174, 215nn.37, 39, 49, 216n.55
Modern industry. See Industrial development
Moh, H.Y., 249n.3
Moh, Mrs., 235n.16, 236n.17, 237n.42, 251n.36
Moral economy (minsheng), 23
Morrison, Miss, 228n.38
Mr. X, 50–51
Mud huts, 37
Mui tsai, 125–26
Municipal Council (Shanghai)
    Child Labor Commission, 77, 98–114
        creation of, 50, 53–54, 79, 100–101
        findings/recommendations, 14–15, 105–08,
            172, 174, 203–04
        legislative efforts/failure, 108–14, 169, 172,
            238nn.59, 62, 67, 239nn.78, 84, 96
        membership/investigative approach, 102,
            235n.16, 236–37nn.18, 19
        witness testimony, 102–05, 209n.67,
            236n.17, 237nn.22, 32, 34, 42, 44, 47
    factory legislation, 149–50, 151
    governing role, xvi-xviii
    Housing Committee, 127
    housing reform, 22, 174
    industrial data collection, 5, 17, 21
    Industrial Section
        Child Protection Section, 125–27
        creation of, 58
        reform efforts, 114–21, 172, 240n.106
        World War II activities, 123–29
            child protection, 125–27
            dispute mediation, 124–25
            economic data collection, 123–24, 173,
                241nn.8, 9

Municipal Council (Shanghai) *(continued)*
  education/training programs, 127, 128–29,
    242*n.32*
  health/safety issues, 127, 128, 129, 174
  housing standards, 127–28, 174
  membership, 239*n.79*
  reform efforts, xi, xiii-xiv, 98–121
  and YWCA, 57, 58, 114, 165, 240*n.107*
Municipal Police (Shanghai), xvii, 125

Naigai Wata Kaisha (cotton mill), 23, 37, 175,
    239*n.96*
Nankai University, 94, 95, 233*nn.123, 131*
Nankai University Statistical Service, 4
Nanking Ministry of Industries, 16
Nanking Theological Seminary, 97, 234*n.148*
Nantao, xvi
Nantao Christian Institute, 33
Nanyang Brothers' Tobacco Company, 6, 146
  as BAT's competitor, 11, 208*n.33*, 209*n.58*
  employee welfare plan, 23
  housing provided, 22
  pay rates/work hours, 18
National Assembly of Industrial Girls (YWCA),
    71, 223–24*n.136*
National Christian Conference (1922), 32, 33,
    73, 74–76, 81, 162, 168, 225–27*nn.5, 6, 7,
    8, 11, 12, 13, 14*
National Christian Conference (1923), 54
National Christian Council of China (NCC), 43,
    225*n.2*
  Biennial Meeting (1931), 93
  child labor, 80, 84, 101
  Committee on Christianizing Economic
    Relations, 59, 83, 85, 86–88, 92, 93–94,
    95, 96
  Conference on the People's Livelihood
    (1931), 89–93, 168, 170
  cooperatives, 88–89, 91–92, 94, 96, 97, 130,
    162, 170–71, 176, 232*n.120*, 233*nn.123,
    124*, 234*n.148*
  employer relations, 162–63, 175
  Industrial Commission. *See* Industrial
    Commission
  Institute of Social and Economic Research,
    80–81, 229*nn.50, 51, 54, 55*
  and labor unions, 168, 252*nn.47, 48*
  National Conference on Christianizing
    Economic Relations (1927), 83–86, 162,
    163, 168, 230*nn.69, 75, 78*
  North China Industrial Service Union, 95–96
  publications, 231*n.80*
    Christian Industry, 77, 83, 227*n.18*, 231*n.80*
    Industrial Reconstruction Series, 78,
      227–28*nn.25, 27*
  reform efforts, xiii, xv, 32, 34–35, 45, 73–97,
    169

National Christian Council of China (NCC)
    (continued)
  Rockefeller grant, 55, 56, 67, 78, 81, 82, 96,
    229*n.54*, 233*n.138*
  Shanghai Committee on the Church and
    Industry, 79–80, 228*nn.38, 40*
  study findings, 21
  university-associated projects, 93–96
  and YMCA, 79, 83
  and YWCA, 50, 54, 58, 60, 67, 79, 83, 168,
    222*n.104*, 252*n.48*
National Conference on Christianizing
    Economic Relations (1927), 83–86, 162,
    163, 168, 230*nn.69, 75, 78*
National Factory Inspection Bureau, 120–21
Nationalist Ministry of Industries, 4
Nationalist movement/government
  early reform efforts, xi, xiii, xiv
  and foreign-owned enterprises, 11
  and ILO, 153
  impact on reform movement, xiv-xvi, 101,
    114, 253–54*n.54*
  industrial production efforts, 9
  and labor unions, xiv, xv, 7–8, 253–54*n.54*
  and reform legislation, xiv, 249*n.56*
  Shanghai invasion, xvi
  and YWCA, 65–66
  See also Kuomintang
NCC. *See* National Christian Council of China
New, Dr., 236*n.17*
Nieh, C.C., 76, 227*n.13*, 236*n.17*, 249–50*n.4*
Nipps, John W., 43–45, 163, 216*n.69*, 217*n.78*
Nishikawa, Mr., 236*n.17*
Noh, H.Y., 235*n.16*
North China Christian Rural Service Union,
    233*n.130*
North China Daily News, 101, 110, 112, 253*n.52*
North China Herald, 100, 110, 112–13,
    238*n.59*, 239*n.84*
North China Industrial Service Union, 95–96
Northern Expedition, 80

Okada, G., 227*n.13*, 235*n.16*
Opium War. *See* First Opium War; Second
    Opium War
Orchard, Dorothy, 16–17
"Outlines of Plan for Model Villages for
    Working People," 38, 215*n.36*
"Outlines of Report on Housing and Social
    Conditions Amomg Industrial Workers in
    Shangahi," 36
Outworkers, 134, 172, 243*n. 58*, 244*nn.66, 67*

Page, Kirby, 35
Pao-kung. See Contract labor system
Pao-kung-t'ou, 14
Parker, G.A., 228*n.27*

Paton, William, 82
Patton, C.E., 227n.21
Patton, G.E., 227n.17
Pay rates/work hours
  child labor, 16, 17, 18, 100, 103–04, 105,
    226n.11, 235n.10
  data collection, 123–24, 173, 241n.131
  dispute mediation, 124–25
  legislation, 25, 213n.144
  overview of industries, 16–18
  research/study findings, 84, 92, 210n.88,
    211nn.90, 93, 226n.8
  wage summary tables, 179–83
  women workers, 17, 18, 47–48, 62, 100, 179,
    211n.92, 226n.11, 230n.75, 235n.10
Pearce, Edward, 227n.13
Penney Foundation, 233n.123
"The People's Livelihood as Revealed by
  Family Budget Studies," 90
Phosphorous poisoning, 20, 21, 79, 107, 174,
  211n.112
"Phossy-jaw." See Phosphorous poisoning
Platt, B.S., 21
Pone, M. Camille, 116, 149–50, 240n.105
Porcelain industry, 4
Pottery industry, 89
Powell, J.B., 235n.15
Pratt, John, 109
Price, Detective Inspector, 236n.17
Price, Frank, 234n.148
Printing industry
  apprenticeships, 209n.67
  child labor, 99, 107, 239n.96
  health/safety issues, 21
  industry profile, 5, 7, 11
  pay rates/work hours, 16, 18
Private property, 85
Protestant Church of America, 73
Provisional Court (Shanghai), xvii
Provisional Factory Regulations (1923), 53,
  101, 102, 110, 145, 157, 175, 184–88,
  213n.142, 249n.56
Public Works Department (International
  Settlement), 14

Rao, W.T., 223–24n.136
Ratepayers, xiv, xvii, 80, 108, 110–11, 116,
  127, 170, 239n.79
Rawlinson, Frank, 76, 77, 82, 217n.78,
  225–26n.5, 227–28nn.17, 25, 230n.69
Rawski, Thomas, 5, 7, 9–10, 11, 18, 20
Read, Bernard, 21
Reconnaissance Committee, 81, 170, 229nn.42,
  50, 51
Recruitment, employee, 13–16
  apprenticeships, 13–14, 25, 172,
    209–10nn.67, 69

Recruitment, employee (continued)
  contract labor system, 13, 14–15, 84, 172,
    210n.76
  freely negotiated agreement, 13, 15
  Green Gang, 8, 15–16, 20
Refugee camps, 122, 127, 131, 132, 241n.5,
  242nn.42, 48
Remer, C.F., 10, 31, 74, 76, 209n.52, 218n.19,
  219n.29, 229n.50
"Report on Industrial and Social Survey," 33
Returned laborers, 29–30
Rickshaw pullers, 12, 18, 23, 37, 40, 120,
  209n.61
Rietveld, Harriet, 54, 58, 221n.69, 230n.69,
  253–54n.54
Rigby, Richard, 239n.78
Riggs, Charles, 245n.106
Robbins, Mrs. Raymond, 218n.15
Rockefeller, John D., Jr., 34, 42, 54–56, 57, 67,
  81, 161, 216n.69
Rockefeller Foundation grants
  ILO, 148
  National Christian Council, 55, 56, 67, 78, 81,
    82, 96, 170, 229n.54, 233n.138
  YMCA, 42, 43, 44, 45, 55–56, 67, 217n.82
  YWCA, 54–56, 57, 67–68, 167, 220n.51,
    223n.123
Rowntree, Sebohm, 34, 35, 88
Rubber industry, 7, 9–10, 20, 21
Rural-urban mobility, 12–13, 172
Russell, Maud, 223n.131, 253–54n.54
Russia, 10, 11, 23

Safety issues. See Health/safety issues
Saint John's University (Shanghai), 78
Sarvis, Mr., 229n.50
Schooling. See Education/training programs
Schwenning, G.T., 42–43, 56
Second Opium War (1856–60), xvi
Senger, Miss, 233n.124
Sewell, William, 94, 245n.106
Sexual abuse, 48
Shanghai
  Bureau of Social Affairs, 4, 19, 99, 120, 123,
    124, 173, 211n.101, 241n.131
  Chapei, xvi, 37, 46, 58–59, 166, 251n.36
  First Special District Court, xvii, 116, 119,
    125, 129
  French Concession, xi, xvi, 116, 122, 150,
    206n.22
  housing reform, 22, 37, 174
  International Settlement. See International
    Settlement
  Mixed Court, xiv, xvii
  model village construction, 41
  Municipal Council. See Municipal Council
  Municipal Police, xvii, 125

Shanghai *(continued)*
  Nanking supervision of, xvi, 206*n.20*
  Nantao, xvi
  Nationalist invasion, xvi
  pay rates/work hours, 16, 17, 18, 180
  Provisional Court, xvii
  Woosung, xvi
  and worker migration, 12–13, 172
  YWCA model center, 63–64, 67, 71, 72, 130,
    131, 224*n.140*
Shanghai Committee on the Church and
    Industry (NCC), 79–80, 228*nn.38, 40*
Shanghai Community Church, 126
Shanghai International Industrial Service
    League, 80, 229*n.44*
Shanghai Missionary Association, 76
Shanghai Power Company, 41
Shanghai Rotary Club, 38, 51–52
Shanghai University, 94
Shaw, George Bernard, 34
Shedd, Charles C., 31, 163
Shin Tak-hing, 54, 57, 219*n.36*
Shipbuilding industry, 18, 107, 209*n.67*
Shipway, G.W., 236*n.17*, 237*n.42*
Silcock, H.T., 94
Silk industry
  child labor, 99, 103, 106, 237*n.34*, 239*n.96*,
    239–40*n.98*
  health/safety issues, 20, 174
  industry profile, 5, 6, 8, 9
  pay rates/work hours, 16, 18
  women workers, 6, 47, 58–59, 168,
    208*n.27*
  worker profile, 208*n.27*
  YWCA's Chapei center, 58–59
Silver prices, 8
Sing, T.S., 227*n.21*
Sinicization. *See* Nationalist
    movement/government
Sino-Japanese War (1937), xiv, 5, 9, 19–20, 42,
    122, 123, 151
Sisterhood societies, 48
Skinner, C.A., 236*n.17*, 237*n.34*
Small-scale industry, 88, 91–92, 93, 94
Smith, Constance, 219*n.34*
Snow, Edgar, 138
Sokolsky, George, 238*n.59*, 251*n.23*
Soong Mei-ling, 54, 57, 220*n.63*, 235*n.16*
"Statement of Industrial Work," 44–45
Stone, Mary, 30
Strand, David, 18, 23
Stuart, Leighton, 233*n.130*
Student Workers' Conference (YWCA; 1922),
    53, 219*n.38*
Su, George, 236*n.17*
Sun Chuan-fang, 166
Sun Yat-sen, 40, 175

Tao, L.K., 81
T'ao Ling, 61, 230*n.69*
Tata Steel Company (India), 109
Tawney, R.W., 51
Taxation policies, 8
Tayler, J.B., 34, 49, 73, 81, 87–89, 90, 91–92,
    93–96, 97, 138, 141, 143, 144, 162–63,
    170–71, 176, 217*n.78*, 229*n.55*, 231*nn.83,
    94*, 232*nn.98, 120*, 233*nn.124, 126, 130,
    131, 139*, 234*n.148*, 245*n.88*, 246*n.116*
Tchou, M.T. (Thomas; Chu Mu-ch'eng), 21–22,
    32, 33, 34–36, 37, 38, 41, 42, 43, 46, 76,
    77, 90–91, 156, 163, 165, 173, 174,
    216*nn.52, 60*, 227–28*nn.17, 18, 25*,
    229*n.50*, 230*n.69*, 248*nn.30, 32*
Thoburn, Helen, 50, 227*n.18*, 253–54*n.54*
Thomas, Albert, 148, 153
Threefold labor standard, 75, 76
Tientsin, 99, 114
  YWCA industrial program, 61–63, 71, 72,
    130, 224–25*nn.140, 143, 145*, 242*n.36*
Ting, Miss, 60
Tinghsien project, 206*n.12*
Tobacco industry
  child labor, 99, 106–07, 235*n.10*, 239*n.96*
  employee welfare plans, 23
  foreign investment/ownership, 11, 209*nn.56, 58*
  housing, 22
  industry profile, 5, 6, 9
  pay rates/work hours, 16, 18, 235*n.10*
Trade Union Law (1929), xiv, 25, 65
Trade unions. *See* Unions, labor
Training. *See* Education/training programs
Transpacific liberalism, xiii, 205*n.9*
Treaty of Nanking, xvi
Treaty of Shimenoseki, 3
Treaty ports, xi, xvi, 3, 11, 12, 138, 147, 170
Tsha, T.Y., 17, 18, 123
Tsien, Mr., 236*n.17*
Tsur, Y.T., 233*n.130*

Unemployment, 19–20, 173, 211*nn.101, 102,
    104, 105*, 226*n.11*
Unions, labor
  child labor, 210*n.76*
  and Christian church, 84
  Dockers' Union (Hankow), 155, 248*n.46*
  employee welfare plans, 23–24, 213*n.145*
  and ILO, 145–46, 151, 153, 155, 249*n.54*
  and Kuomintang, 7–8, 87, 90–91, 148, 153,
    166, 169, 208–09*n.43*, 248*n.48*,
    252–53*nn.42, 49*
  Labor Union Law, 90–91, 166, 168, 175
  and National Christian Council, 168,
    252*nn.47, 48*
  and Nationalist movement/government, xiv,
    xv, 7–8, 253–54*n.54*

Unions, labor *(continued)*
  studies of, 90–91
  welfare workers' intermediary role, 163–68
  and women workers, 68–69, 70, 164–68, 176, 252*n.42*
  and YMCA, 163–64, 250–51*n.22*
  and YWCA, 60, 68–69, 70, 164–68, 176, 221*n.85*, 223*n.134*, 251*nn.23, 28, 35, 36*, 252*nn.42, 43*
United Front, 169, 253–54*n.54*
United States, 8, 109
  industrial investment/ownership, 10, 11
University of Nanking, 142
Urban-rural mobility, 12–13, 172

Van Kleeck, Mary, 88
Versailles peace conference (1919), xiv
Vocational registration, 131

Wages. *See* Pay rates/work hours
Wagner, Augusta, 5, 14, 25, 112, 150, 155, 157–58, 234*n.145*
Wales, Nym, 138
Wallace, E.W., 227*n.21*
Wang, Miss, 236*n.17*, 237*n.42*
Wang, William, 87
Ward, Harry, 35
Ward, H. Lipson, 235*n.16*
Washington Conference (1919), 145
Watson, Angus, 88
Williams, George, 29
Wilson, E.O., 233*n.130*
Women in Industry in the Chapei, Hongkew and Pootung Districts of Shanghai, 61
Women in Tients in Industries, 61
Women's Clubs, 101, 109, 113–14, 235*n.15*
Women workers, 12
  agricultural sector, 98
  "amusement" occupations, 126
  apprenticeships, 209–10*n.69*
  and Confucian values, 99
  contract labor system, 14, 15, 48, 125
  cotton industry, 6, 15, 21, 47, 168, 208*n.24*, 211*n.92*, 217*n.4*
  domestic service. *See Mui tsai*
  education/training programs, 40, 61–63, 64, 69, 164–65, 174–75, 223*n.132*
  gender-related obligations, 48
  general profile, 47–48
  handicraft industry, 74, 98
  health/safety issues, 20, 21, 174, 226*nn.8, 11*, 230*n.75*
  and labor unions, 68–69, 70, 164–68, 176, 252*n.42*
  legislation, 25, 46
  match industry, 47

Women workers *(continued)*
  pay rates/work hours, 17, 18, 47–48, 62, 100, 179, 211*n.92*, 226*n.11*, 230*n.75*, 235*n.10*
  reform efforts. *See* National Christian Council of China; Young Women's Christian Association
  sexual abuse, 48
  silk industry, 6, 47, 58–59, 168, 208*n.27*
  sisterhood societies, 48
  tobacco industry, 6, 47
  YWCA industrial cooperatives, 130, 133–37, 243–44*nn.56, 57, 58, 59, 62, 63, 64, 65, 66, 67, 72*
Wong, Jennings, 153, 247*n.26*
Wong, W.H., 233*n.130*
Woo, S.M., 227*n.21*
Woodsmall, Ruth, 130–31
Wool industry, 89
Woosung, xvi
Woo Tao-yin, 236*n.17*, 237*n.34*
Workers' rights, xiv
Work hours. *See* Pay rates/work hours
Workmen's Compensation Act (District of Columbia, U.S.A.), xvii, 129, 206*n.21*
World Missionary Conference (1910), 73
World's Committee (YMCA), xii, 220*n.47*
World's Committee (YWCA), xii, xiii, 53, 164, 167, 220*n.47*
World's Student Christian Federation, 74
World War I, 3
World War II, 122–44
  Chinese Industrial Cooperative Movement, 123, 130, 133–34, 136, 138–44, 170–71, 176, 245*nn.101, 106*, 246*nn.116, 117, 118*, 254*n.55*
    See also Indusco
  Industrial Section activities, 123–29
    child protection, 125–27
    dispute mediation, 124–25
    economic data collection, 123–24, 241*nn.8, 9*
    education/training programs, 127, 128–29, 242*n.32*
    health/safety issues, 127, 128, 129, 174
    housing standards, 127–28, 174
    refugee camps, 122, 127, 131, 132, 241*n.5*, 242*nn.42, 48*
    YWCA work, 123, 129–38, 242–45*nn.42, 48, 49, 56, 57, 58, 59, 62, 63, 64, 65, 66, 67, 72, 84*
Wusih, YWCA model center, 64–65, 68, 71, 72, 91, 222*n.108*, 224*n.143*

Yang, Gladys, 233*n.126*
Yangtze Engineering Works, 33
Yangtzepoo Social Center, 33
Yard, J.M., 227*n.21*

Yeh Kung-chia, 5, 6, 7
Yen, James, xii, xiii, 205n.9, 215n.34
  Mass Education Movement, xii, xv, 29, 174,
    206n.12
Yenching University, 94, 96, 97, 233n.131,
    234nn.145, 147
Yen Chung-p'ing, 207n.18
Young Men's Christian Association (YMCA),
    88
  and child labor, 35, 36
  Commission on Labor Problems, xii
  evangelization, 39
  and ILO, 146, 246–47n.6
  industrial extension work, 30–32, 35–36, 169,
    213n.5, 214–15nn.9, 31
  International Committee, xiii, xv-xvi, 44, 45,
    55, 56, 161, 206nn.15, 17, 220n.47,
    250n.5
  and Kuomintang, 44
  and labor unions, 163–64, 250–51n.22
  Model Village, 36–42, 43, 46, 60, 63, 169,
    174, 215nn.37, 39, 49, 216n.55
  and National Christian Council, 79, 83
  reform efforts, xi, xii, xiii, xv, 29–46, 172,
    173, 217n.82
  relations with employers, 160–61, 162,
    249nn.3, 4
  research/study findings, 21–22, 32–36, 173,
    214nn.28, 29
  and returned laborers, 29–30
  and Rockefeller grant, 42, 43, 44, 45, 55–56,
    67, 217n.82
  threefold labor standard, 76–77
  World's Committee, xii, 220n.47
  and YWCA, 60, 253–54n.54
Young Women's Christian Association
    (YWCA)
  and ILO, 146, 246n.6
  Industrial Advisory Committee, xii
  Industrial Secretaries' Conferences, 59–60,
    68, 69, 70, 162, 166, 167, 170, 223n.131
  and Kuomintang, 60, 221n.84, 253–54n.54
  and labor unions, 60, 68–69, 70, 164–68, 176,
    221n.85, 223n.134, 251nn.23, 28, 35,
    36, 252nn.42, 43
  National Assembly of Industrial Girls, 71,
    223–24n.136
  and National Christian Council, 50, 54, 58,
    60, 67, 79, 83, 168, 222n.104, 252n.48
  and Nationalist movement/government, 65–66

Young Women's Christian Association
    (YWCA) (continued)
  organization development/direction, xii-xiii,
    66–72, 87, 224n.137
  reform efforts, xi, xv, 29, 33, 47–72, 169–70,
    172–73, 206n.13, 218n.10, 222n.109,
    250n.10, 252n.46
  Chapei center, 58–59, 166, 251n.36
  Chefoo industrial program, 71, 72, 130,
    224–25nn.140, 145
  child labor, 50, 53–54, 57, 101, 161–62,
    164, 218n.20
  education/training programs, 40, 78,
    134–35, 137, 138, 165–66, 174–75,
    221n.84, 223n.132
  employer-based approach, 50–52, 161–62,
    170, 250n.9
  government-sponsored programs, 65–66
  information gathering, 60–61
  Shanghai center, 63–64, 67, 71, 72, 130,
    131, 224n.140
  Tientsin industrial program, 61–63, 71, 72,
    130, 224–25nn.140, 143, 145, 242n.36
  welfare worker training, 52–53
  Wusih center, 64–65, 68, 71, 72, 91,
    222n.108, 224n.143
  and Rockefeller grant, 54–56, 57, 67–68, 167,
    220n.51, 223n.123
  and Shanghai Municipal Council, 57, 58, 114,
    165, 240n.107
  Student Workers' Conference (1922), 53,
    219n.38
  threefold labor standard, 76
  World's Committee, xii, xiii, 53, 164, 167,
    220n.47
  World War II activities, 123, 129–38,
    242nn.42, 48, 49, 244n.84
  industrial cooperatives, 130, 133–37,
    243–44nn.56, 57, 58, 59, 62, 63, 64,
    65, 66, 67, 72
  and YMCA, 60, 253–54n.54
Young Workers' Employment Contract, 126
Yui, David, 45
YWCA. See Young Women's Christian
    Association

Zung Wei-tsung, 49, 50, 54, 57, 74, 76, 77, 169,
    218nn.19, 22, 220n.65, 227–28nn.17, 18,
    25, 38, 229n.50, 236n.17, 237–38nn.34, 52

Robin Porter hold degrees in international relations and in Chinese history from McGill University, and a doctorate in modern Chinese history from the School of Oriental and African Studies, University of London. He has lived and worked in China, and is a Chinese speaker.

Dr. Porter has taught Chinese history and politics at Concordia University in Canada, at Murdoch and Melbourne Universities in Australia, and is now head of the Chinese Business Centre at Keele University in England. In the 1980s, he was adviser to the China Trade Group of the British automotive industry.